The Library Freedom Act

Libraries have the freedom to acquire their collections.

Libraries have the freedom to circulate
materials in their collections.

Libraries guarantee the privacy of their patrons.

Libraries oppose any type of censorship.

When libraries are imperiled,
librarians will join together
to secure their freedom.

library wars
Love & War

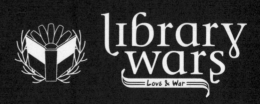

library wars

⎯ Love & War ⎯

11

STORY & ART BY *Kiiro Yumi*   ORIGINAL CONCEPT BY *Hiro Arikawa*

library wars

Love & War

Contents

CHAPTER 49

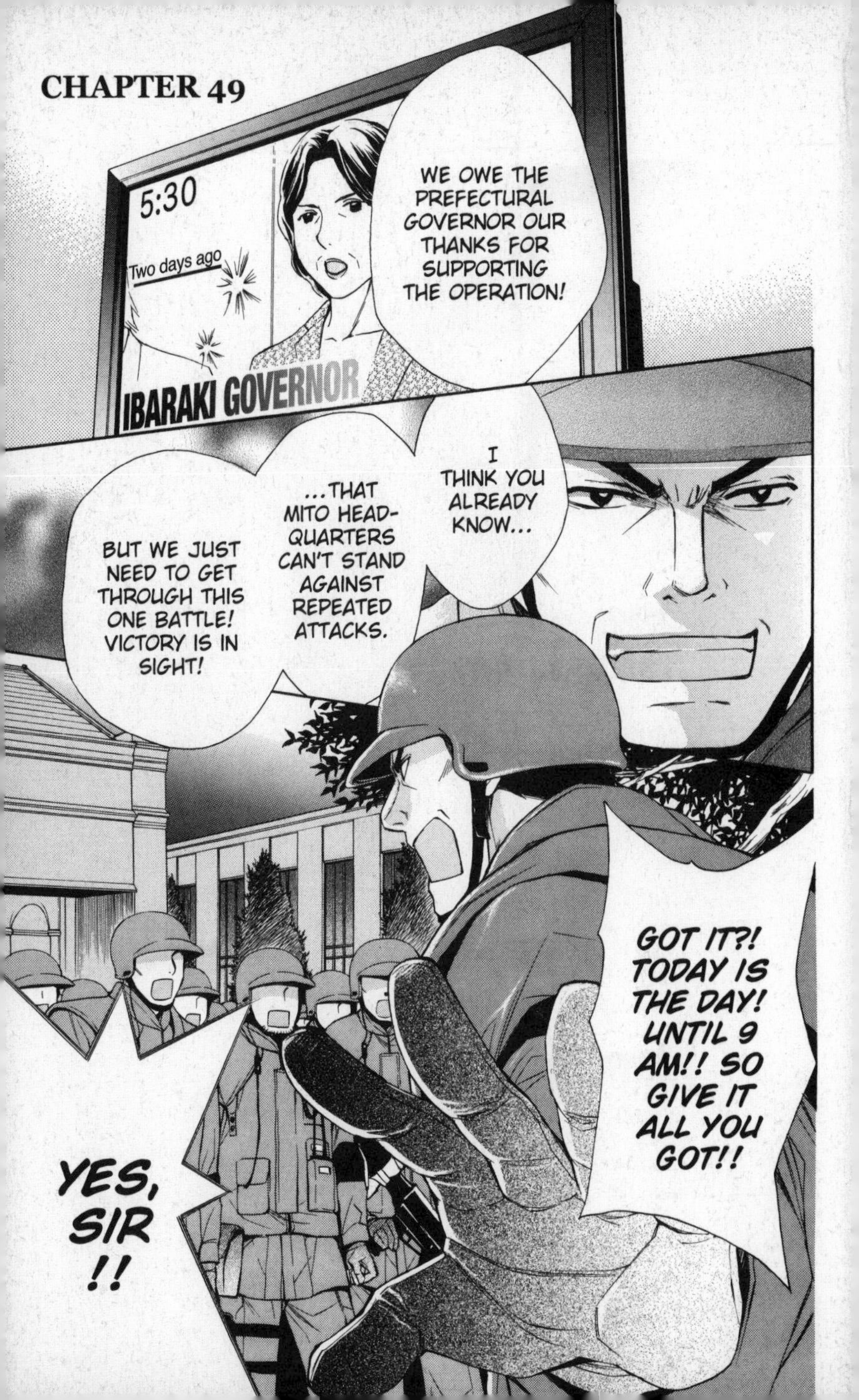
5:30
Two days ago
IBARAKI GOVERNOR
WE OWE THE PREFECTURAL GOVERNOR OUR THANKS FOR SUPPORTING THE OPERATION!
I THINK YOU ALREADY KNOW...
...THAT MITO HEAD-QUARTERS CAN'T STAND AGAINST REPEATED ATTACKS.
BUT WE JUST NEED TO GET THROUGH THIS ONE BATTLE! VICTORY IS IN SIGHT!
GOT IT?! TODAY IS THE DAY! UNTIL 9 AM!! SO GIVE IT ALL YOU GOT!!
YES, SIR !!

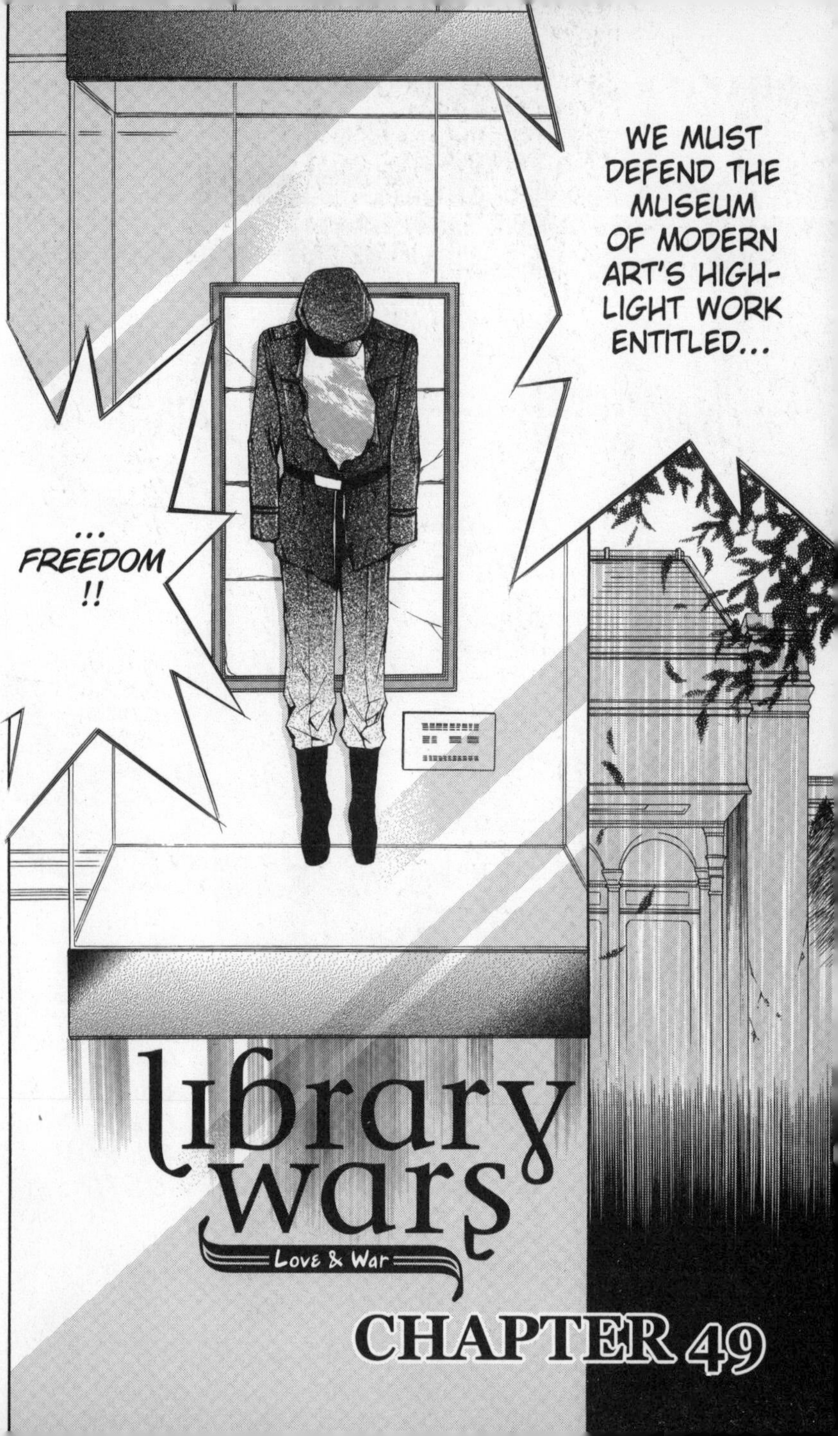
WE MUST DEFEND THE MUSEUM OF MODERN ART'S HIGH-LIGHT WORK ENTITLED...
... FREEDOM !!
library wars
Love & War
CHAPTER 49

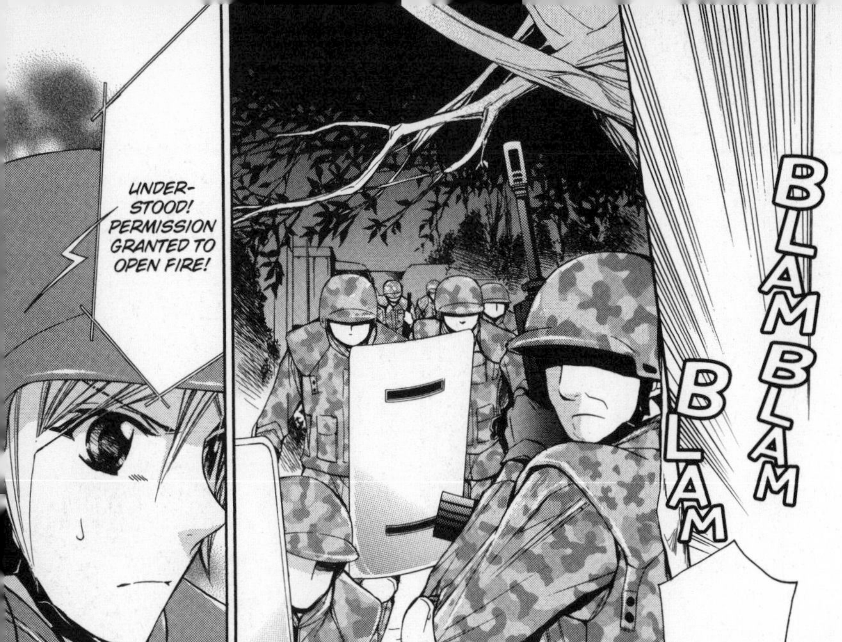
BLAM BLAM
BLAM
I HEAR GUNFIRE NEAR THE LIBRARY!
THEY'RE HERE!
IT'S THE MEDIA BETTER-MENT COMMITTEE!
UNDER-STOOD! PERMISSION GRANTED TO OPEN FIRE!
Battles usually begin...

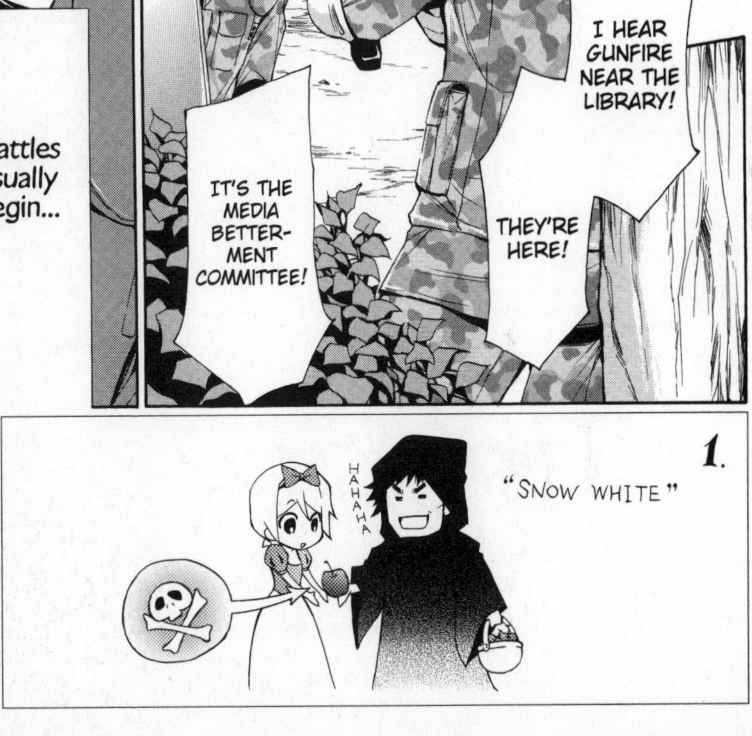
1.
"SNOW WHITE"
HAHAHA

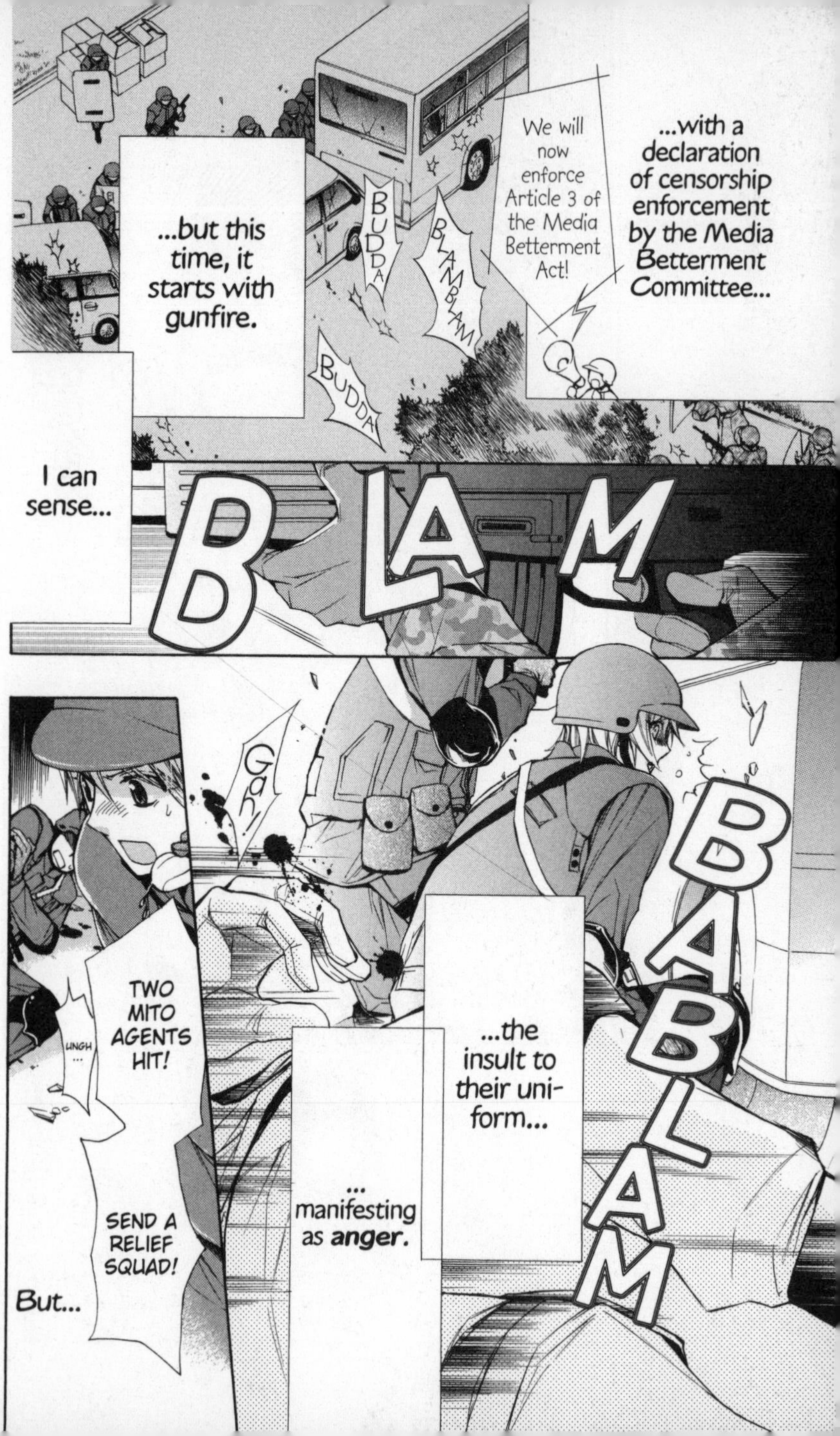
...with a declaration of censorship enforcement by the Media Betterment Committee...
We will now enforce Article 3 of the Media Betterment Act!
BLAMBLAM
BUDDA
...but this time, it starts with gunfire.
BUDDA
BLAM
I can sense...
BABLAM
Gah!
...the insult to their uniform...
... manifesting as **anger**.
TWO MITO AGENTS HIT!
UNGH ...
SEND A RELIEF SQUAD!
But...

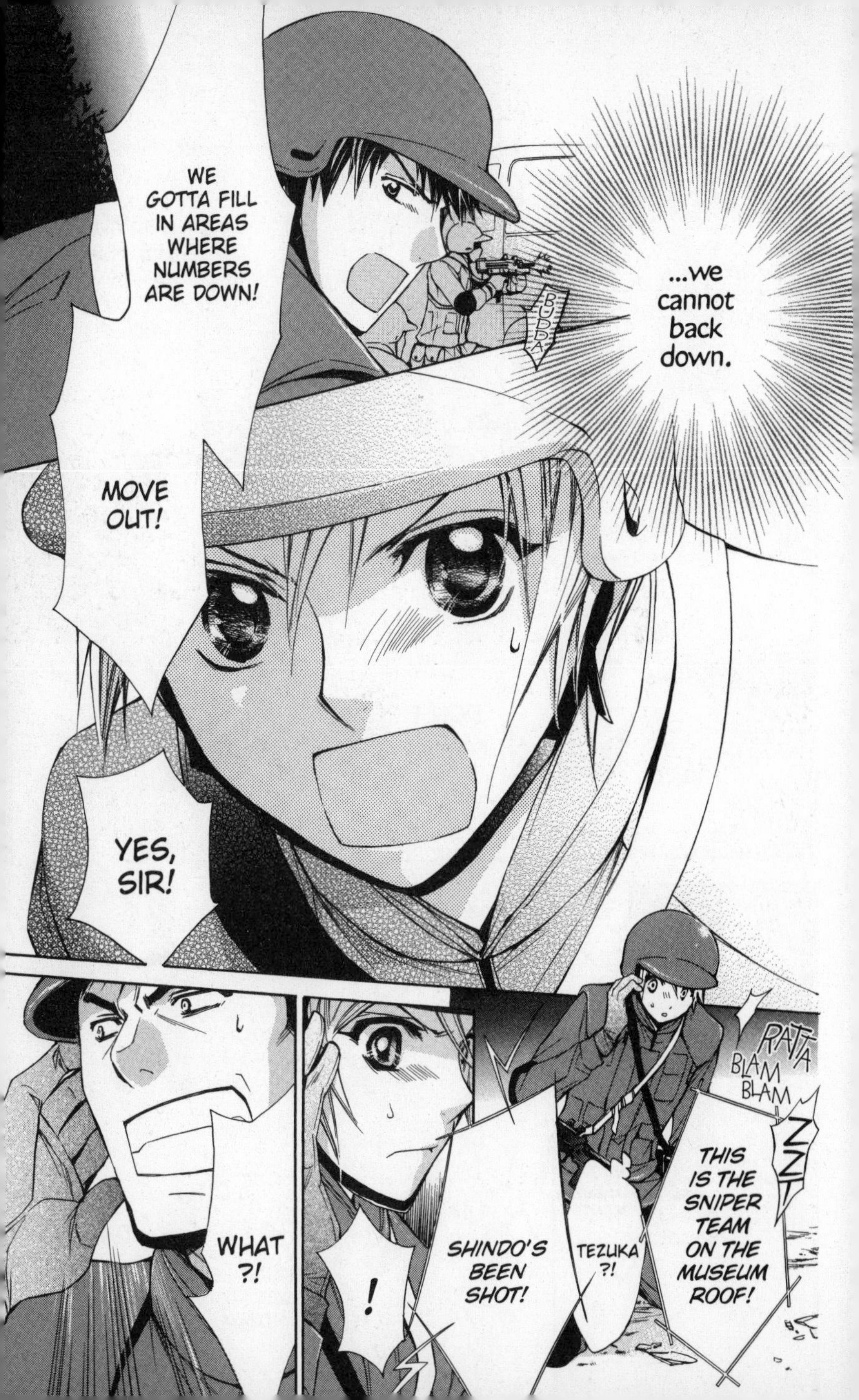
...we cannot back down.
BUDDA
WE GOTTA FILL IN AREAS WHERE NUMBERS ARE DOWN!
MOVE OUT!
YES, SIR!
RATTA BLAM BLAM
ZZZT
THIS IS THE SNIPER TEAM ON THE MUSEUM ROOF!
TEZUKA?!
SHINDO'S BEEN SHOT!
!
WHAT?!

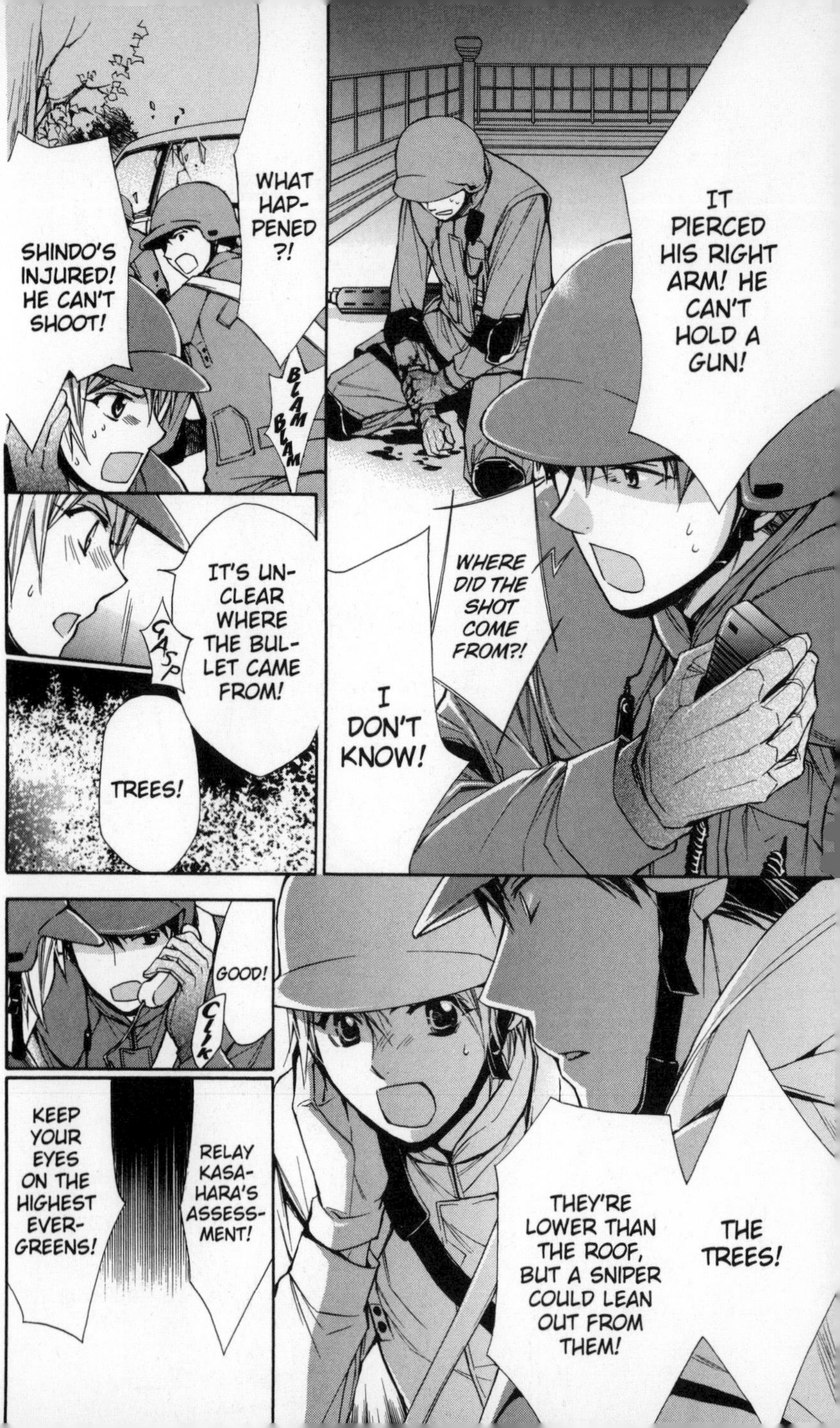
IT PIERCED HIS RIGHT ARM! HE CAN'T HOLD A GUN!
WHERE DID THE SHOT COME FROM?!
I DON'T KNOW!
WHAT HAP-PENED?!
SHINDO'S INJURED! HE CAN'T SHOOT!
BLAM BLAM
IT'S UN-CLEAR WHERE THE BUL-LET CAME FROM!
GASP
TREES!
THE TREES!
THEY'RE LOWER THAN THE ROOF, BUT A SNIPER COULD LEAN OUT FROM THEM!
GOOD!
CLIK
RELAY KASA-HARA'S ASSESS-MENT!
KEEP YOUR EYES ON THE HIGHEST EVER-GREENS!

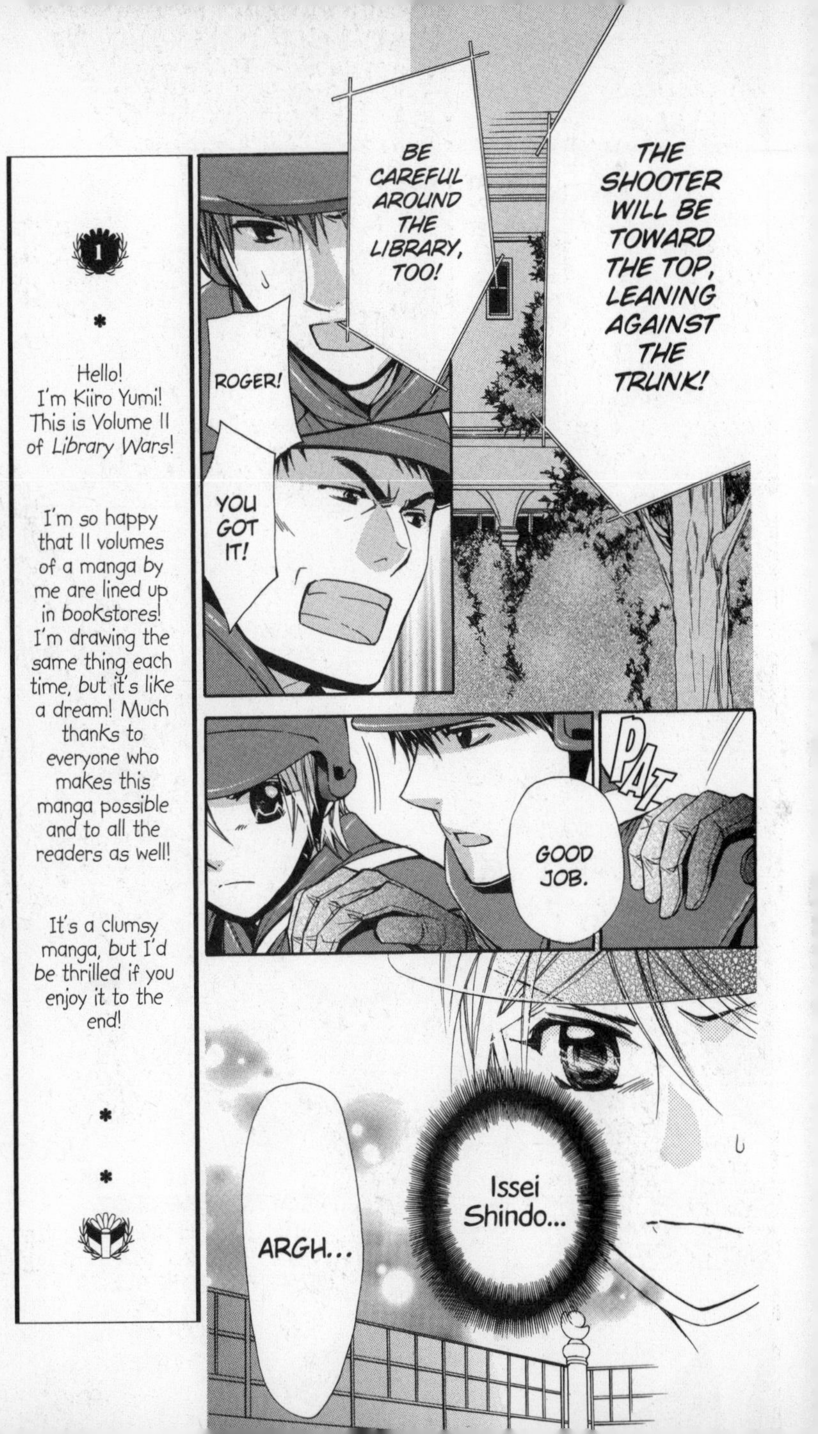
THE SHOOTER WILL BE TOWARD THE TOP, LEANING AGAINST THE TRUNK!
BE CAREFUL AROUND THE LIBRARY, TOO!
ROGER!
YOU GOT IT!
PAT
GOOD JOB.
Issei Shindo...
ARGH...

1

*

Hello! I'm Kiiro Yumi! This is Volume 11 of *Library Wars*!

I'm so happy that 11 volumes of a manga by me are lined up in bookstores! I'm drawing the same thing each time, but it's like a dream! Much thanks to everyone who makes this manga possible and to all the readers as well!

It's a clumsy manga, but I'd be thrilled if you enjoy it to the end!

*

*

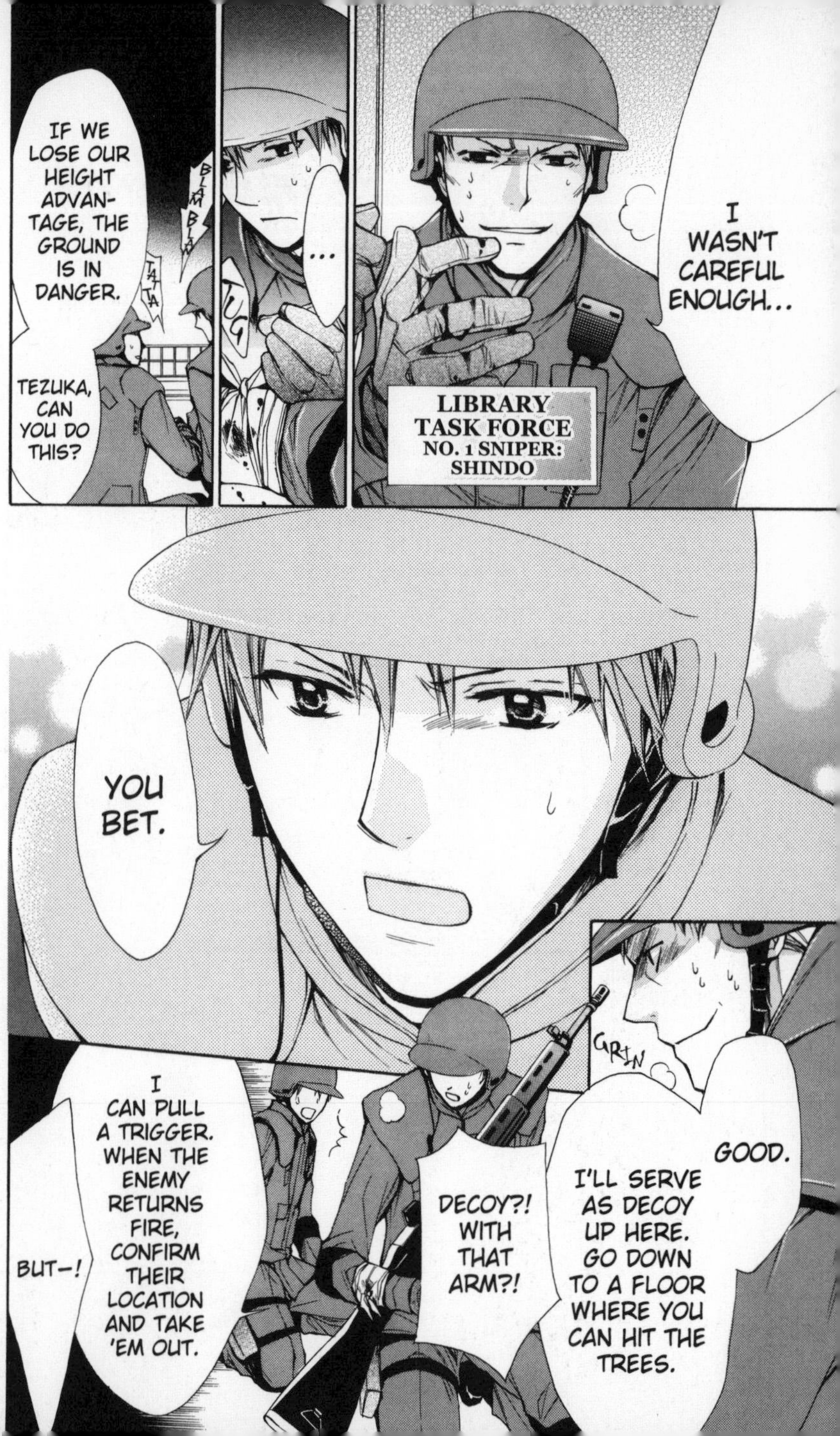
I WASN'T CAREFUL ENOUGH...
LIBRARY TASK FORCE NO. 1 SNIPER: SHINDO
...
TUG
BLAM BLAM
IF WE LOSE OUR HEIGHT ADVANTAGE, THE GROUND IS IN DANGER.
TA TA
TEZUKA, CAN YOU DO THIS?
YOU BET.
GRIN
GOOD.
I'LL SERVE AS DECOY UP HERE. GO DOWN TO A FLOOR WHERE YOU CAN HIT THE TREES.
DECOY?! WITH THAT ARM?!
I CAN PULL A TRIGGER. WHEN THE ENEMY RETURNS FIRE, CONFIRM THEIR LOCATION AND TAKE 'EM OUT.
BUT—!

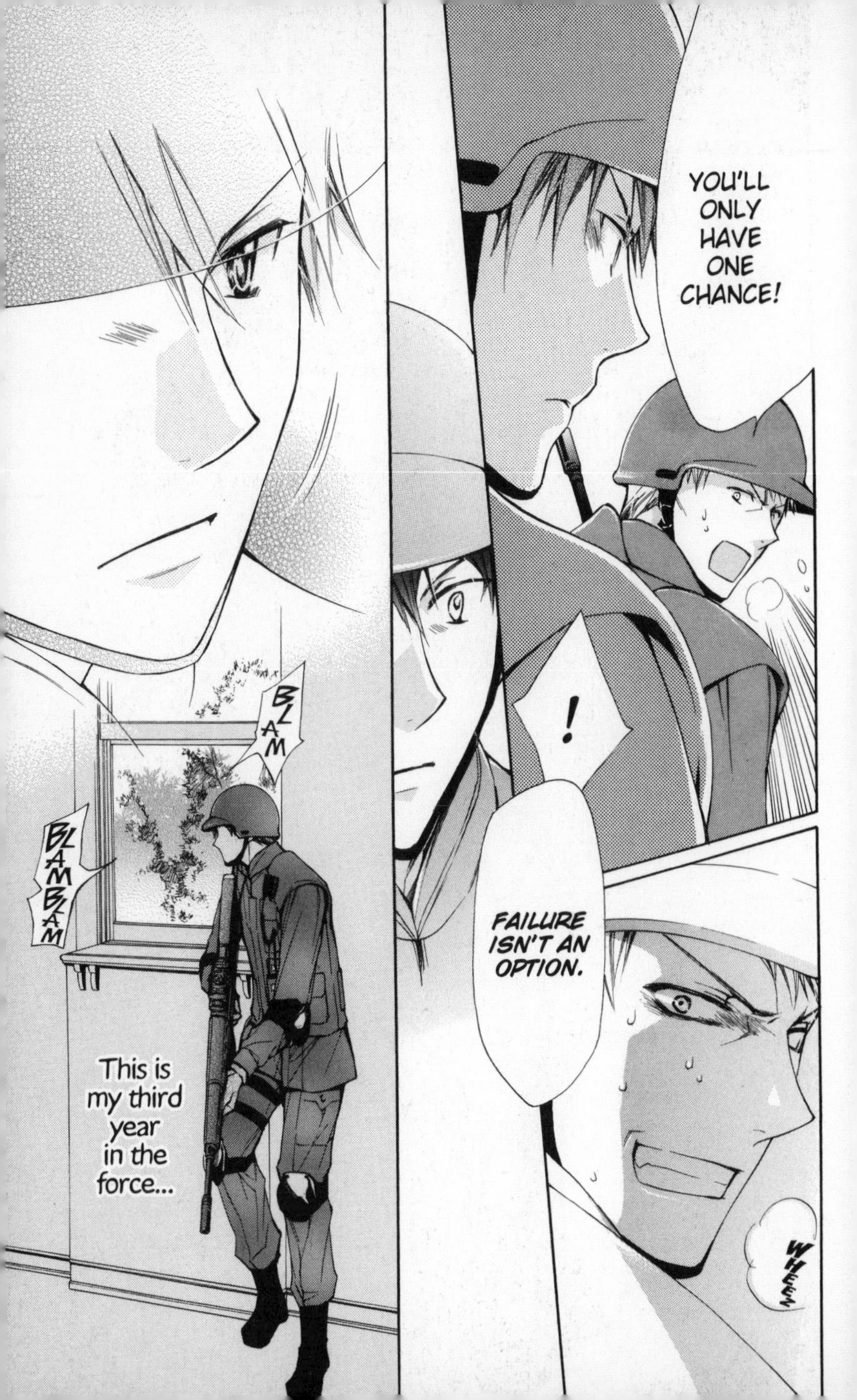
YOU'LL ONLY HAVE ONE CHANCE!
!
FAILURE ISN'T AN OPTION.
WHEEZ
BLAM
BLAMBLAM
This is my third year in the force...

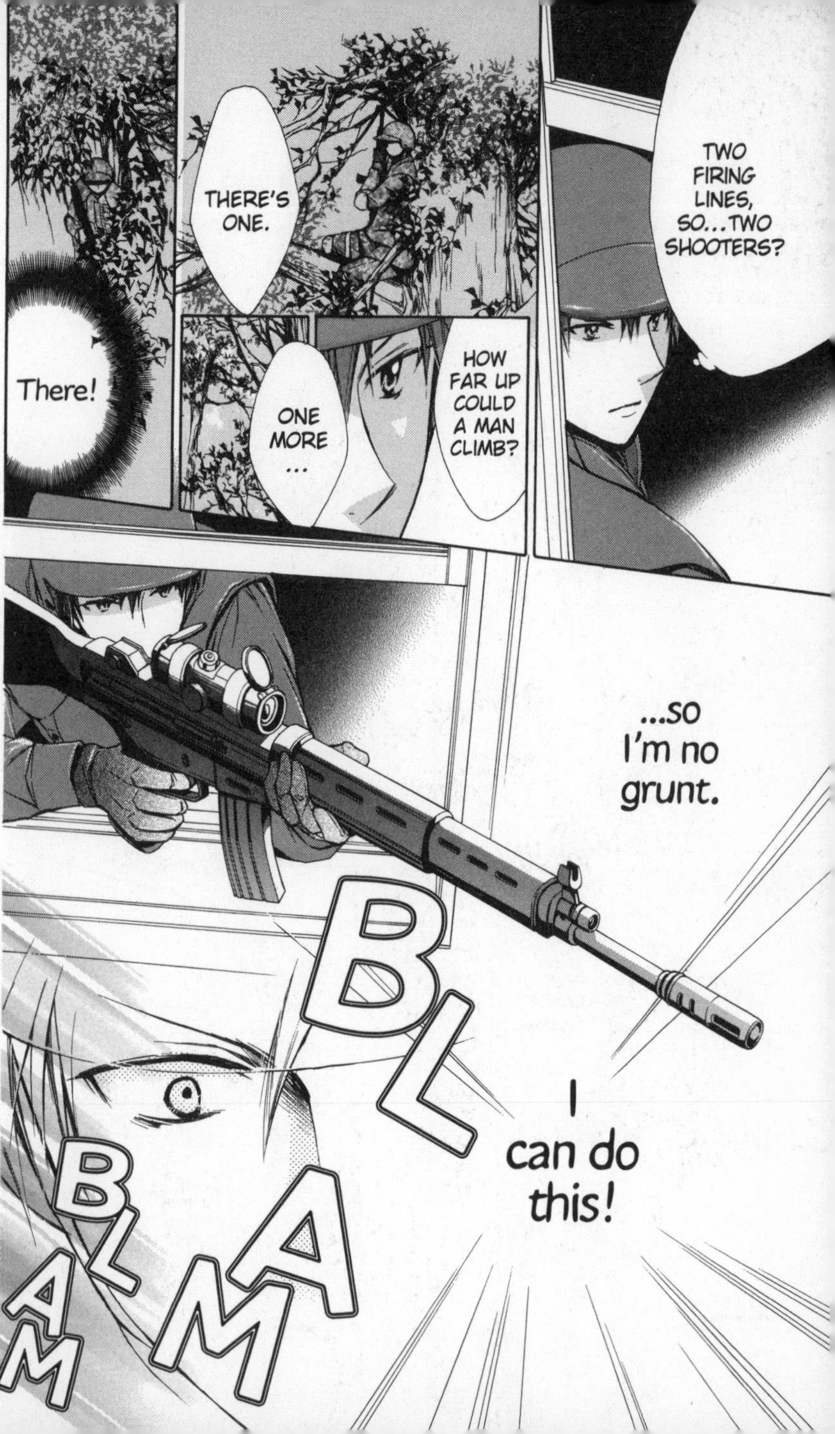
TWO FIRING LINES, SO...TWO SHOOTERS?
THERE'S ONE.
HOW FAR UP COULD A MAN CLIMB?
ONE MORE ...
There!
...so I'm no grunt.
BLAM
I can do this!
BLAM

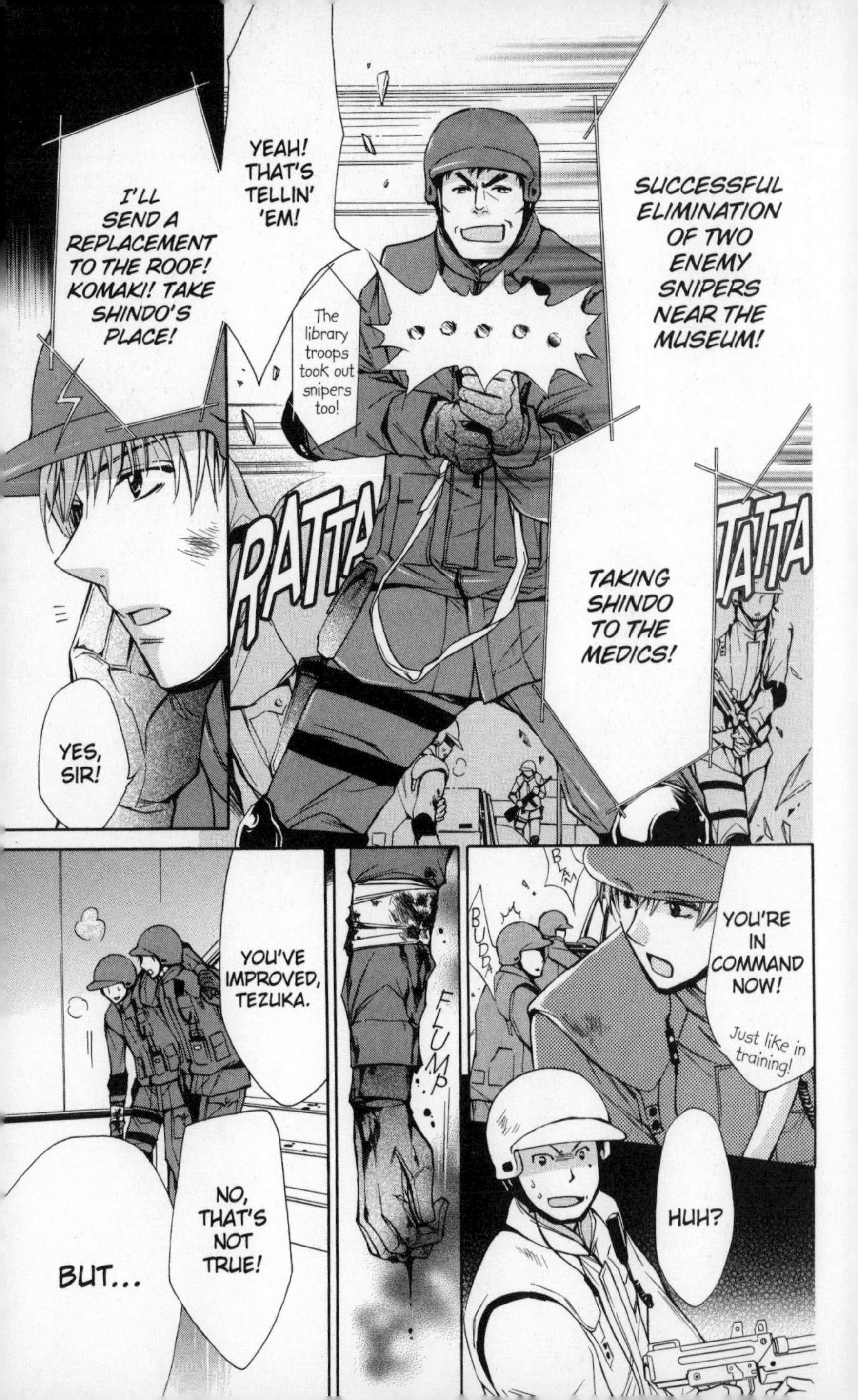
SUCCESSFUL ELIMINATION OF TWO ENEMY SNIPERS NEAR THE MUSEUM!
YEAH! THAT'S TELLIN' 'EM!
I'LL SEND A REPLACEMENT TO THE ROOF! KOMAKI! TAKE SHINDO'S PLACE!
The library troops took out snipers too!
TATTA
TAKING SHINDO TO THE MEDICS!
RATTA
YES, SIR!
BLAM
BUDDA
YOU'RE IN COMMAND NOW!
Just like in training!
HUH?
FLUMP
YOU'VE IMPROVED, TEZUKA.
NO, THAT'S NOT TRUE!
BUT...

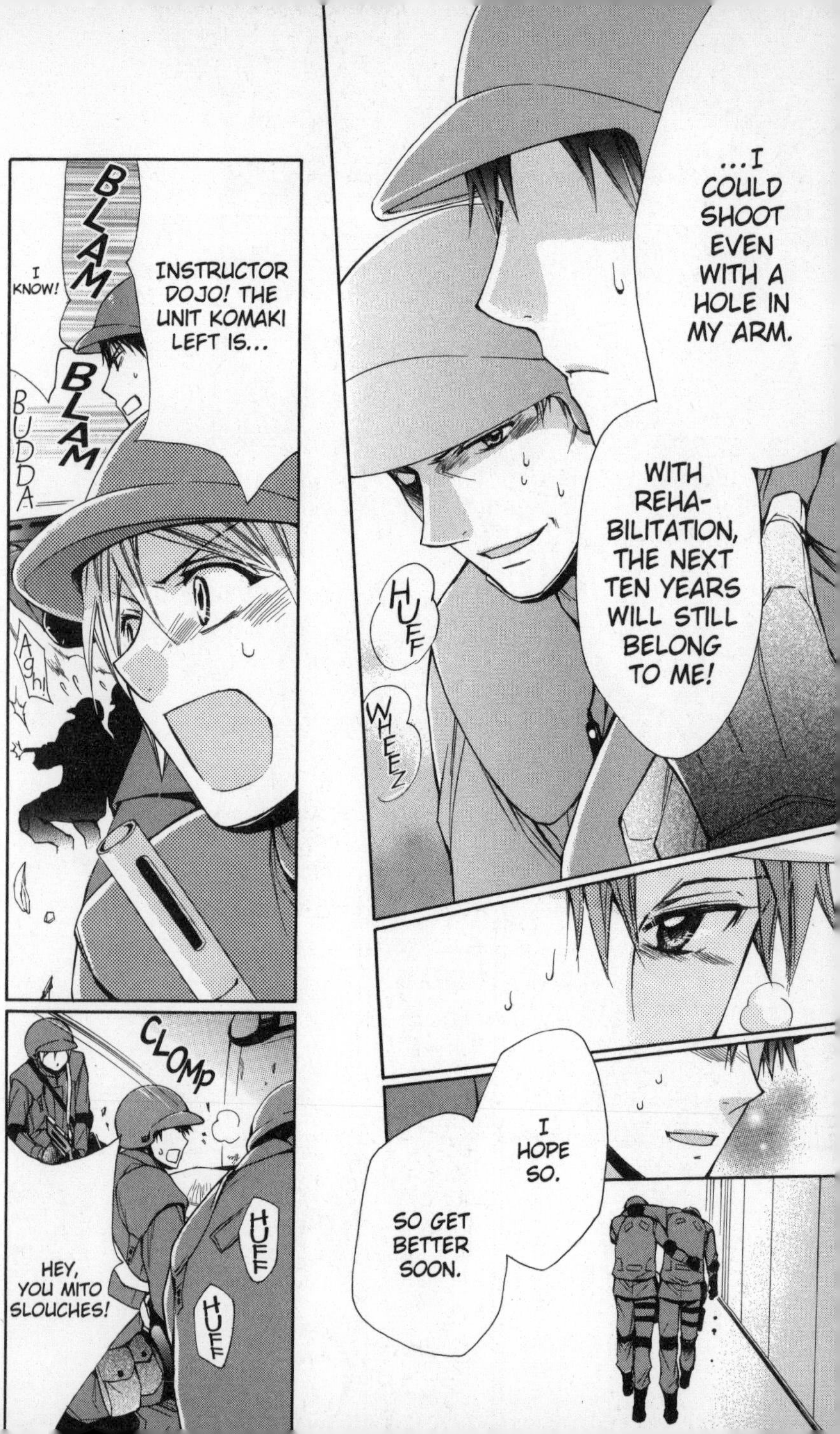
...I COULD SHOOT EVEN WITH A HOLE IN MY ARM.
WITH REHA-BILITATION, THE NEXT TEN YEARS WILL STILL BELONG TO ME!
HUFF
WHEEZ
I HOPE SO.
SO GET BETTER SOON.
INSTRUCTOR DOJO! THE UNIT KOMAKI LEFT IS...
I KNOW!
BLAM
BLAM
BLAM
BUDDA
Agh!
CLOMP
HUFF
HUFF
HEY, YOU MITO SLOUCHES!

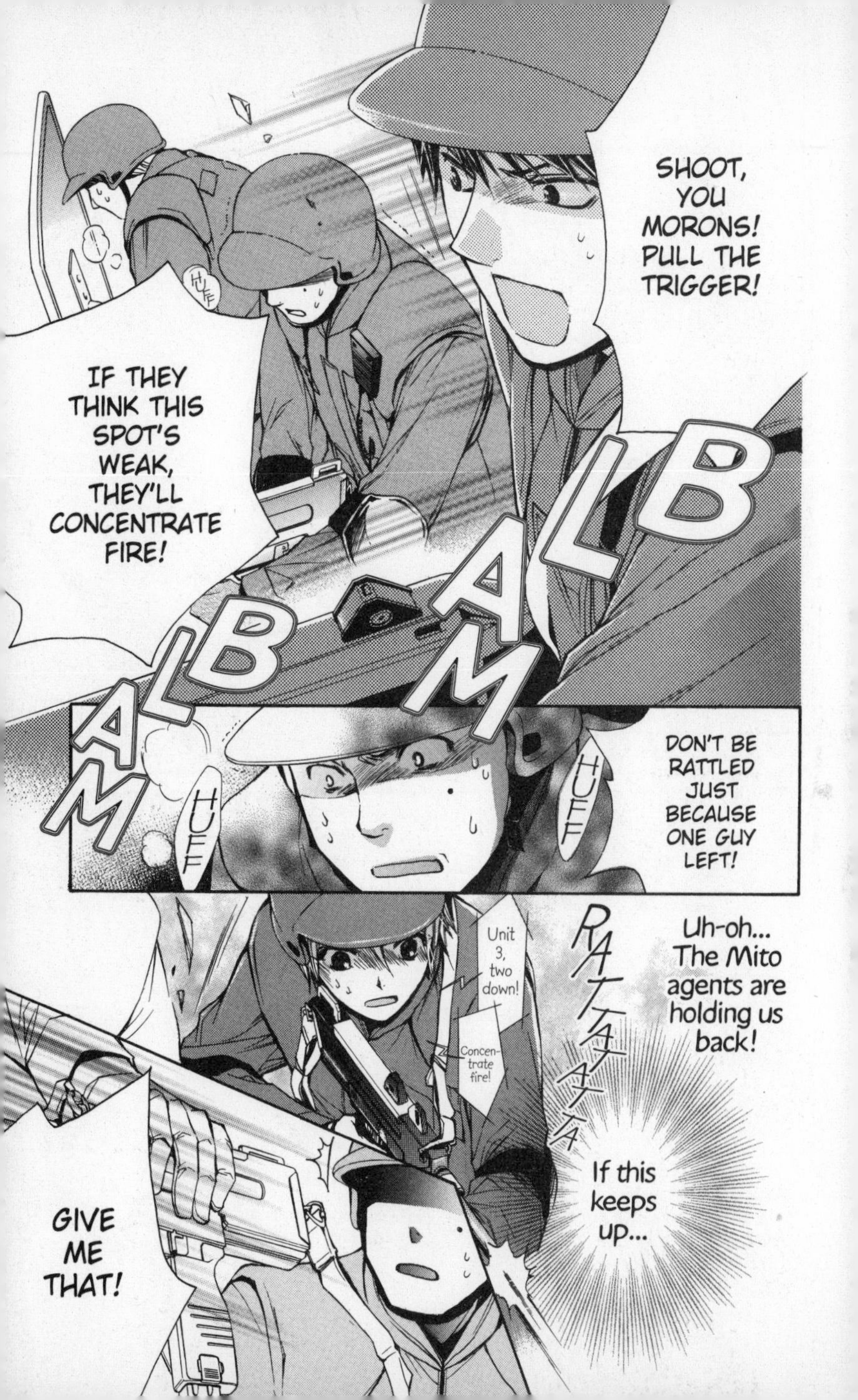
SHOOT, YOU MORONS! PULL THE TRIGGER!
HUFF
IF THEY THINK THIS SPOT'S WEAK, THEY'LL CONCENTRATE FIRE!
BLAM
BLAM
DON'T BE RATTLED JUST BECAUSE ONE GUY LEFT!
HUFF
HUFF
Uh-oh... The Mito agents are holding us back!
RATATATATA
Unit 3, two down!
Concentrate fire!
If this keeps up...
GIVE ME THAT!

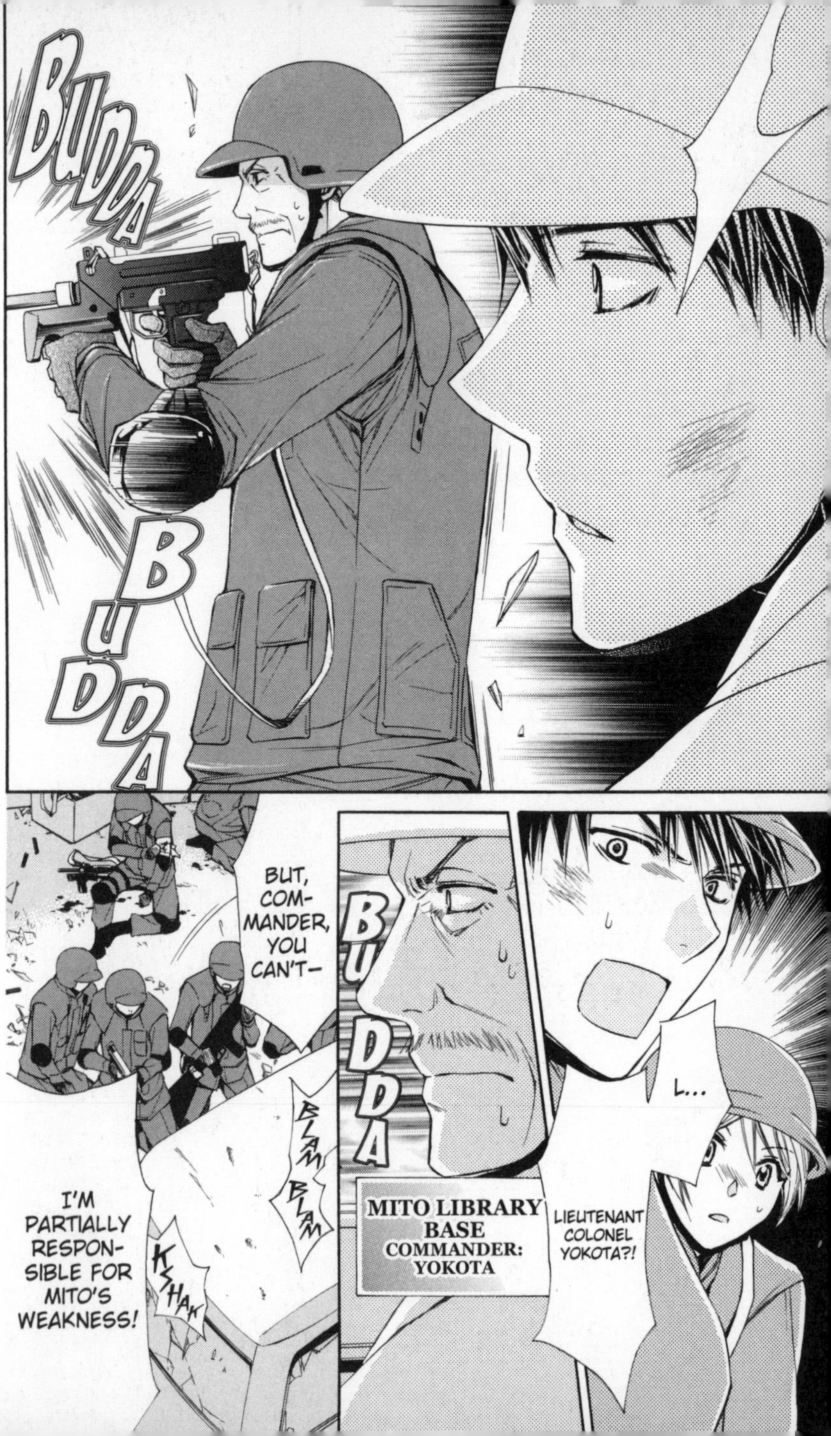
BUDDA
BUDDA
L...
LIEUTENANT COLONEL YOKOTA?!
MITO LIBRARY BASE
COMMANDER: YOKOTA
BUDDA
BUT, COMMANDER, YOU CAN'T—
BLAM BLAM
KSHAK
I'M PARTIALLY RESPONSIBLE FOR MITO'S WEAKNESS!

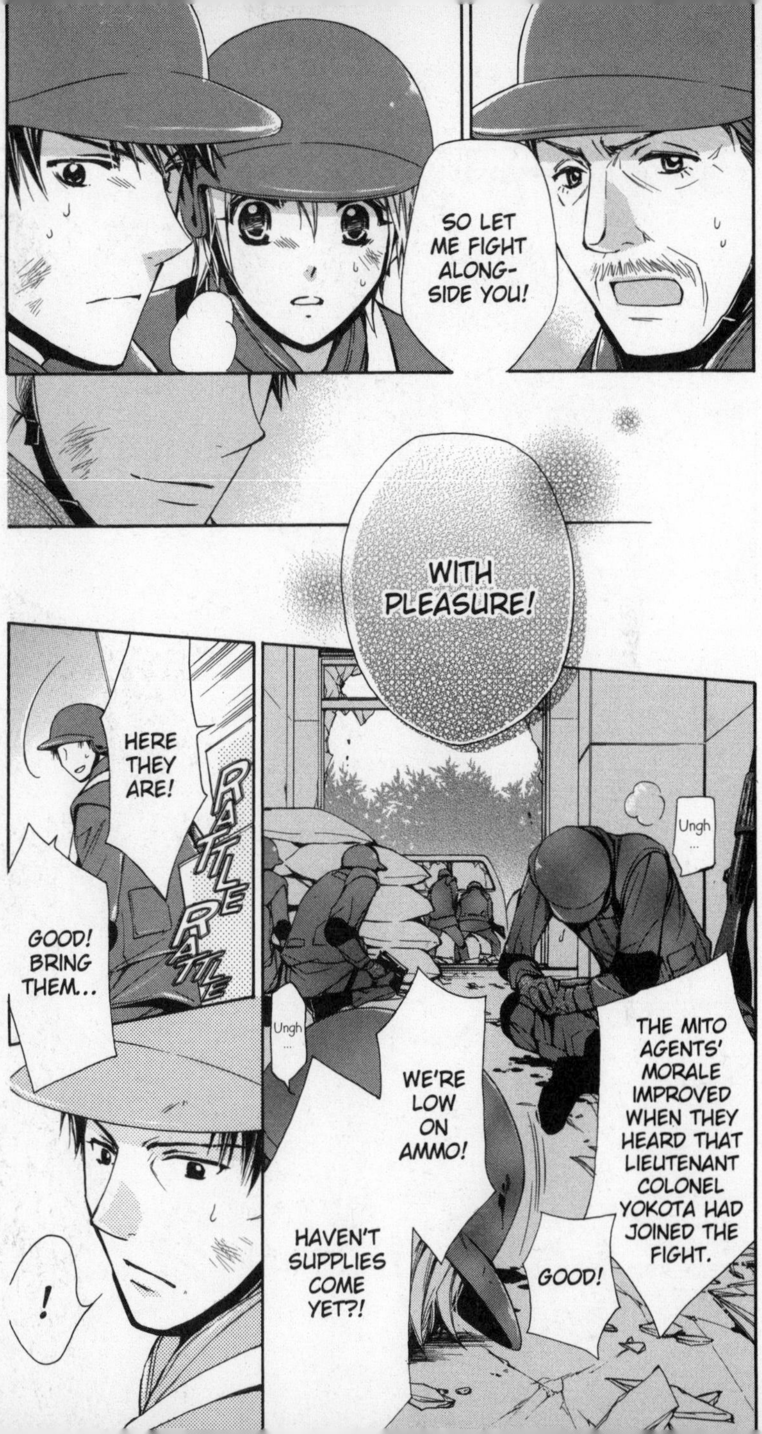

SO LET ME FIGHT ALONG-SIDE YOU!
WITH PLEASURE!
Ungh...
THE MITO AGENTS' MORALE IMPROVED WHEN THEY HEARD THAT LIEUTENANT COLONEL YOKOTA HAD JOINED THE FIGHT.
WE'RE LOW ON AMMO!
Ungh...
GOOD!
HAVEN'T SUPPLIES COME YET?!
HERE THEY ARE!
RATTLE RATTLE
GOOD! BRING THEM...
!

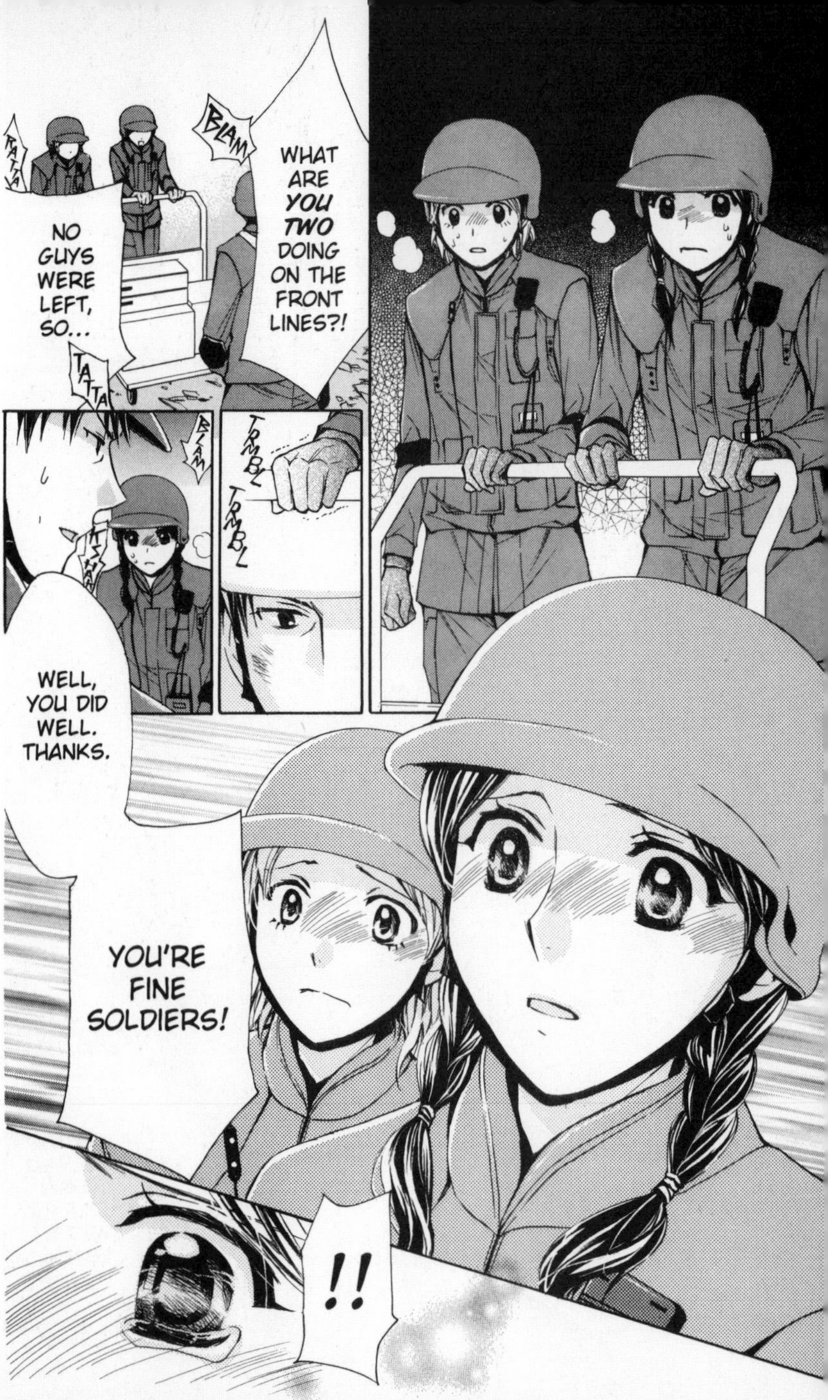
BLAM
WHAT ARE YOU TWO DOING ON THE FRONT LINES?!
RATTA
NO GUYS WERE LEFT, SO...
TATTA
TRMBL TRMBL
BLAM
KSHAH
WELL, YOU DID WELL. THANKS.
YOU'RE FINE SOLDIERS!
!!

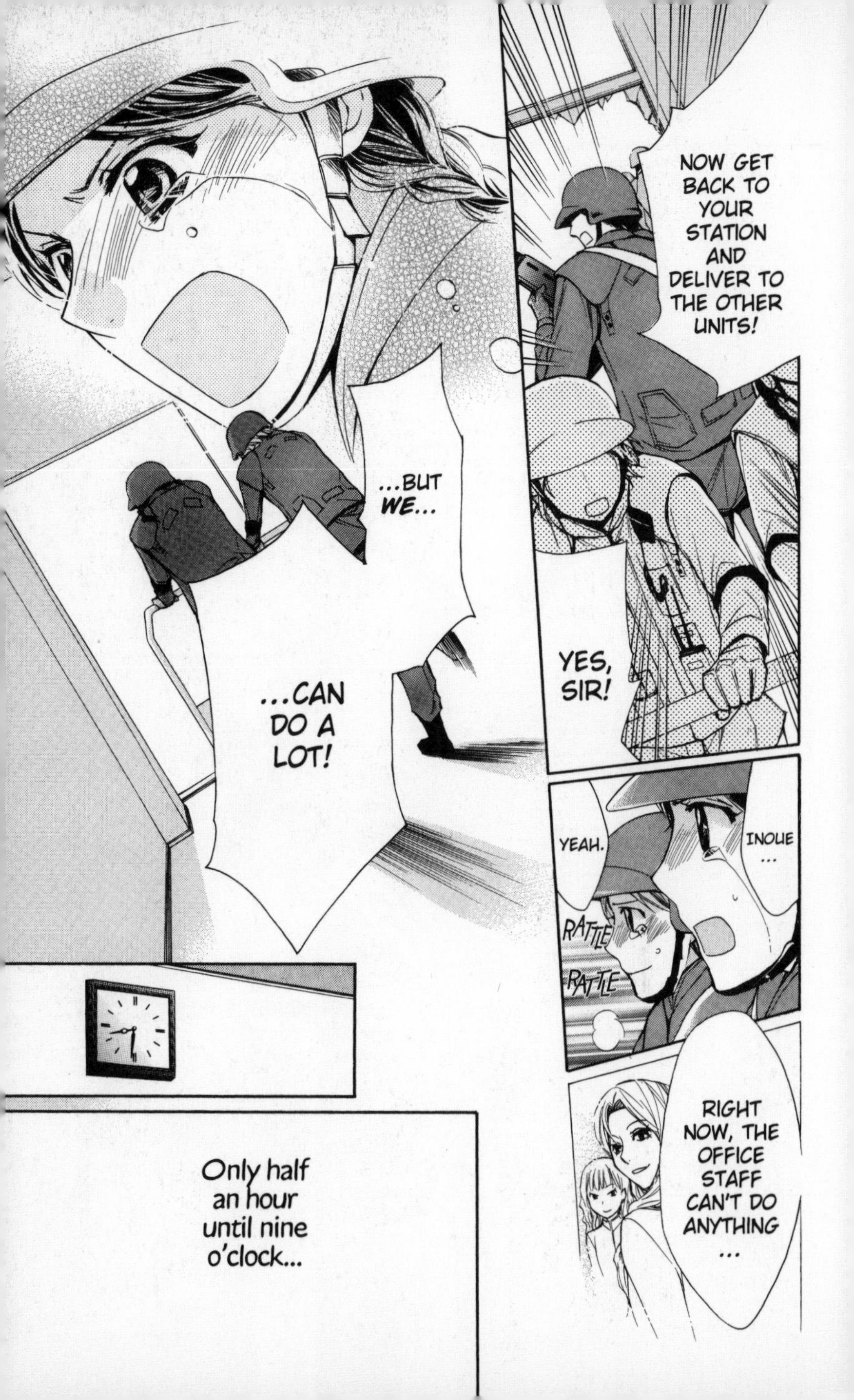
NOW GET BACK TO YOUR STATION AND DELIVER TO THE OTHER UNITS!
YES, SIR!
INOUE...
YEAH.
RATTLE
RATTLE
RIGHT NOW, THE OFFICE STAFF CAN'T DO ANYTHING...
...BUT WE...
...CAN DO A LOT!
Only half an hour until nine o'clock...

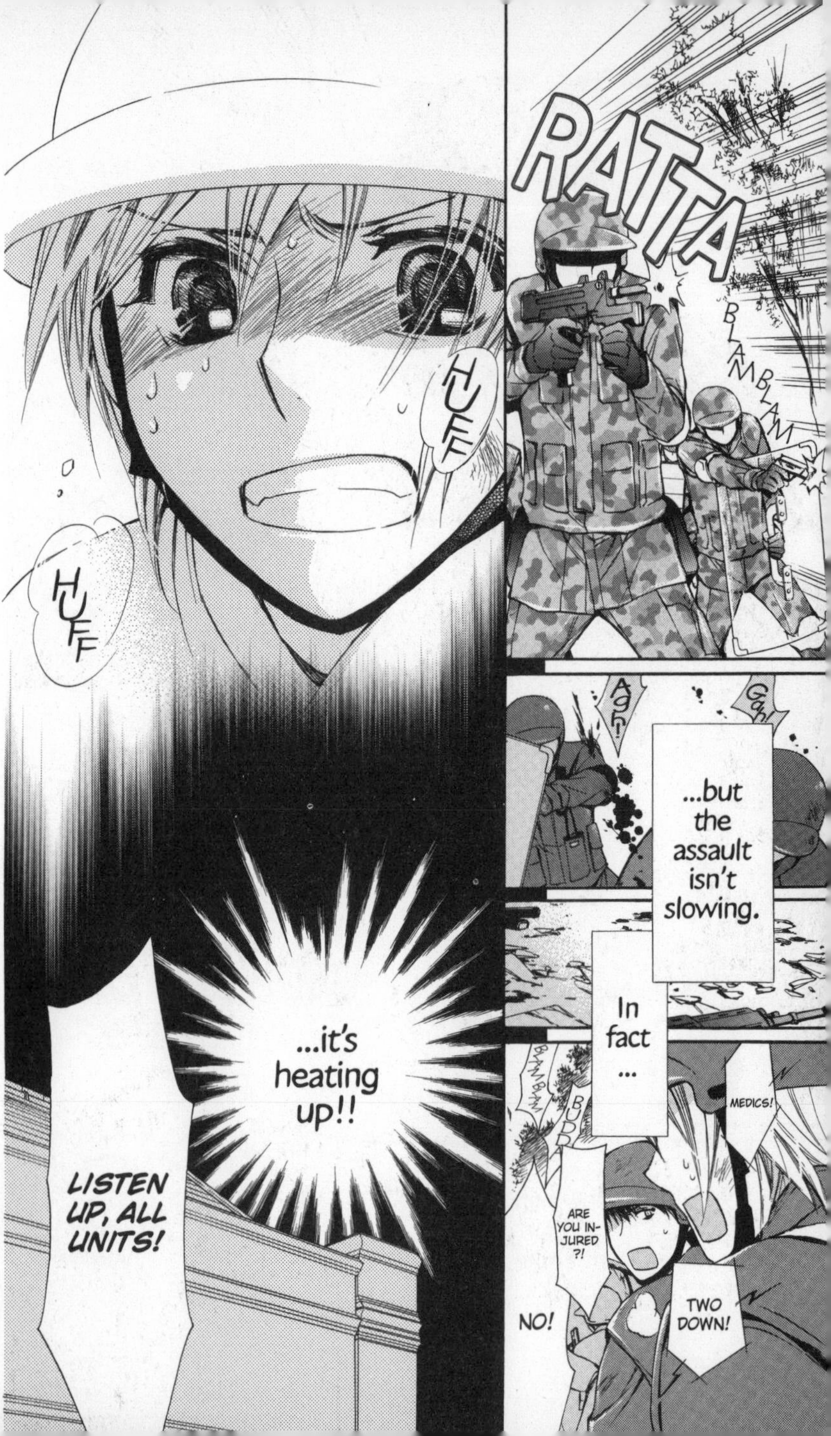
RATTA
BLAMBLAM
Agh!
Gah!
...but the assault isn't slowing.
In fact ...
BLAMBLAM
BUDD
MEDICS!
ARE YOU IN-JURED?!
TWO DOWN!
NO!
HUFF
HUFF
...it's heating up!!
LISTEN UP, ALL UNITS!

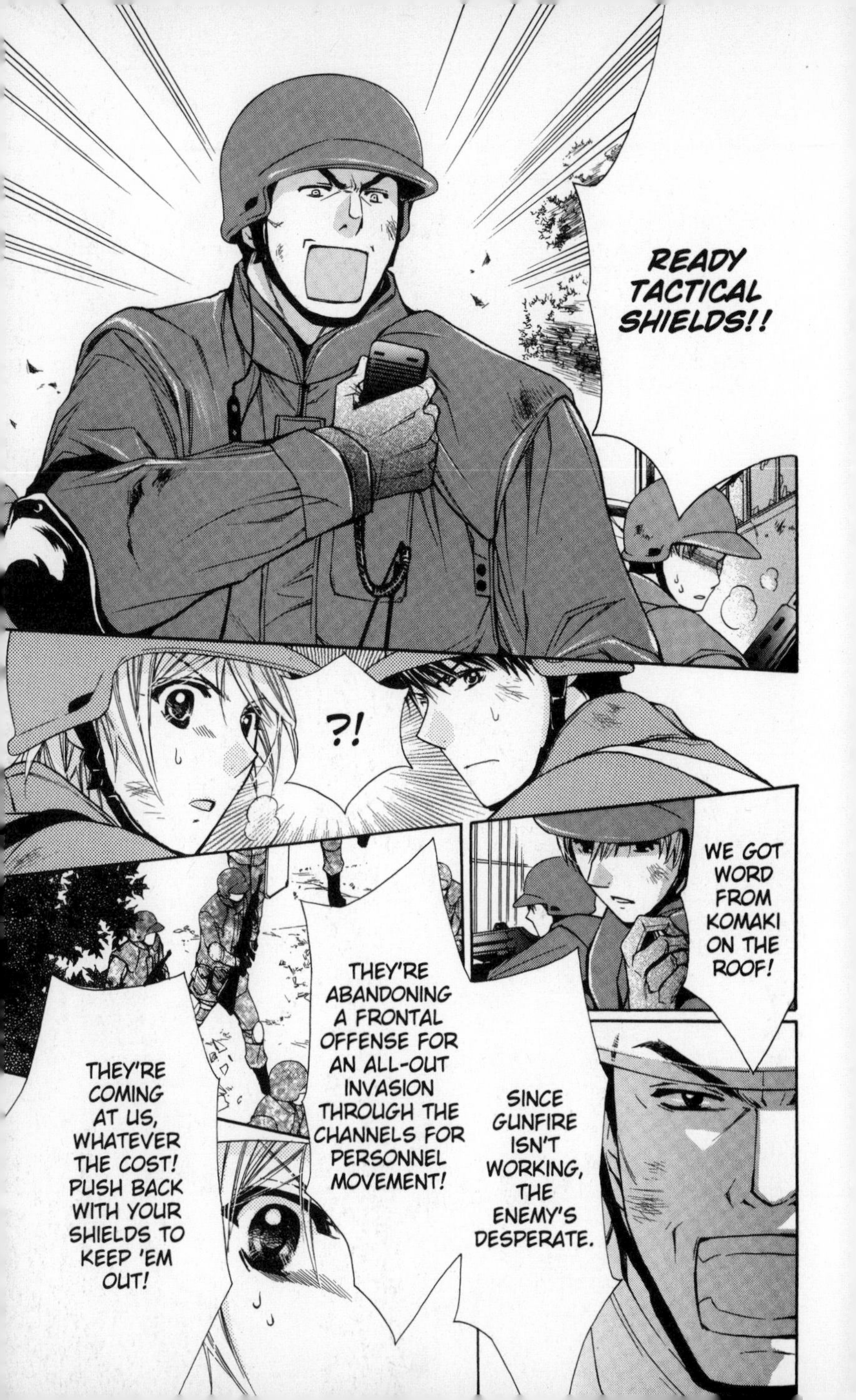
READY TACTICAL SHIELDS!!
?!
WE GOT WORD FROM KOMAKI ON THE ROOF!
THEY'RE ABANDONING A FRONTAL OFFENSE FOR AN ALL-OUT INVASION THROUGH THE CHANNELS FOR PERSONNEL MOVEMENT!
SINCE GUNFIRE ISN'T WORKING, THE ENEMY'S DESPERATE.
THEY'RE COMING AT US, WHATEVER THE COST! PUSH BACK WITH YOUR SHIELDS TO KEEP 'EM OUT!

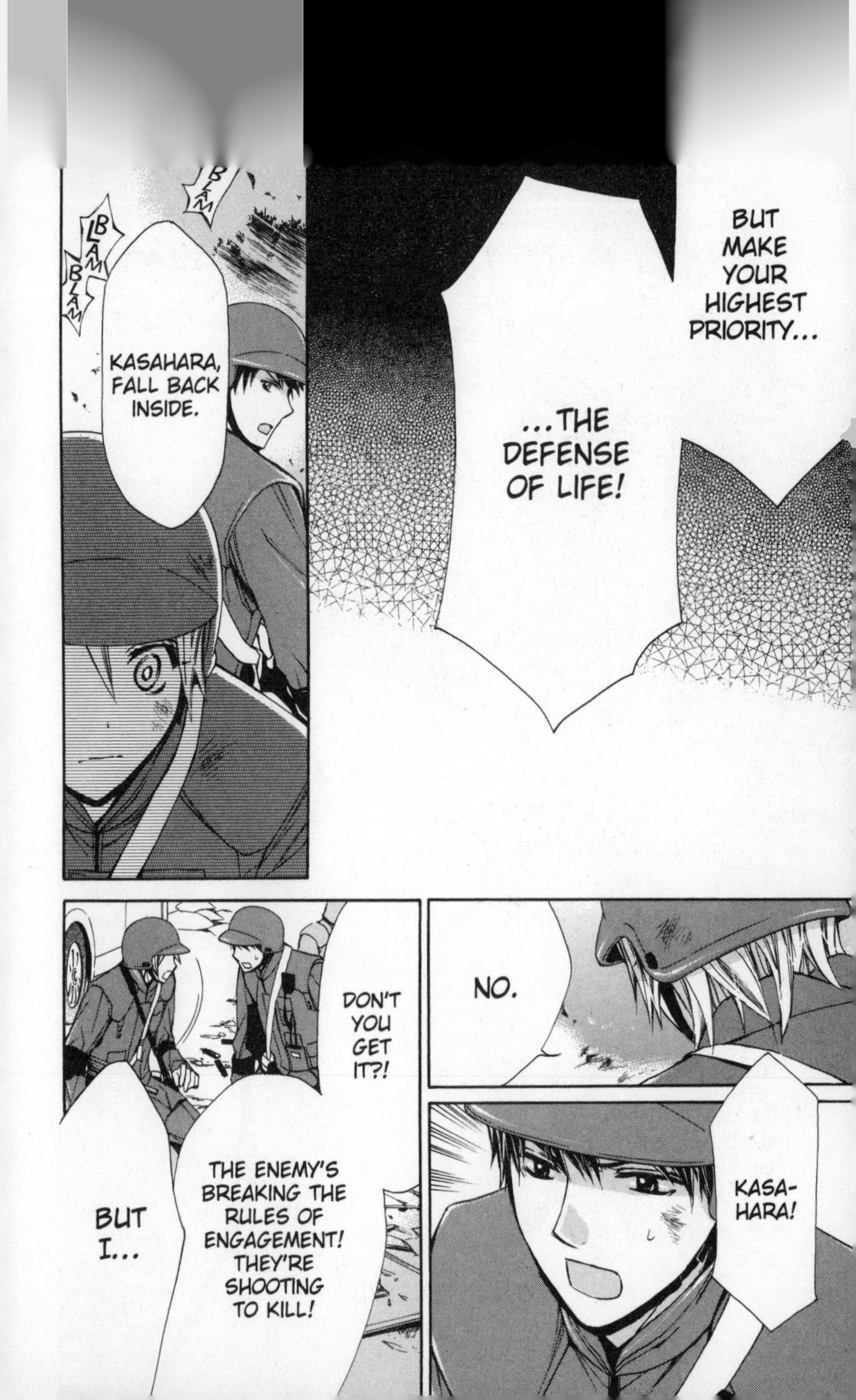
BUT MAKE YOUR HIGHEST PRIORITY...
...THE DEFENSE OF LIFE!
BLAM
BLAM
BLAM
KASAHARA, FALL BACK INSIDE.
NO.
KASA-HARA!
DON'T YOU GET IT?!
THE ENEMY'S BREAKING THE RULES OF ENGAGEMENT! THEY'RE SHOOTING TO KILL!
BUT I...

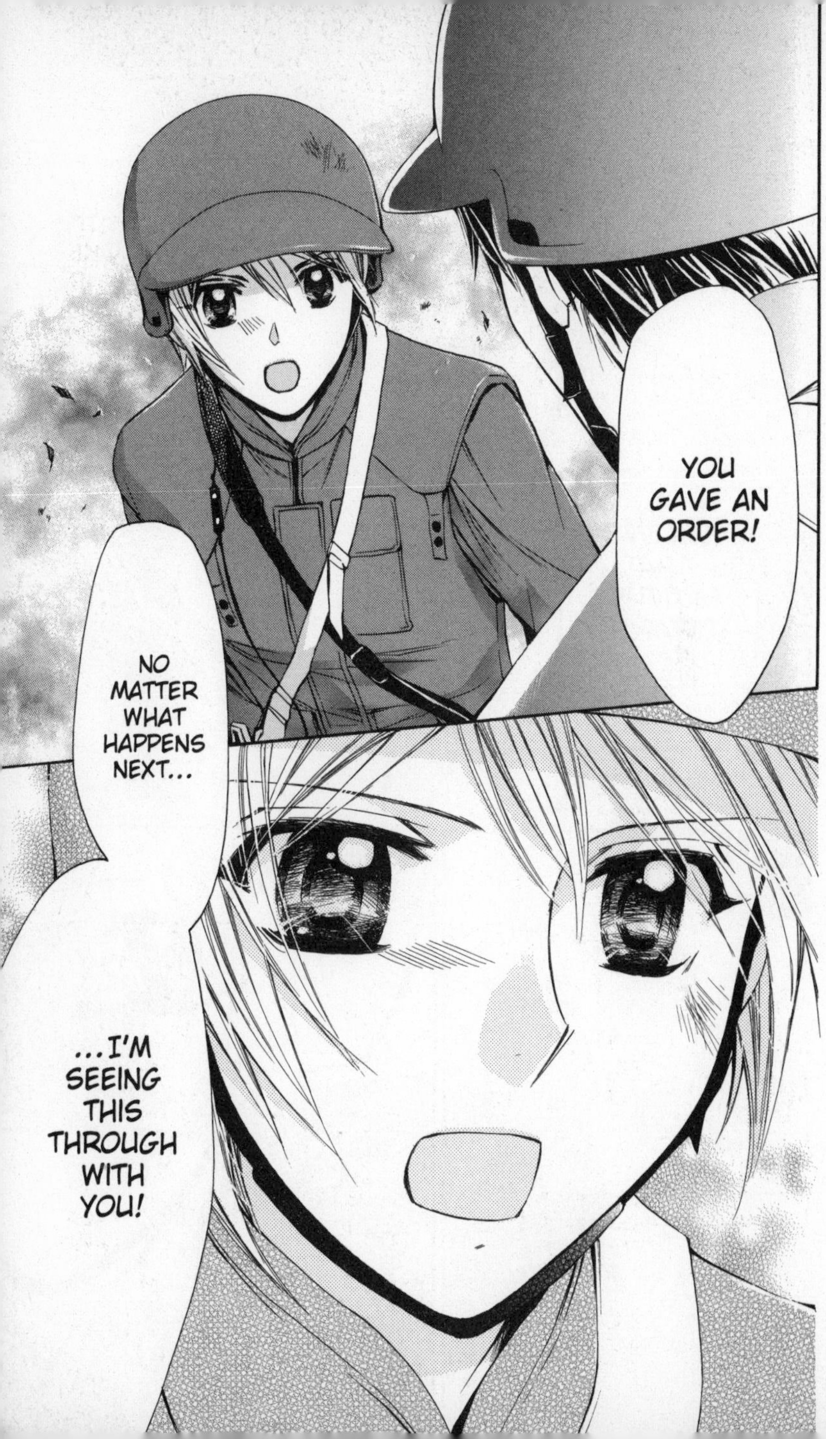
YOU GAVE AN ORDER!
NO MATTER WHAT HAPPENS NEXT...
...I'M SEEING THIS THROUGH WITH YOU!

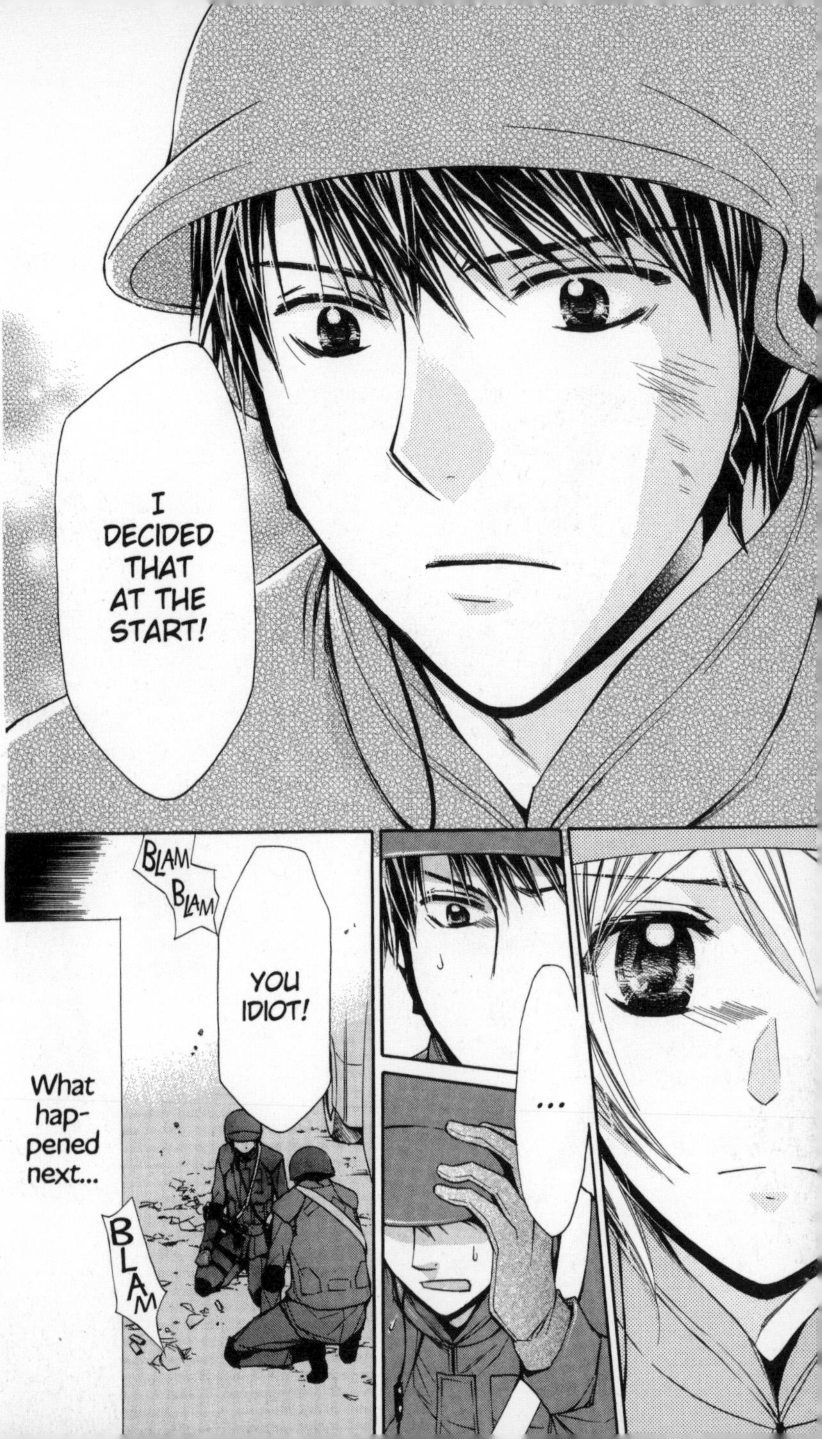
I DECIDED THAT AT THE START!
...
BLAM BLAM
YOU IDIOT!
What hap-pened next...
BLAM

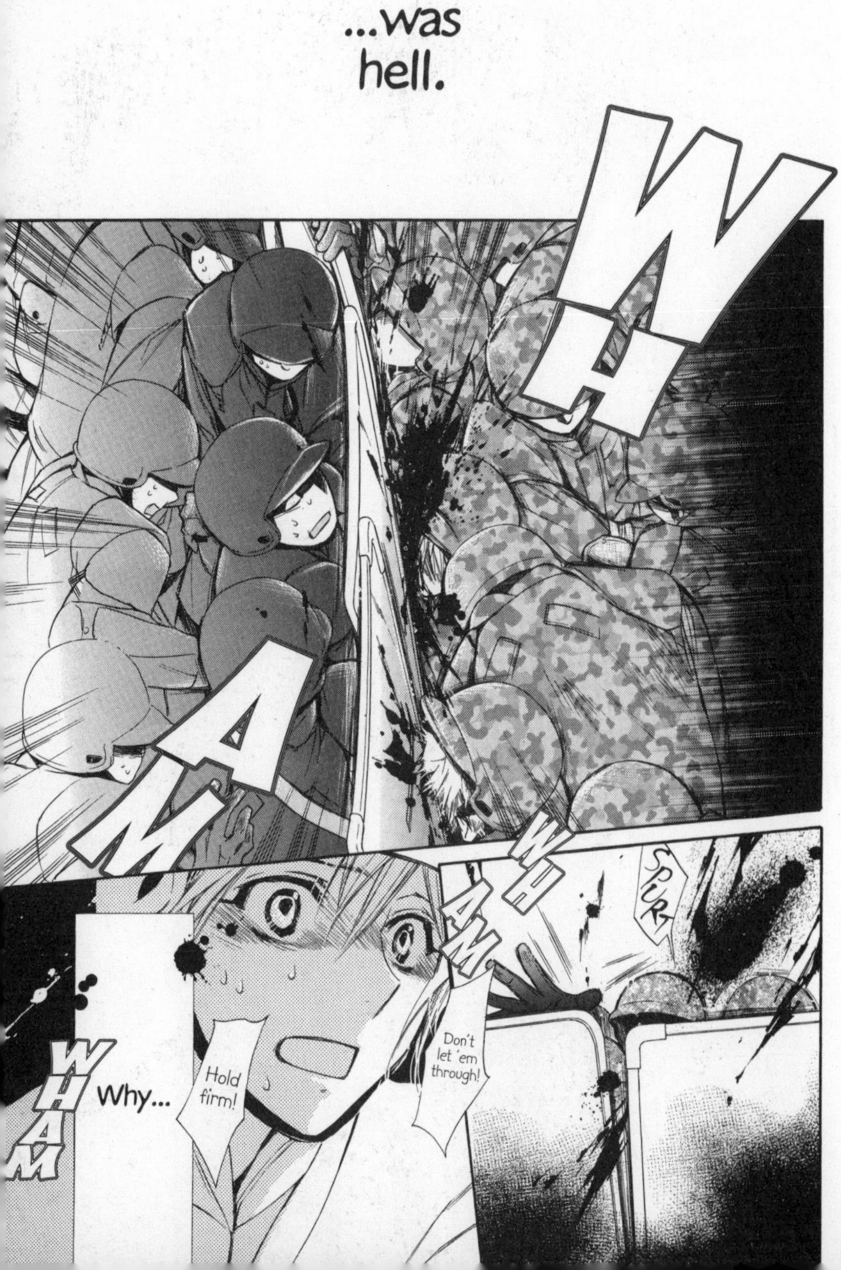
...was hell.
WHAM
WHAM
SPURT
Don't let 'em through!
Hold firm!
Why...
WHAM

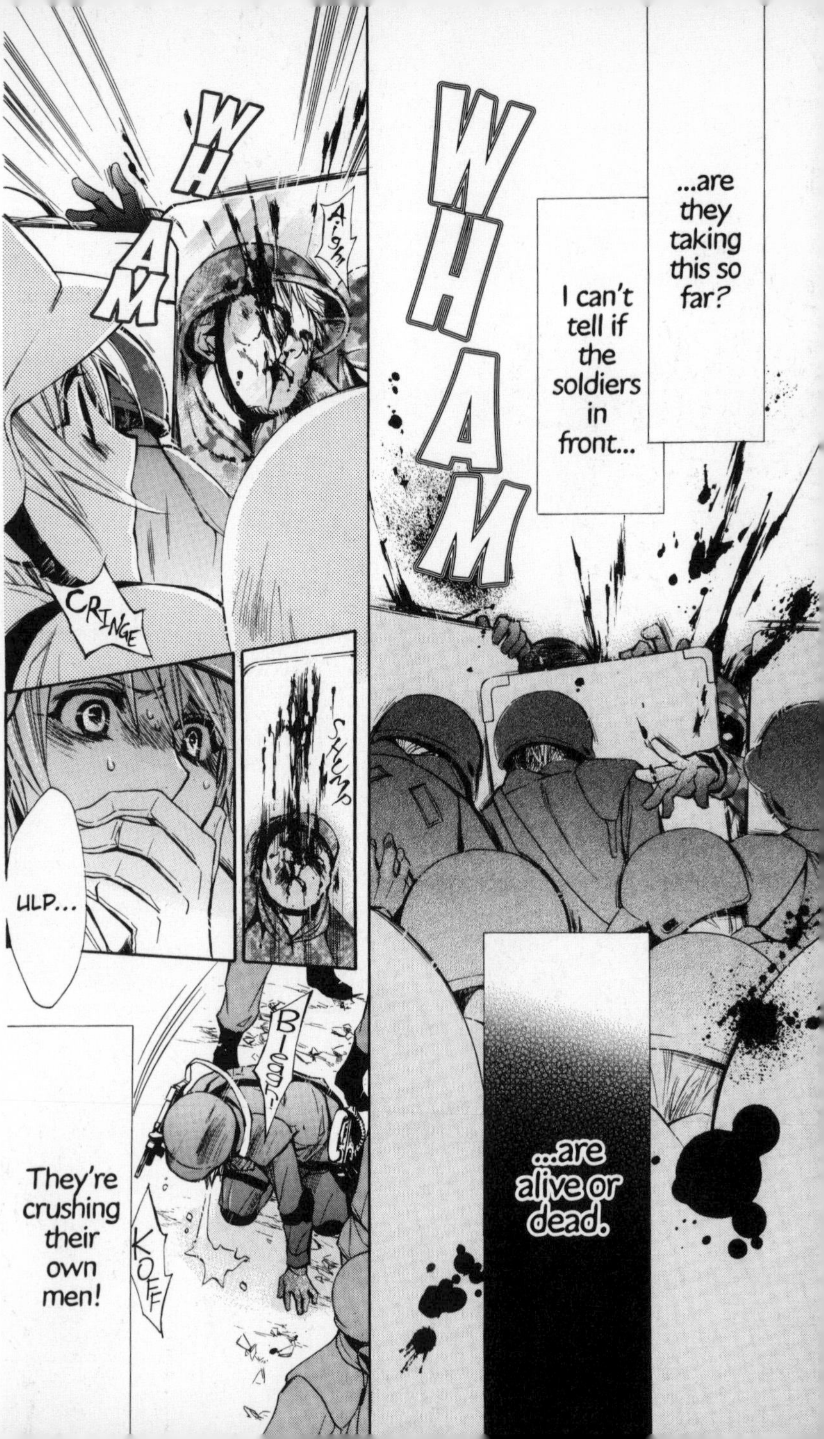
...are they taking this so far?
I can't tell if the soldiers in front...
WHAM
...are alive or dead.
WHAM
Aigh!
CRINGE
SHUMP
ULP...
Bleagh!
KOFF
They're crushing their own men!

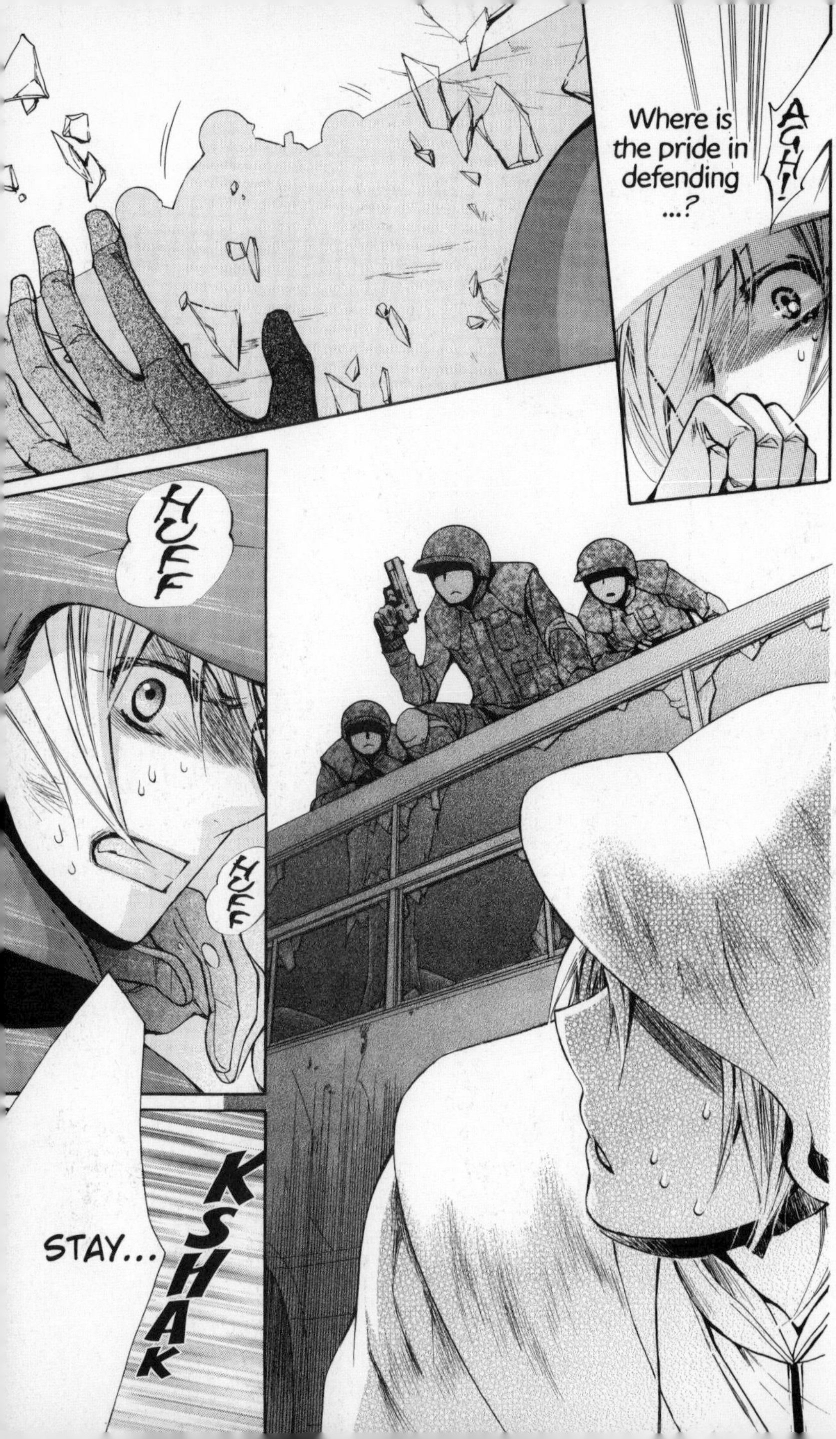
Where is the pride in defending ...?
AGH!
HUFF
HUFF
STAY...
KSHAK

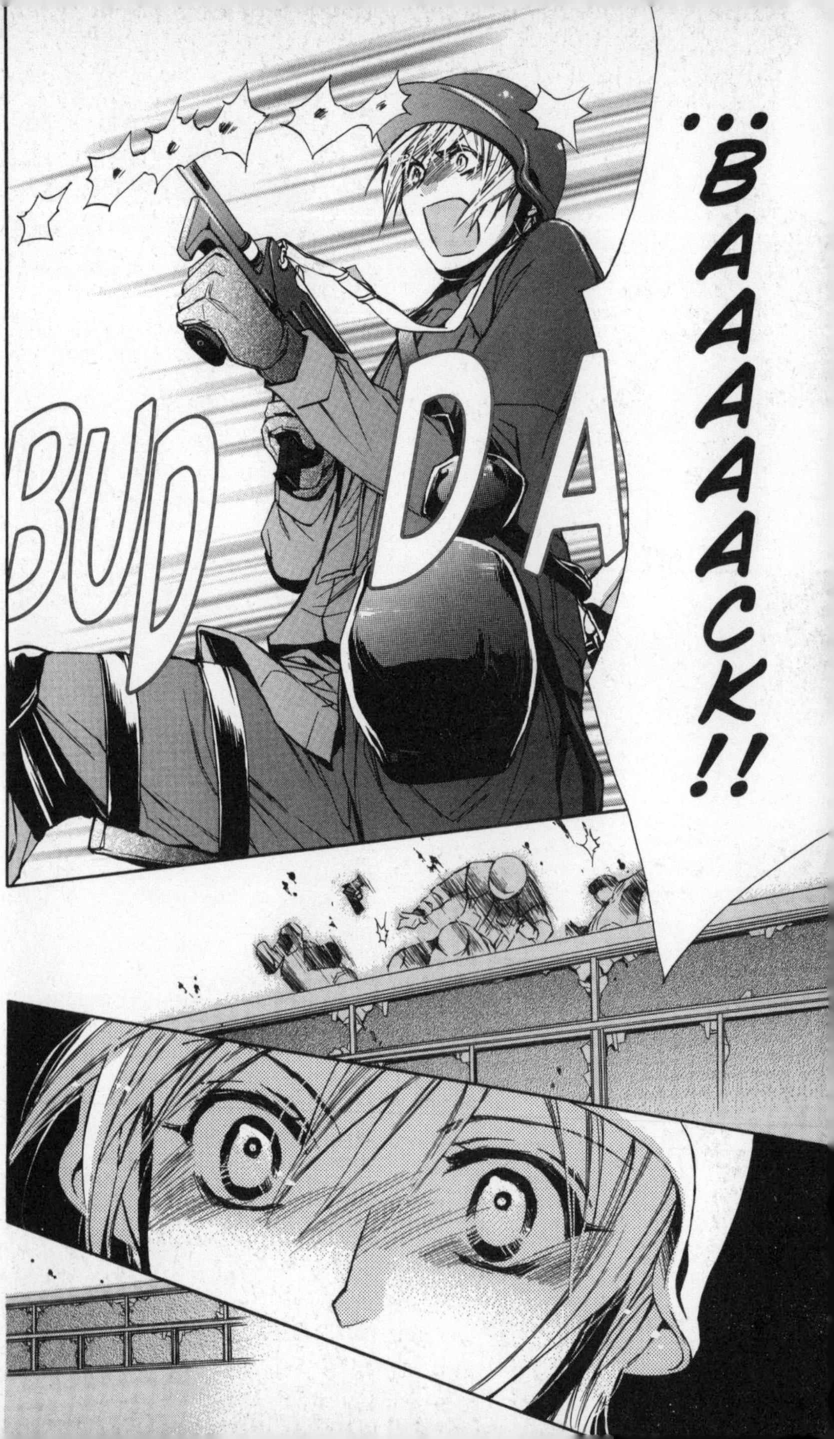
BAAAAACK!!
BUD DA

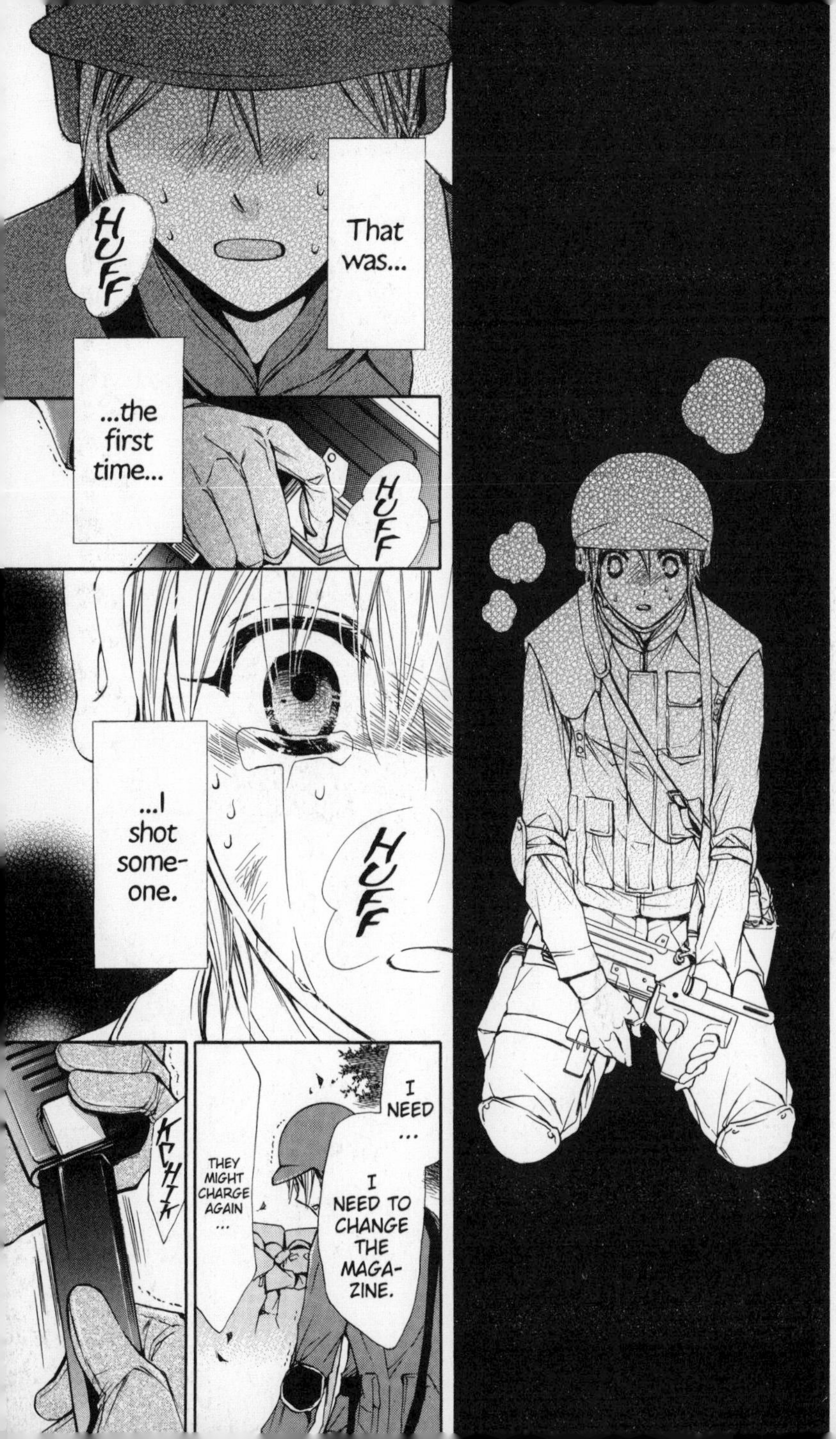
That was...
HUFF
...the first time...
HUFF
HUFF
...I shot some-one.
I NEED...
I NEED TO CHANGE THE MAGA-ZINE.
THEY MIGHT CHARGE AGAIN...
KCHIK

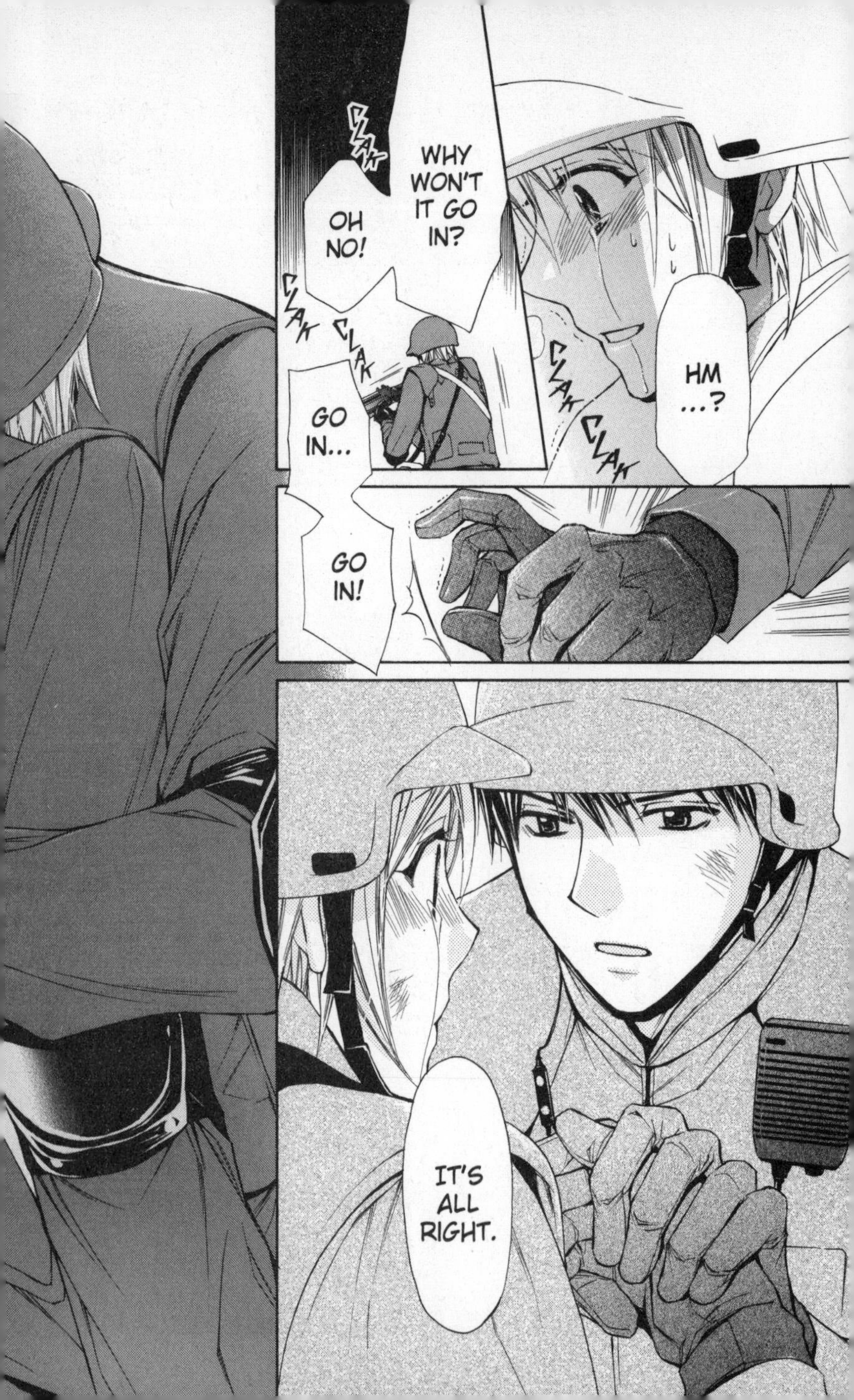
HM ...?
CLAK CLAK
WHY WON'T IT GO IN?
CLAK
OH NO!
CLAK
CLAK
GO IN...
GO IN!
IT'S ALL RIGHT.

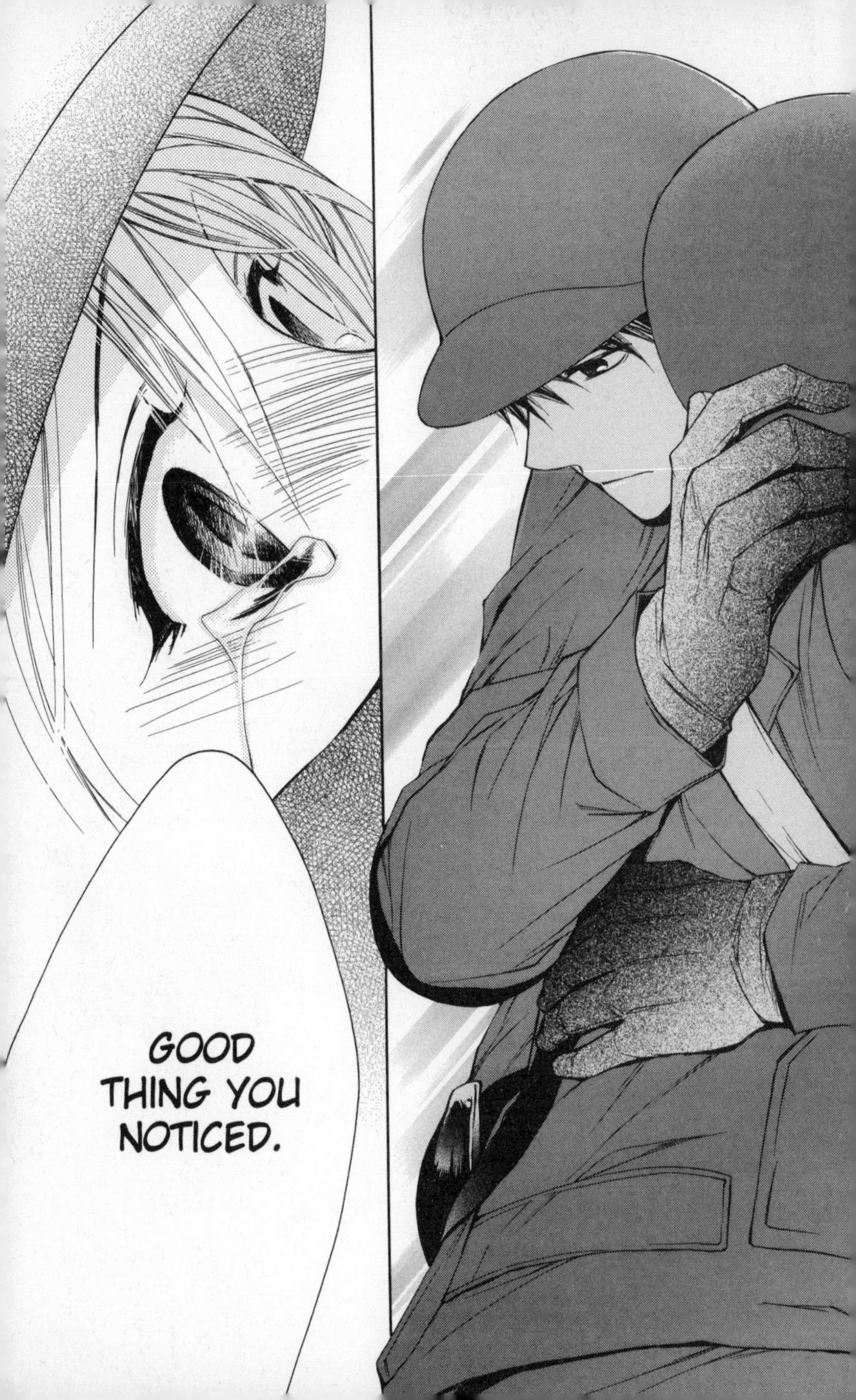
GOOD THING YOU NOTICED.

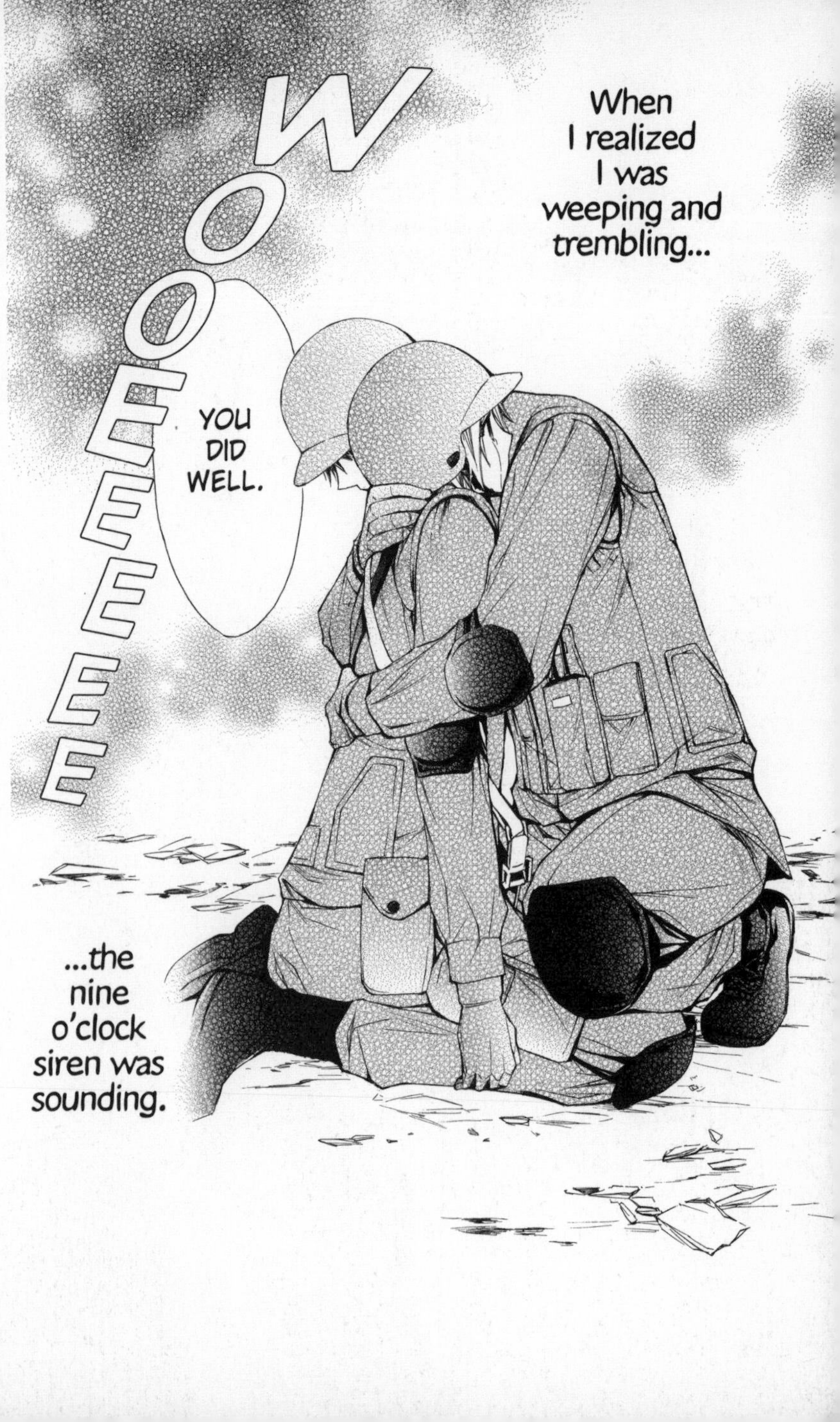
When I realized I was weeping and trembling...
WOOEEEEEE
YOU DID WELL.
...the nine o'clock siren was sounding.

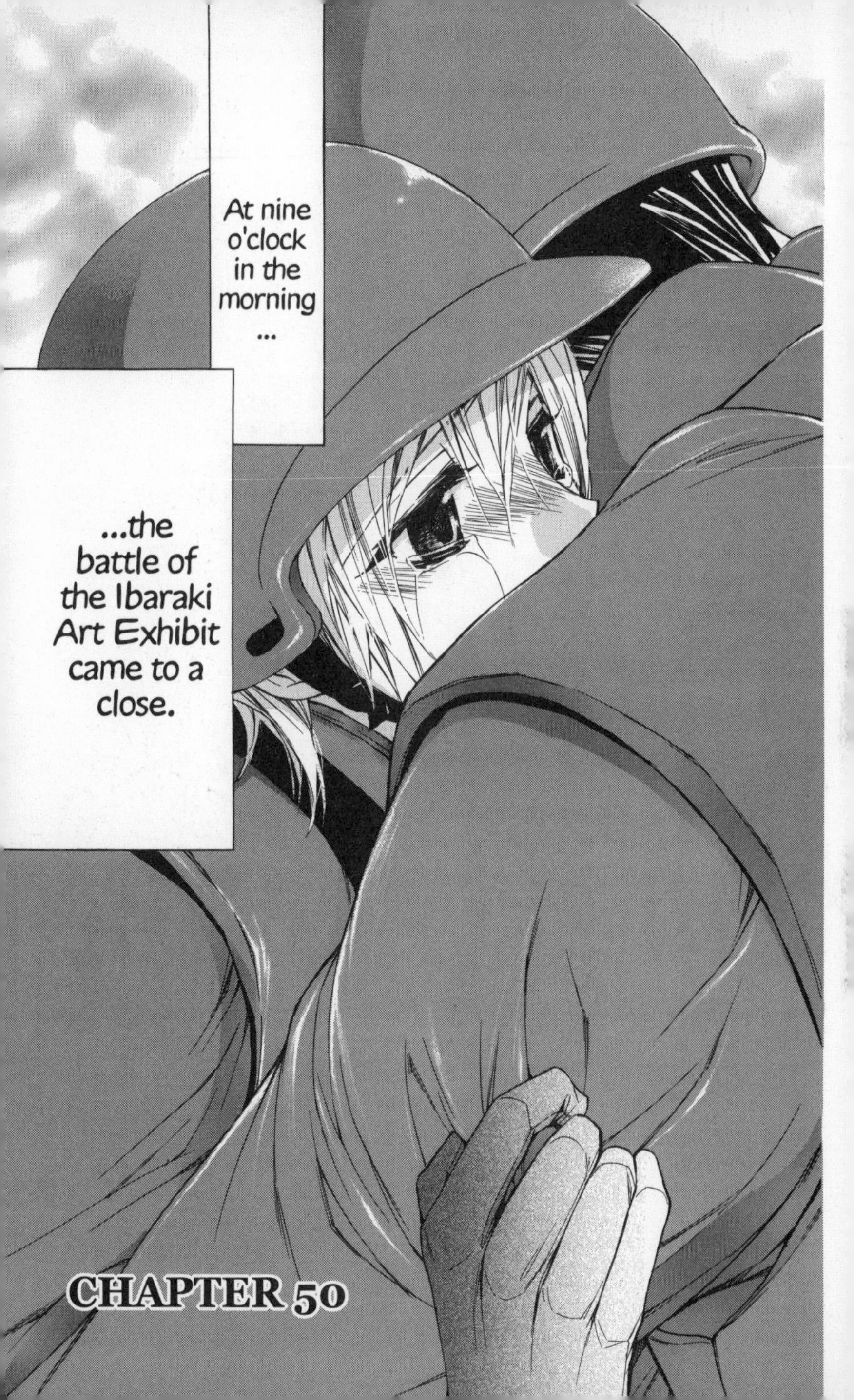
At nine o'clock in the morning ...
...the battle of the Ibaraki Art Exhibit came to a close.
CHAPTER 50

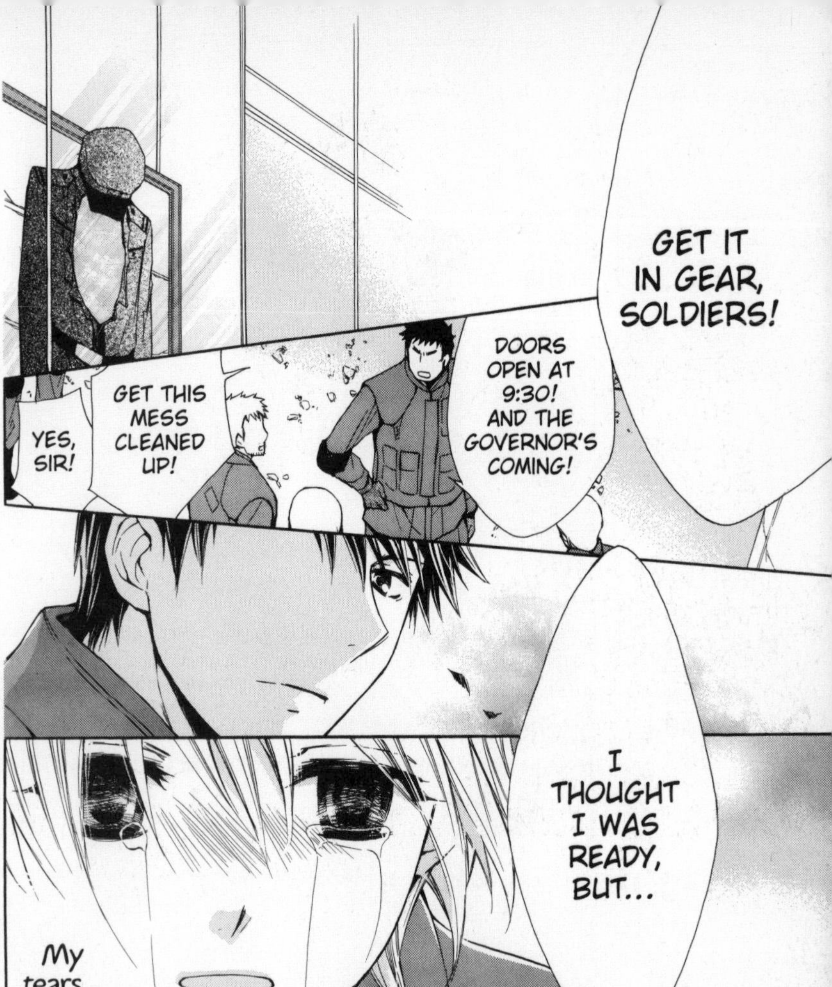
GET IT IN GEAR, SOLDIERS!
DOORS OPEN AT 9:30! AND THE GOVERNOR'S COMING!
GET THIS MESS CLEANED UP!
YES, SIR!
I THOUGHT I WAS READY, BUT...
My tears...

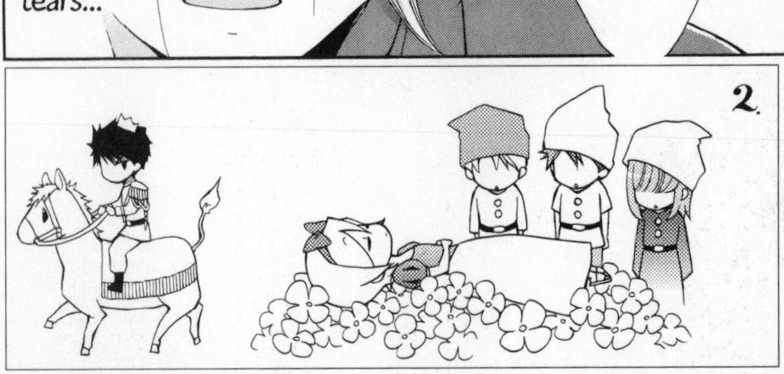
2.

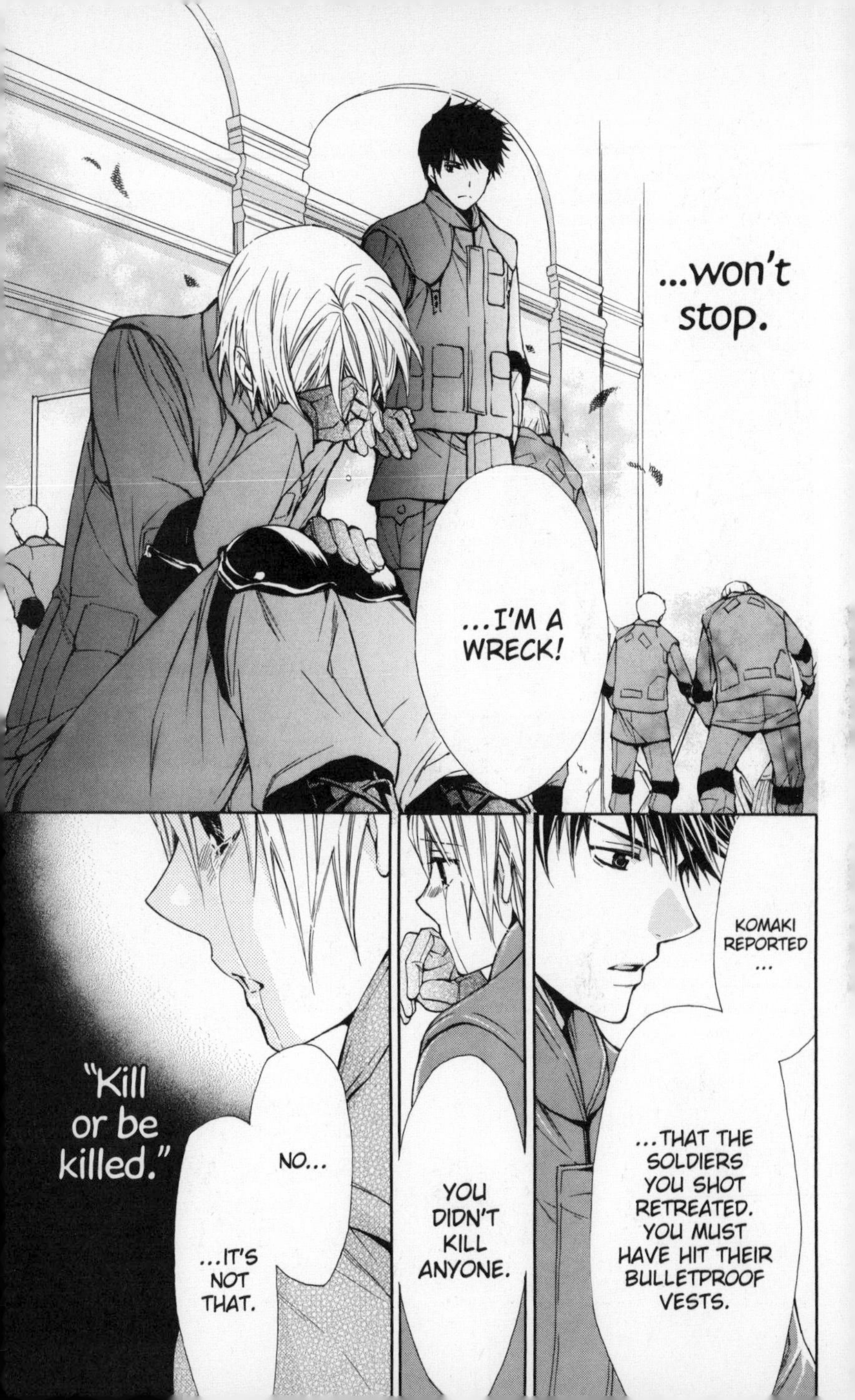
...won't stop.
...I'M A WRECK!
KOMAKI REPORTED ...
...THAT THE SOLDIERS YOU SHOT RETREATED. YOU MUST HAVE HIT THEIR BULLETPROOF VESTS.
YOU DIDN'T KILL ANYONE.
NO...
...IT'S NOT THAT.
“Kill or be killed.”

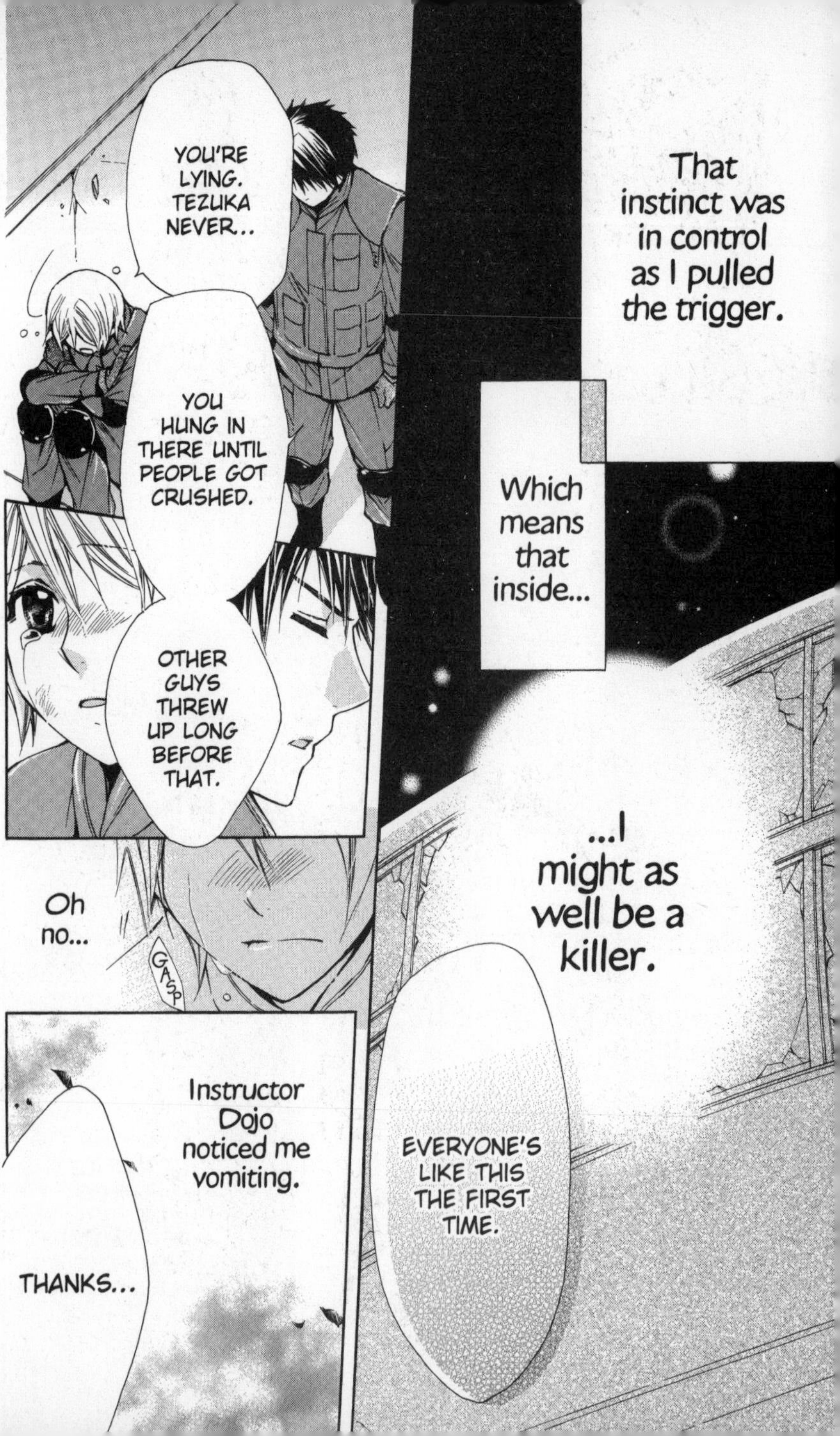
That instinct was in control as I pulled the trigger.
Which means that inside...
...I might as well be a killer.
EVERYONE'S LIKE THIS THE FIRST TIME.
YOU'RE LYING. TEZUKA NEVER...
YOU HUNG IN THERE UNTIL PEOPLE GOT CRUSHED.
OTHER GUYS THREW UP LONG BEFORE THAT.
Oh no...
GASP
Instructor Dojo noticed me vomiting.
THANKS...

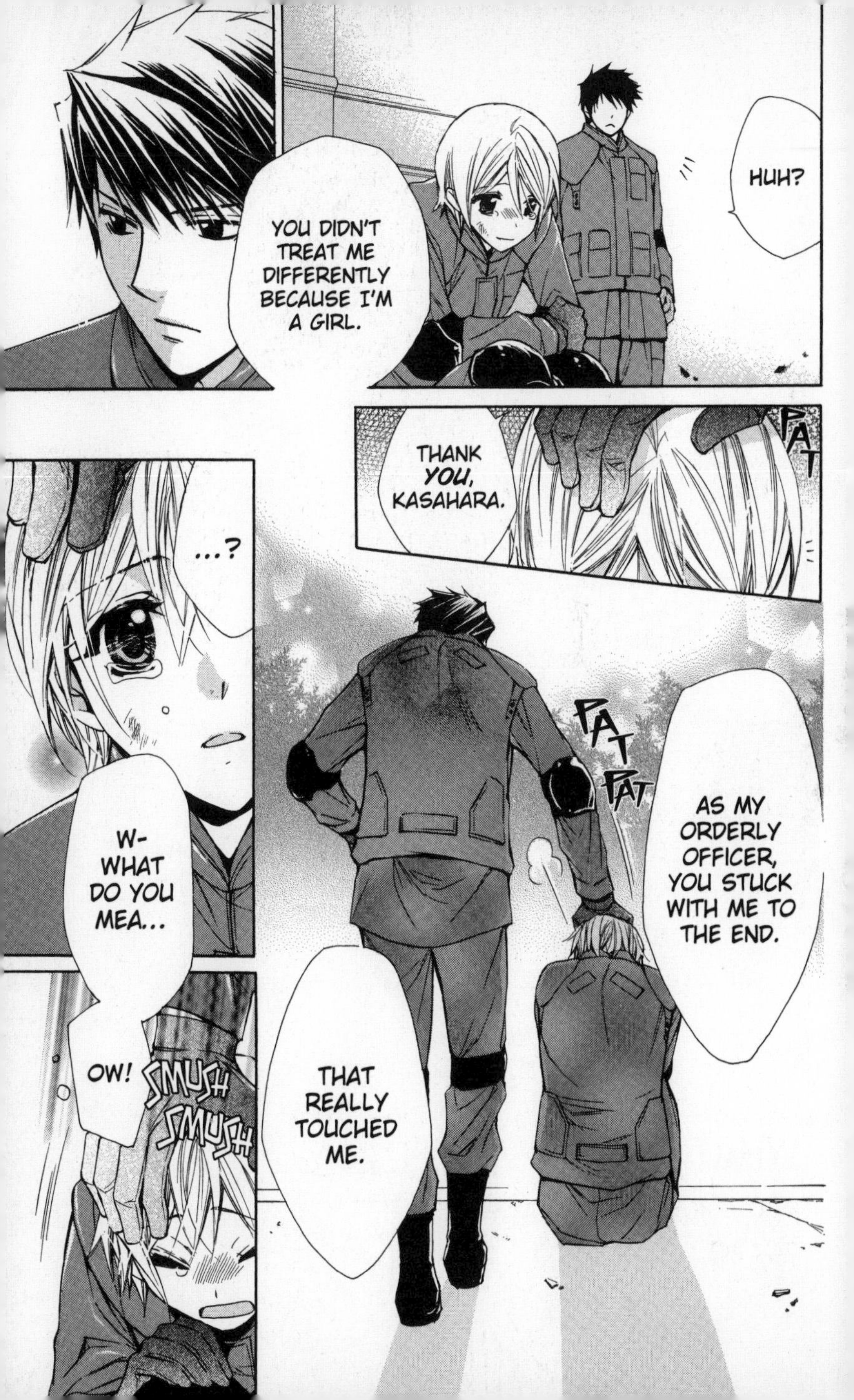
HUH?
YOU DIDN'T TREAT ME DIFFERENTLY BECAUSE I'M A GIRL.
PAT
THANK YOU, KASAHARA.
AS MY ORDERLY OFFICER, YOU STUCK WITH ME TO THE END.
PAT PAT
THAT REALLY TOUCHED ME.
...?
W-WHAT DO YOU MEA...
OW!
SMUSH SMUSH

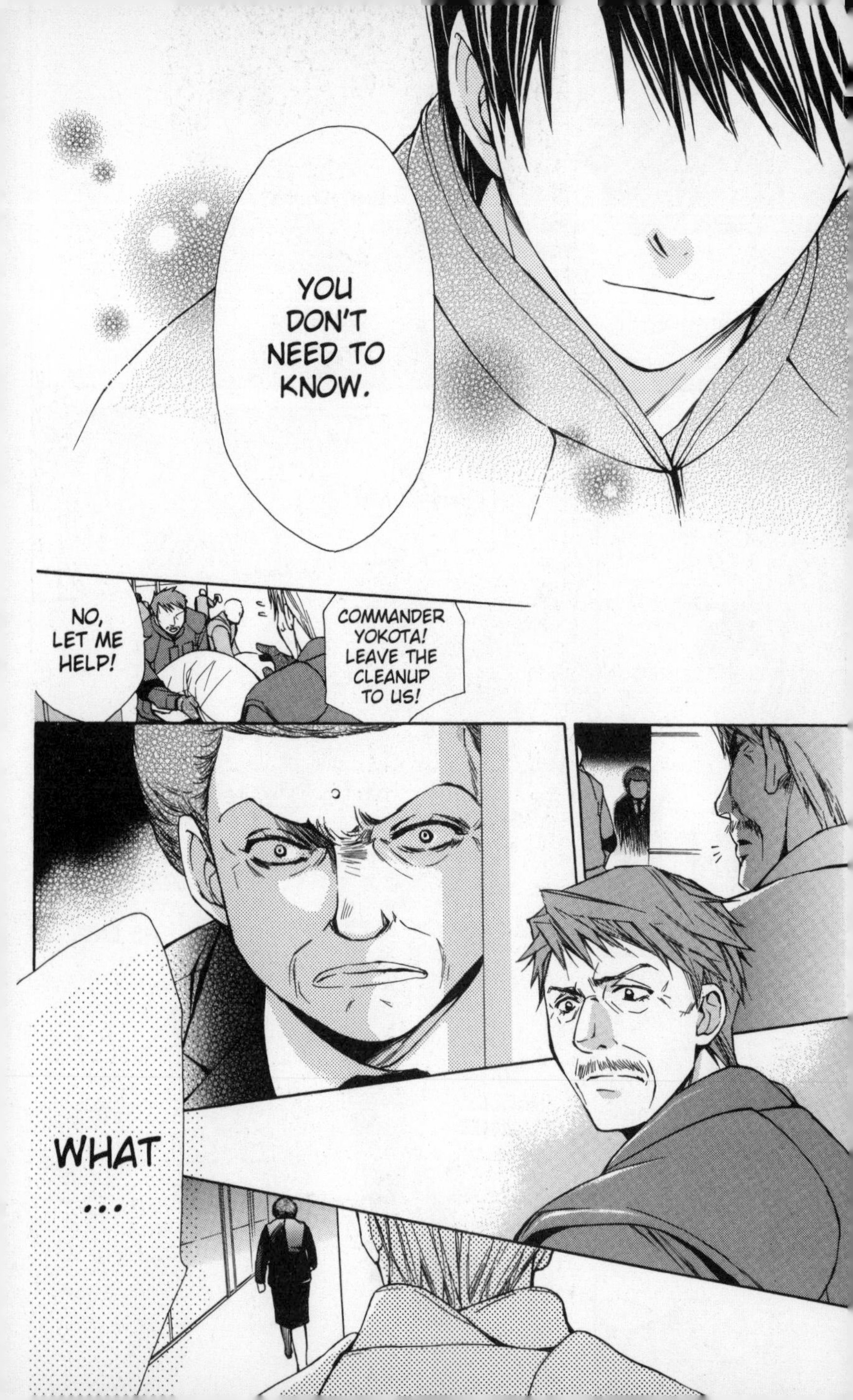
YOU DON'T NEED TO KNOW.
COMMANDER YOKOTA! LEAVE THE CLEANUP TO US!
NO, LET ME HELP!
WHAT ...

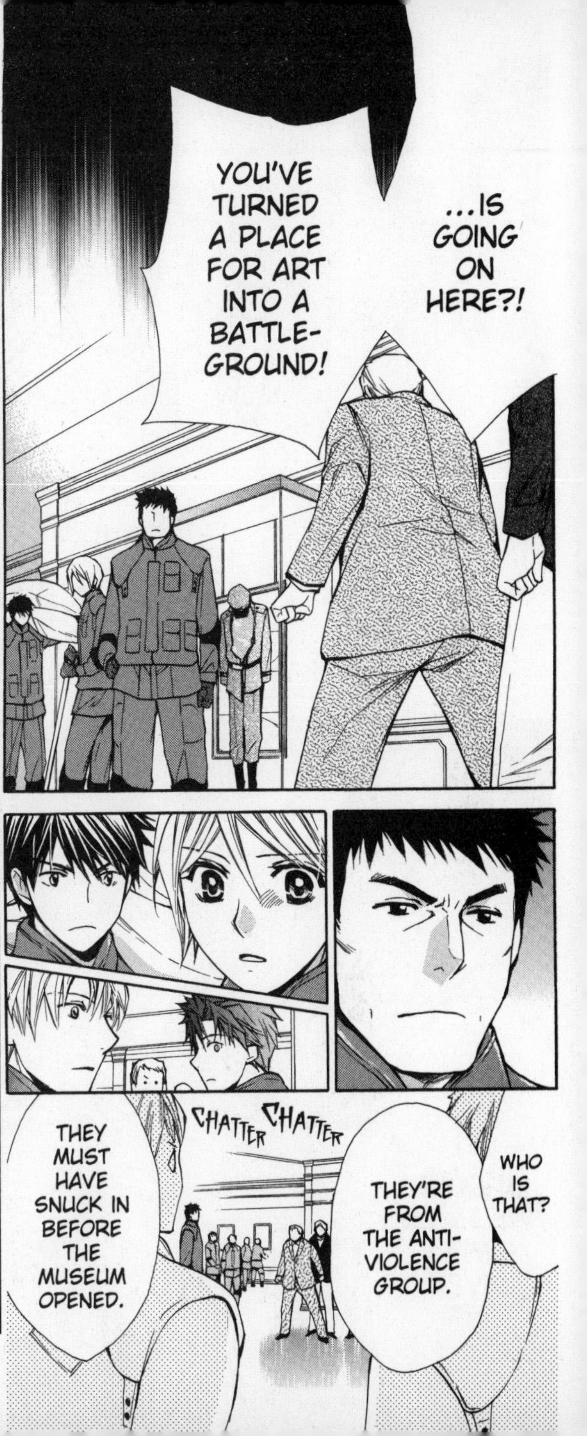
...IS GOING ON HERE?!
YOU'VE TURNED A PLACE FOR ART INTO A BATTLE-GROUND!
WHO IS THAT?
THEY'RE FROM THE ANTI-VIOLENCE GROUP.
CHATTER CHATTER
THEY MUST HAVE SNUCK IN BEFORE THE MUSEUM OPENED.

2

*

In Volume 10 I mentioned the anime movie of *Library Wars*, but the live-action movie is slated to come out in April 2013, which is when Volume 11 comes out! I'm so looking forward to it!! Everyone on the cast fits their characters perfectly. Everyone in the Library Forces will look cute or cool!

Personally, the cast member who most surprised me plays Tezuka. When I was a child, I didn't watch *Kamen Rider*. The first *Rider* I really watched was *Fourze*, so I was like, "Whoa, it's Gen-chan!" (lol) I love Gen-chan. I can't wait!!

*

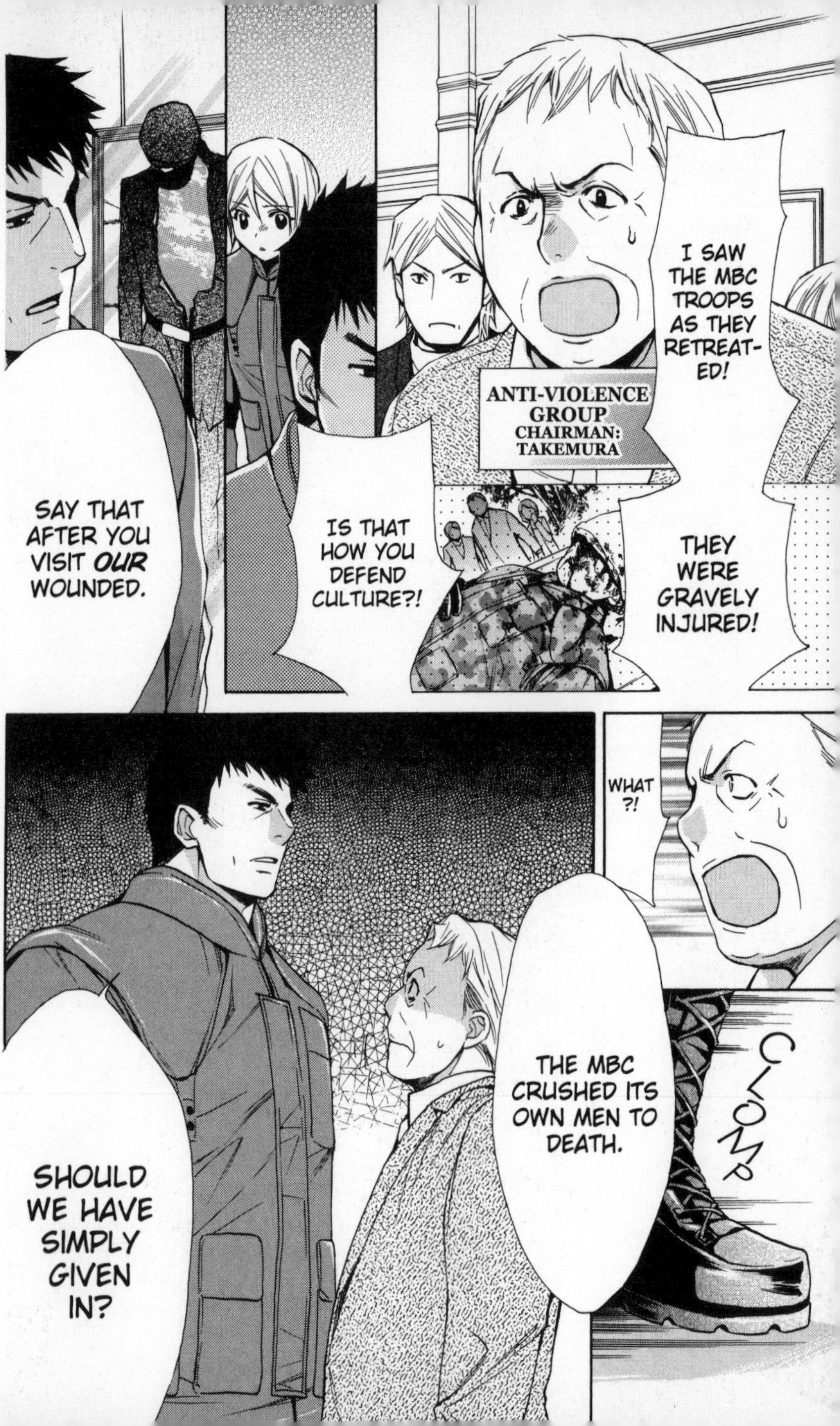
I SAW THE MBC TROOPS AS THEY RETREAT-ED!
ANTI-VIOLENCE GROUP CHAIRMAN: TAKEMURA
THEY WERE GRAVELY INJURED!
IS THAT HOW YOU DEFEND CULTURE?!
SAY THAT AFTER YOU VISIT *OUR* WOUNDED.
WHAT?!
CLOMP
THE MBC CRUSHED ITS OWN MEN TO DEATH.
SHOULD WE HAVE SIMPLY GIVEN IN?

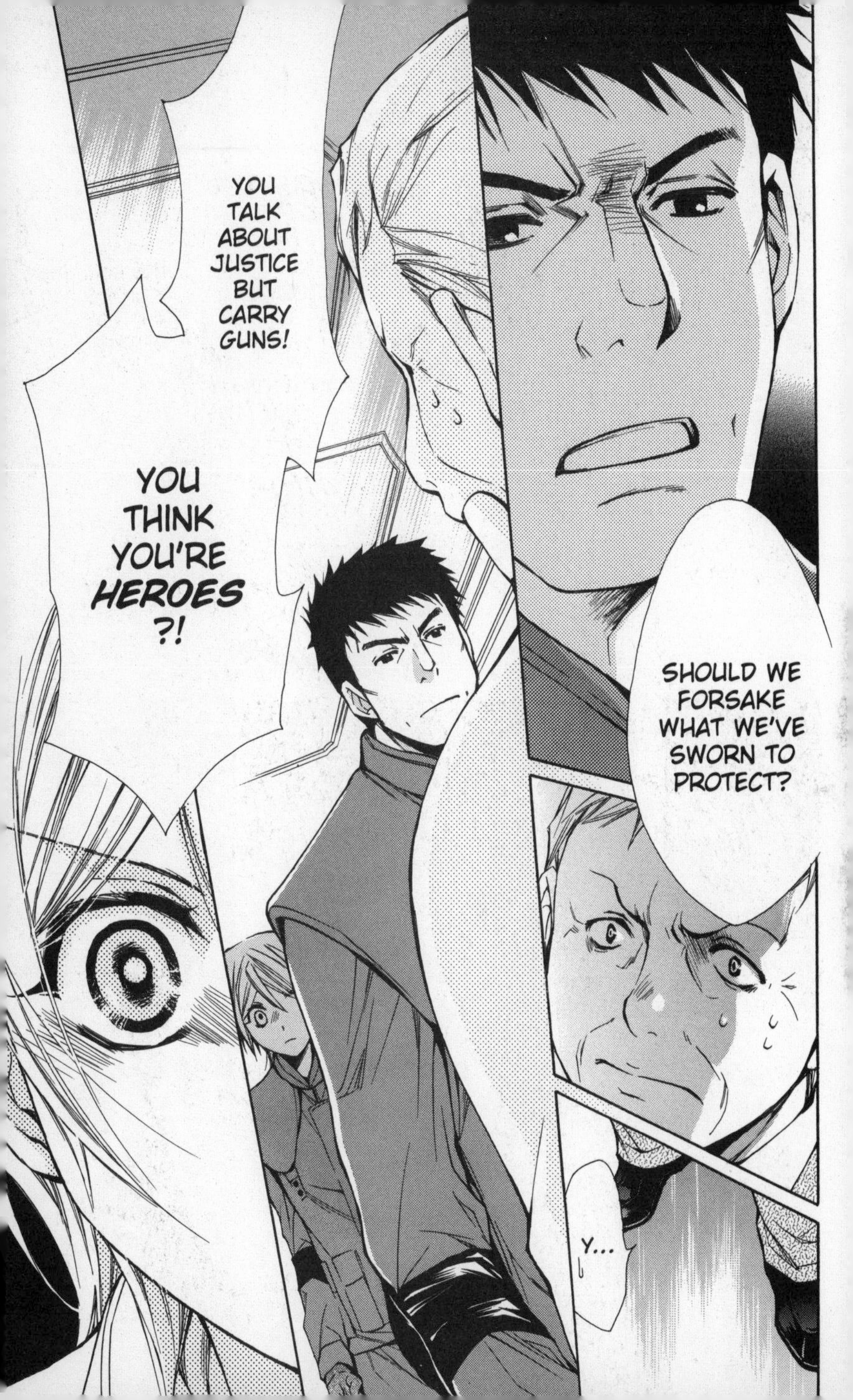
YOU TALK ABOUT JUSTICE BUT CARRY GUNS!
YOU THINK YOU'RE *HEROES* ?!
SHOULD WE FORSAKE WHAT WE'VE SWORN TO PROTECT?
Y...

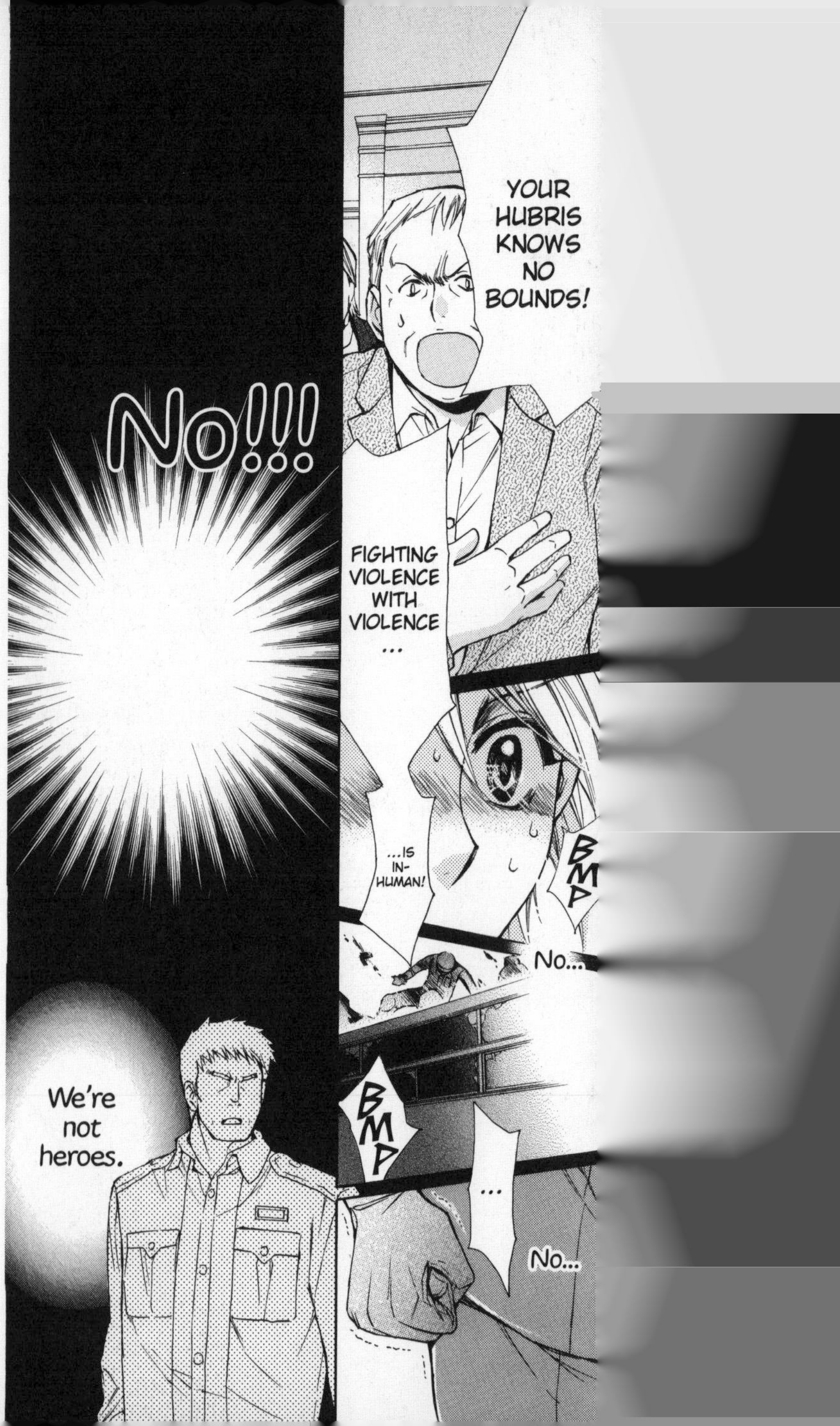
YOUR HUBRIS KNOWS NO BOUNDS!
FIGHTING VIOLENCE WITH VIOLENCE...
...IS IN-HUMAN!
BMP
No...
BMP
...
No...
No!!!
We're not heroes.

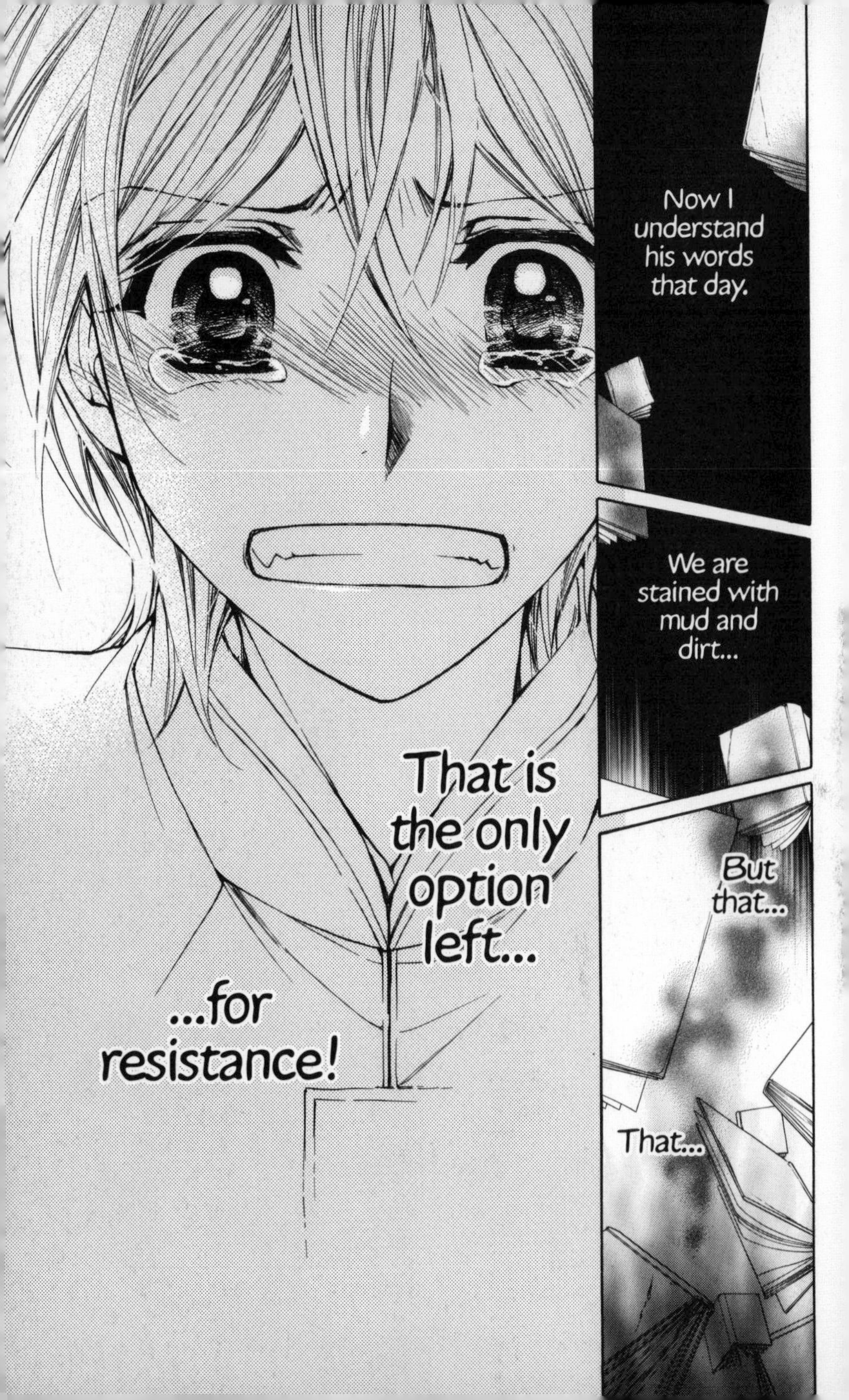

Now I understand his words that day.
We are stained with mud and dirt...
But that...
That...
That is the only option left...
...for resistance!

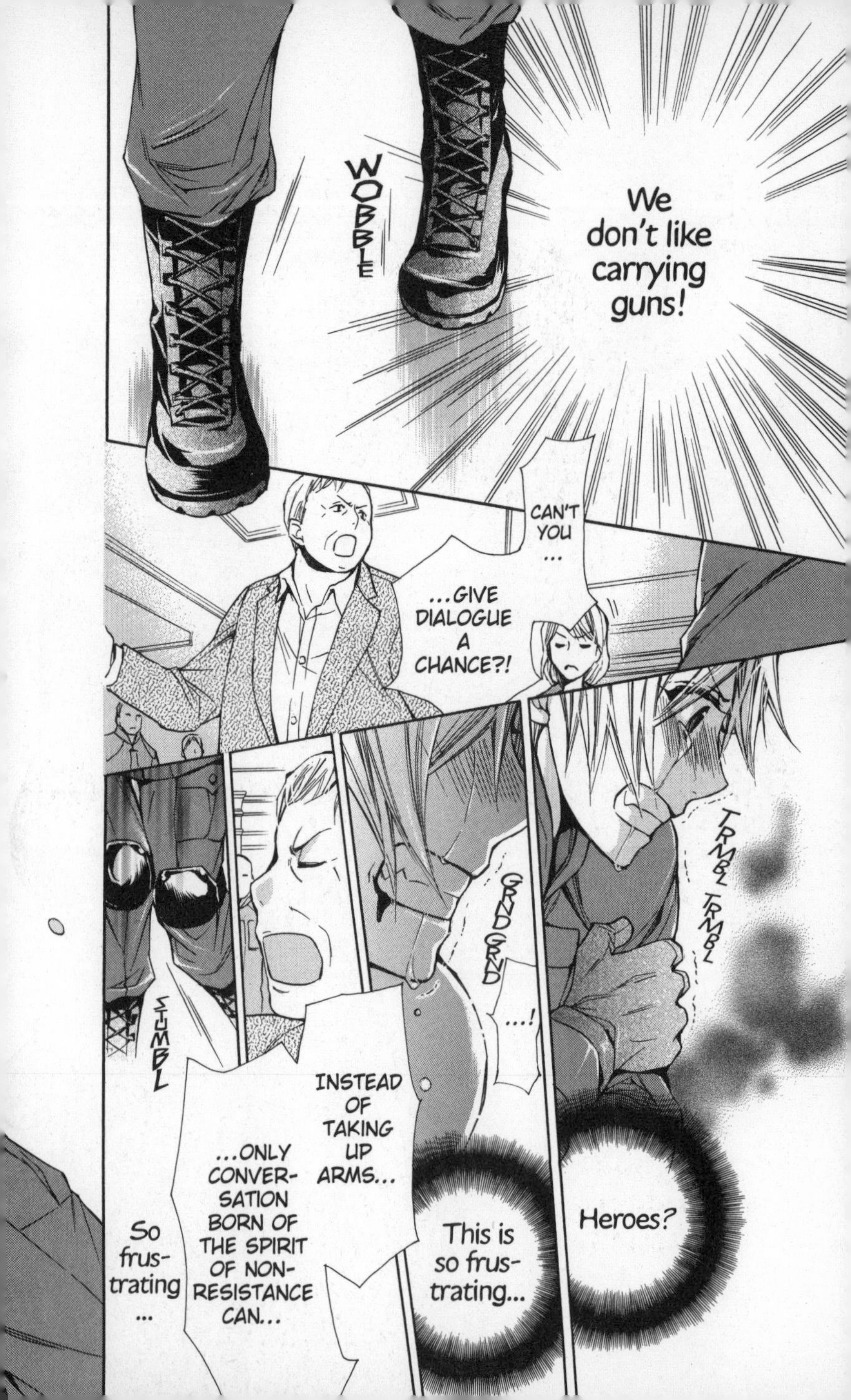
We don't like carrying guns!
WOBBLE
CAN'T YOU...
...GIVE DIALOGUE A CHANCE?!
TRMBL TRMBL
Heroes?
GRND GRND
...!
This is so frus-trating...
INSTEAD OF TAKING UP ARMS...
...ONLY CONVER-SATION BORN OF THE SPIRIT OF NON-RESISTANCE CAN...
STUMBL
So frus-trating...

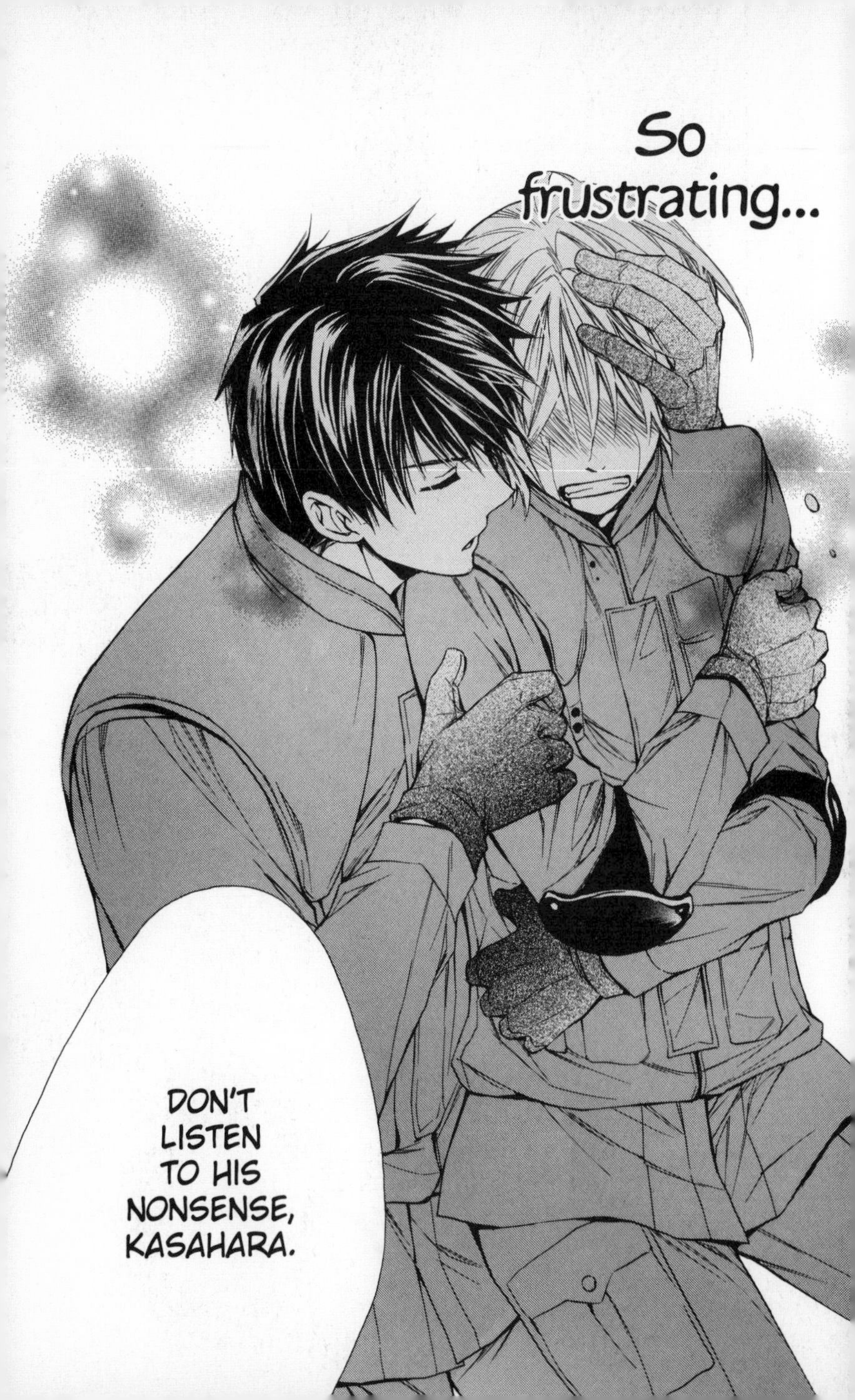
So frustrating...
DON'T LISTEN TO HIS NONSENSE, KASAHARA.

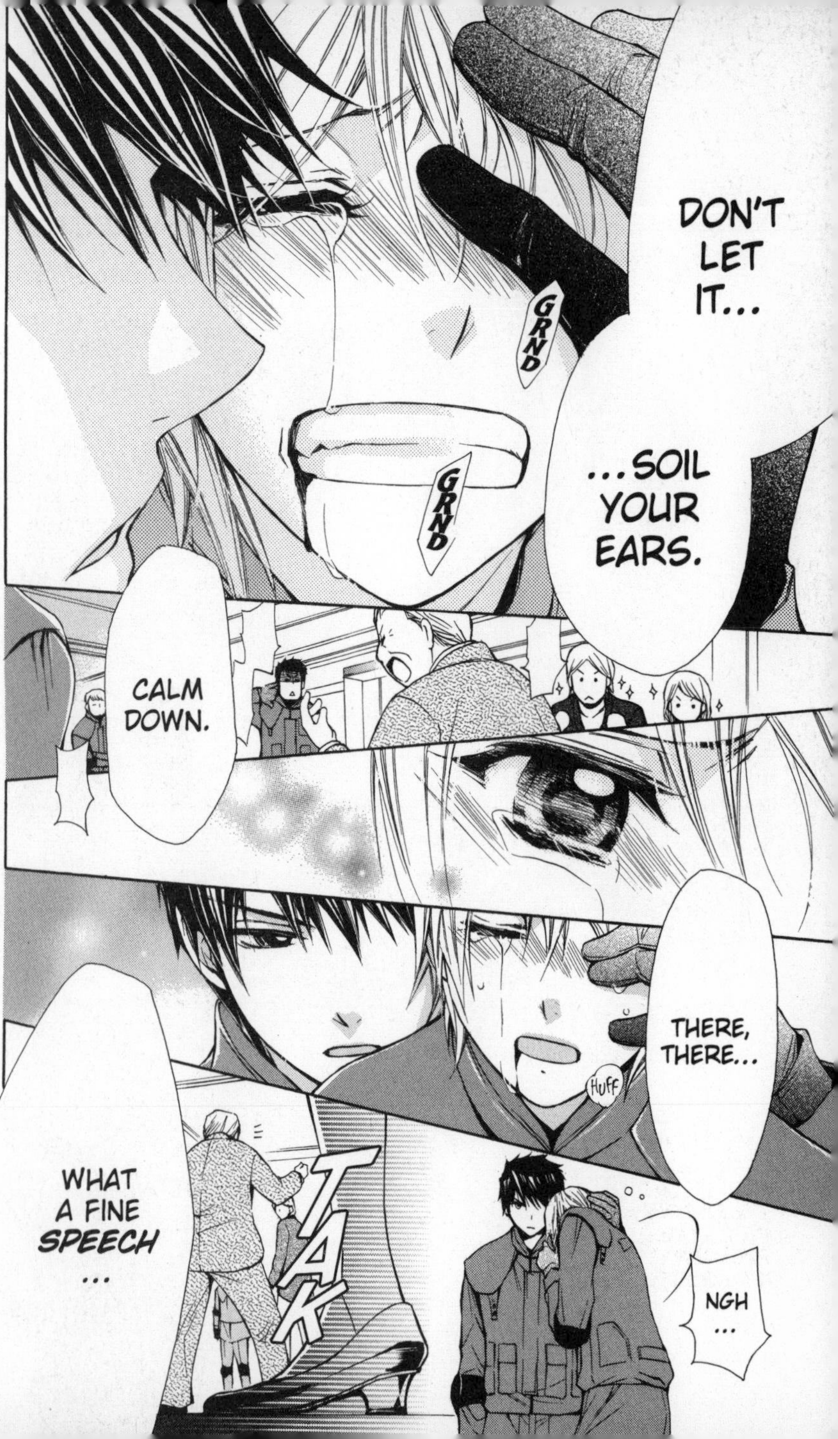
DON'T LET IT...
...SOIL YOUR EARS.
GRND
GRND
CALM DOWN.
THERE, THERE...
HUFF
NGH ...
TAK
WHAT A FINE SPEECH ...

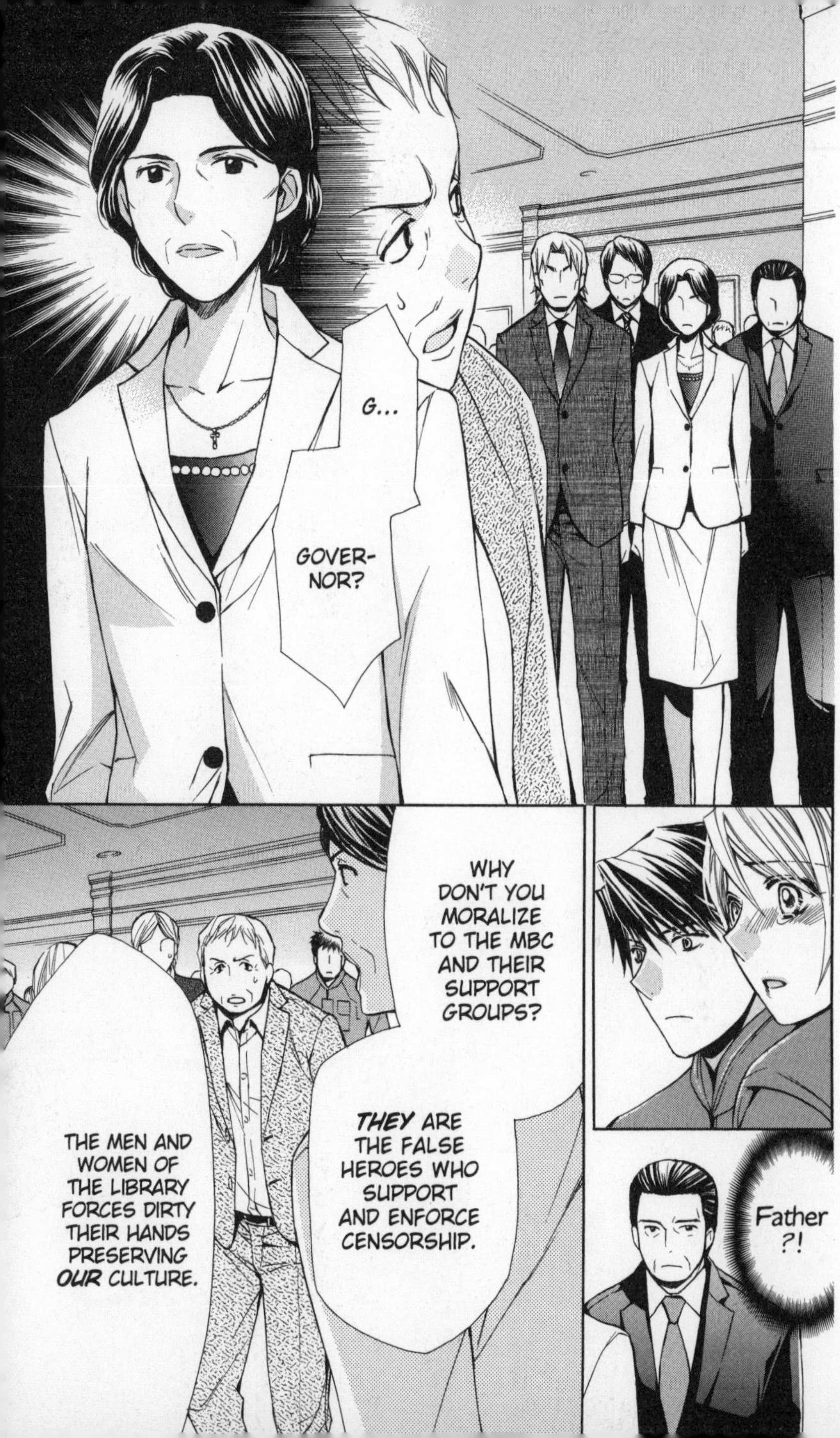
G...
GOVER-NOR?
Father?!
WHY DON'T YOU MORALIZE TO THE MBC AND THEIR SUPPORT GROUPS?
THEY ARE THE FALSE HEROES WHO SUPPORT AND ENFORCE CENSORSHIP.
THE MEN AND WOMEN OF THE LIBRARY FORCES DIRTY THEIR HANDS PRESERVING OUR CULTURE.

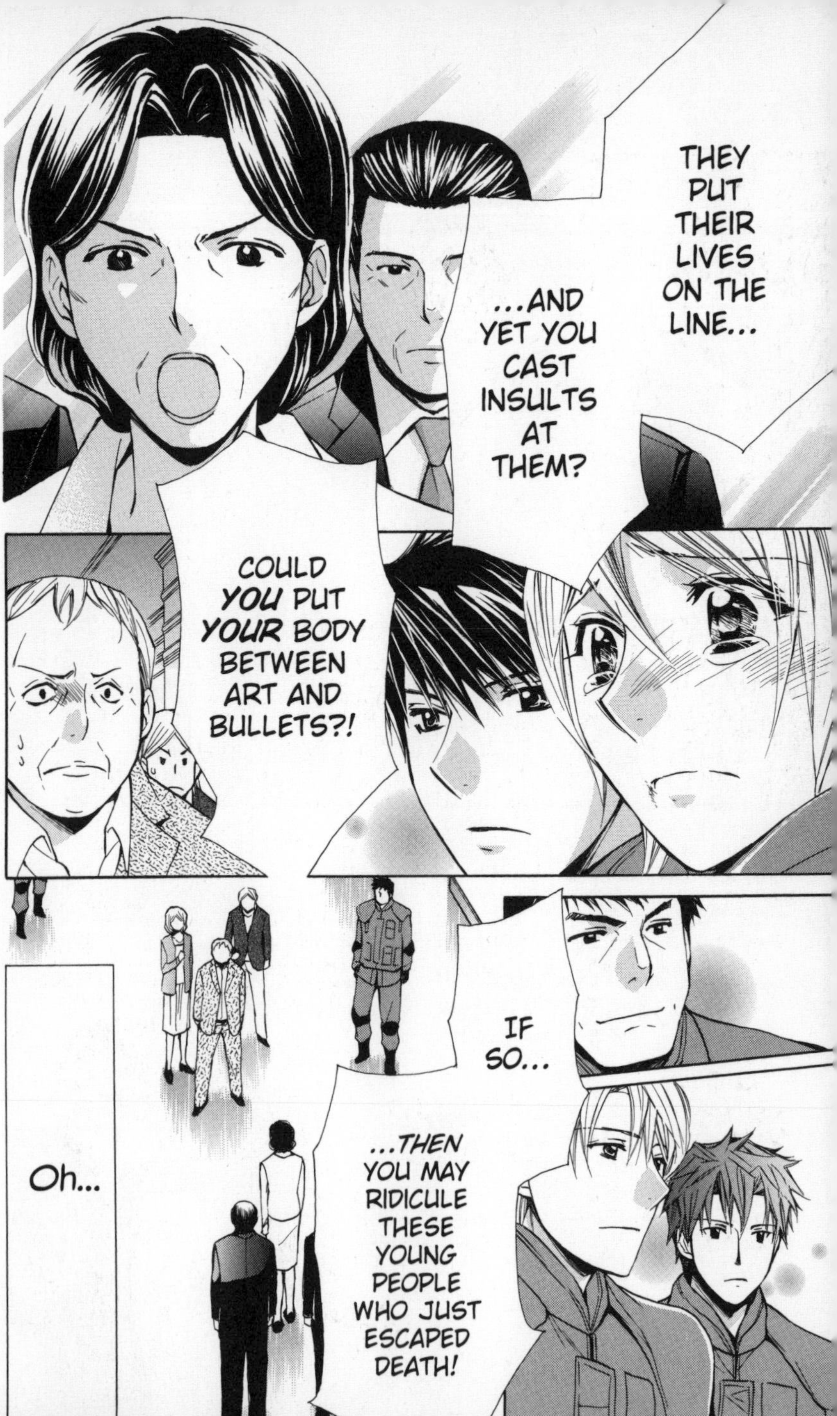
THEY PUT THEIR LIVES ON THE LINE...
...AND YET YOU CAST INSULTS AT THEM?
COULD *YOU* PUT *YOUR* BODY BETWEEN ART AND BULLETS?!
IF SO...
...*THEN* YOU MAY RIDICULE THESE YOUNG PEOPLE WHO JUST ESCAPED DEATH!
Oh...

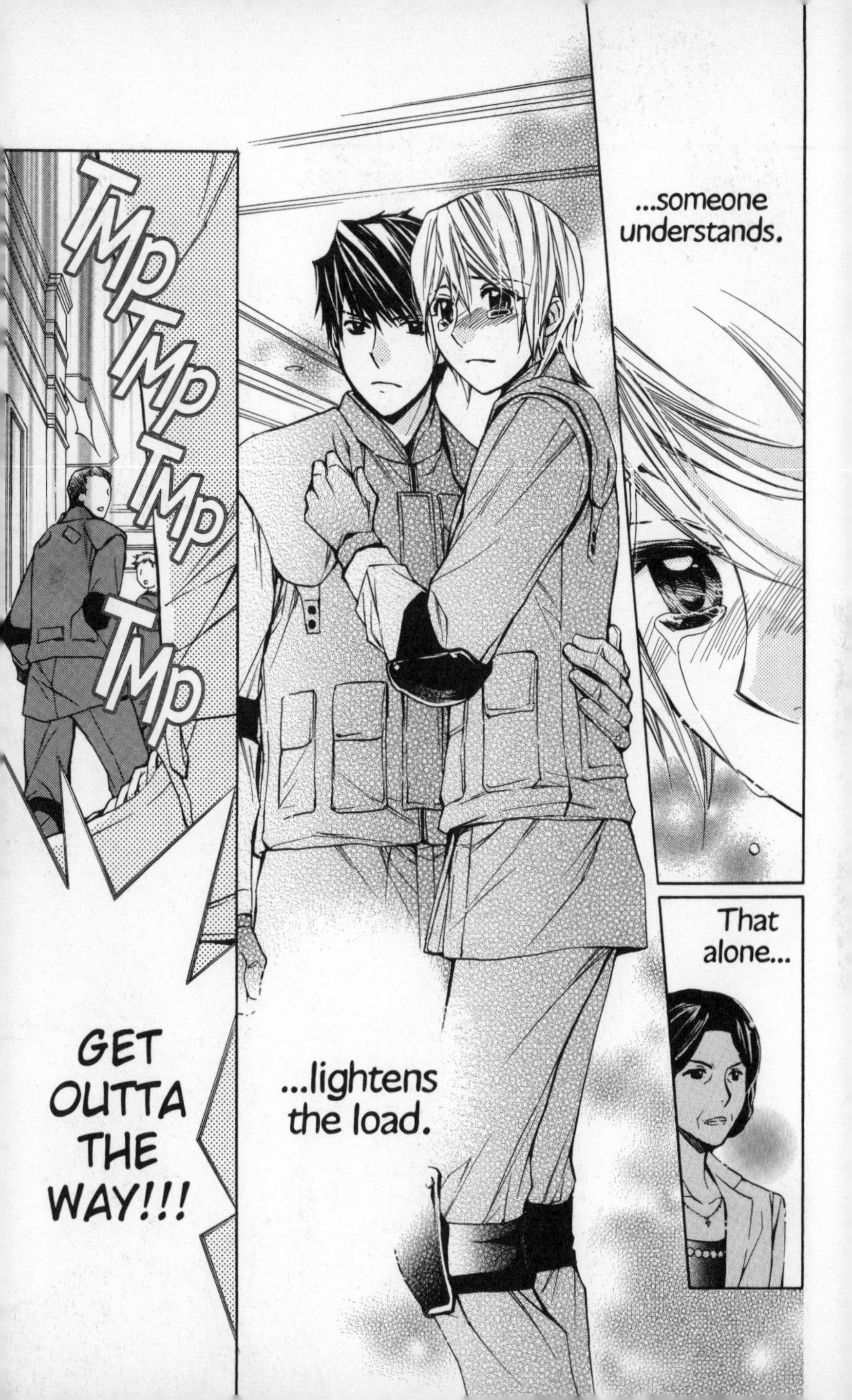
...someone understands.
That alone...
...lightens the load.
TMP TMP TMP TMP
GET OUTTA THE WAY!!!

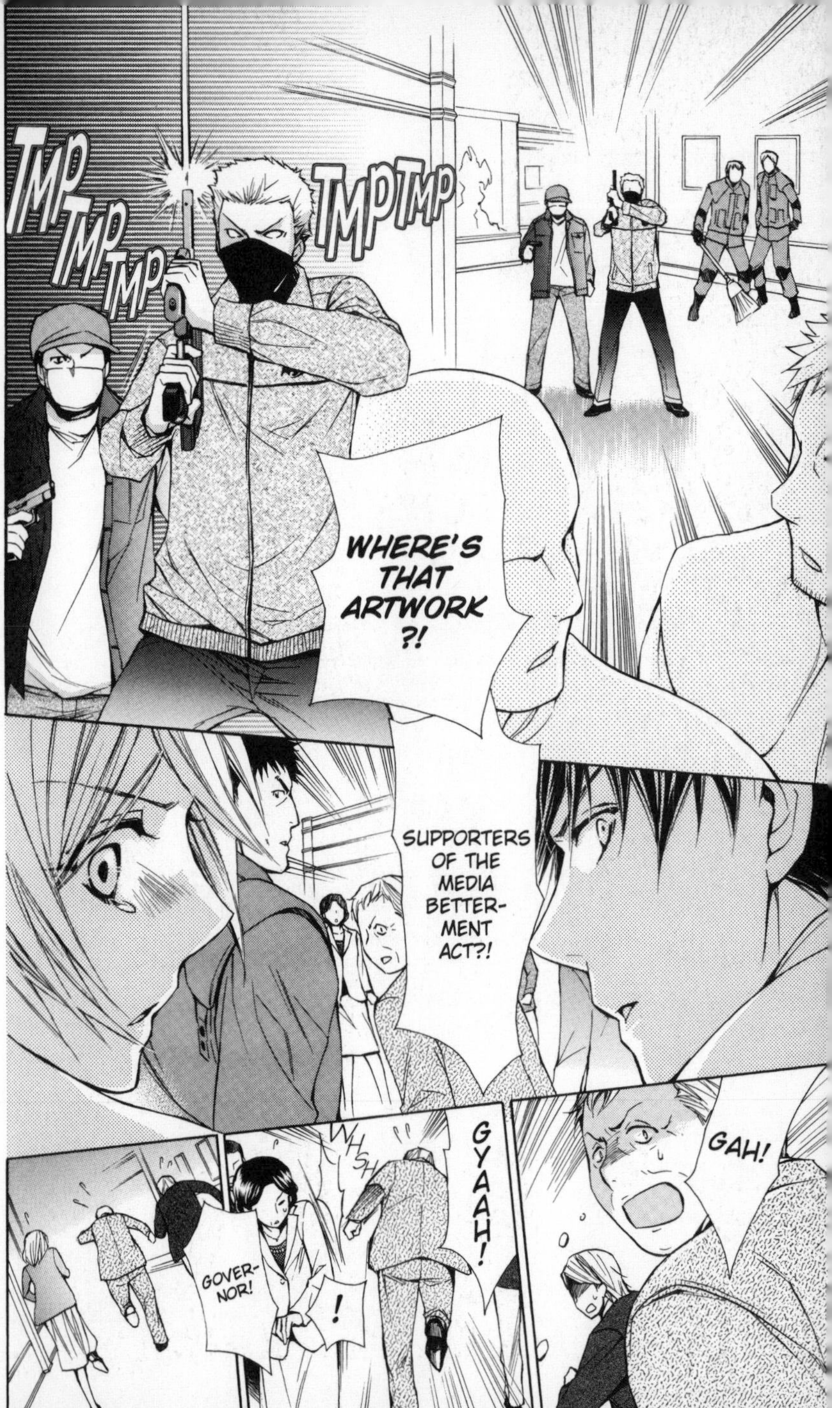
TMPTMP
TMP TMP TMP TMP
WHERE'S THAT ARTWORK?!
SUPPORTERS OF THE MEDIA BETTER-MENT ACT?!
GAH!
GYAAAH!
WHSH
!
GOVER-NOR!

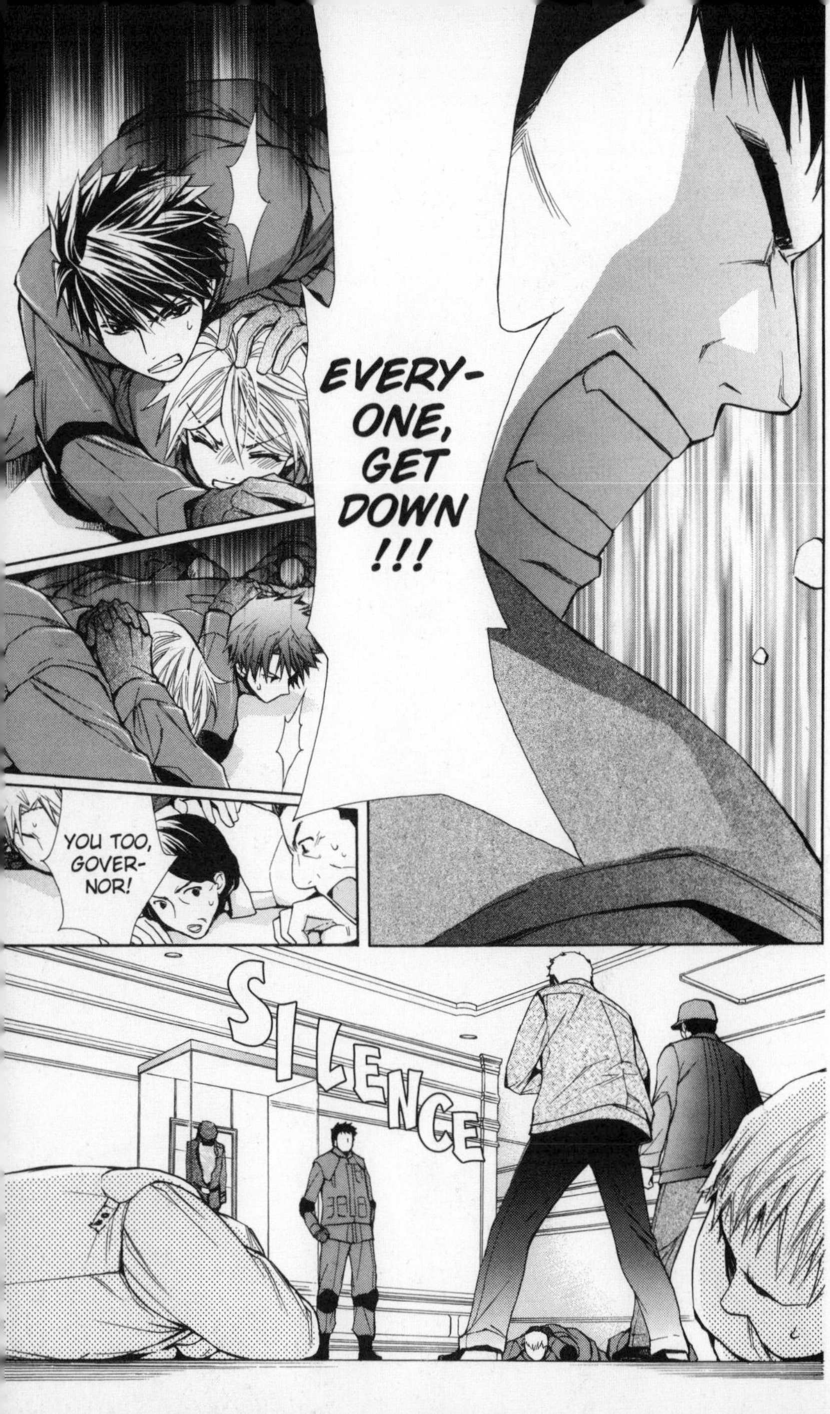
EVERY-ONE, GET DOWN!!!
YOU TOO, GOVER-NOR!
SILENCE

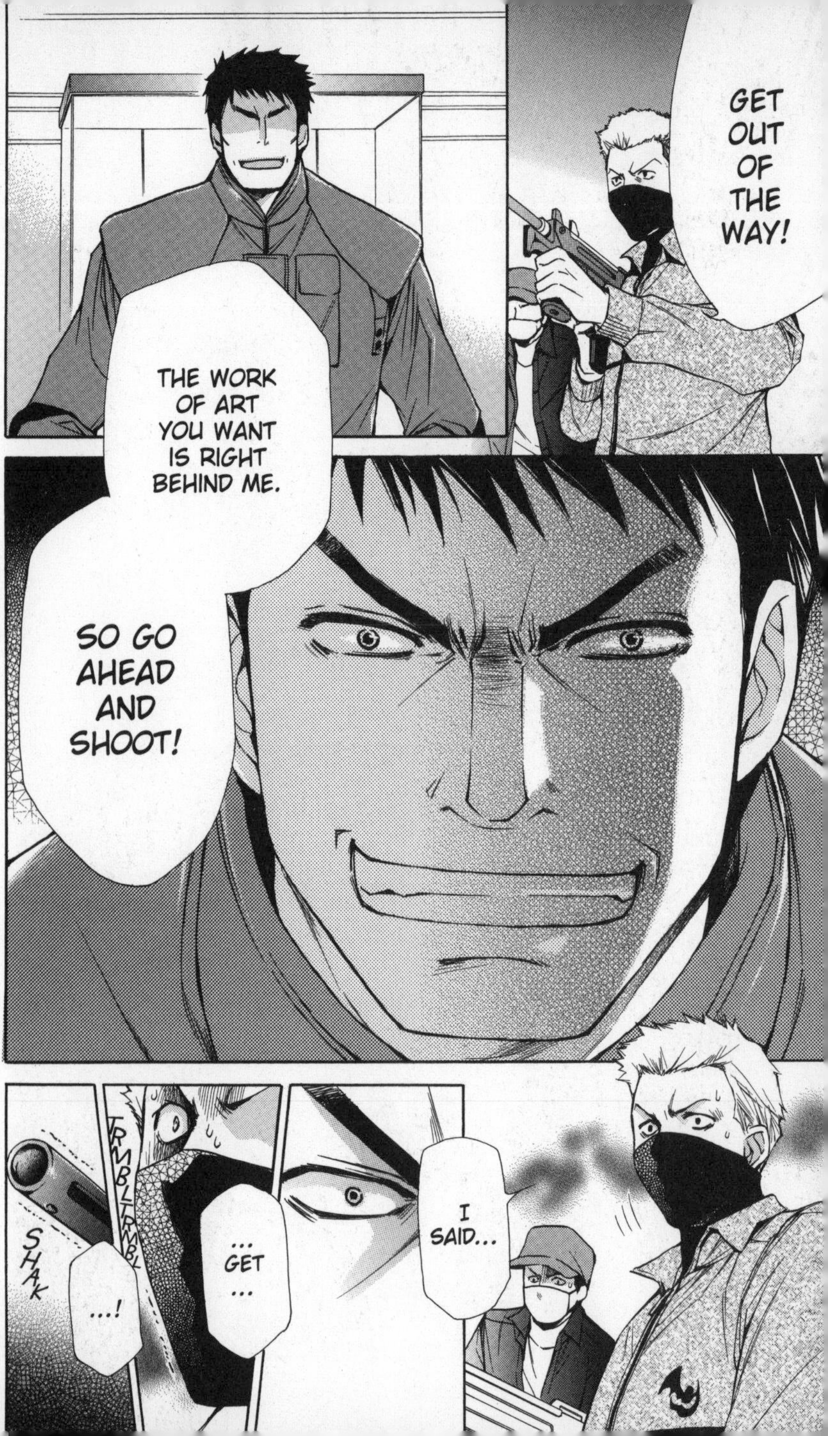
GET OUT OF THE WAY!
THE WORK OF ART YOU WANT IS RIGHT BEHIND ME.
SO GO AHEAD AND SHOOT!
I SAID...
...GET...
TRMBL TRMBL
...!
SHAK

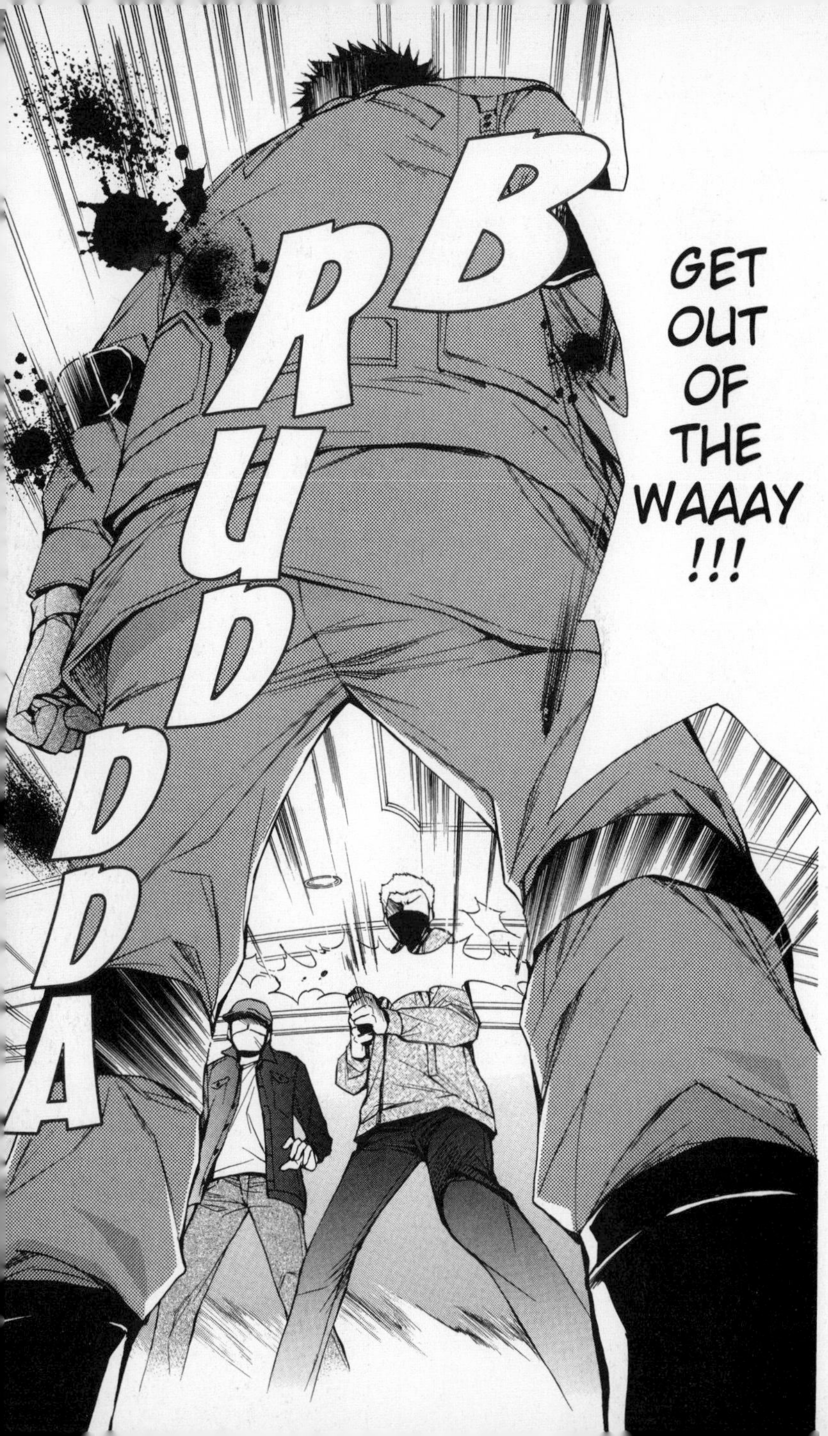
GET OUT OF THE WAAAY!!!
BRADDUDDA

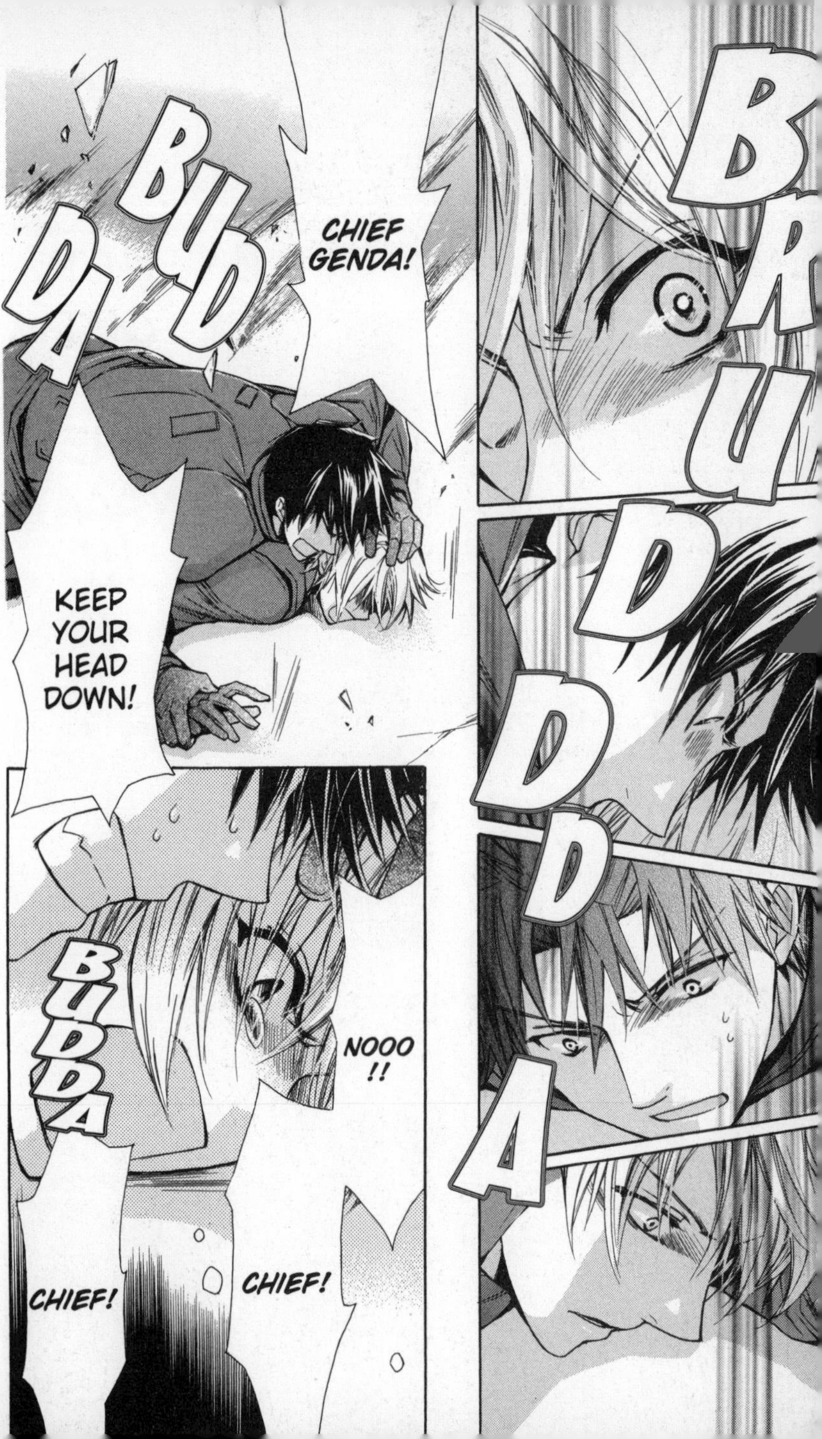
BRUDDDDA
BUDDA
CHIEF GENDA!
KEEP YOUR HEAD DOWN!
NOOO !!
BUDDA
CHIEF!
CHIEF!

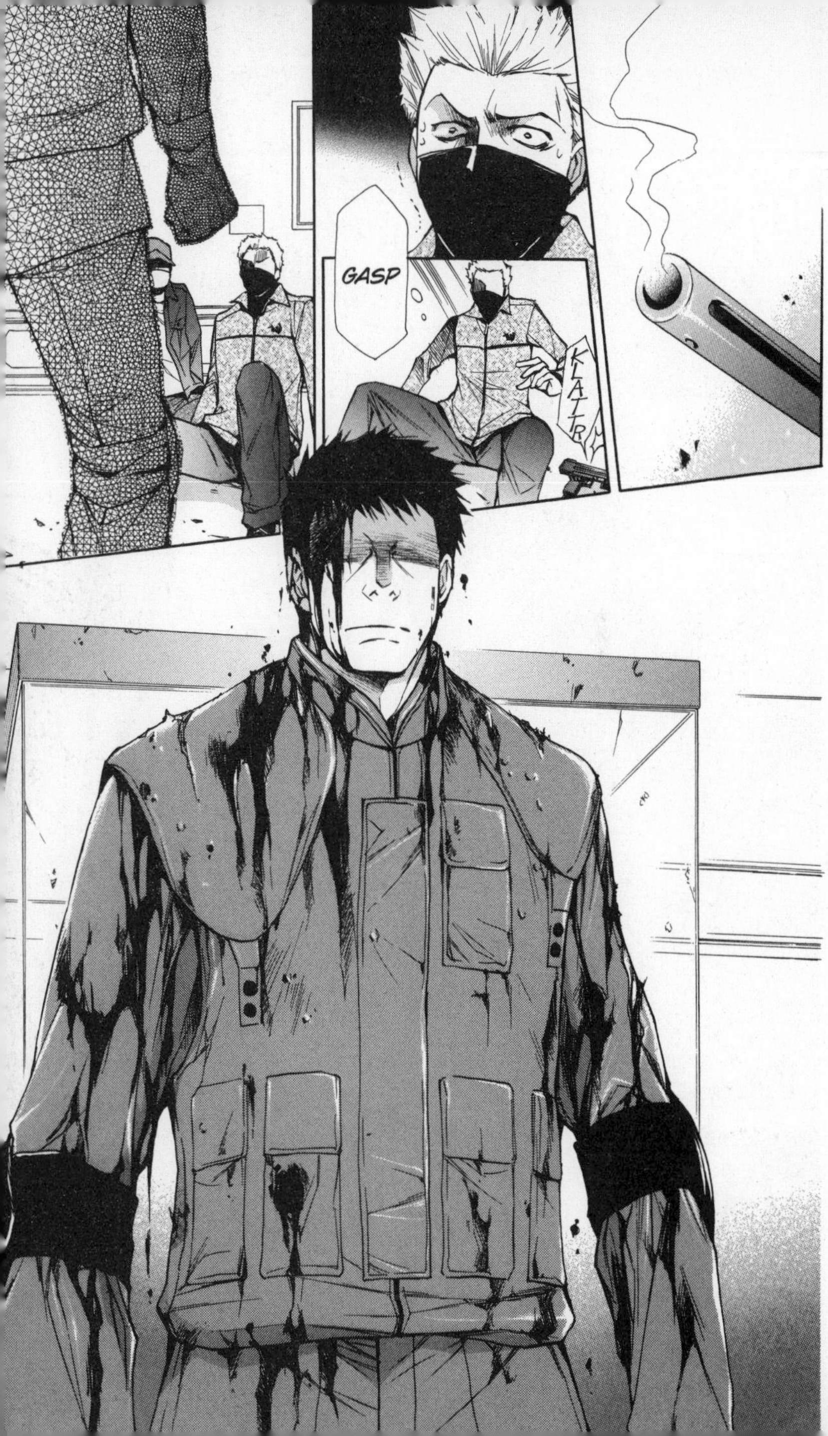
GASP
KLATTR

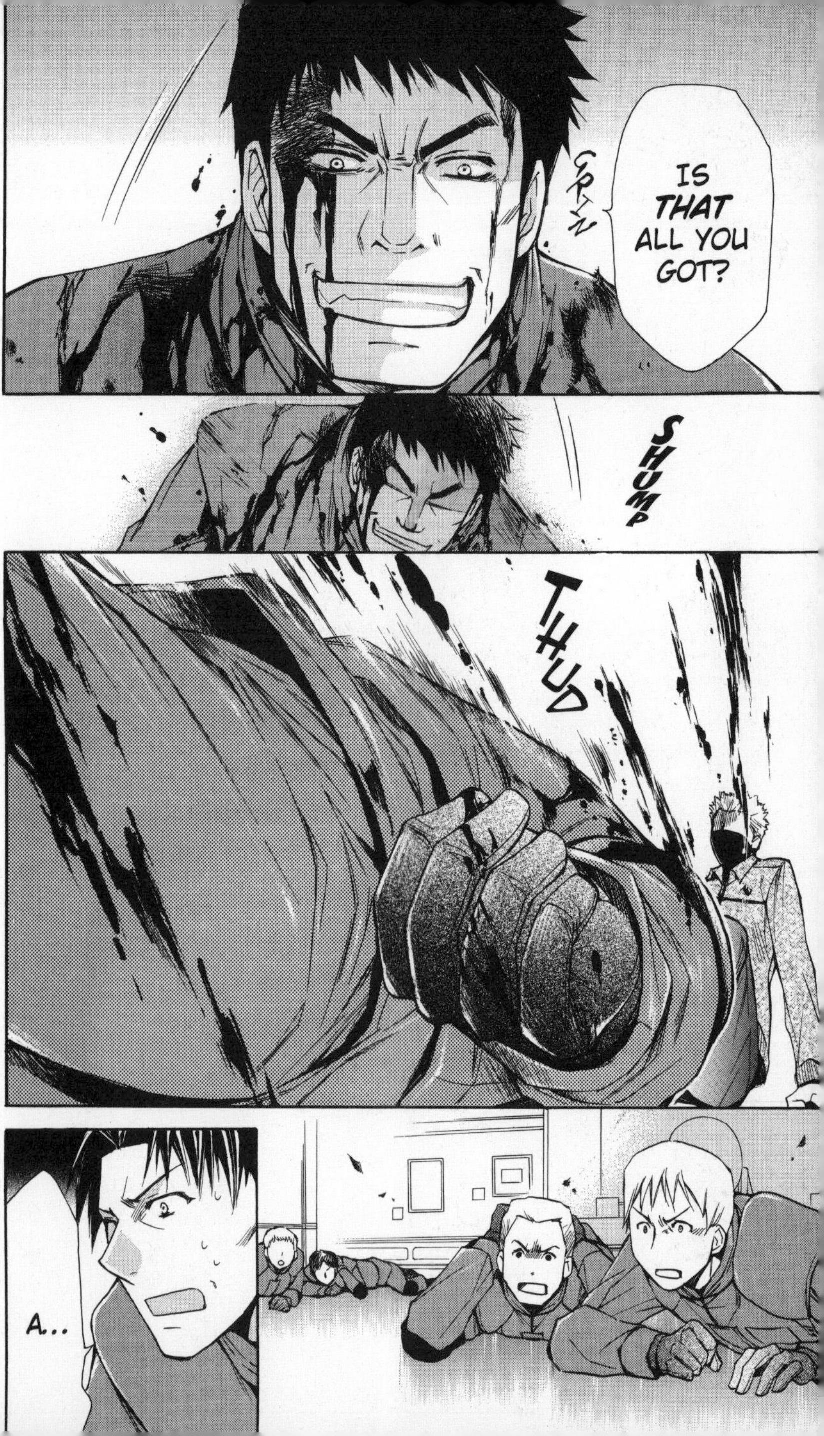
IS THAT ALL YOU GOT?
GRIN
SHUMP
THUD
A...

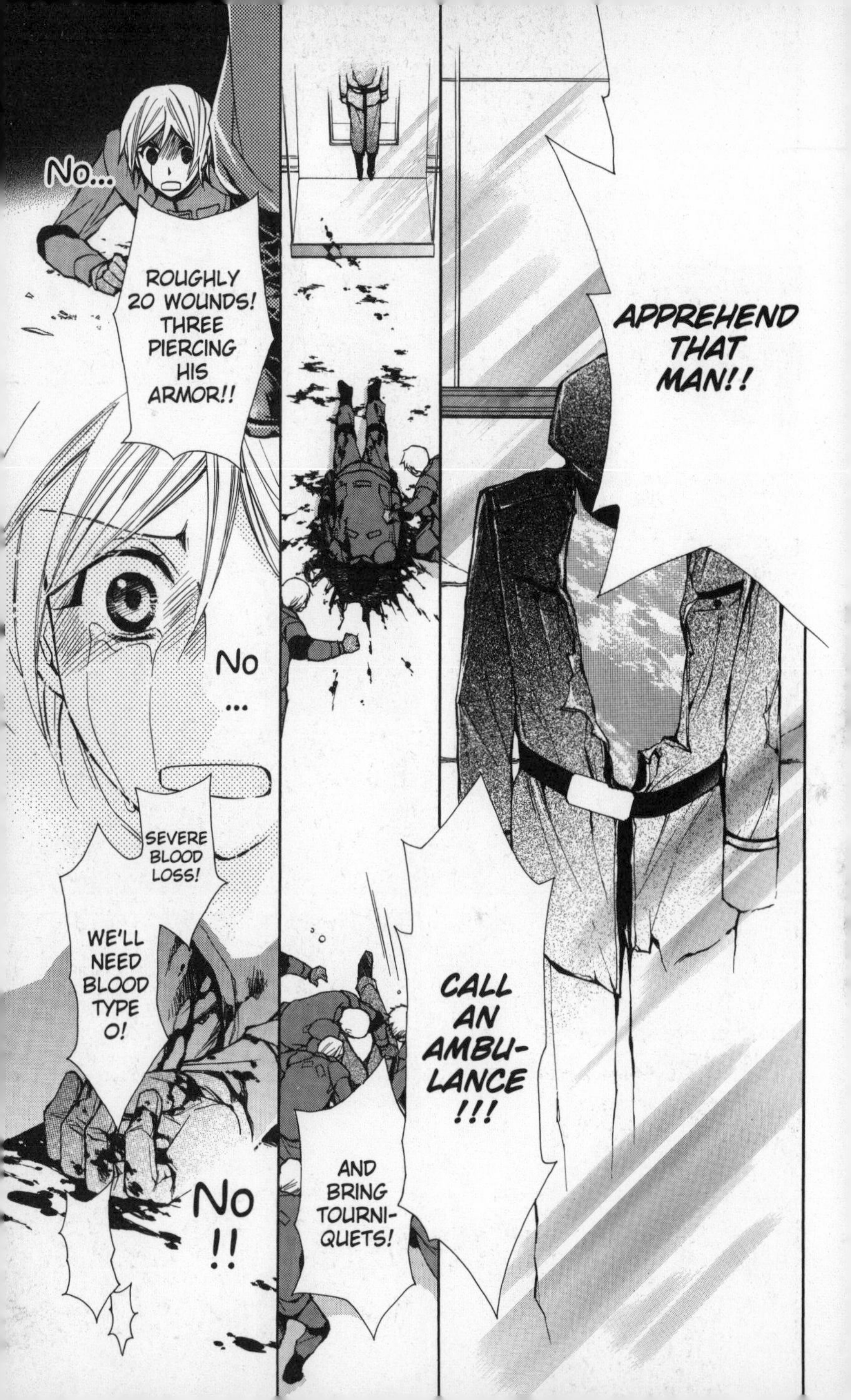
APPREHEND THAT MAN!!
CALL AN AMBU-LANCE!!!
AND BRING TOURNI-QUETS!
No...
ROUGHLY 20 WOUNDS! THREE PIERCING HIS ARMOR!!
No ...
SEVERE BLOOD LOSS!
WE'LL NEED BLOOD TYPE O!
No !!

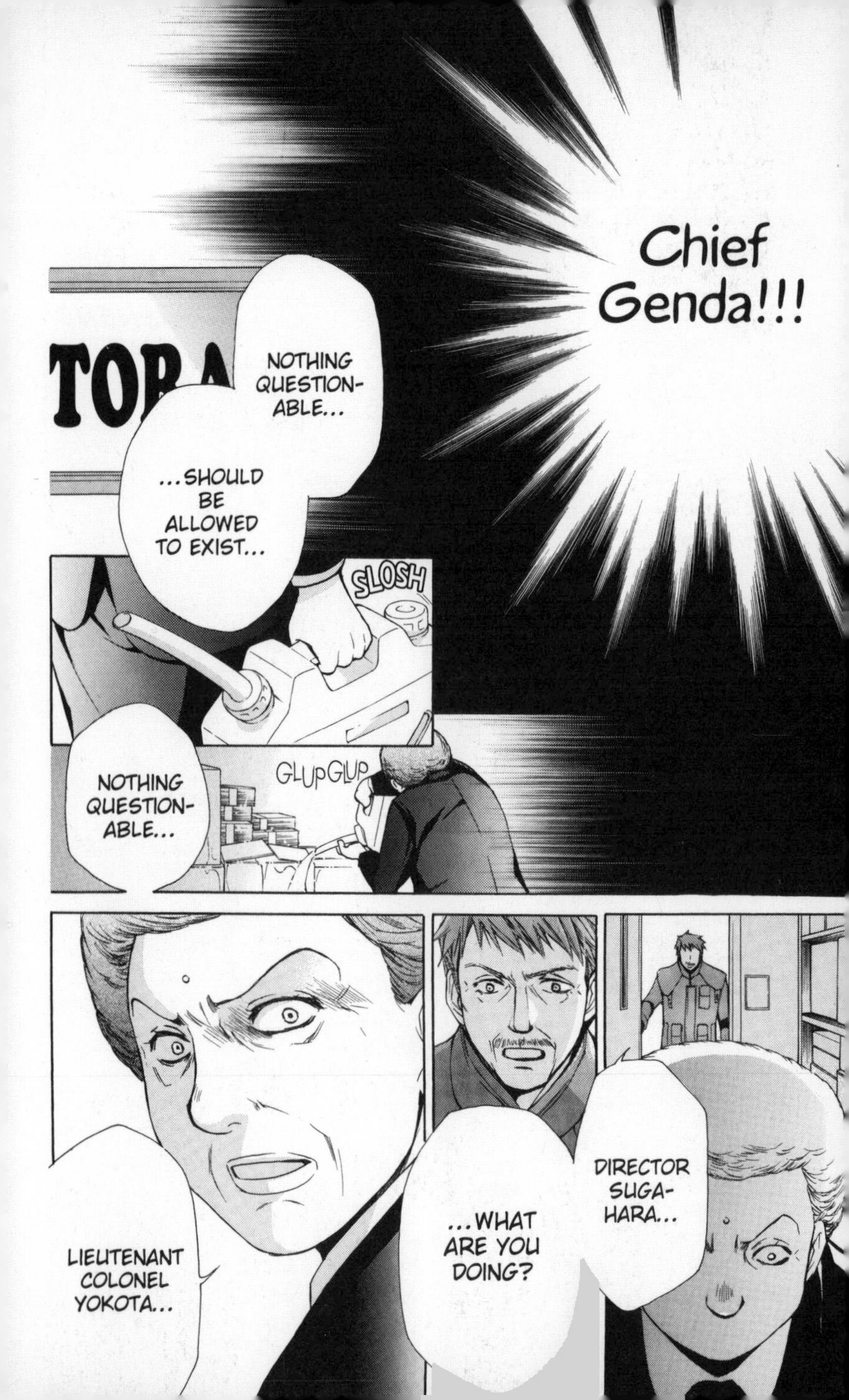
Chief Genda!!!
NOTHING QUESTION-ABLE...
...SHOULD BE ALLOWED TO EXIST...
SLOSH
GLUPGLUP
NOTHING QUESTION-ABLE...
DIRECTOR SUGA-HARA...
...WHAT ARE YOU DOING?
LIEUTENANT COLONEL YOKOTA...

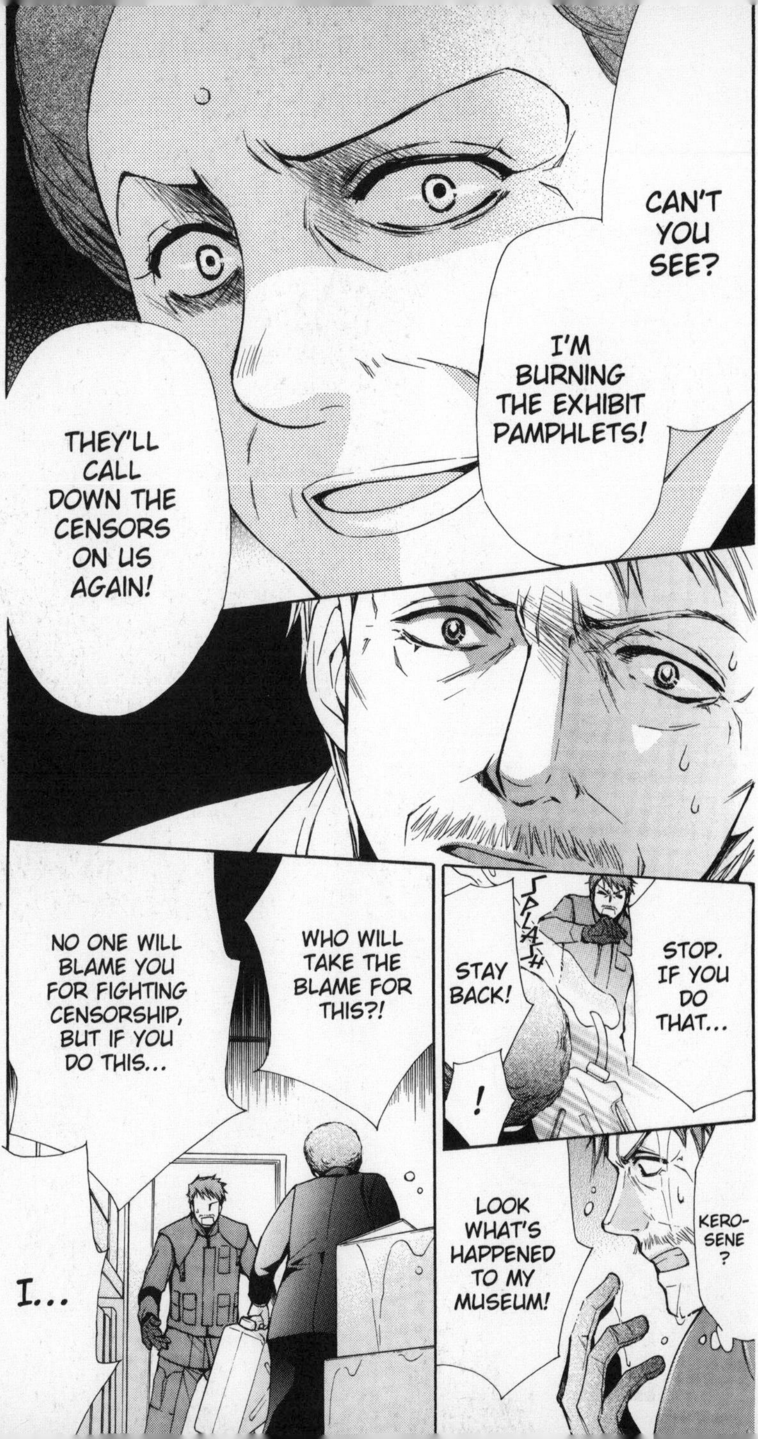
CAN'T YOU SEE?
I'M BURNING THE EXHIBIT PAMPHLETS!
THEY'LL CALL DOWN THE CENSORS ON US AGAIN!
STOP. IF YOU DO THAT...
SPLASH
STAY BACK!
!
KERO-SENE?
LOOK WHAT'S HAPPENED TO MY MUSEUM!
WHO WILL TAKE THE BLAME FOR THIS?!
NO ONE WILL BLAME YOU FOR FIGHTING CENSORSHIP, BUT IF YOU DO THIS...
I...

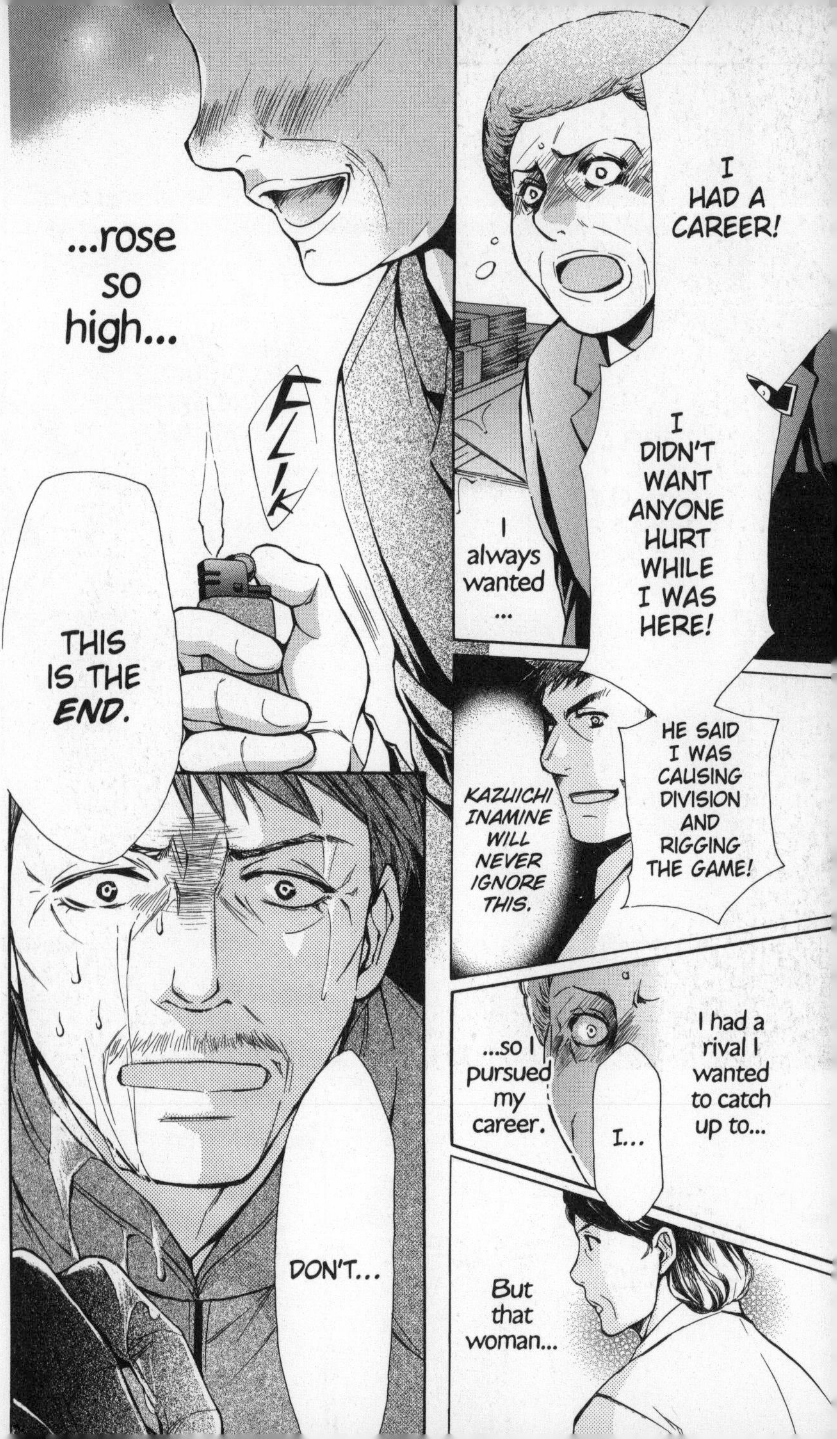
I HAD A CAREER!
I DIDN'T WANT ANYONE HURT WHILE I WAS HERE!
I always wanted ...
HE SAID I WAS CAUSING DIVISION AND RIGGING THE GAME!
KAZUICHI INAMINE WILL NEVER IGNORE THIS.
I had a rival I wanted to catch up to...
I...
...so I pursued my career.
But that woman...
...rose so high...
FLIK
THIS IS THE END.
DON'T...

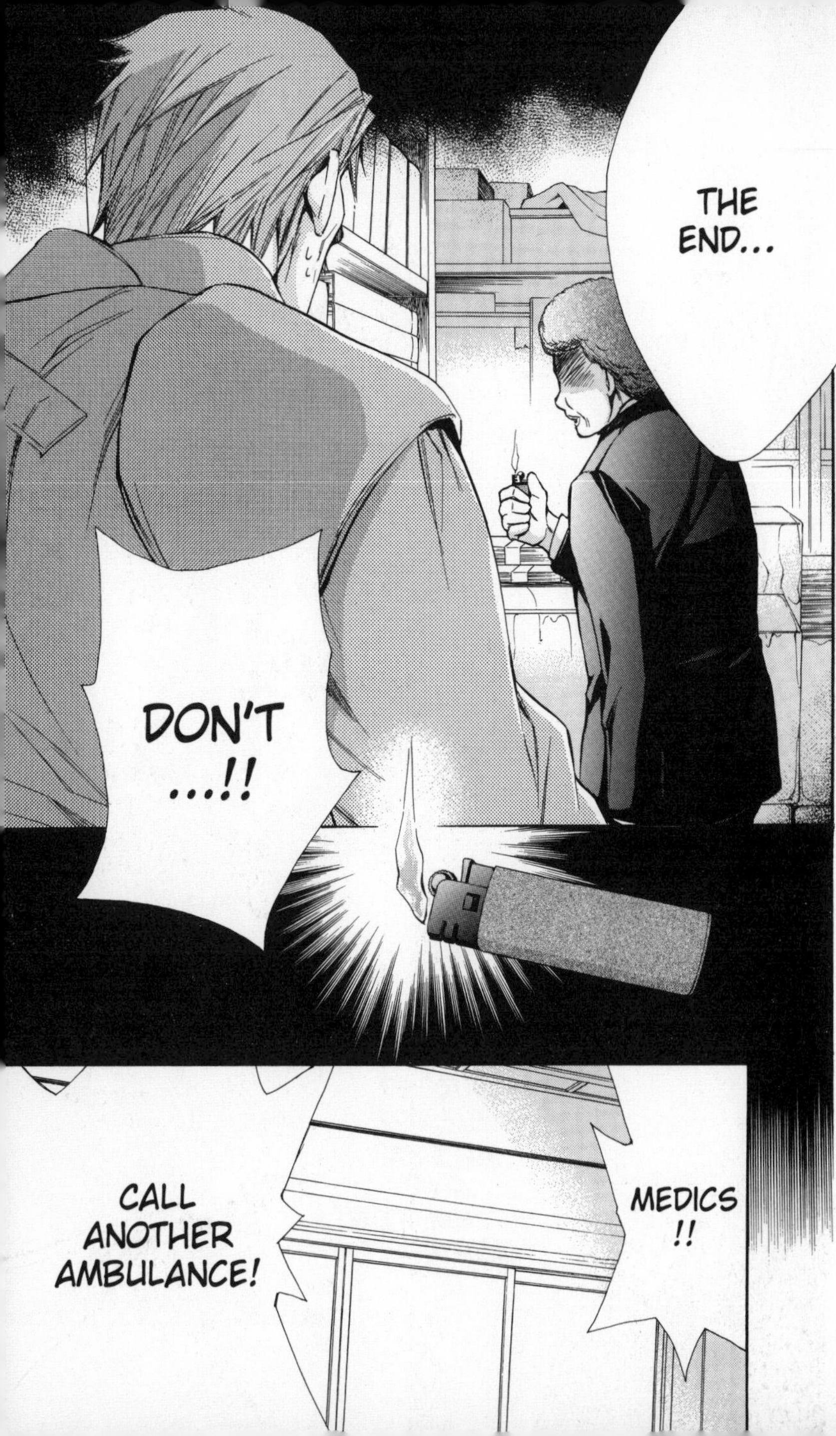
THE END...
DON'T ...!!
MEDICS !!
CALL ANOTHER AMBULANCE!

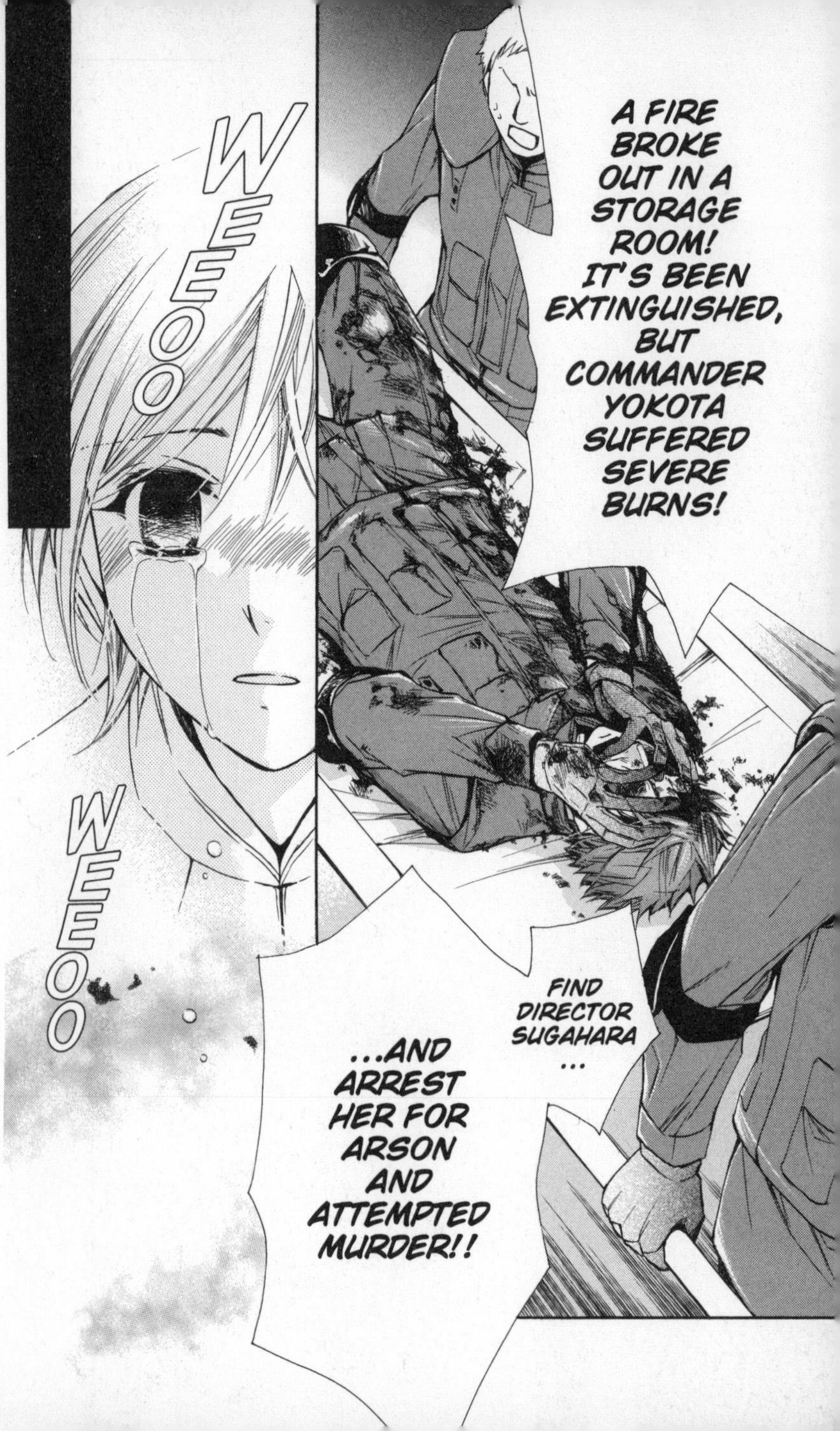
A FIRE BROKE OUT IN A STORAGE ROOM! IT'S BEEN EXTINGUISHED, BUT COMMANDER YOKOTA SUFFERED SEVERE BURNS!
FIND DIRECTOR SUGAHARA ...
...AND ARREST HER FOR ARSON AND ATTEMPTED MURDER!!
WEEOO
WEEOO

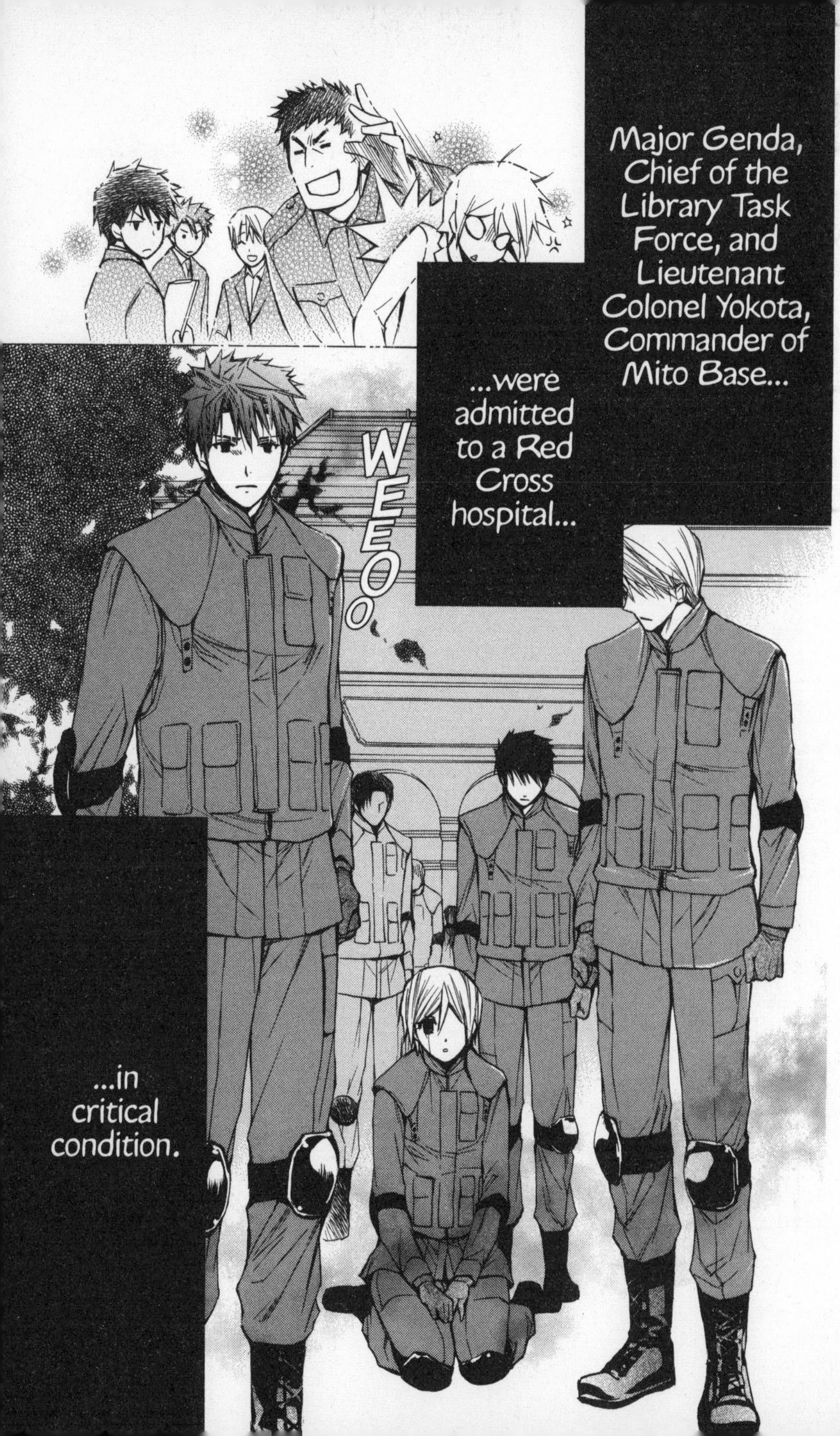
Major Genda, Chief of the Library Task Force, and Lieutenant Colonel Yokota, Commander of Mito Base...
...were admitted to a Red Cross hospital...
WEEOO
...in critical condition.

Secret Admirer part 10

Previously on Secret Admirer

Moburo Agohige has a crush on Iku Kasahara, but it never sees the light of day.

*There's lots of lovey-dovey going on, and Chief got shot up, so his depression is 80 percent worse than usual.

Agohige looks pretty down...

What a sorry sight!

...

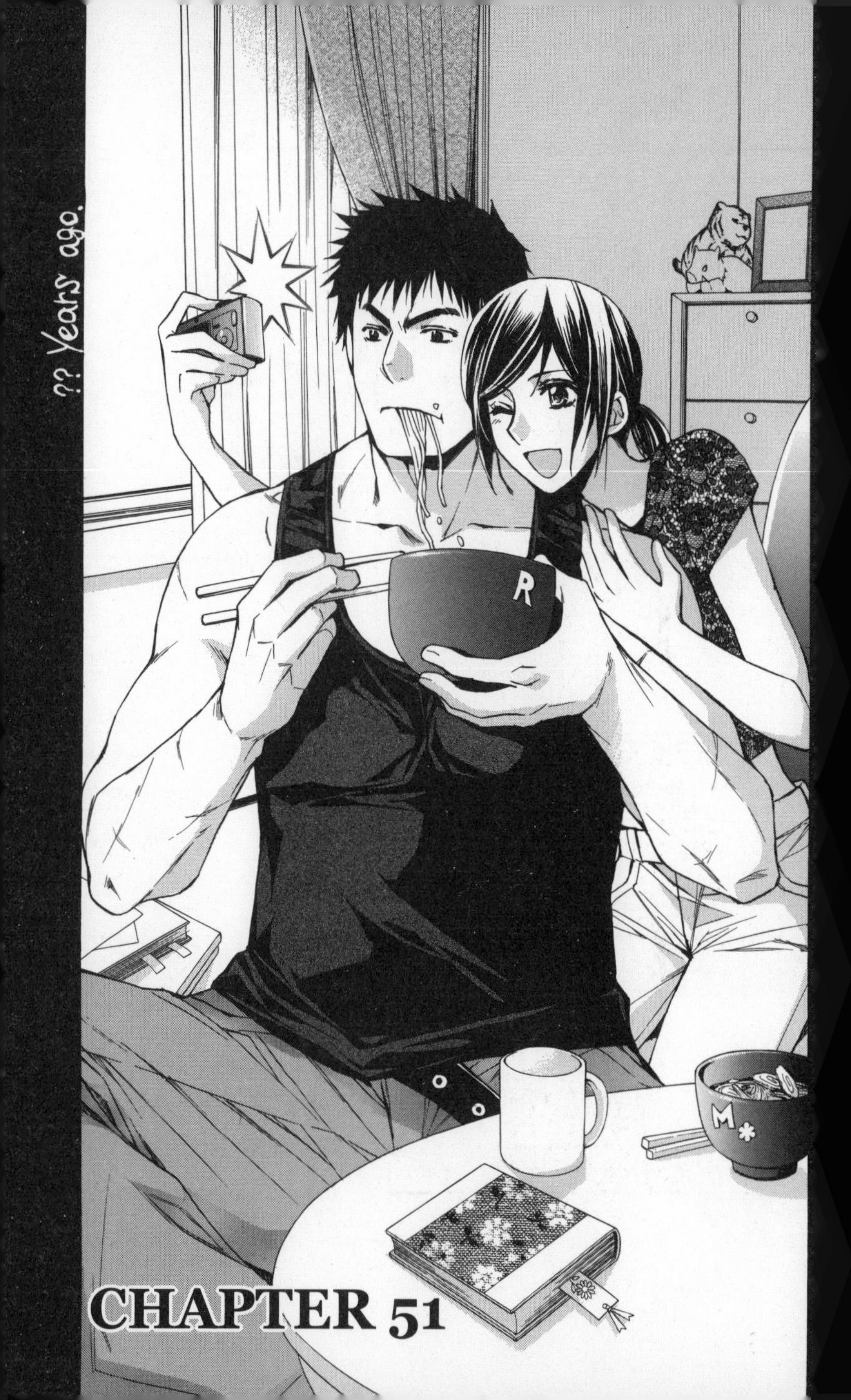
?? Years ago.
R
M

CHAPTER 51

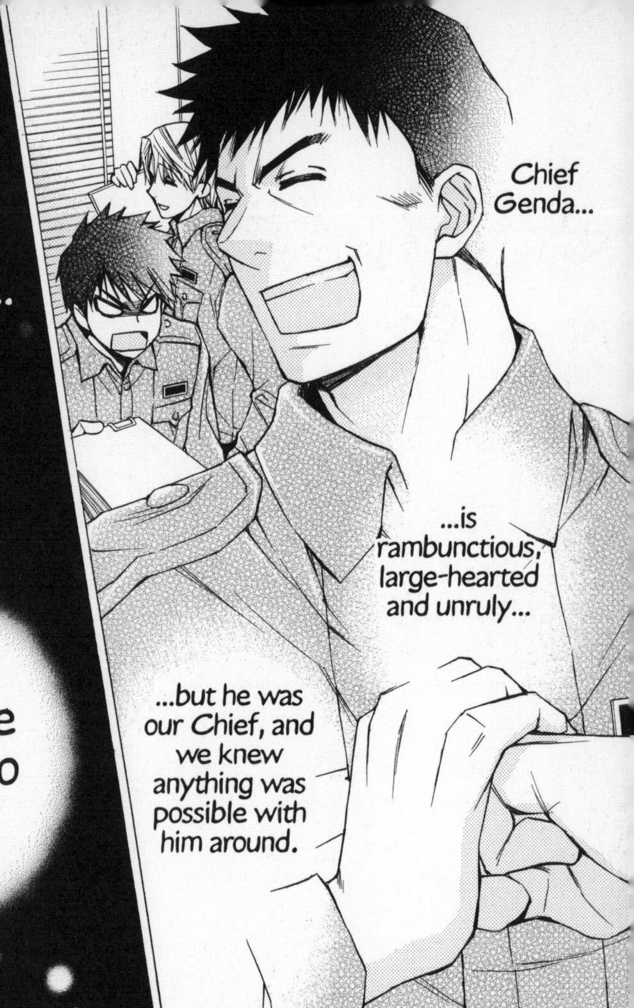
Chief Genda...
...is rambunctious, large-hearted and unruly...
...but he was our Chief, and we knew anything was possible with him around.

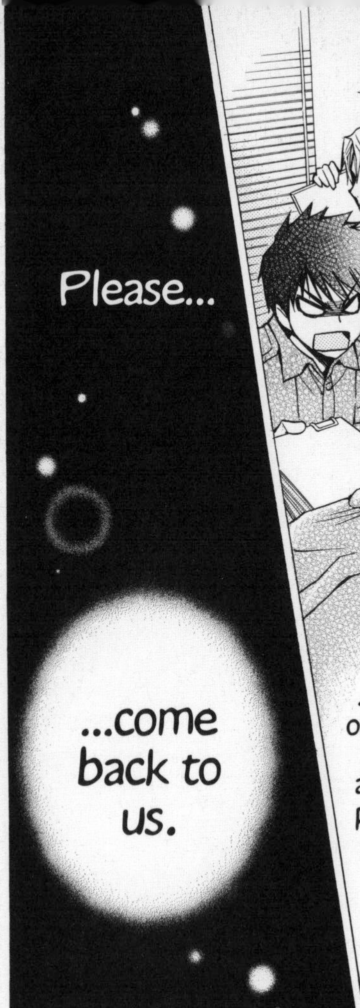
Please...
...come back to us.

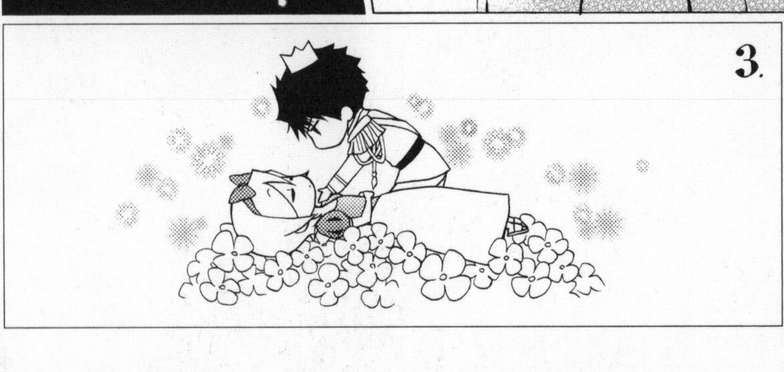
3.

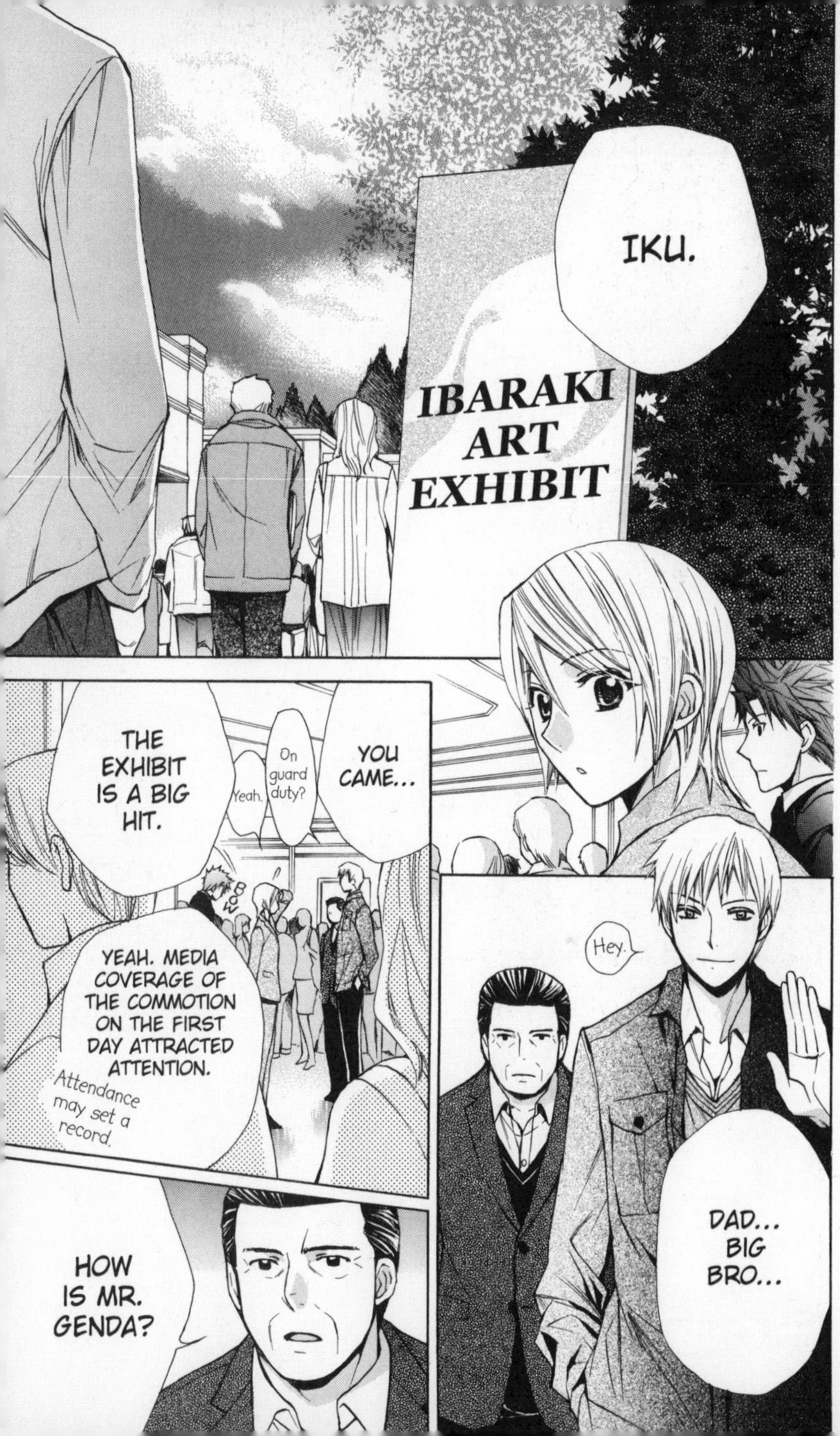
IKU.
IBARAKI ART EXHIBIT
Hey.
DAD... BIG BRO...
YOU CAME...
On guard duty?
Yeah.
THE EXHIBIT IS A BIG HIT.
BOW
YEAH. MEDIA COVERAGE OF THE COMMOTION ON THE FIRST DAY ATTRACTED ATTENTION.
Attendance may set a record.
HOW IS MR. GENDA?

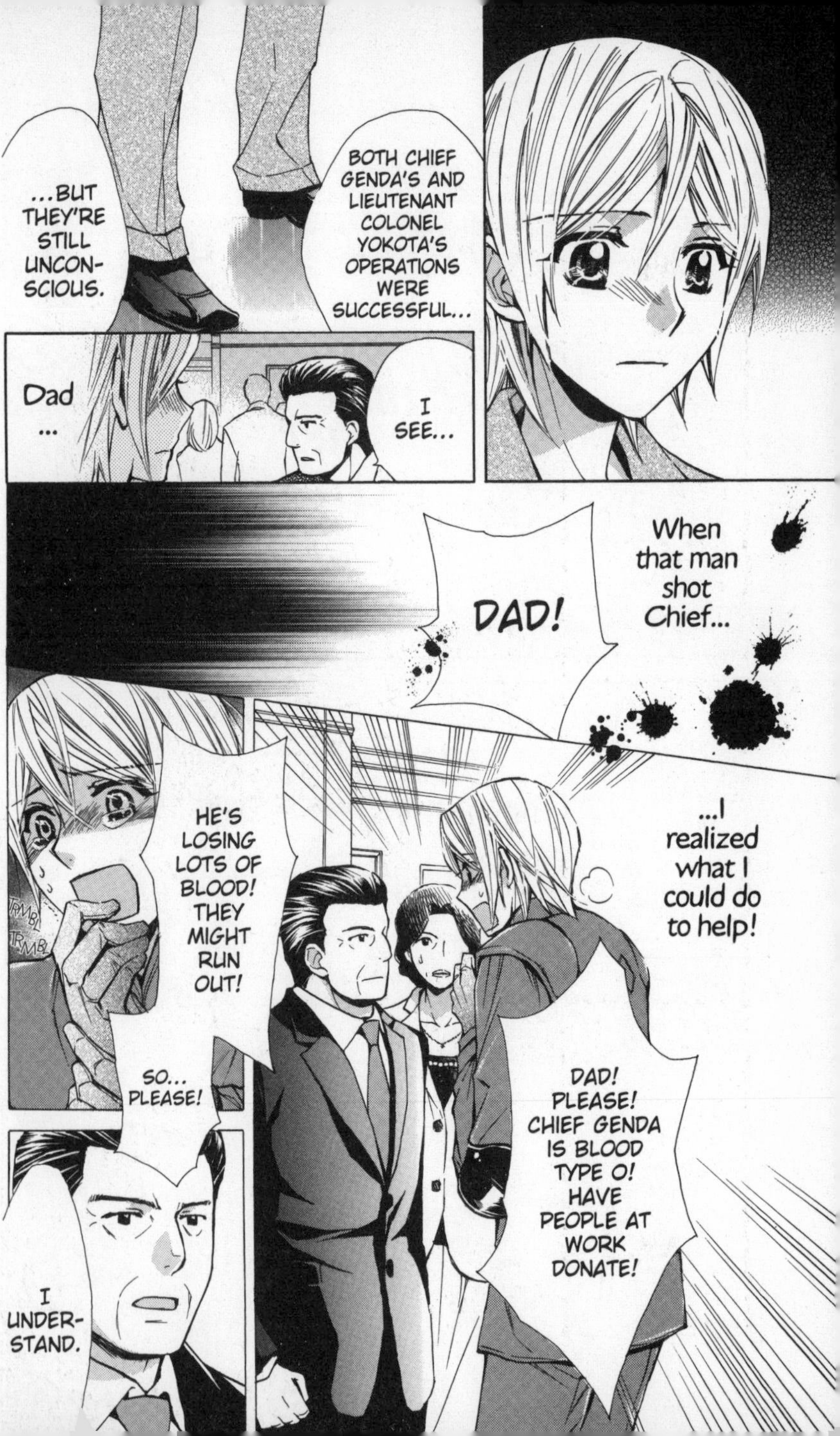
BOTH CHIEF GENDA'S AND LIEUTENANT COLONEL YOKOTA'S OPERATIONS WERE SUCCESSFUL...
...BUT THEY'RE STILL UNCON-SCIOUS.
I SEE...
Dad ...
When that man shot Chief...
DAD!
...I realized what I could do to help!
DAD! PLEASE! CHIEF GENDA IS BLOOD TYPE O! HAVE PEOPLE AT WORK DONATE!
HE'S LOSING LOTS OF BLOOD! THEY MIGHT RUN OUT!
TRMBL
TRMBL
SO... PLEASE!
I UNDER-STAND.

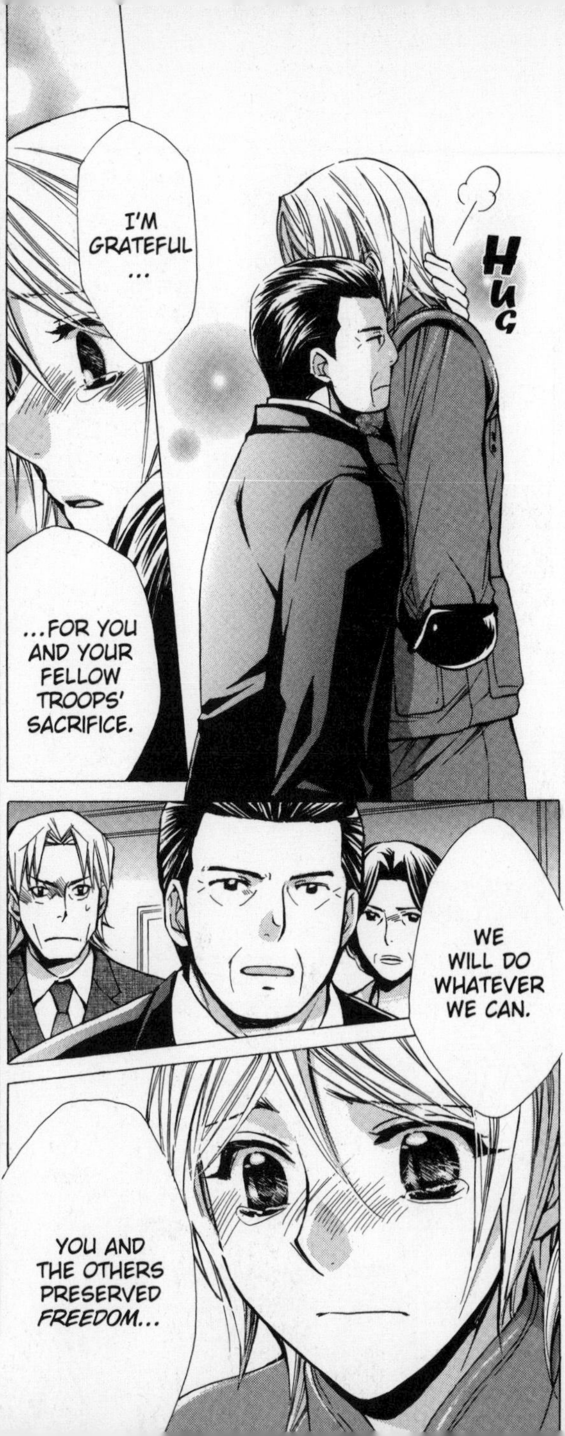
HUG
I'M GRATEFUL...
...FOR YOU AND YOUR FELLOW TROOPS' SACRIFICE.
WE WILL DO WHATEVER WE CAN.
YOU AND THE OTHERS PRESERVED FREEDOM...

3

*

Speaking of movies, my most favorite movies in the whole world are *The Hobbit*, which came out not long ago, and *The Lord of the Rings* series, so I can't help but be excited. Thinking about immersing myself in that world for another three movies makes me practically come apart at the seams!

In *The Lord of the Rings*, I was intensely interested in the king of the humans, but this time I'm *absorbed* in the king of the dwarves. (lol) I'd only ever thought of dwarves as squat and cute, but they can be handsome, too! My mistake! I was totally fooled!

*

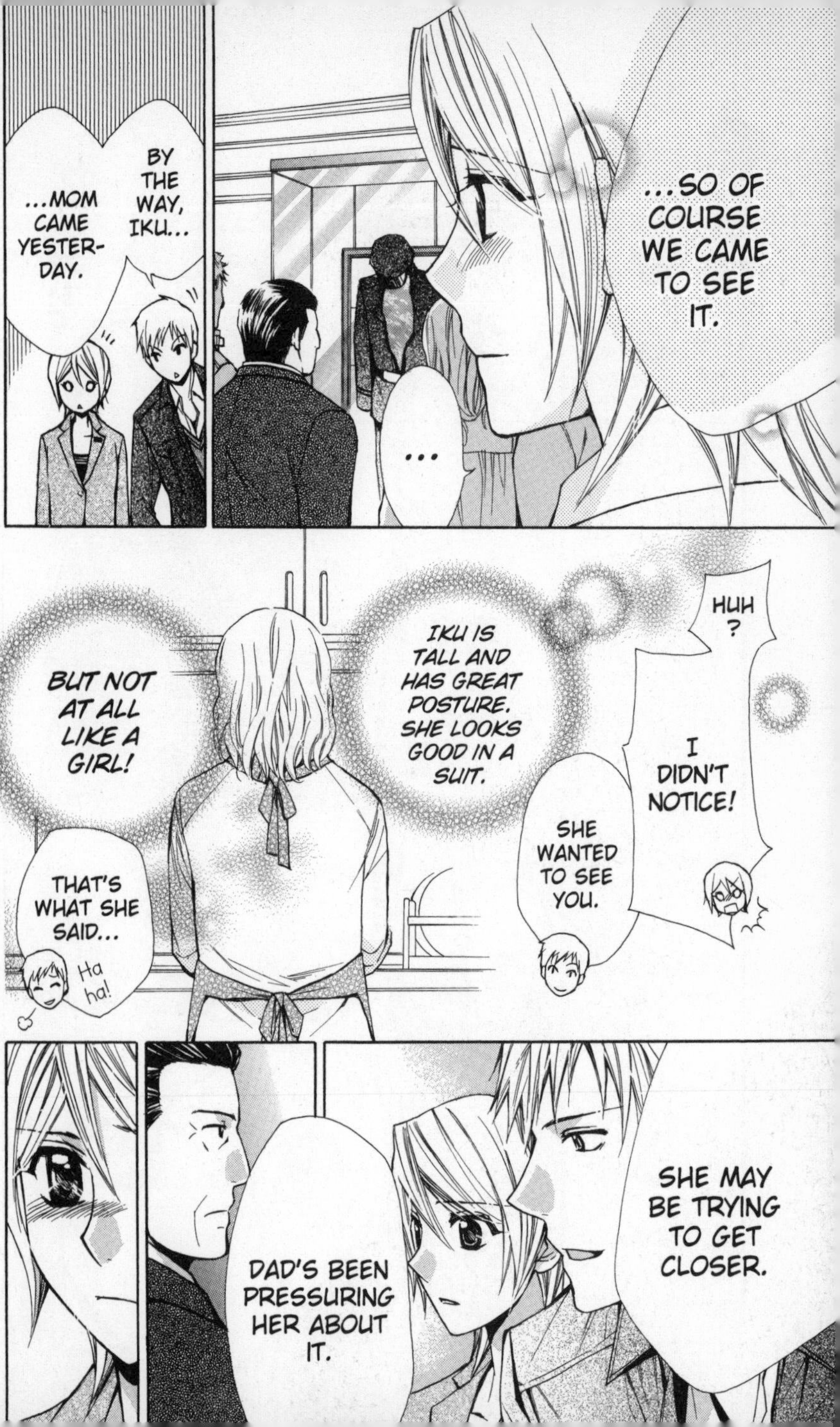
...SO OF COURSE WE CAME TO SEE IT.
...
BY THE WAY, IKU...
...MOM CAME YESTER-DAY.
HUH?
I DIDN'T NOTICE!
SHE WANTED TO SEE YOU.
IKU IS TALL AND HAS GREAT POSTURE. SHE LOOKS GOOD IN A SUIT.
BUT NOT AT ALL LIKE A GIRL!
THAT'S WHAT SHE SAID...
Ha ha!
SHE MAY BE TRYING TO GET CLOSER.
DAD'S BEEN PRESSURING HER ABOUT IT.

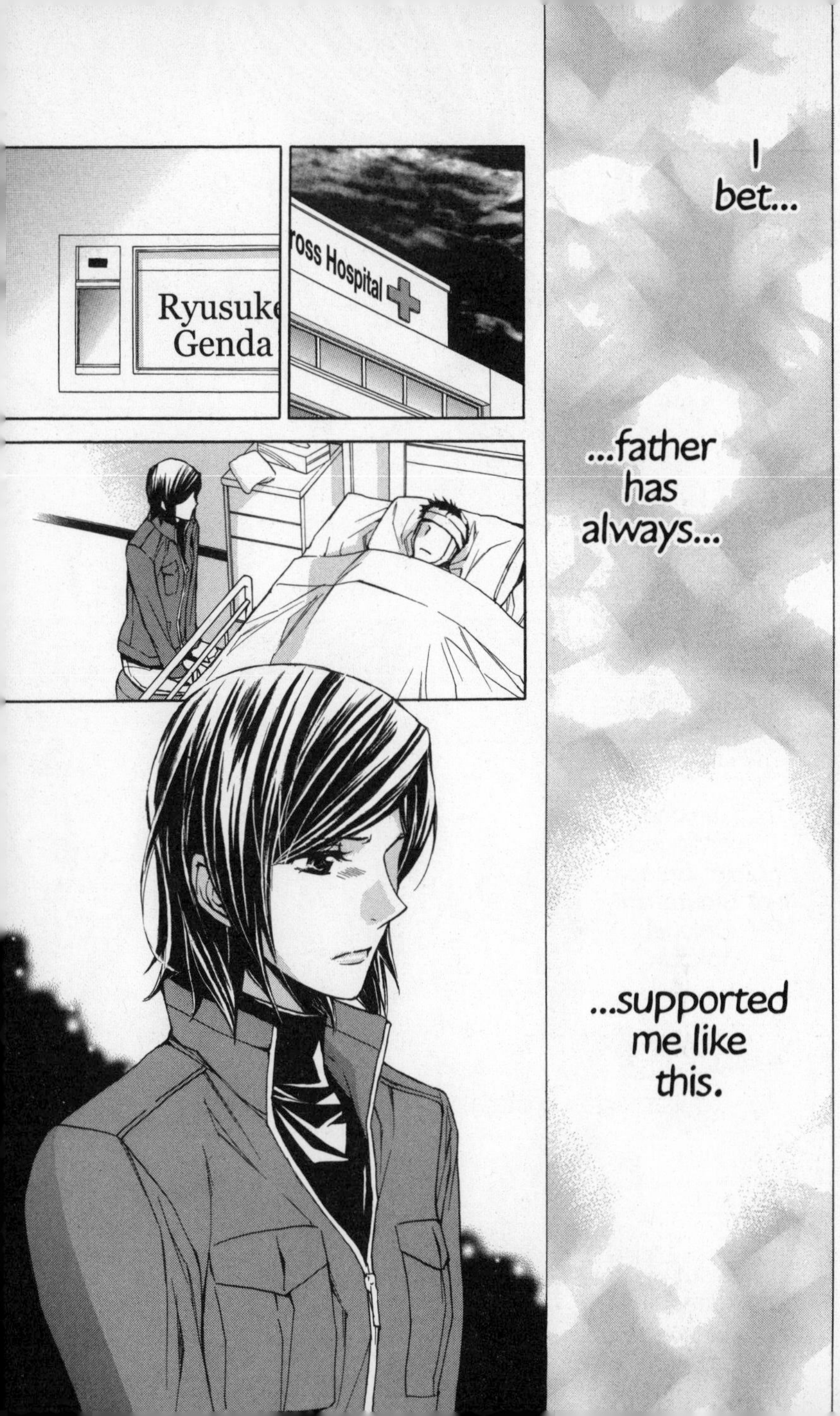
I bet...
...father has always...
...supported me like this.
ross Hospital
Ryusuke Genda

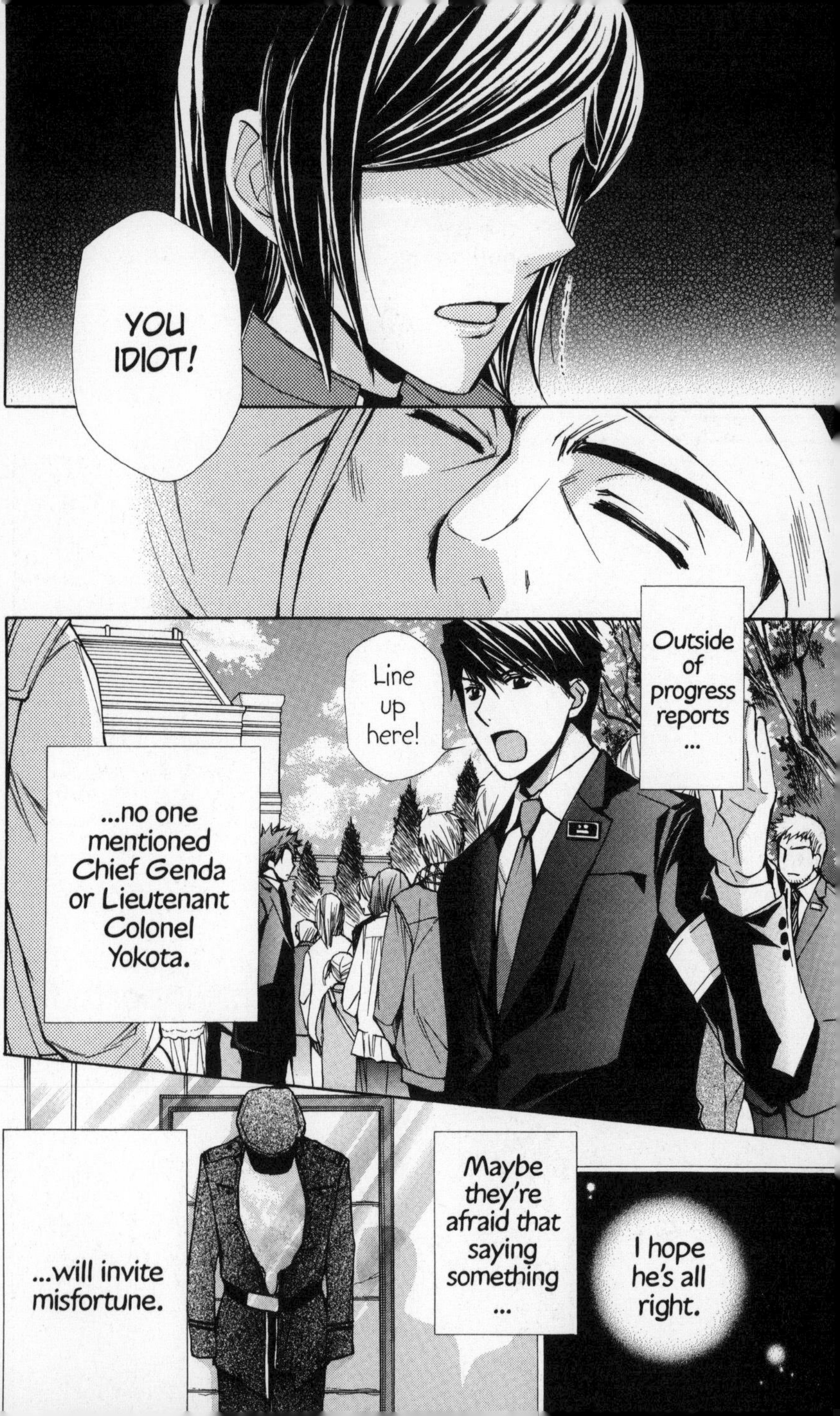
YOU IDIOT!
Outside of progress reports ...
Line up here!
...no one mentioned Chief Genda or Lieutenant Colonel Yokota.
I hope he's all right.
Maybe they're afraid that saying something ...
...will invite misfortune.

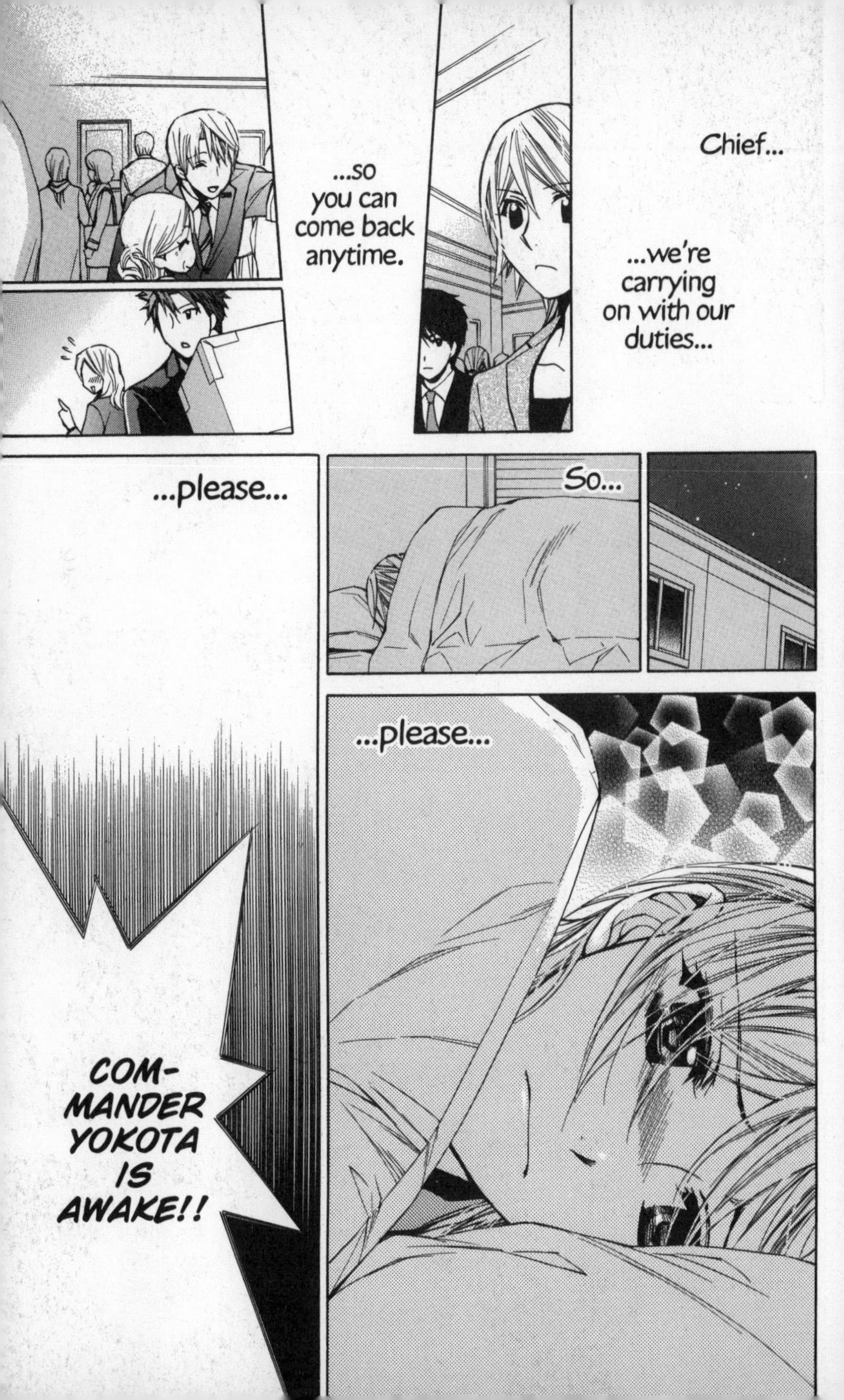

Chief...
...we're carrying on with our duties...
...so you can come back anytime.
So...
...please...
...please...
COM-MANDER YOKOTA IS AWAKE!!

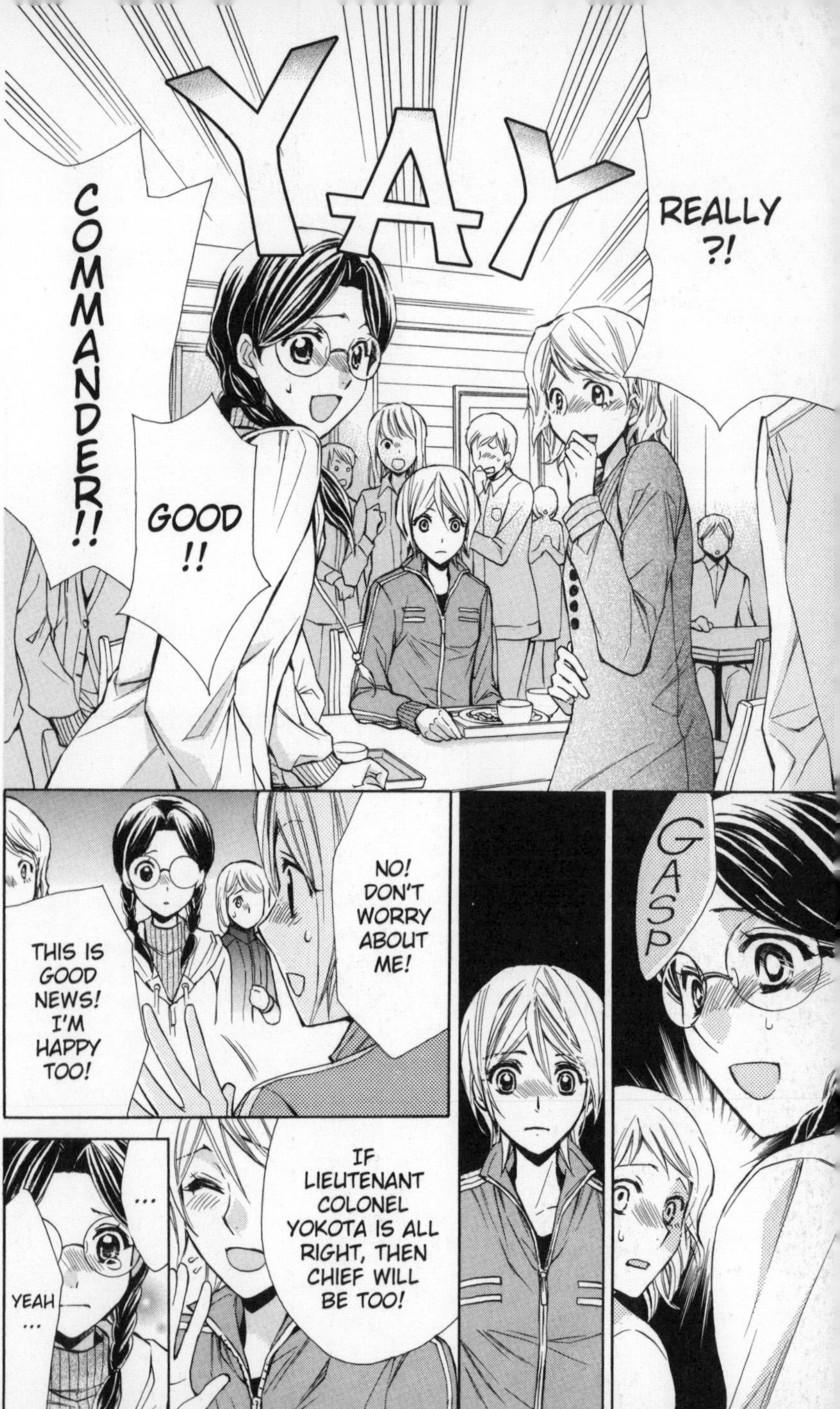
YAY
REALLY ?!
COMMANDER!!
GOOD !!
GASP
NO! DON'T WORRY ABOUT ME!
THIS IS GOOD NEWS! I'M HAPPY TOO!
IF LIEUTENANT COLONEL YOKOTA IS ALL RIGHT, THEN CHIEF WILL BE TOO!
...
YEAH ...

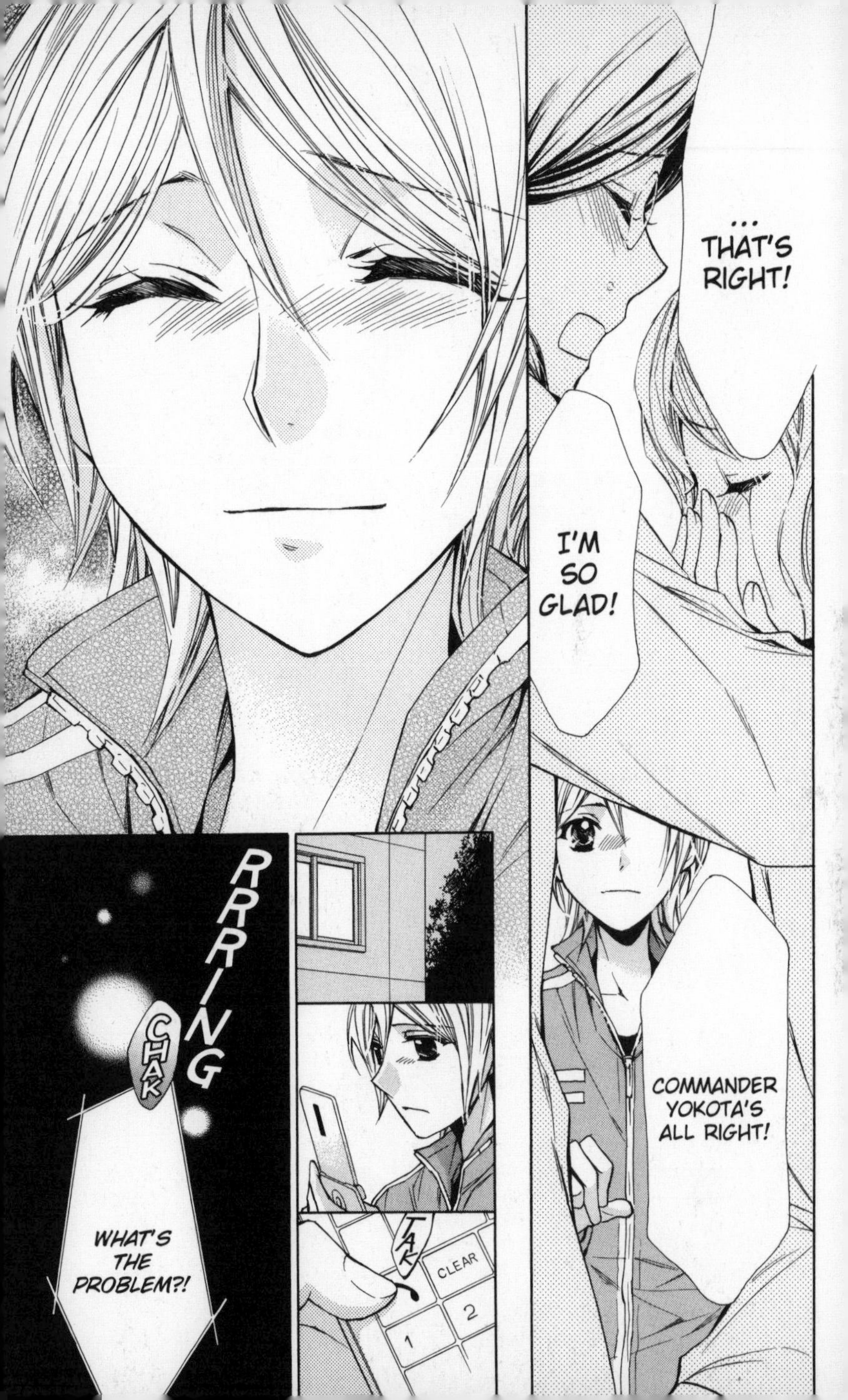
...THAT'S RIGHT!
I'M SO GLAD!
COMMANDER YOKOTA'S ALL RIGHT!
TAK
CLEAR
2
1
RRRING
CHAK
WHAT'S THE PROBLEM?!

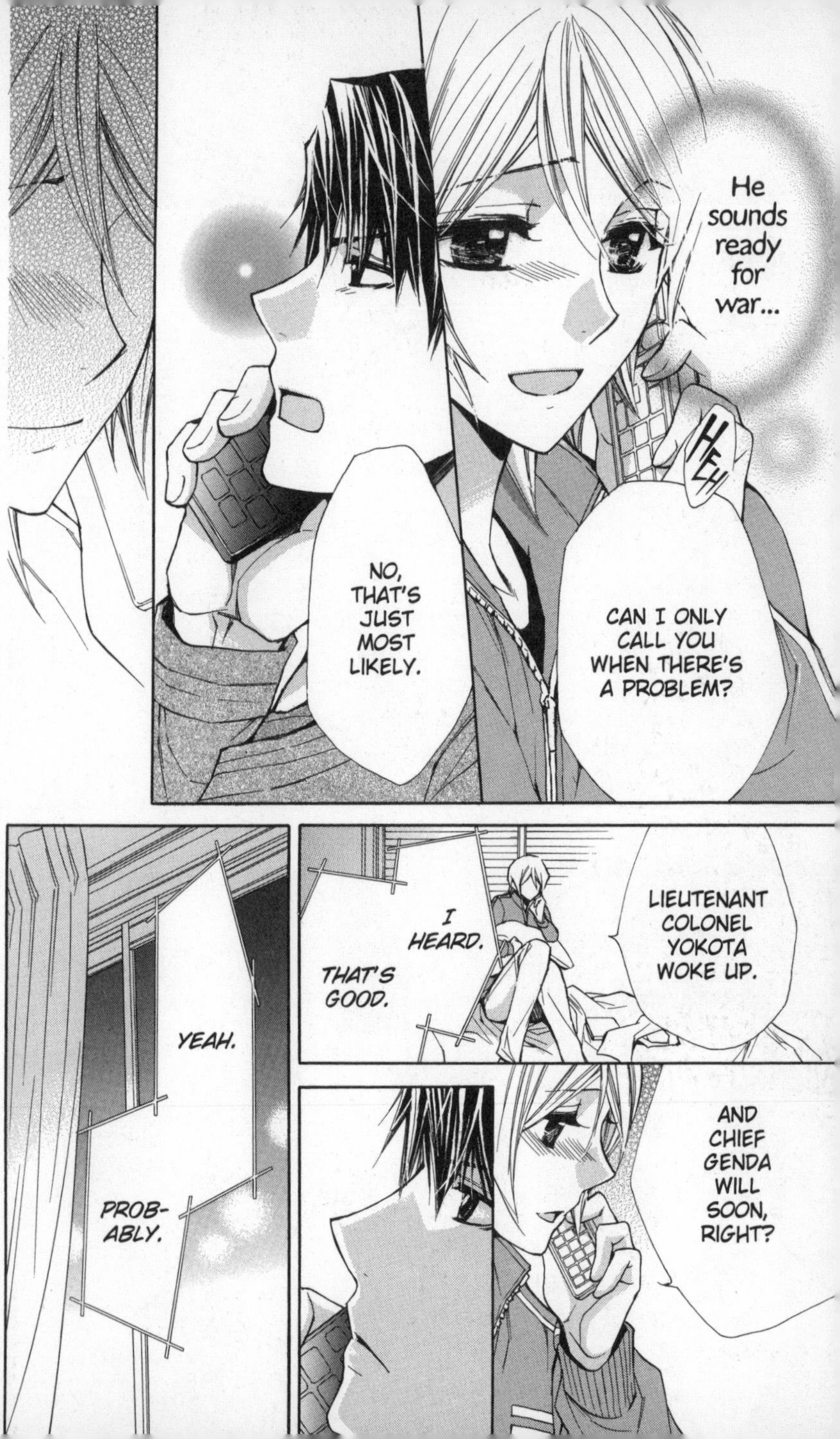
He sounds ready for war...
HEH
CAN I ONLY CALL YOU WHEN THERE'S A PROBLEM?
NO, THAT'S JUST MOST LIKELY.
LIEUTENANT COLONEL YOKOTA WOKE UP.
I HEARD.
THAT'S GOOD.
AND CHIEF GENDA WILL SOON, RIGHT?
YEAH.
PROB-ABLY.

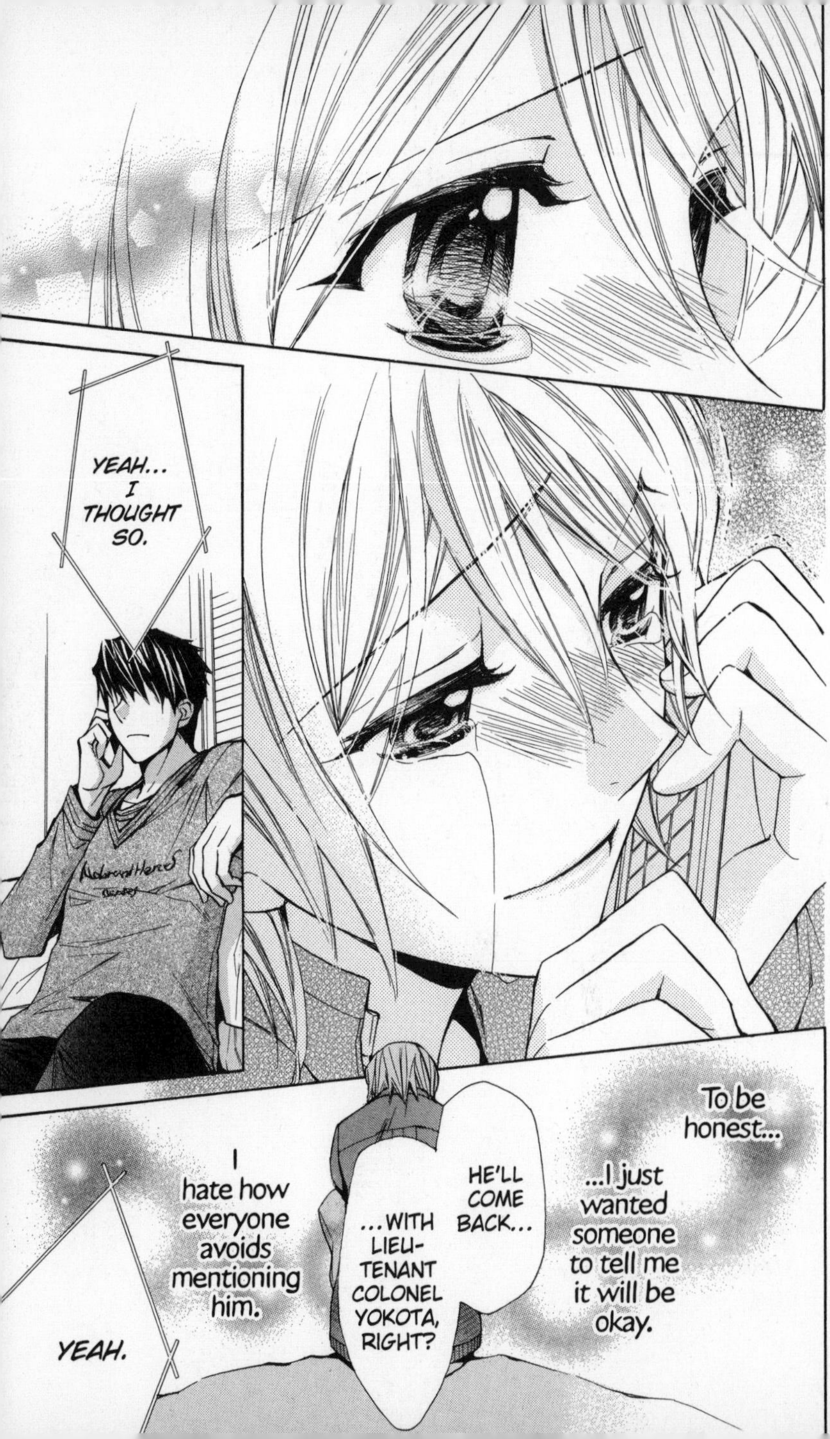
YEAH... I THOUGHT SO.
To be honest...
...I just wanted someone to tell me it will be okay.
HE'LL JUST COME BACK...
...WITH LIEUTENANT COLONEL YOKOTA, RIGHT?
I hate how everyone avoids mentioning him.
YEAH.

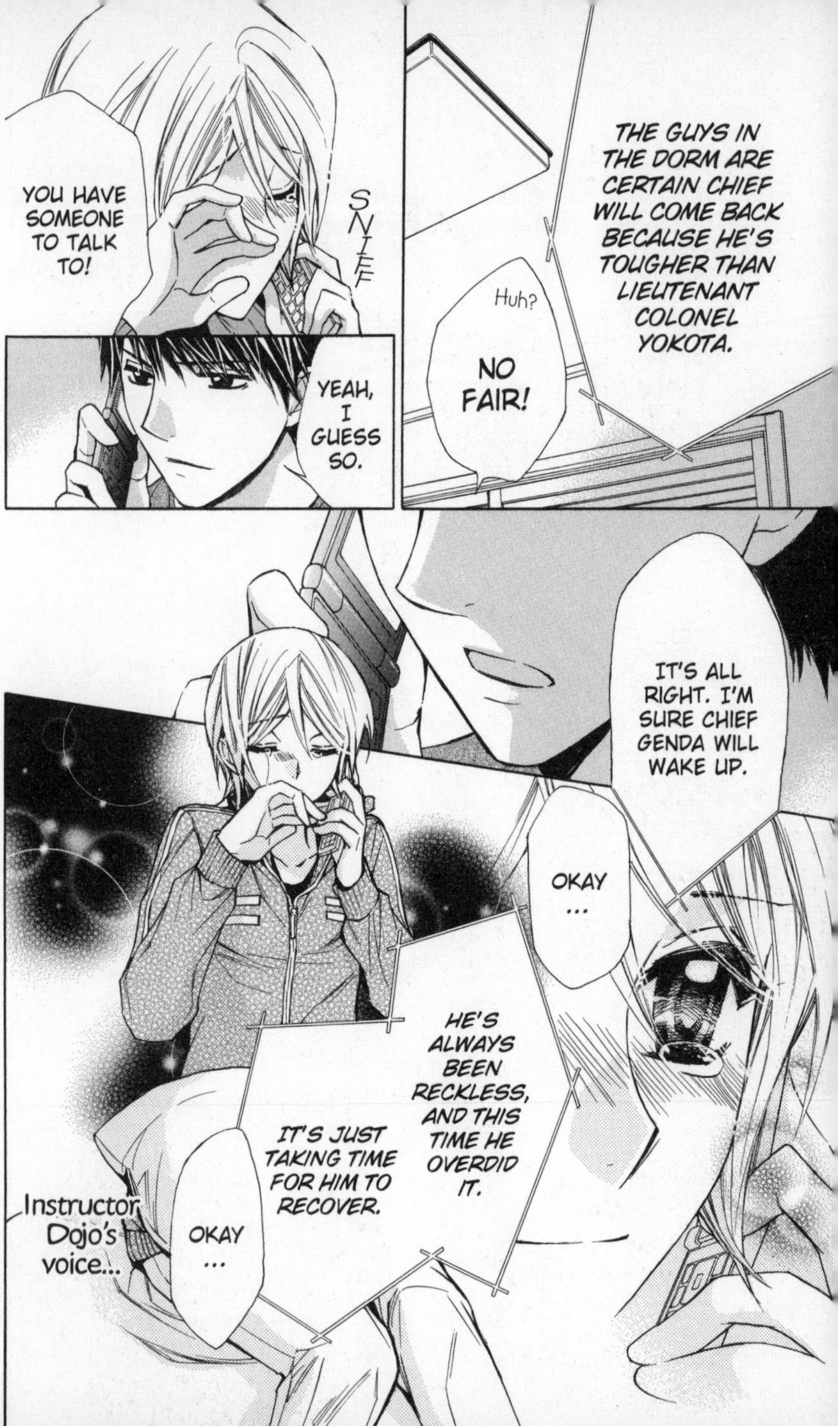
THE GUYS IN THE DORM ARE CERTAIN CHIEF WILL COME BACK BECAUSE HE'S TOUGHER THAN LIEUTENANT COLONEL YOKOTA.
Huh?
NO FAIR!
YOU HAVE SOMEONE TO TALK TO!
SNIFF
YEAH, I GUESS SO.
IT'S ALL RIGHT. I'M SURE CHIEF GENDA WILL WAKE UP.
OKAY ...
HE'S ALWAYS BEEN RECKLESS, AND THIS TIME HE OVERDID IT.
IT'S JUST TAKING TIME FOR HIM TO RECOVER.
OKAY ...
Instructor Dojo's voice...

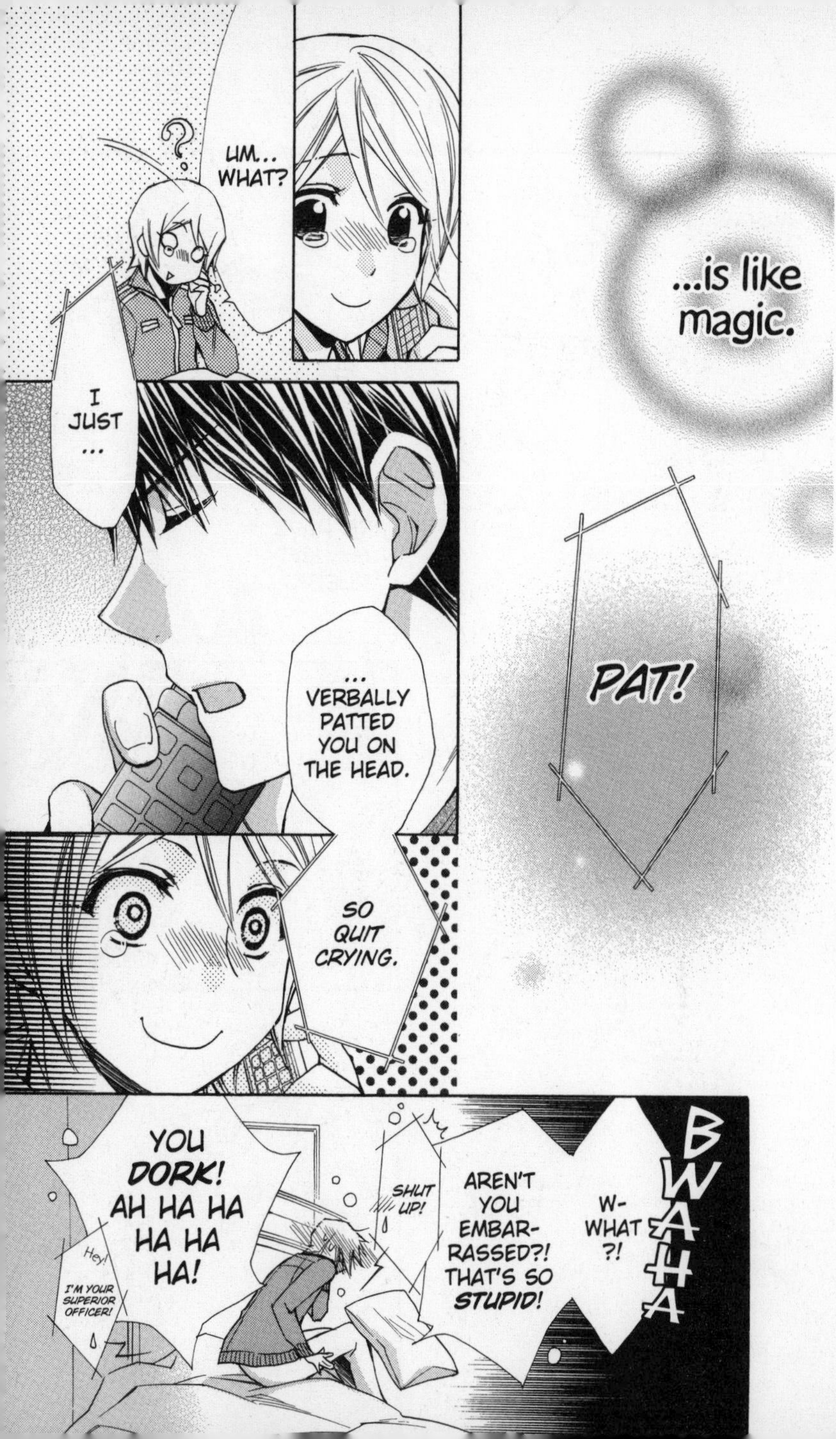

...is like magic.
PAT!
UM... WHAT?
I JUST ...
... VERBALLY PATTED YOU ON THE HEAD.
SO QUIT CRYING.
BWAHAHA
W-WHAT ?!
AREN'T YOU EMBARRASSED?! THAT'S SO STUPID!
SHUT UP!
YOU DORK! AH HA HA HA HA HA!
Hey!
I'M YOUR SUPERIOR OFFICER!

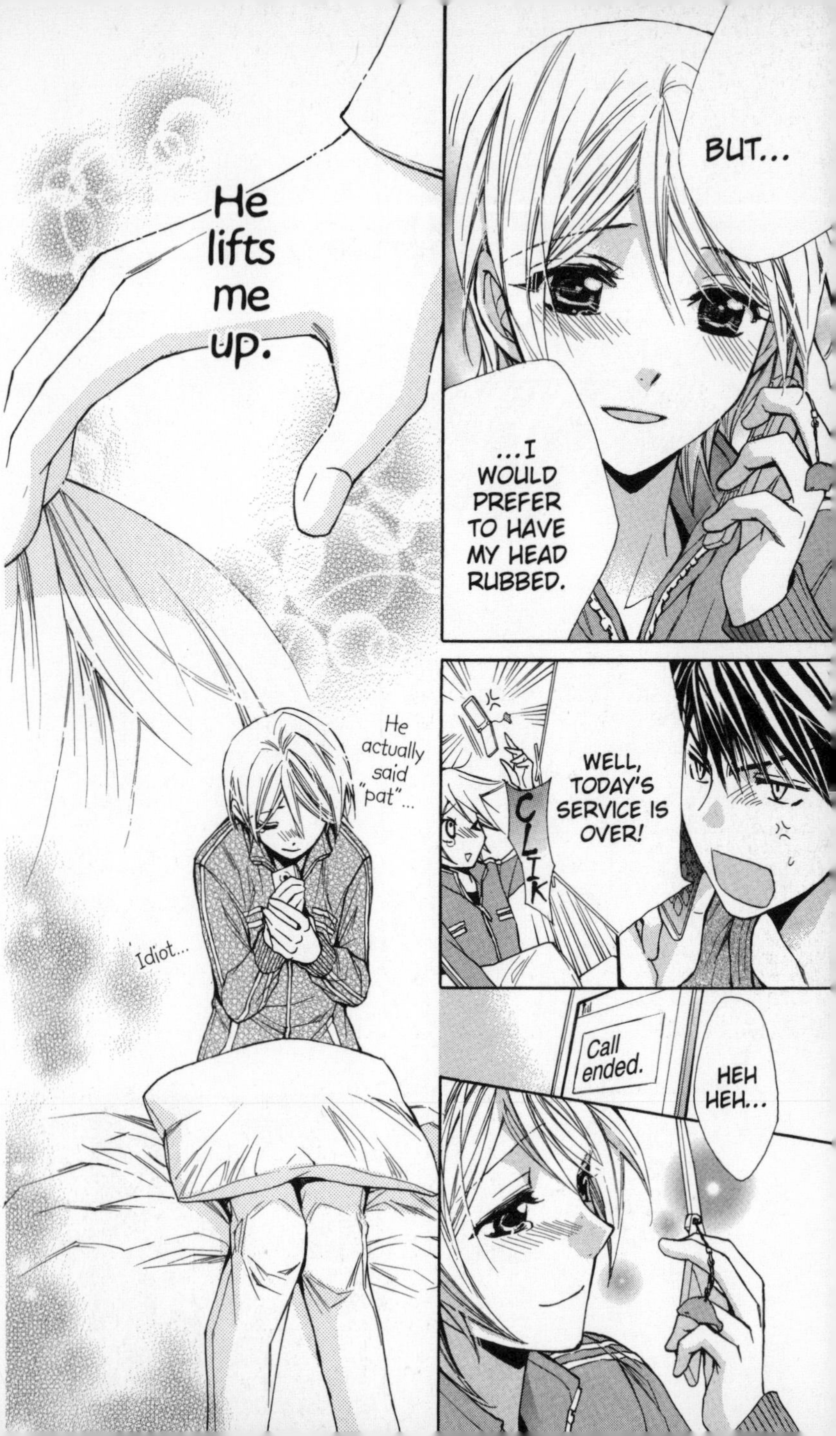
BUT...
...I WOULD PREFER TO HAVE MY HEAD RUBBED.
WELL, TODAY'S SERVICE IS OVER!
CLIK
Call ended.
HEH HEH...
He lifts me up.
He actually said "pat"...
Idiot...

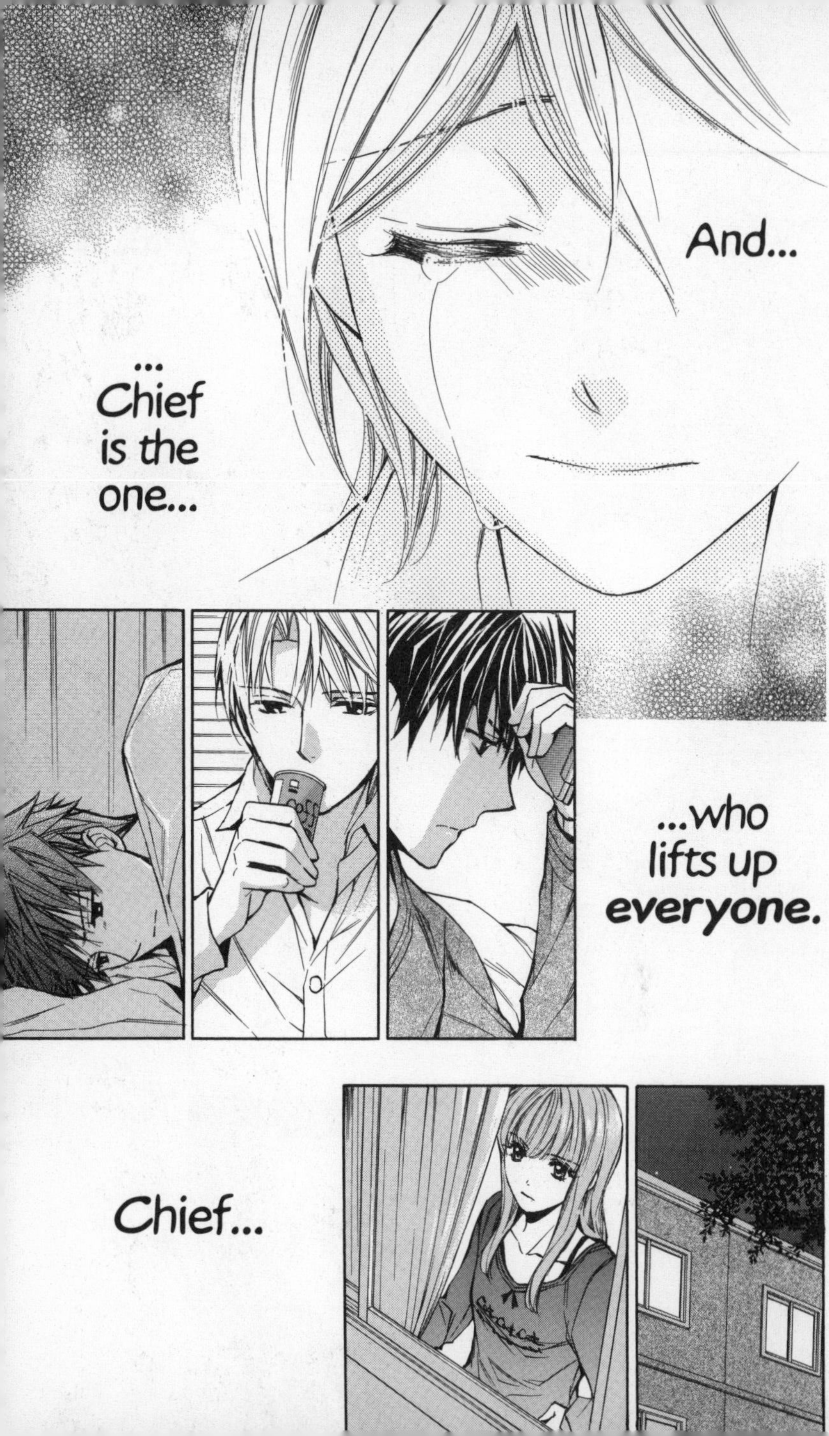
And...
...Chief is the one...
...who lifts up everyone.
Chief...

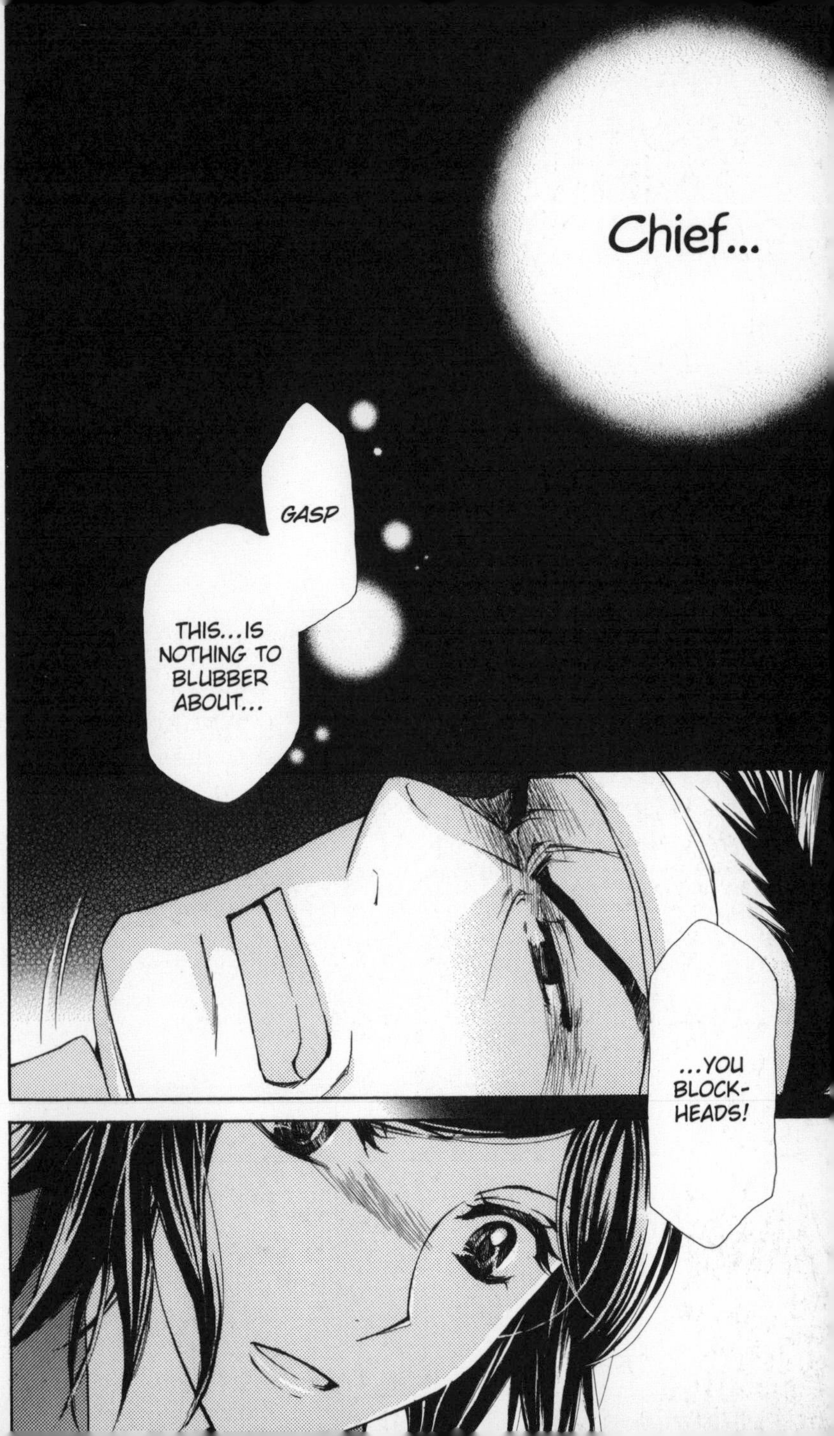
Chief...
GASP
THIS...IS NOTHING TO BLUBBER ABOUT...
...YOU BLOCK-HEADS!

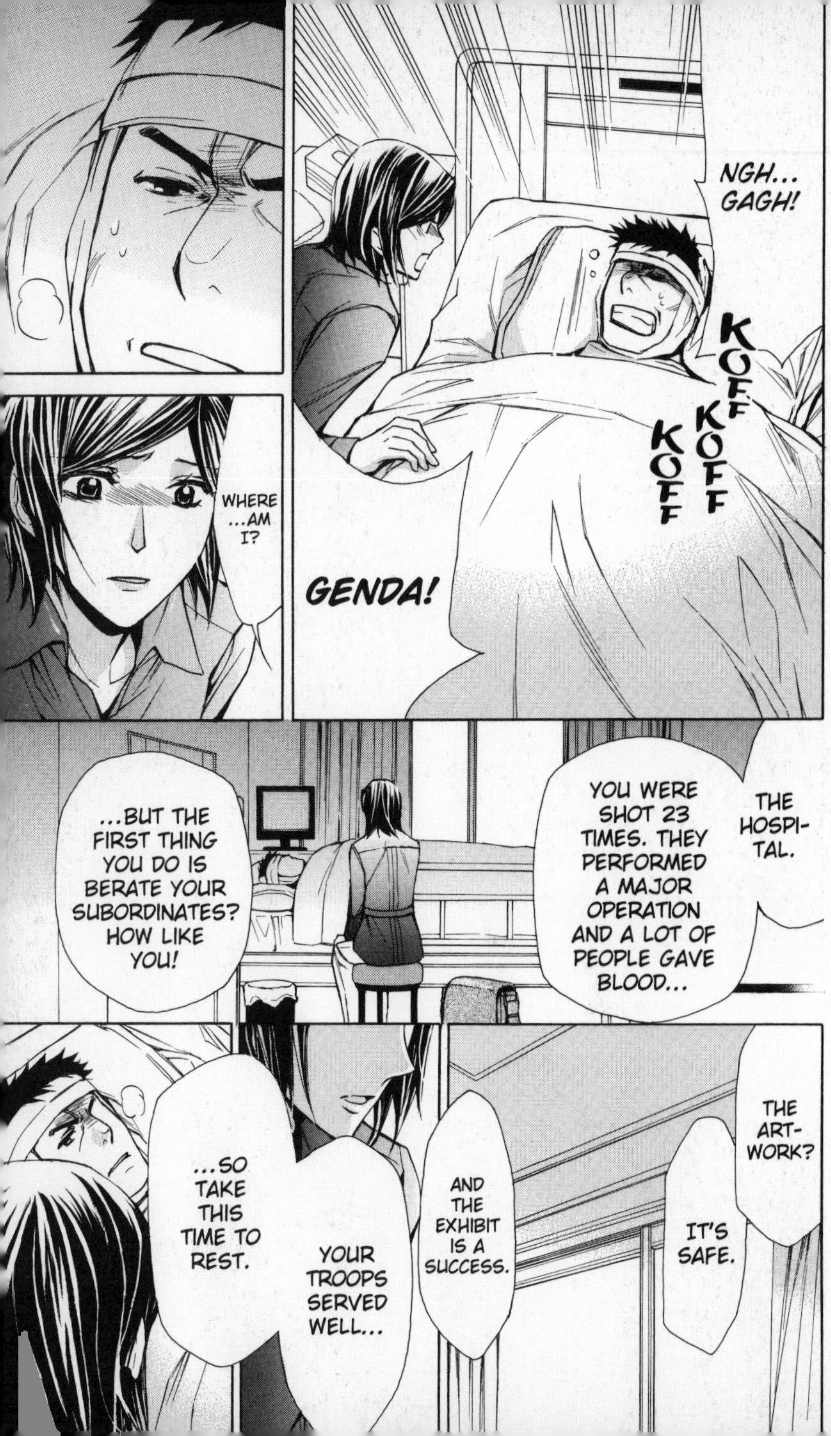
NGH... GAGH!
KOFF KOFF KOFF
GENDA!
WHERE ...AM I?
THE HOSPI-TAL.
YOU WERE SHOT 23 TIMES. THEY PERFORMED A MAJOR OPERATION AND A LOT OF PEOPLE GAVE BLOOD...
...BUT THE FIRST THING YOU DO IS BERATE YOUR SUBORDINATES? HOW LIKE YOU!
THE ART-WORK?
IT'S SAFE.
AND THE EXHIBIT IS A SUCCESS.
YOUR TROOPS SERVED WELL...
...SO TAKE THIS TIME TO REST.

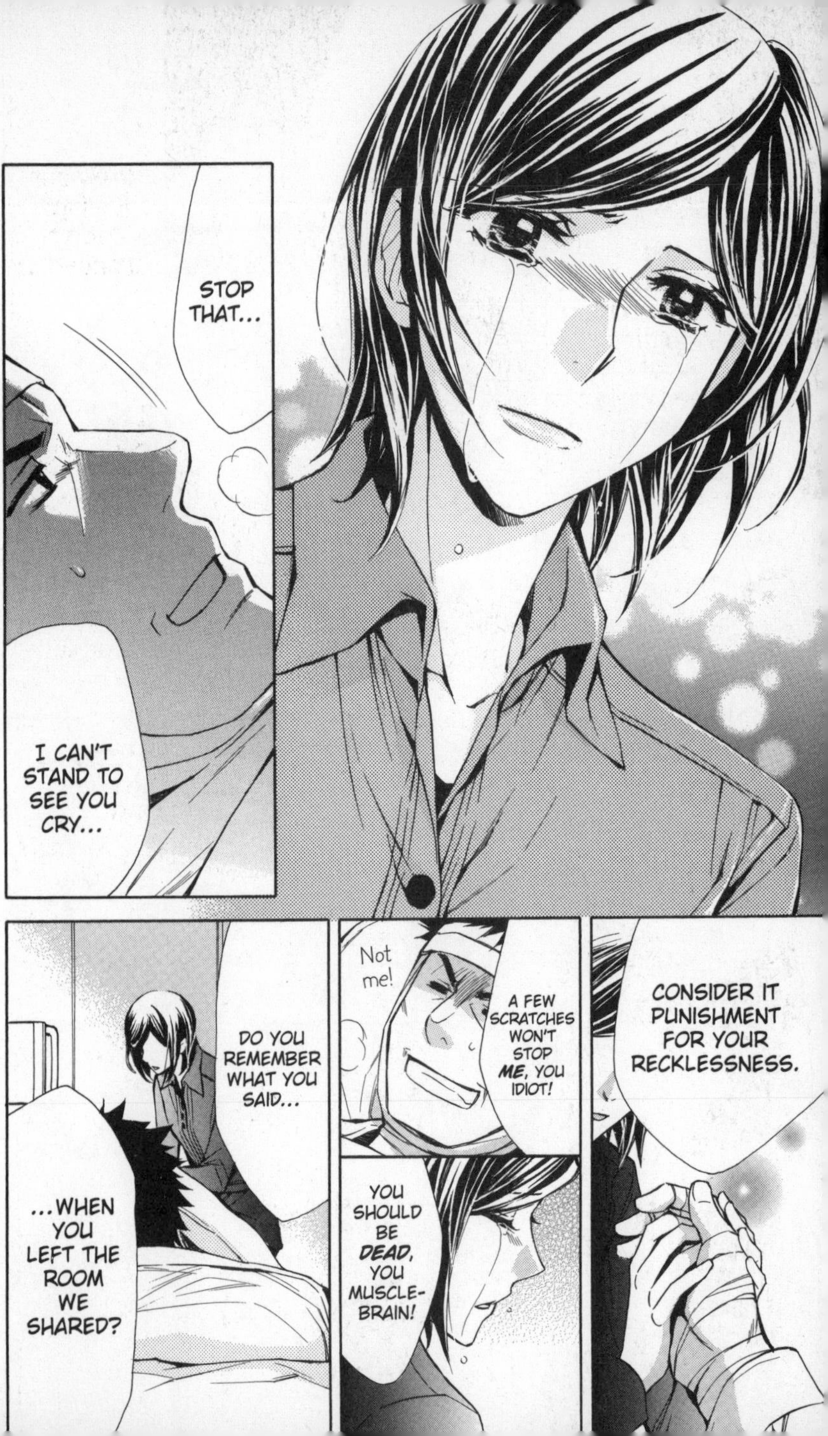
STOP THAT...
I CAN'T STAND TO SEE YOU CRY...
CONSIDER IT PUNISHMENT FOR YOUR RECKLESSNESS.
A FEW SCRATCHES WON'T STOP *ME*, YOU IDIOT!
Not me!
YOU SHOULD BE *DEAD*, YOU MUSCLE-BRAIN!
DO YOU REMEMBER WHAT YOU SAID...
...WHEN YOU LEFT THE ROOM WE SHARED?

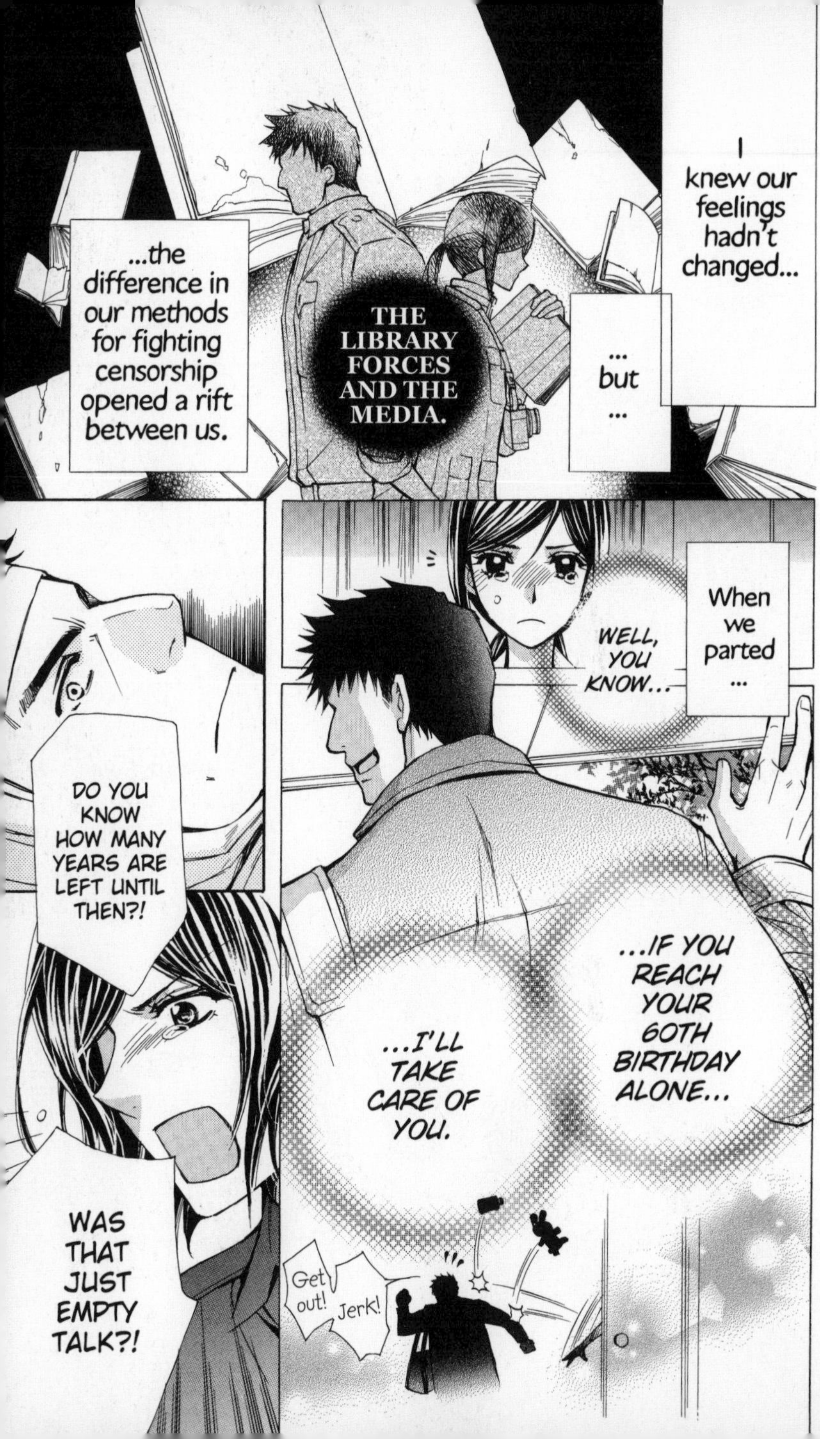
I knew our feelings hadn't changed...
...but...
THE LIBRARY FORCES AND THE MEDIA.
...the difference in our methods for fighting censorship opened a rift between us.
When we parted...
WELL, YOU KNOW...
...IF YOU REACH YOUR 60TH BIRTHDAY ALONE...
...I'LL TAKE CARE OF YOU.
Get out!
Jerk!
DO YOU KNOW HOW MANY YEARS ARE LEFT UNTIL THEN?!
WAS THAT JUST EMPTY TALK?!

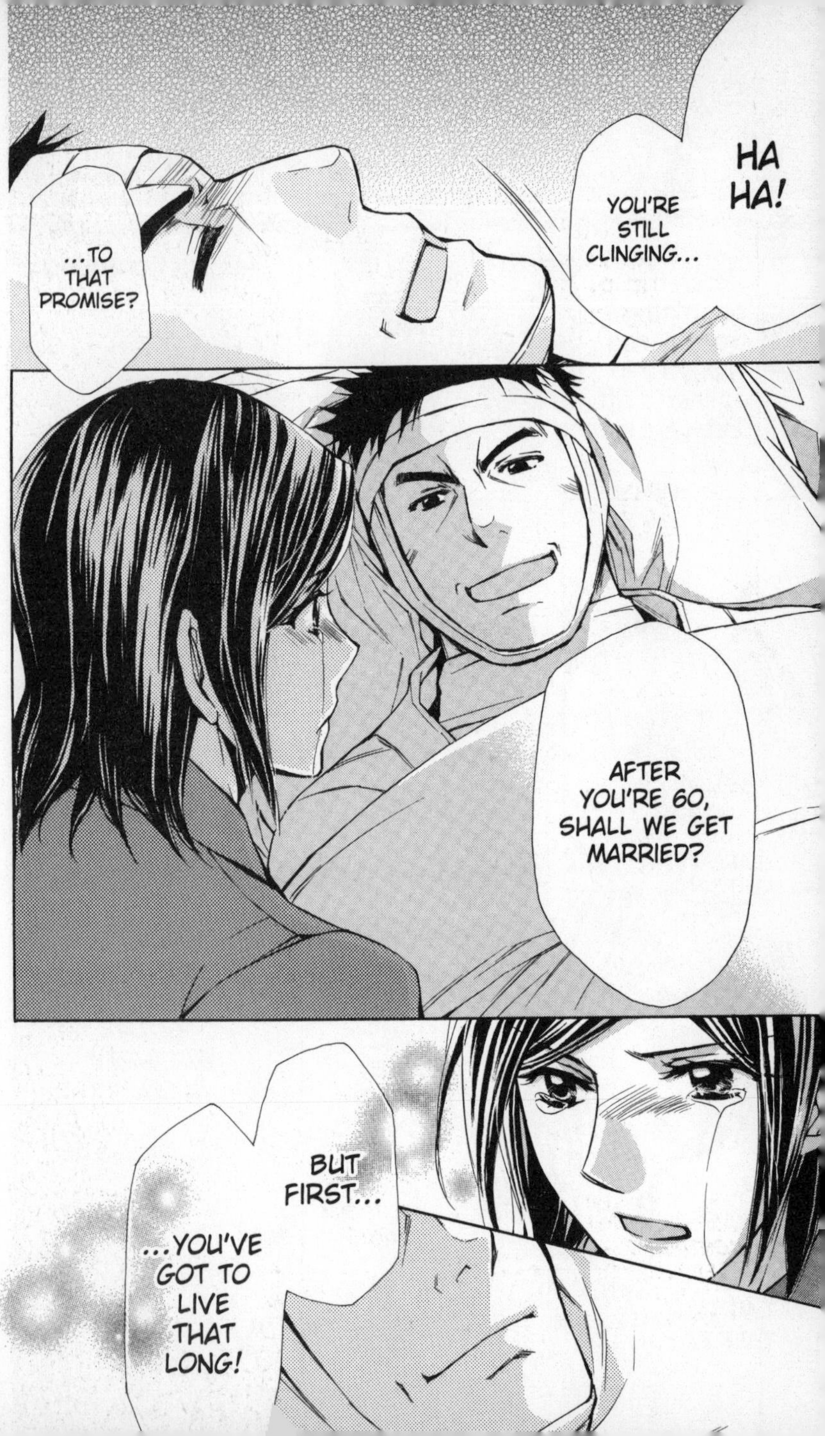
HA HA!
YOU'RE STILL CLINGING...
...TO THAT PROMISE?
AFTER YOU'RE 60, SHALL WE GET MARRIED?
BUT FIRST...
...YOU'VE GOT TO LIVE THAT LONG!

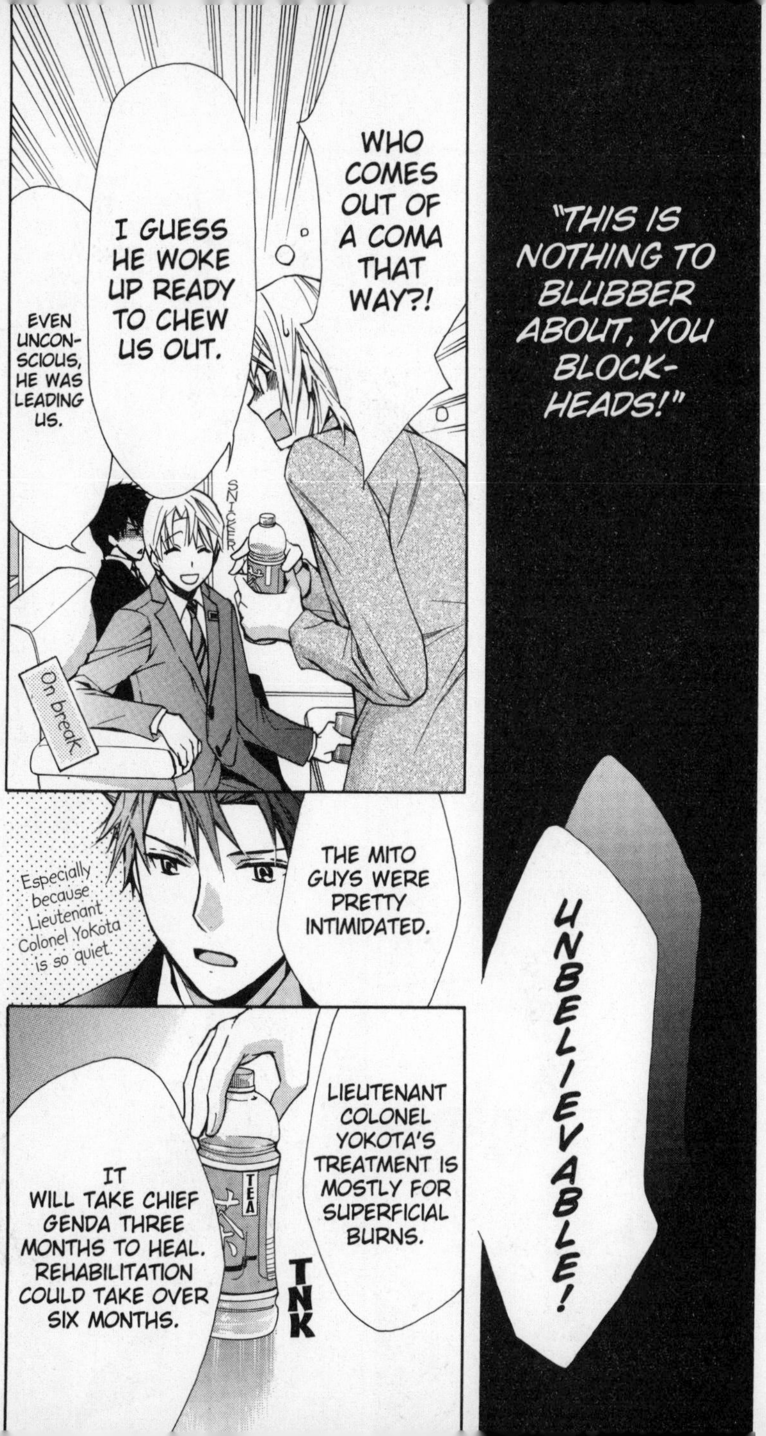
"THIS IS NOTHING TO BLUBBER ABOUT, YOU BLOCKHEADS!"
UNBELIEVABLE!
WHO COMES OUT OF A COMA THAT WAY?!
I GUESS HE WOKE UP READY TO CHEW US OUT.
EVEN UNCONSCIOUS, HE WAS LEADING US.
SNICKER
On break
THE MITO GUYS WERE PRETTY INTIMIDATED.
Especially because Lieutenant Colonel Yokota is so quiet.
LIEUTENANT COLONEL YOKOTA'S TREATMENT IS MOSTLY FOR SUPERFICIAL BURNS.
TNK
TEA
IT WILL TAKE CHIEF GENDA THREE MONTHS TO HEAL. REHABILITATION COULD TAKE OVER SIX MONTHS.

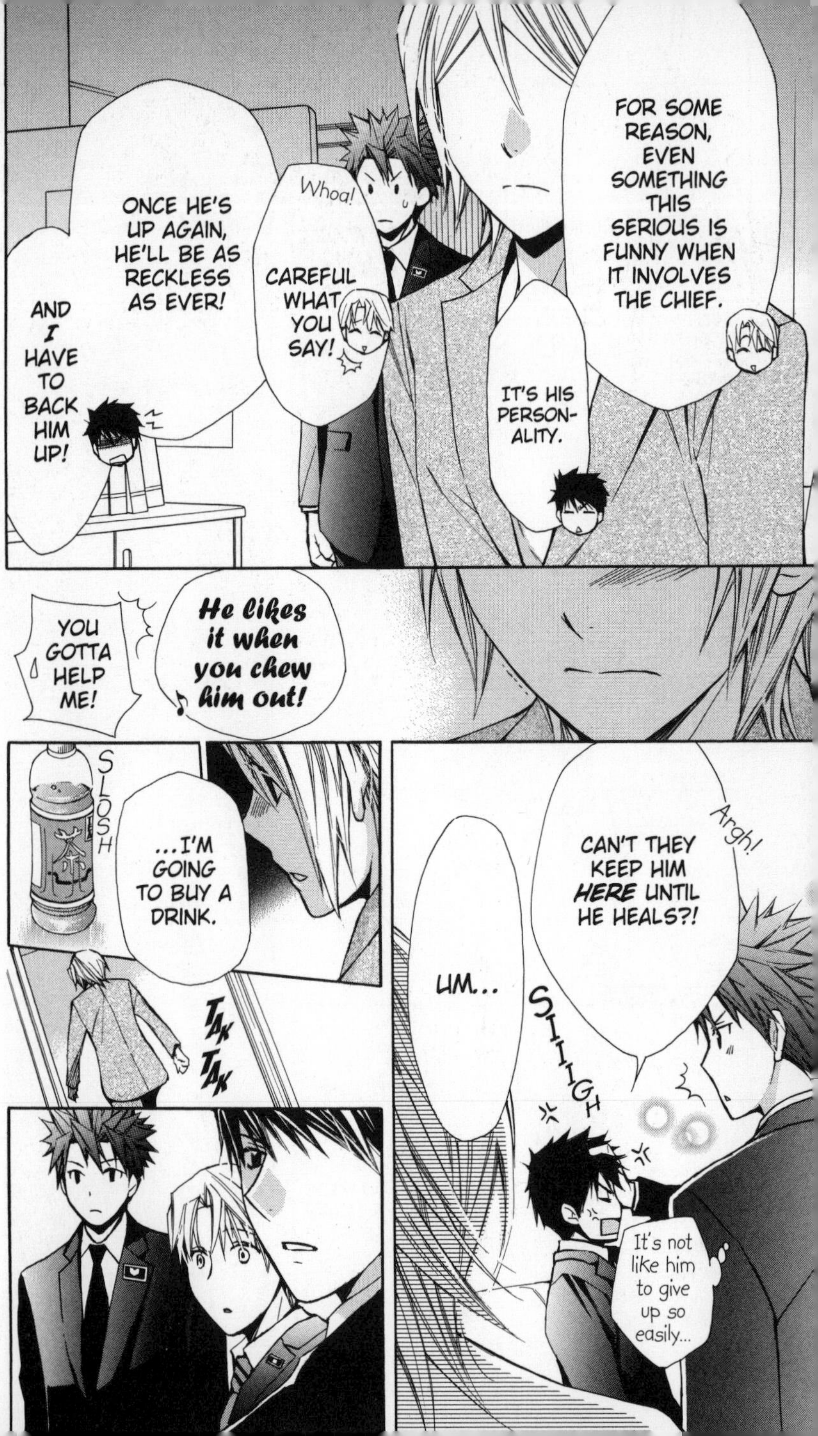
FOR SOME REASON, EVEN SOMETHING THIS SERIOUS IS FUNNY WHEN IT INVOLVES THE CHIEF.
IT'S HIS PERSONALITY.
Whoa!
CAREFUL WHAT YOU SAY!
ONCE HE'S UP AGAIN, HE'LL BE AS RECKLESS AS EVER!
AND *I* HAVE TO BACK HIM UP!
He likes it when you chew him out!
YOU GOTTA HELP ME!
Argh!
CAN'T THEY KEEP HIM *HERE* UNTIL HE HEALS?!
UM...
SIIIGH
It's not like him to give up so easily...
SLOSH
...I'M GOING TO BUY A DRINK.
TAK TAK

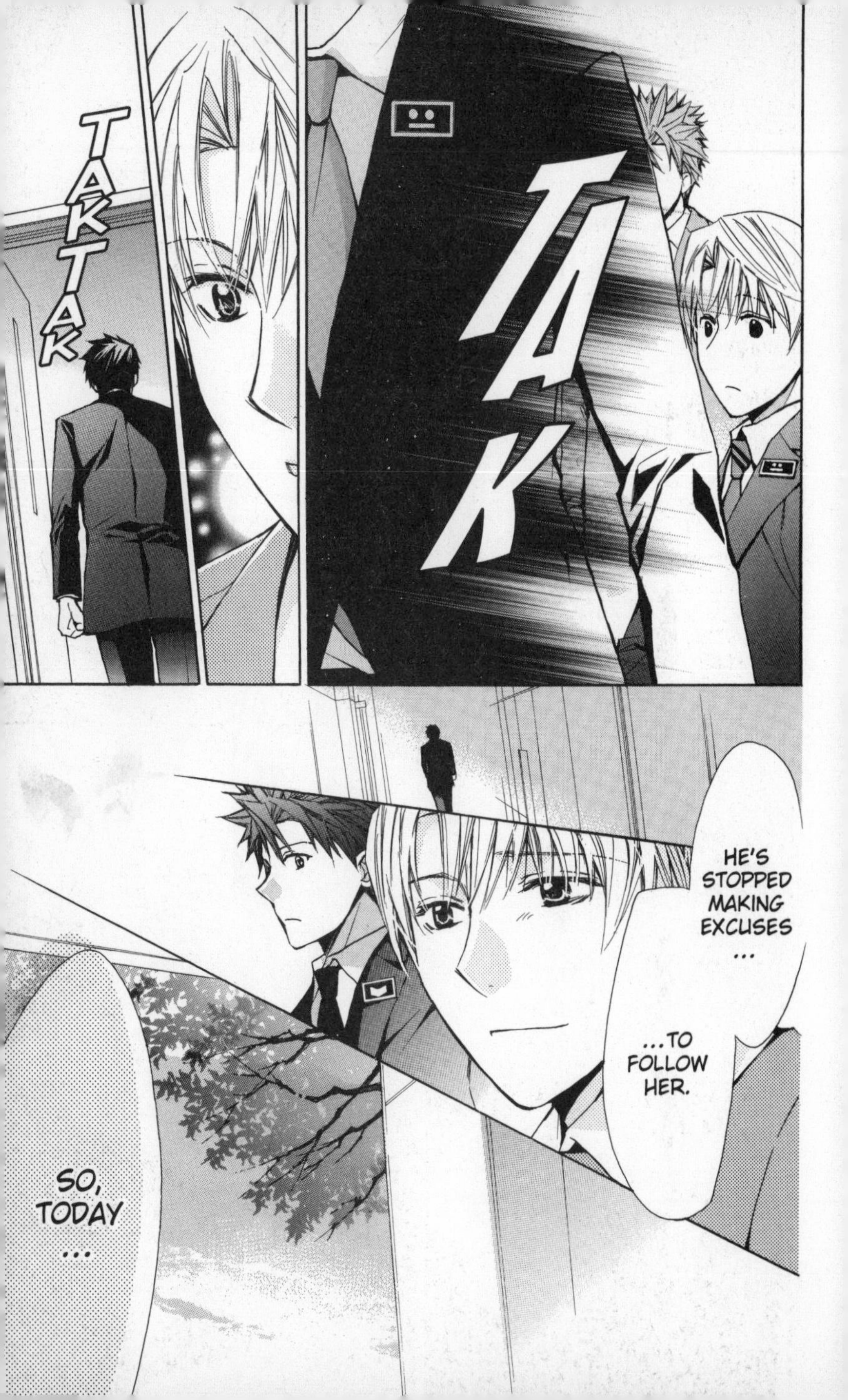
TAK
TAKTAK
HE'S STOPPED MAKING EXCUSES ...
...TO FOLLOW HER.
SO, TODAY ...

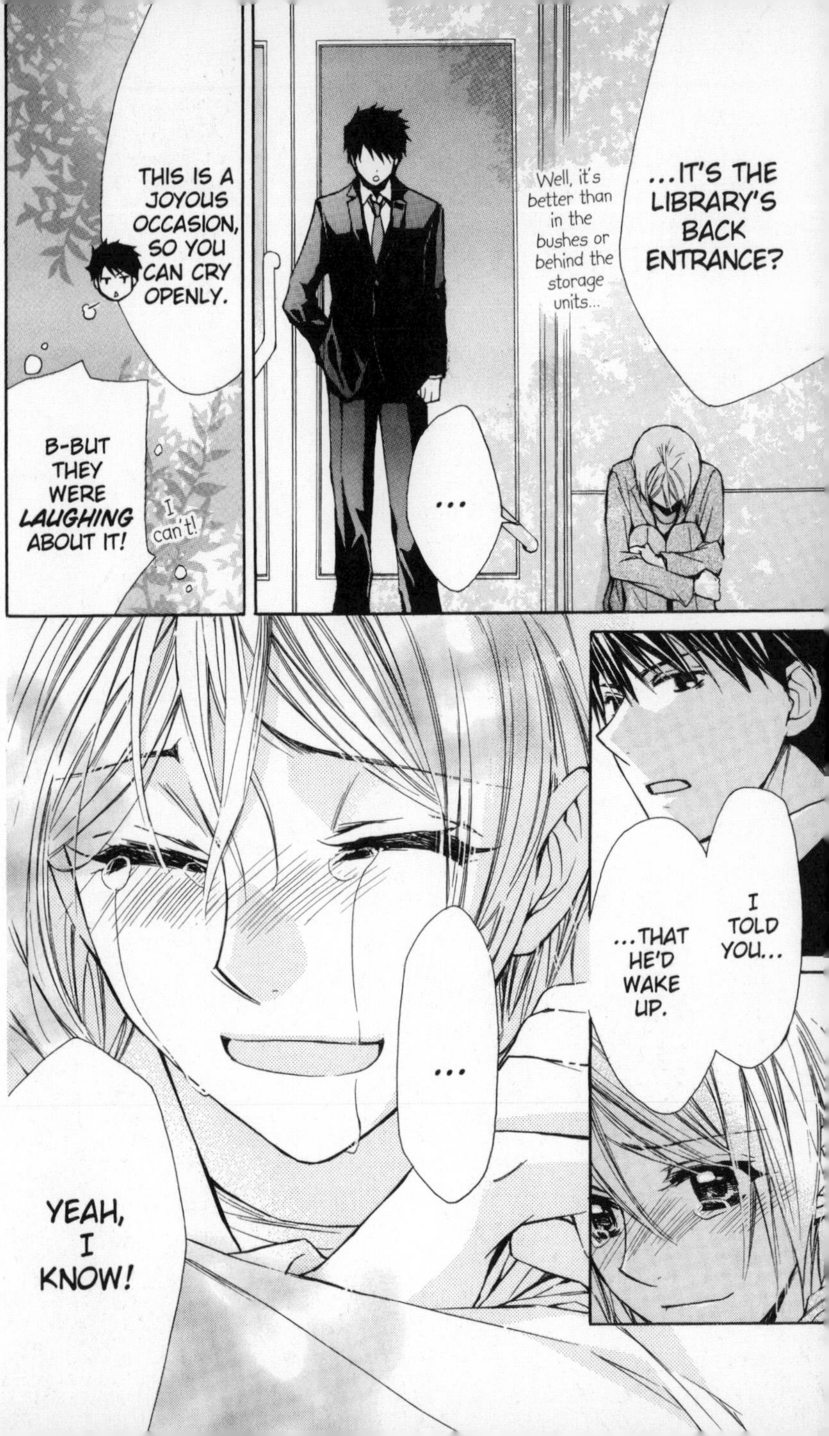
...IT'S THE LIBRARY'S BACK ENTRANCE?
Well, it's better than in the bushes or behind the storage units...
...
THIS IS A JOYOUS OCCASION, SO YOU CAN CRY OPENLY.
B-BUT THEY WERE *LAUGHING* ABOUT IT!
I can't!
I TOLD YOU...
...THAT HE'D WAKE UP.
...
YEAH, I KNOW!

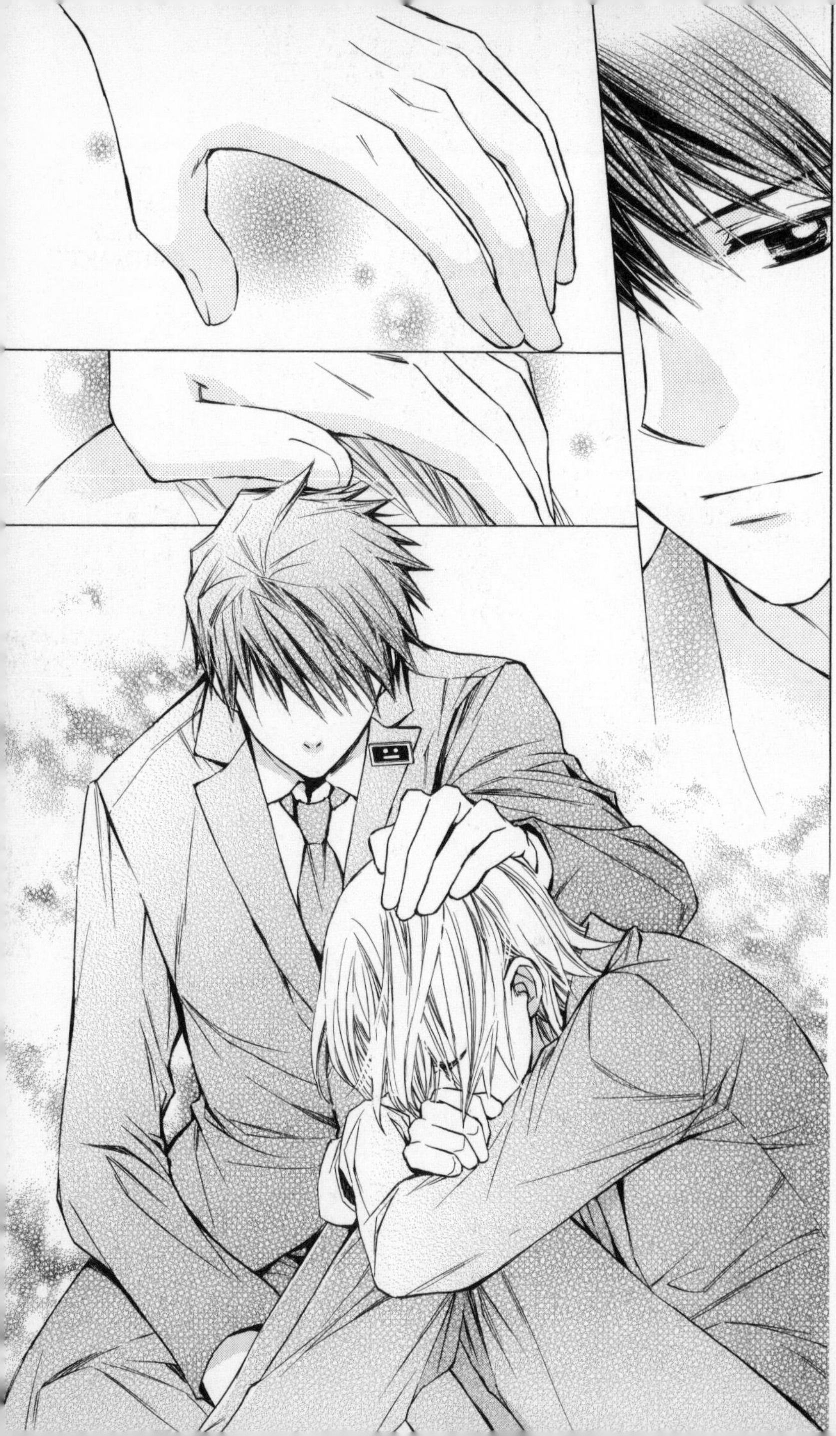

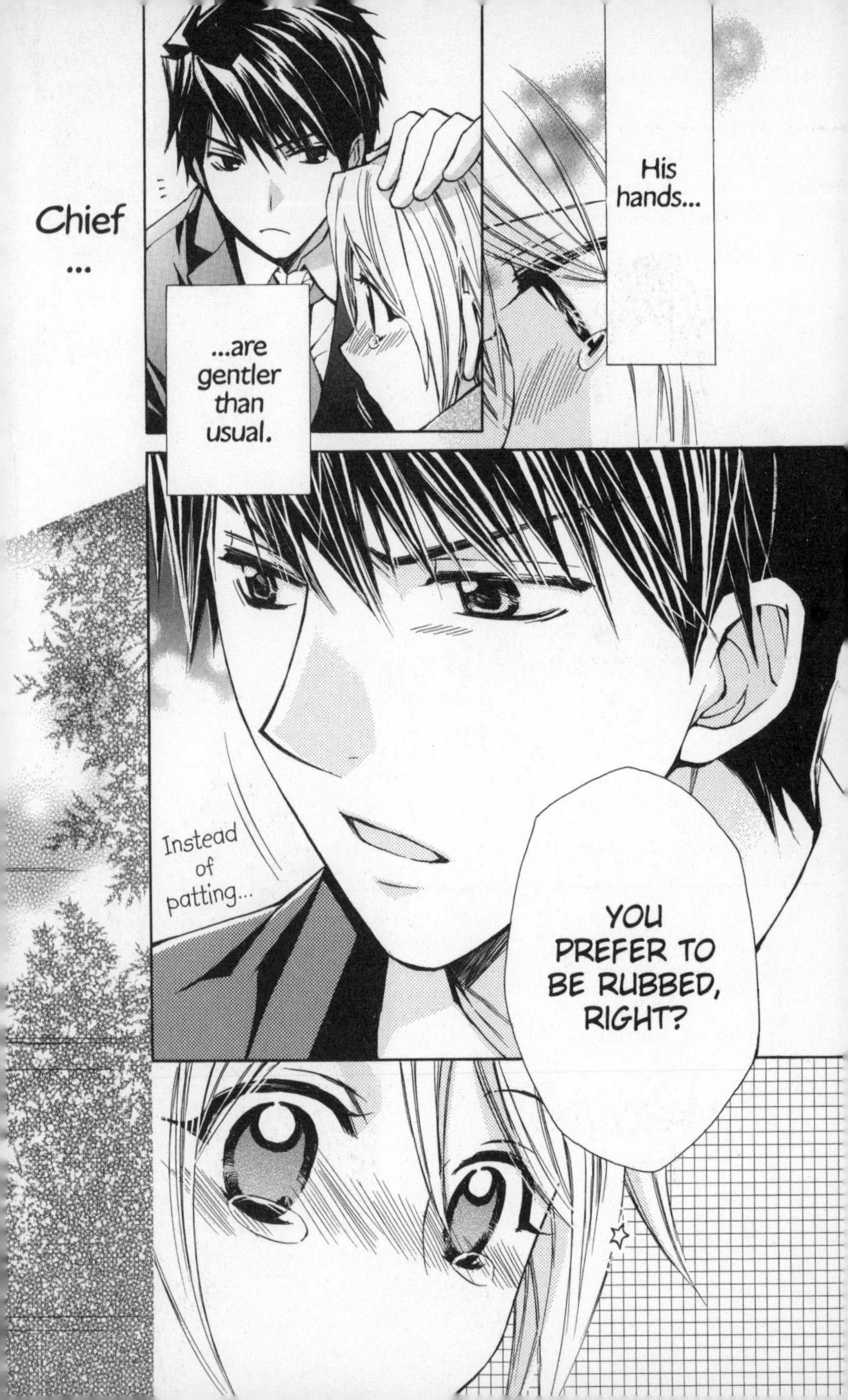
His hands...
...are gentler than usual.
Chief ...
Instead of patting...
YOU PREFER TO BE RUBBED, RIGHT?

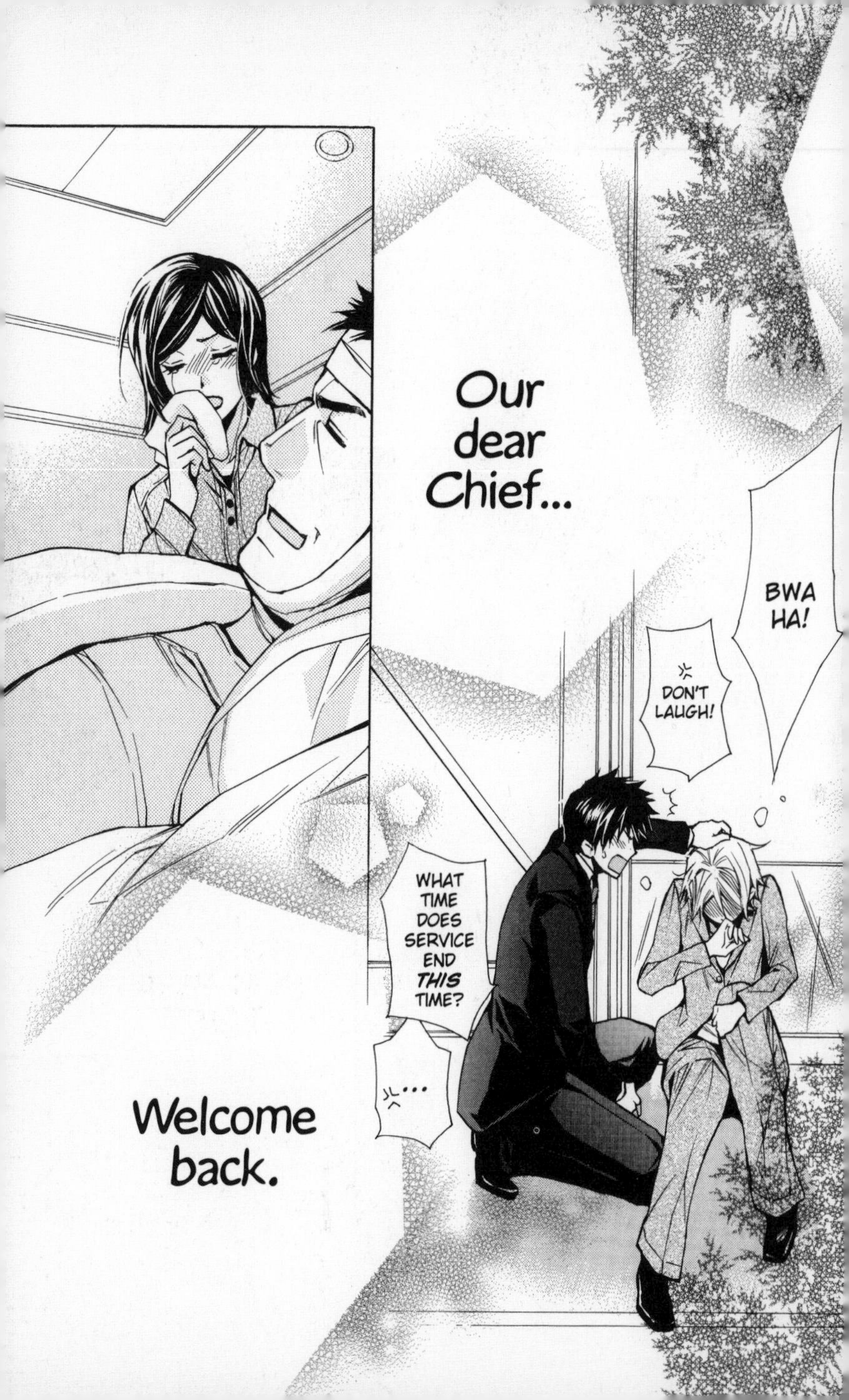

Our dear Chief...
BWA HA!
DON'T LAUGH!
WHAT TIME DOES SERVICE END *THIS* TIME?
...
Welcome back.

Sorta Like a **Massage Ticket**

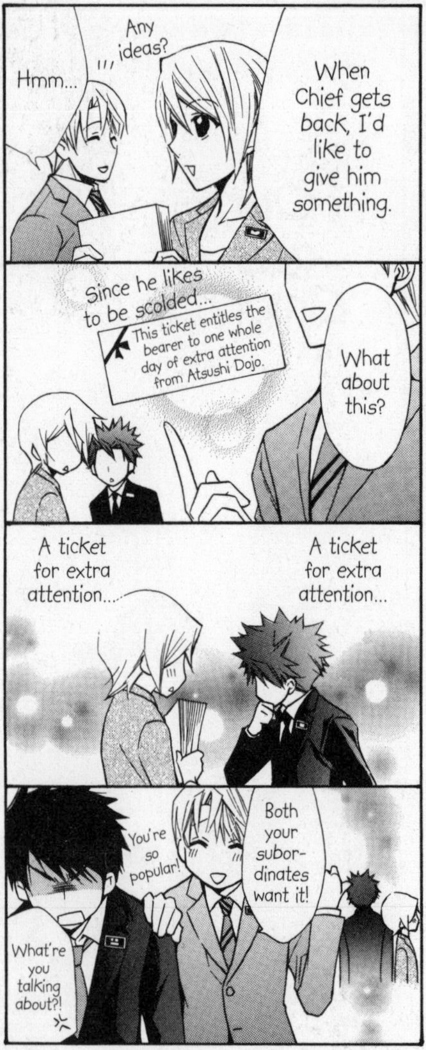
When Chief gets back, I'd like to give him something.
Any ideas?
Hmm...
What about this?
Since he likes to be scolded...
This ticket entitles the bearer to one whole day of extra attention from Atsushi Dojo.
A ticket for extra attention...
A ticket for extra attention...
Both your subordinates want it!
You're so popular!
What're you talking about?!

But you pay attention even without a ticket. ^^
—Komaki

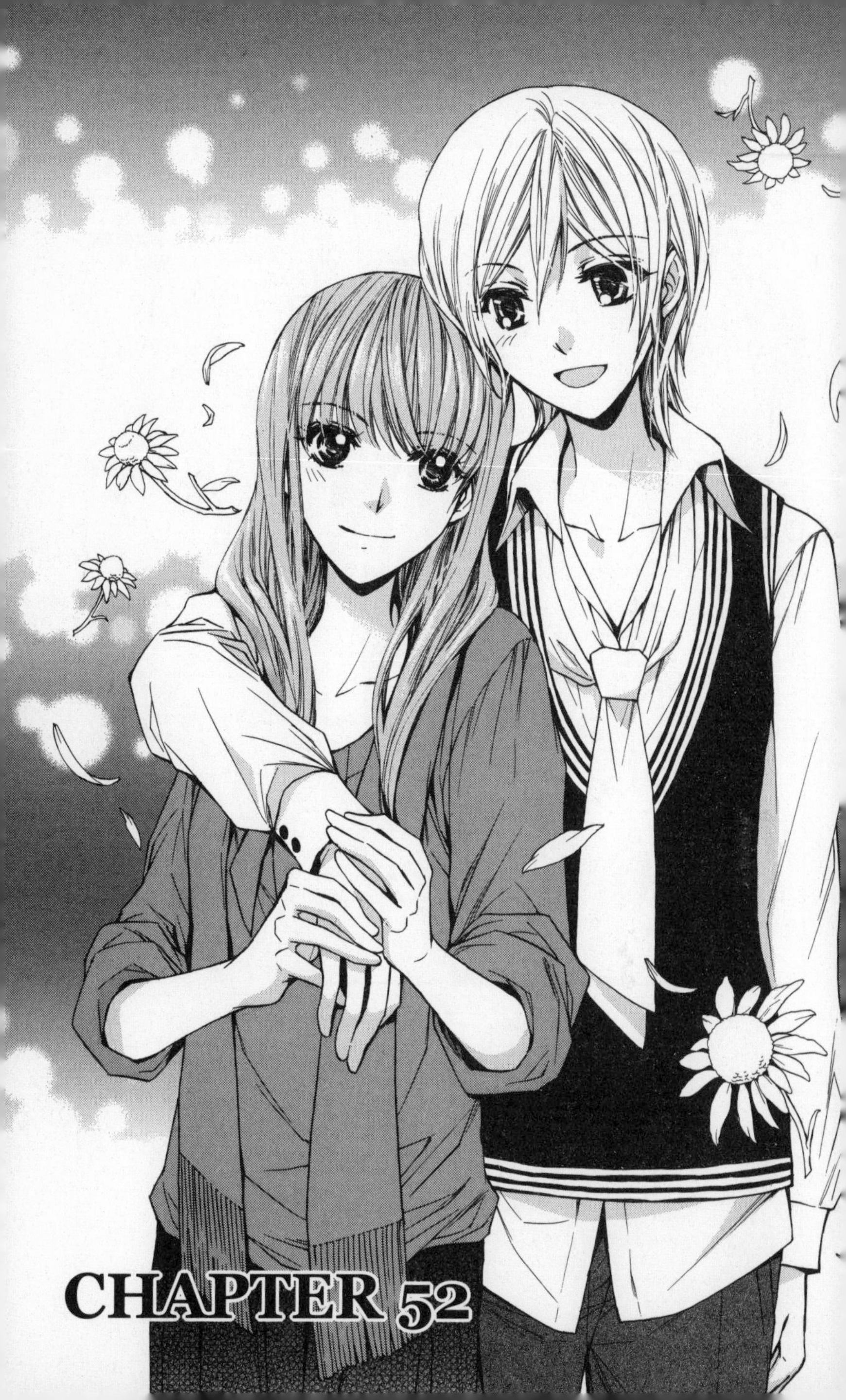
CHAPTER 52

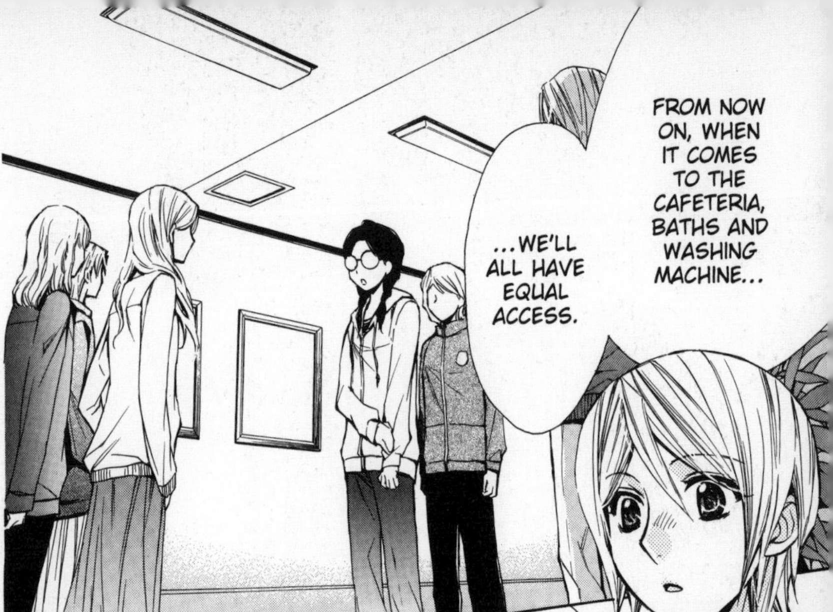
FROM NOW ON, WHEN IT COMES TO THE CAFETERIA, BATHS AND WASHING MACHINE...
...WE'LL ALL HAVE EQUAL ACCESS.
WE'RE NOT SO NAIVE THAT WE'LL SETTLE...
...FOR A MERE APOLOGY ...
...BUT ALL WE WANT RIGHT NOW...
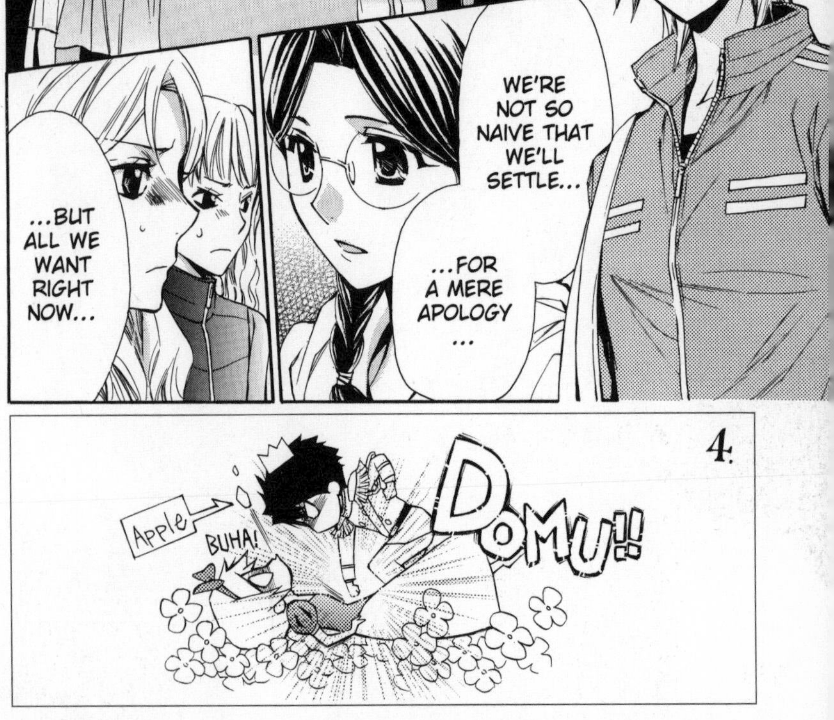
4.
DOMU!!
Apple
BUHA!

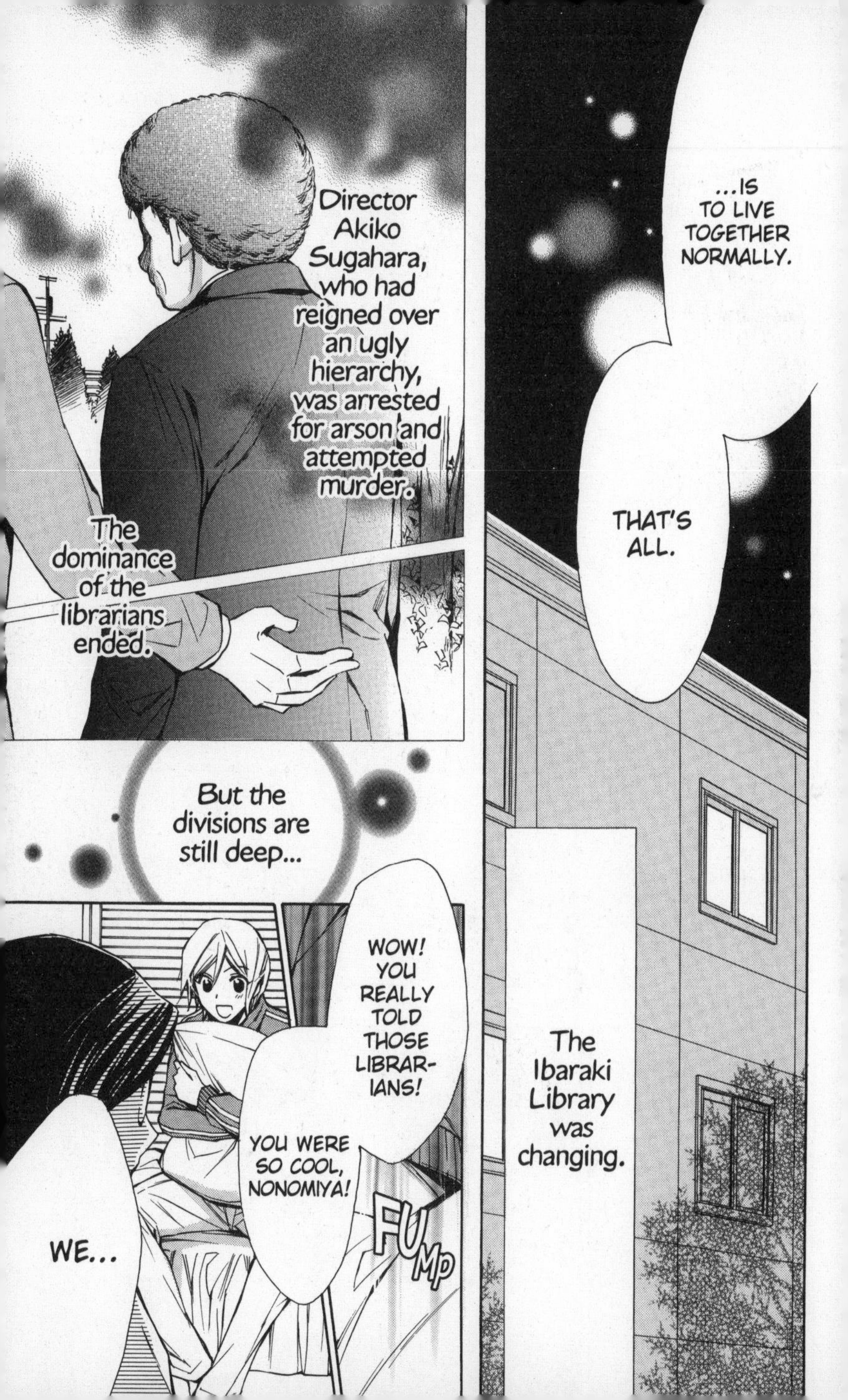
...IS TO LIVE TOGETHER NORMALLY.
THAT'S ALL.
The Ibaraki Library was changing.
Director Akiko Sugahara, who had reigned over an ugly hierarchy, was arrested for arson and attempted murder.
The dominance of the librarians ended.
But the divisions are still deep...
WOW! YOU REALLY TOLD THOSE LIBRAR-IANS!
YOU WERE SO COOL, NONOMIYA!
FUMP
WE...

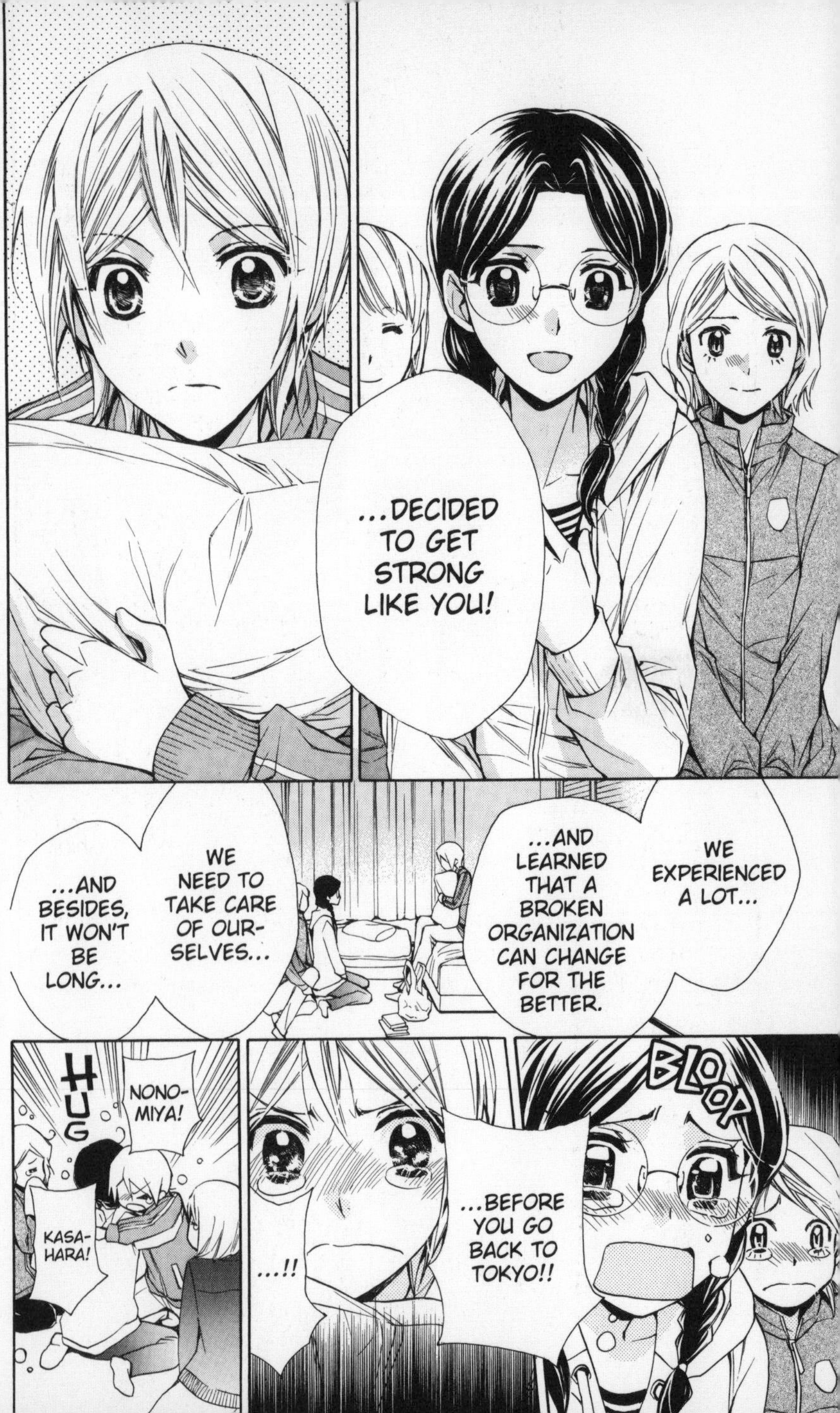
...DECIDED TO GET STRONG LIKE YOU!
WE EXPERIENCED A LOT...
...AND LEARNED THAT A BROKEN ORGANIZATION CAN CHANGE FOR THE BETTER.
WE NEED TO TAKE CARE OF OUR-SELVES...
...AND BESIDES, IT WON'T BE LONG...
BLOOP
...BEFORE YOU GO BACK TO TOKYO!!
...!!
HUG
NONO-MIYA!
KASA-HARA!

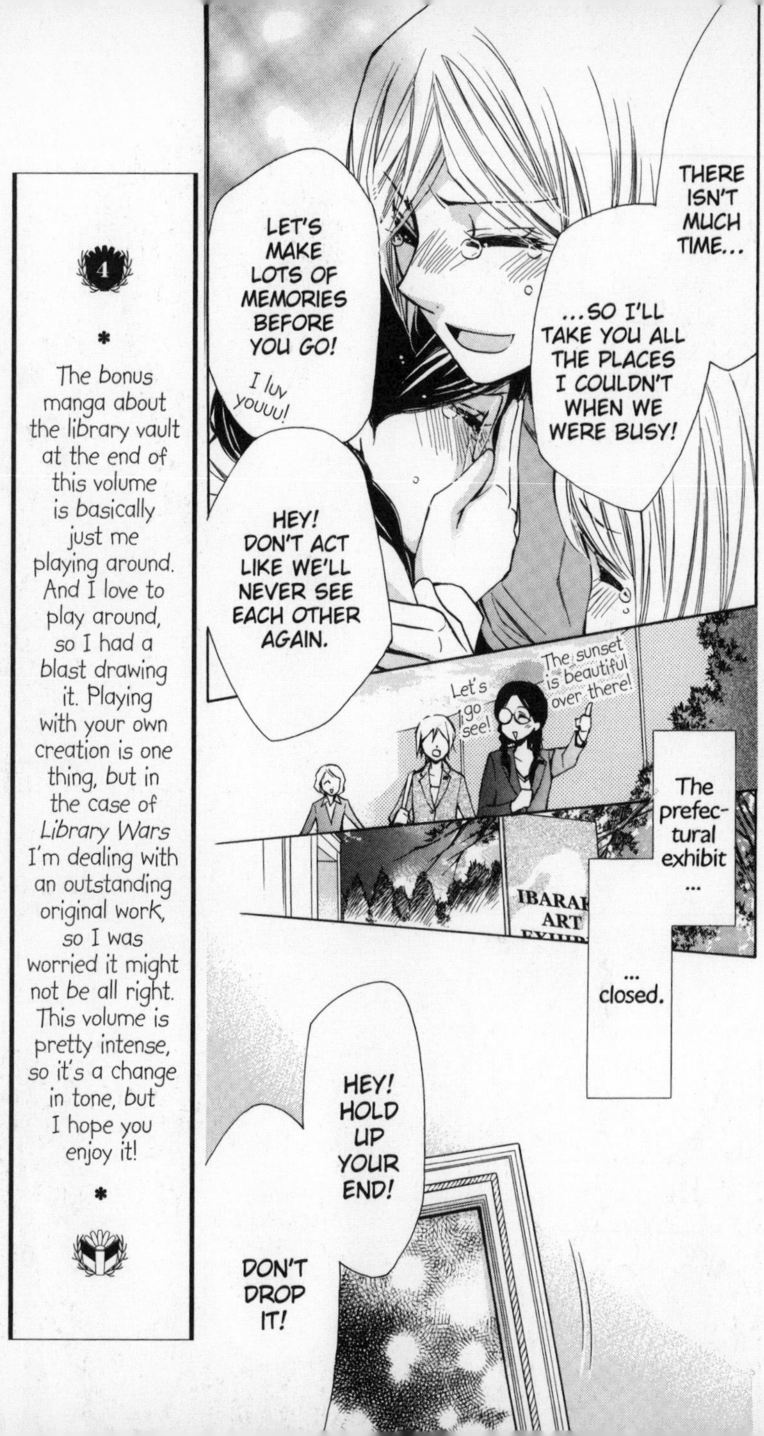
THERE ISN'T MUCH TIME...
...SO I'LL TAKE YOU ALL THE PLACES I COULDN'T WHEN WE WERE BUSY!
LET'S MAKE LOTS OF MEMORIES BEFORE YOU GO!
I luv youuu!
HEY! DON'T ACT LIKE WE'LL NEVER SEE EACH OTHER AGAIN.
The sunset is beautiful over there!
Let's go see!
The prefectural exhibit ...
IBARAK
ART
... closed.
HEY! HOLD UP YOUR END!
DON'T DROP IT!

4

*

The bonus manga about the library vault at the end of this volume is basically just me playing around. And I love to play around, so I had a blast drawing it. Playing with your own creation is one thing, but in the case of *Library Wars* I'm dealing with an outstanding original work, so I was worried it might not be all right. This volume is pretty intense, so it's a change in tone, but I hope you enjoy it!

*

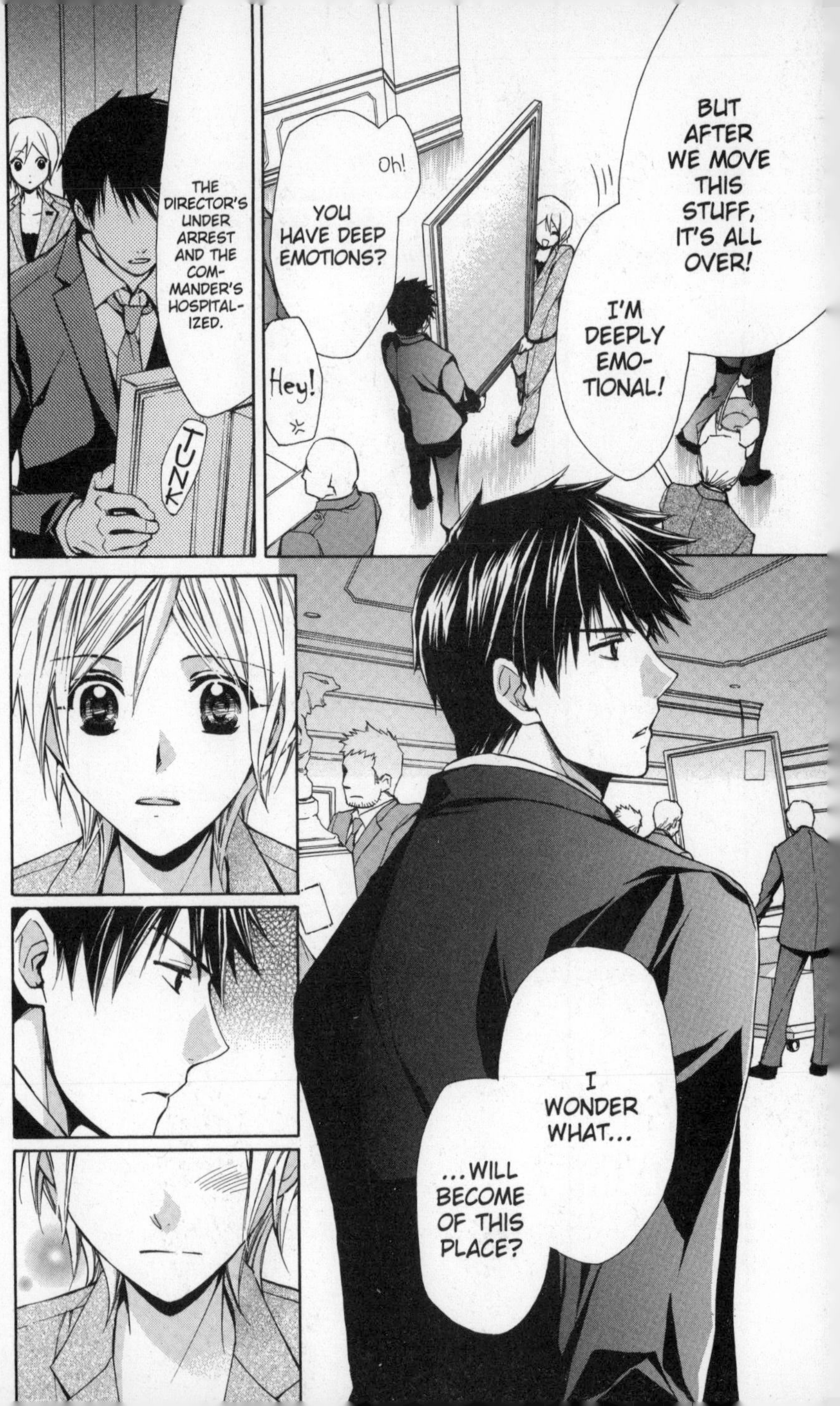
BUT AFTER WE MOVE THIS STUFF, IT'S ALL OVER!
I'M DEEPLY EMO-TIONAL!
Oh!
YOU HAVE DEEP EMOTIONS?
Hey!
THE DIRECTOR'S UNDER ARREST AND THE COM-MANDER'S HOSPITAL-IZED.
JUNK
I WONDER WHAT...
...WILL BECOME OF THIS PLACE?

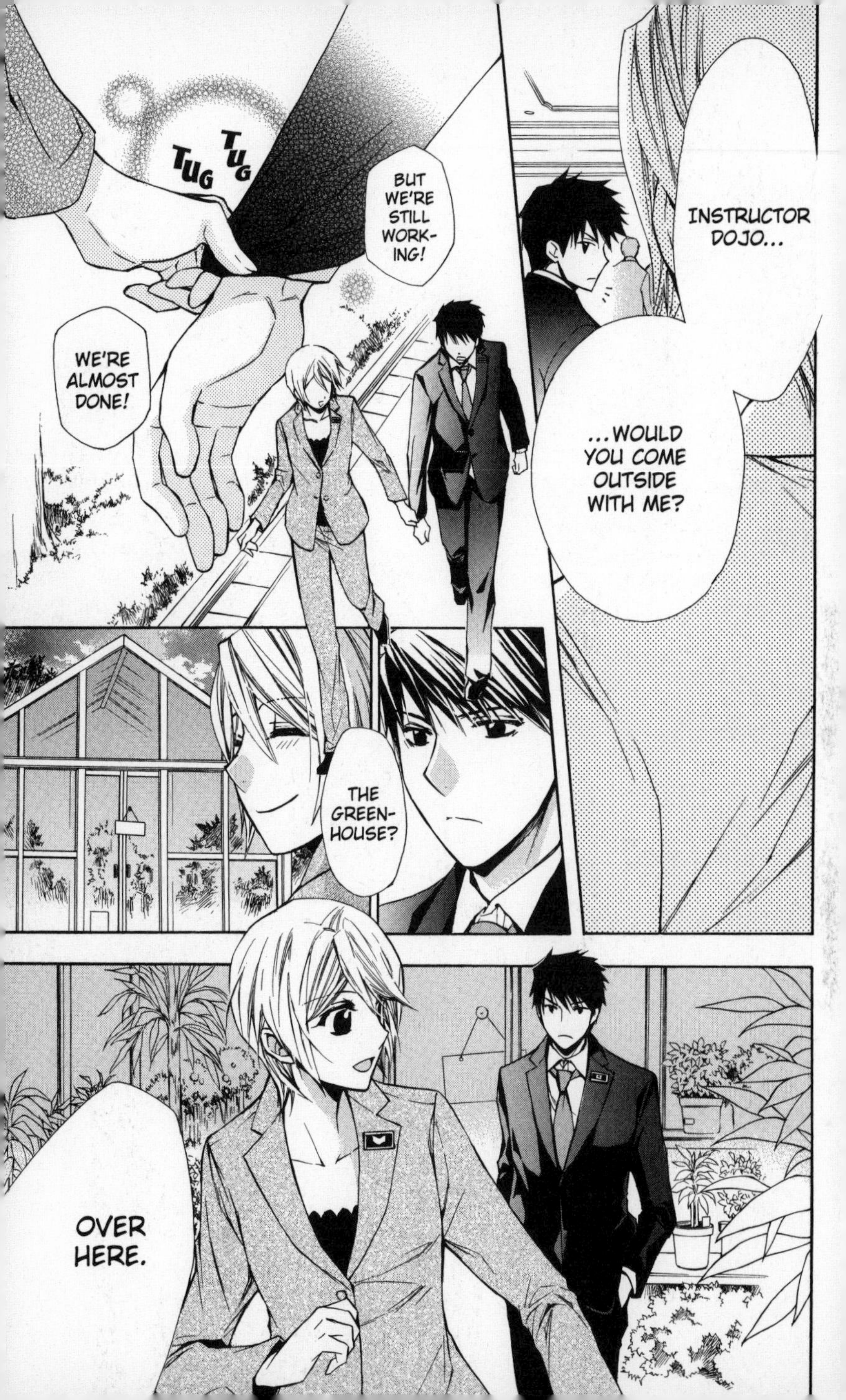
INSTRUCTOR DOJO...
...WOULD YOU COME OUTSIDE WITH ME?
BUT WE'RE STILL WORKING!
TUG TUG
WE'RE ALMOST DONE!
THE GREENHOUSE?
OVER HERE.

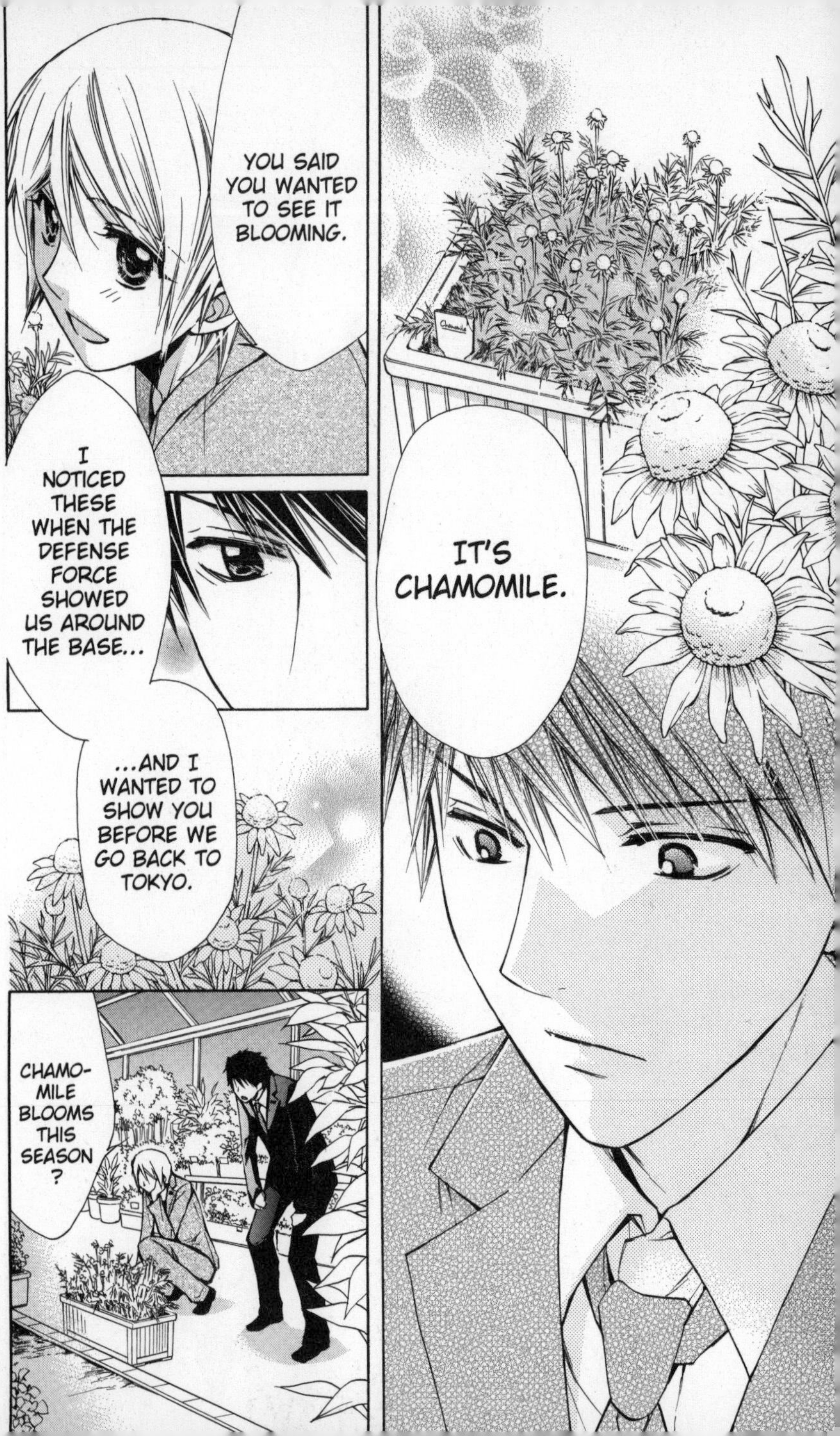
IT'S CHAMOMILE.
YOU SAID YOU WANTED TO SEE IT BLOOMING.
I NOTICED THESE WHEN THE DEFENSE FORCE SHOWED US AROUND THE BASE...
...AND I WANTED TO SHOW YOU BEFORE WE GO BACK TO TOKYO.
CHAMO- MILE BLOOMS THIS SEASON ?

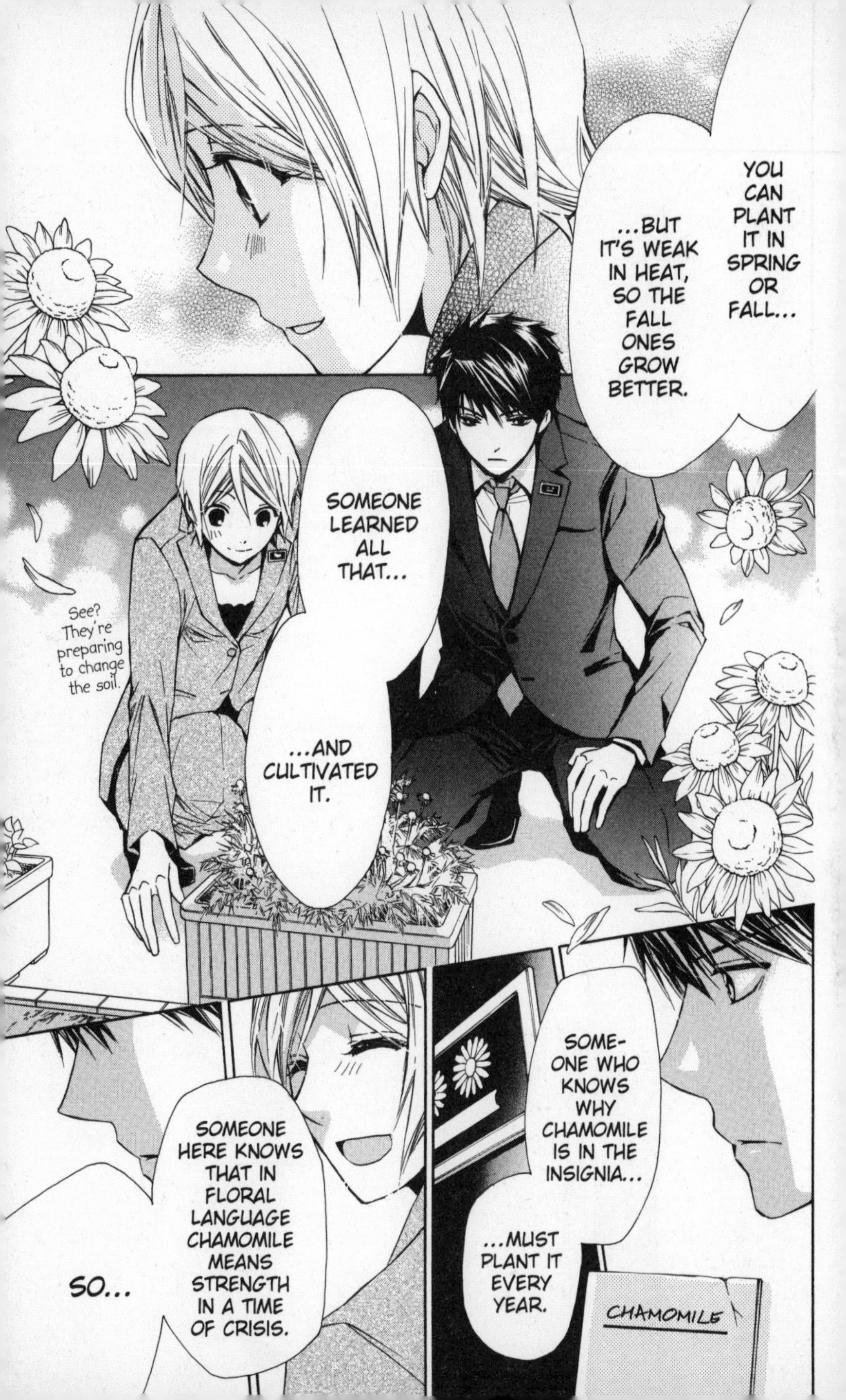
YOU CAN PLANT IT IN SPRING OR FALL...
...BUT IT'S WEAK IN HEAT, SO THE FALL ONES GROW BETTER.
SOMEONE LEARNED ALL THAT...
...AND CULTIVATED IT.
See? They're preparing to change the soil.
SOME-ONE WHO KNOWS WHY CHAMOMILE IS IN THE INSIGNIA...
...MUST PLANT IT EVERY YEAR.
CHAMOMILE
SOMEONE HERE KNOWS THAT IN FLORAL LANGUAGE CHAMOMILE MEANS STRENGTH IN A TIME OF CRISIS.
SO...

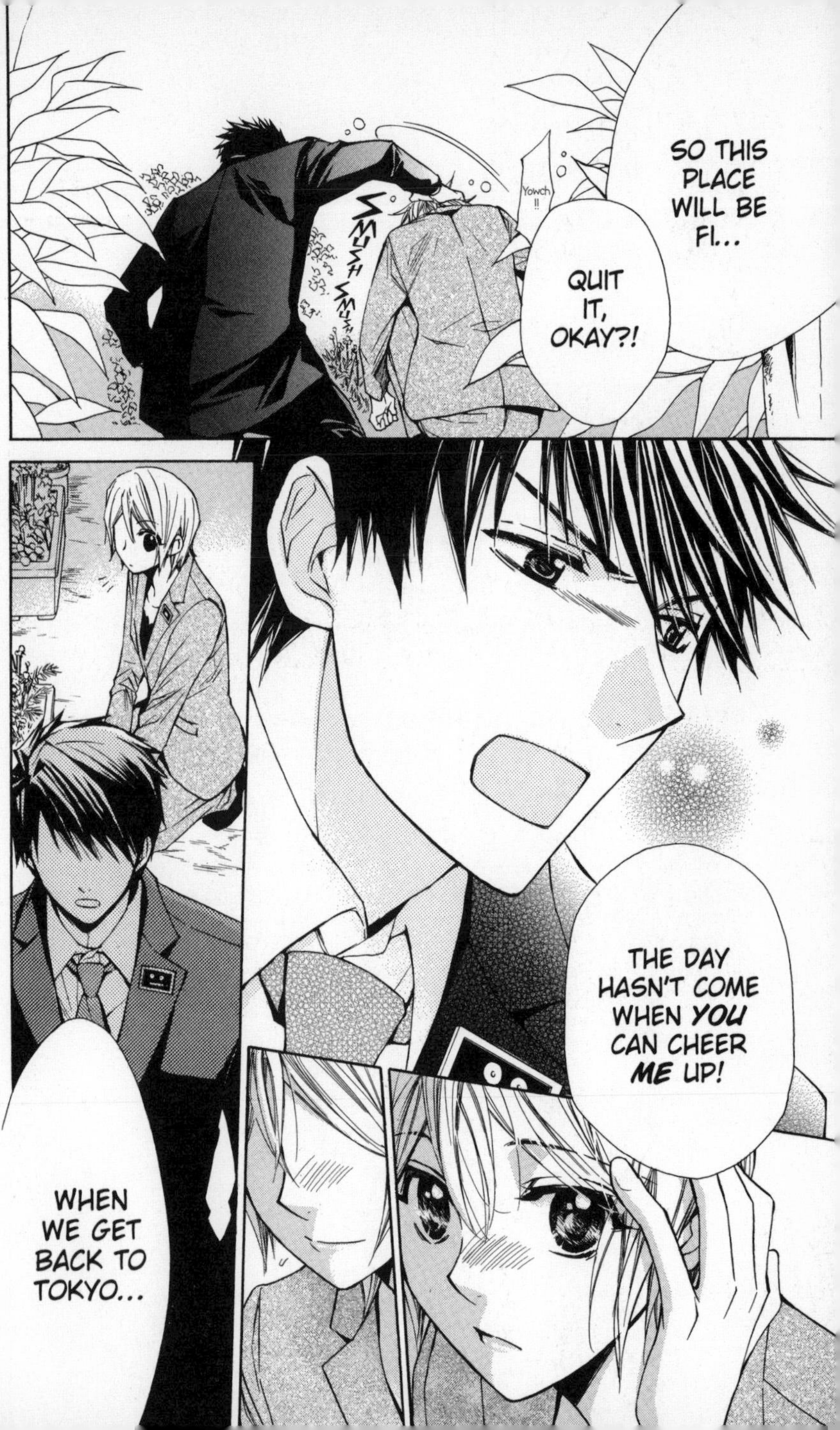
SO THIS PLACE WILL BE FI...
Yowch!!
QUIT IT, OKAY?!
SMUSH SMUSH
THE DAY HASN'T COME WHEN *YOU* CAN CHEER *ME* UP!
WHEN WE GET BACK TO TOKYO...

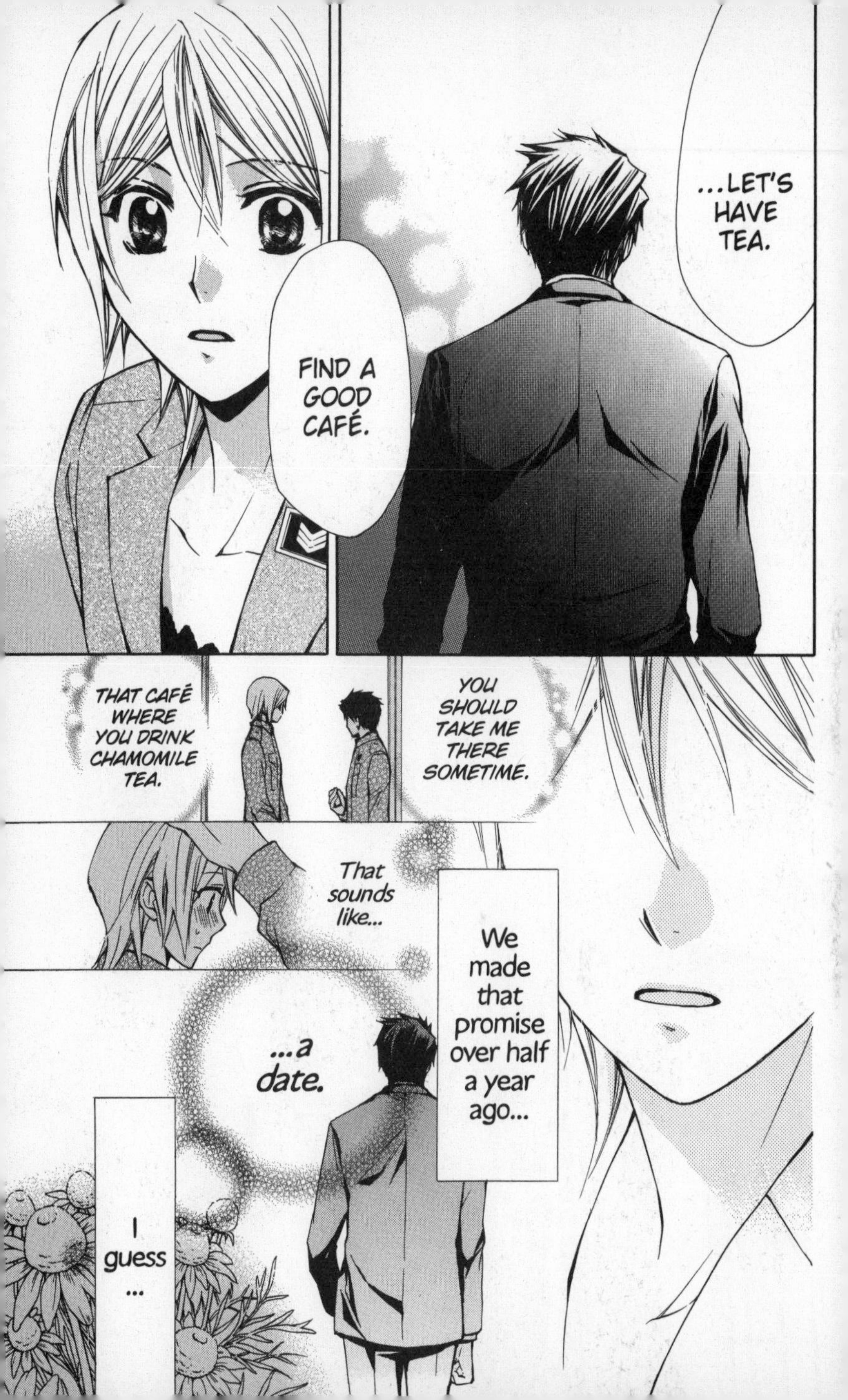

...LET'S HAVE TEA.
FIND A GOOD CAFÉ.
YOU SHOULD TAKE ME THERE SOMETIME.
THAT CAFÉ WHERE YOU DRINK CHAMOMILE TEA.
That sounds like...
We made that promise over half a year ago...
...a date.
I guess ...

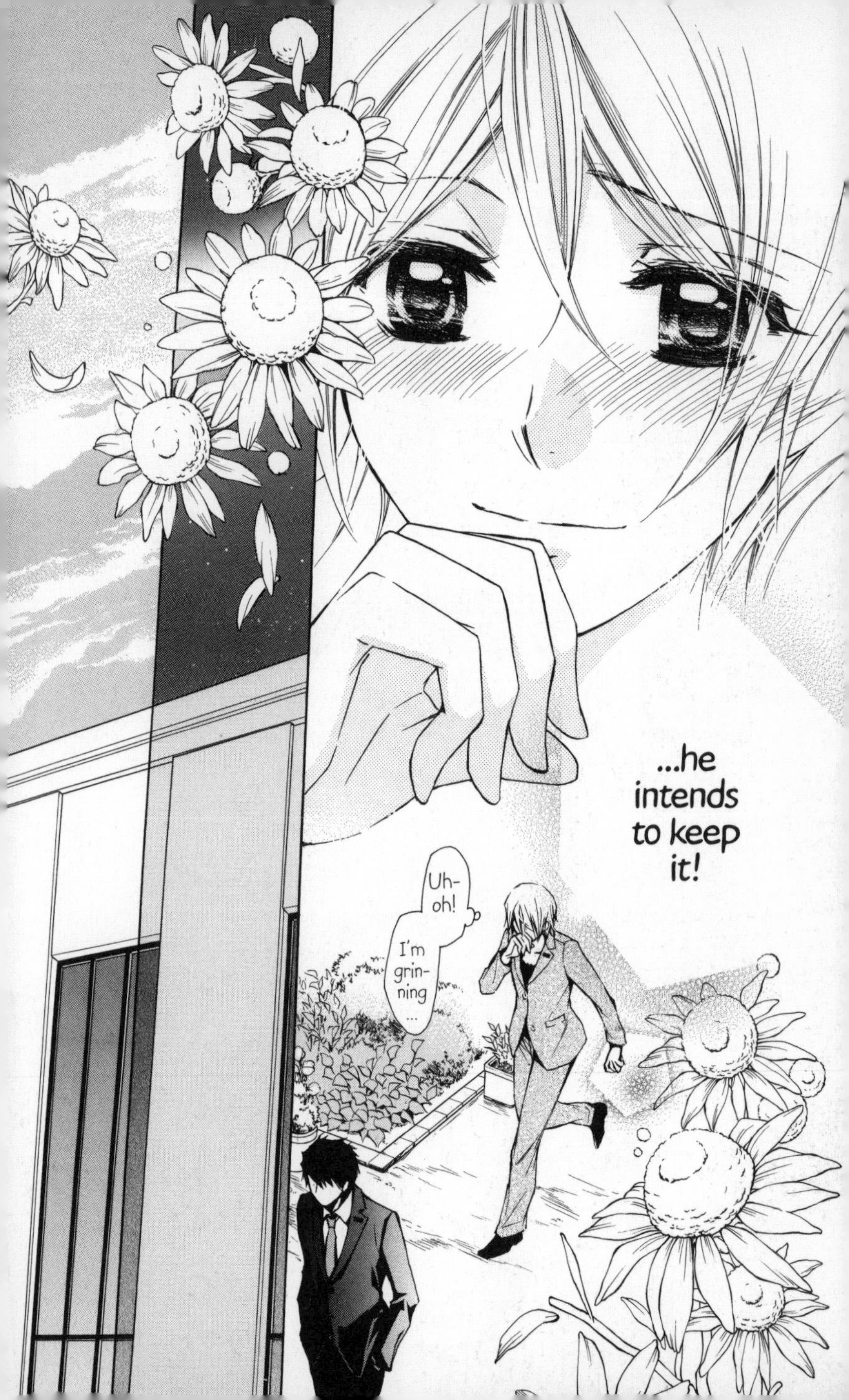
...he intends to keep it!
Uh-oh!
I'm grin-ning...

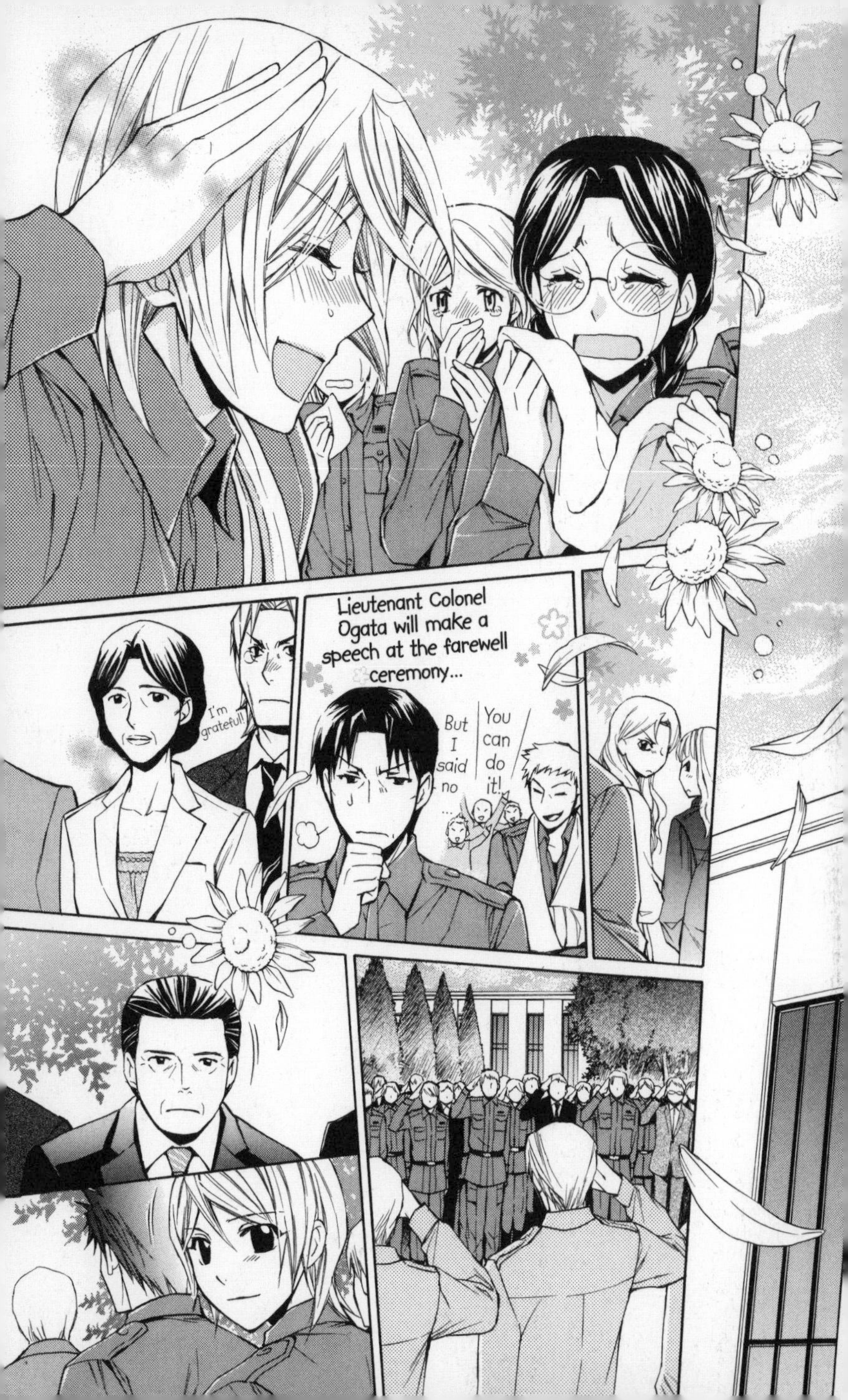
Lieutenant Colonel Ogata will make a speech at the farewell ceremony...
You can do it!
But I said no ...
I'm grateful!

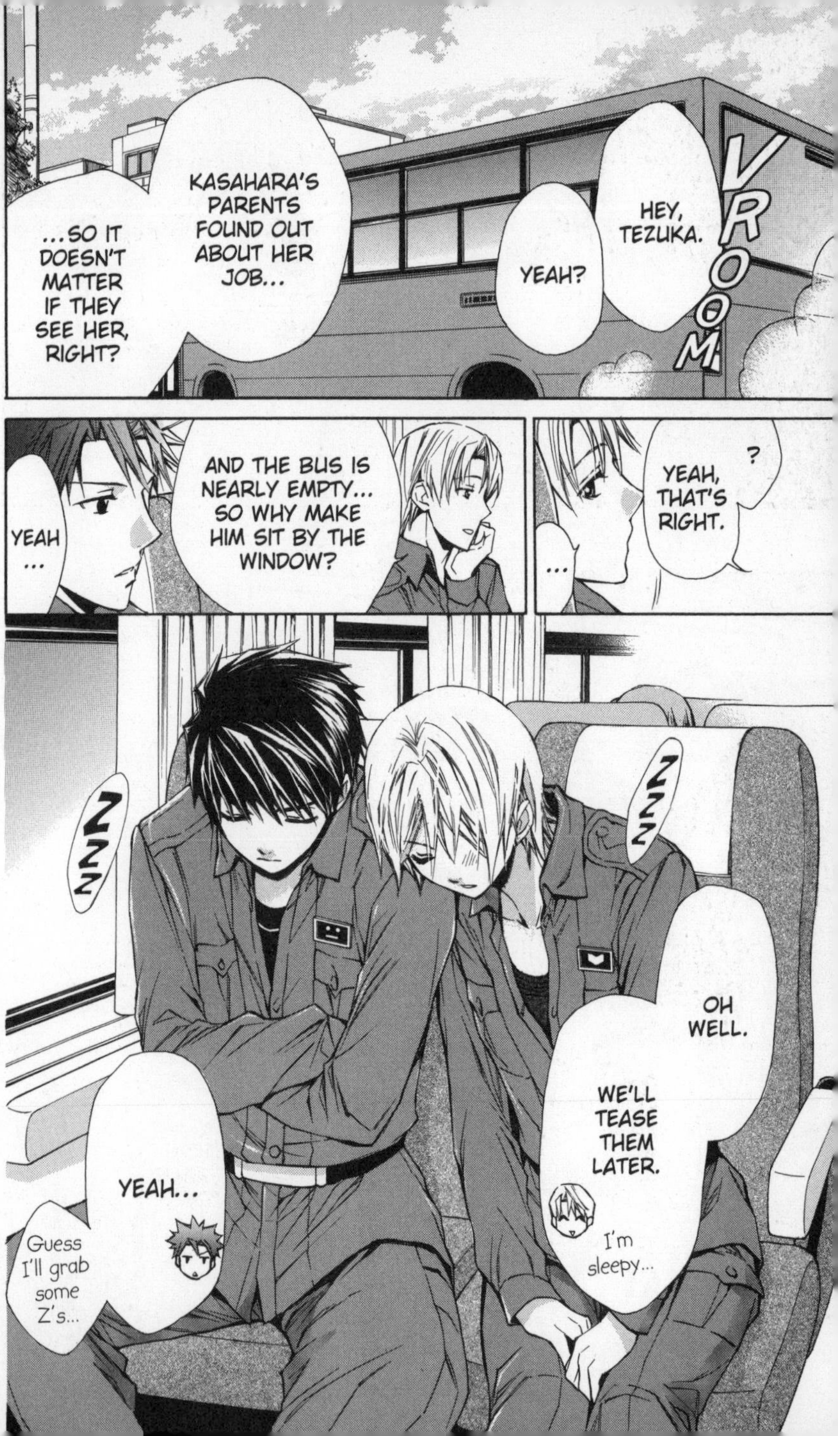
VROOM
HEY, TEZUKA.
YEAH?
KASAHARA'S PARENTS FOUND OUT ABOUT HER JOB...
...SO IT DOESN'T MATTER IF THEY SEE HER, RIGHT?
?
YEAH, THAT'S RIGHT.
...
AND THE BUS IS NEARLY EMPTY... SO WHY MAKE HIM SIT BY THE WINDOW?
YEAH ...
ZZZ
OH WELL.
WE'LL TEASE THEM LATER.
I'm sleepy...
ZZZ
YEAH...
Guess I'll grab some Z's...

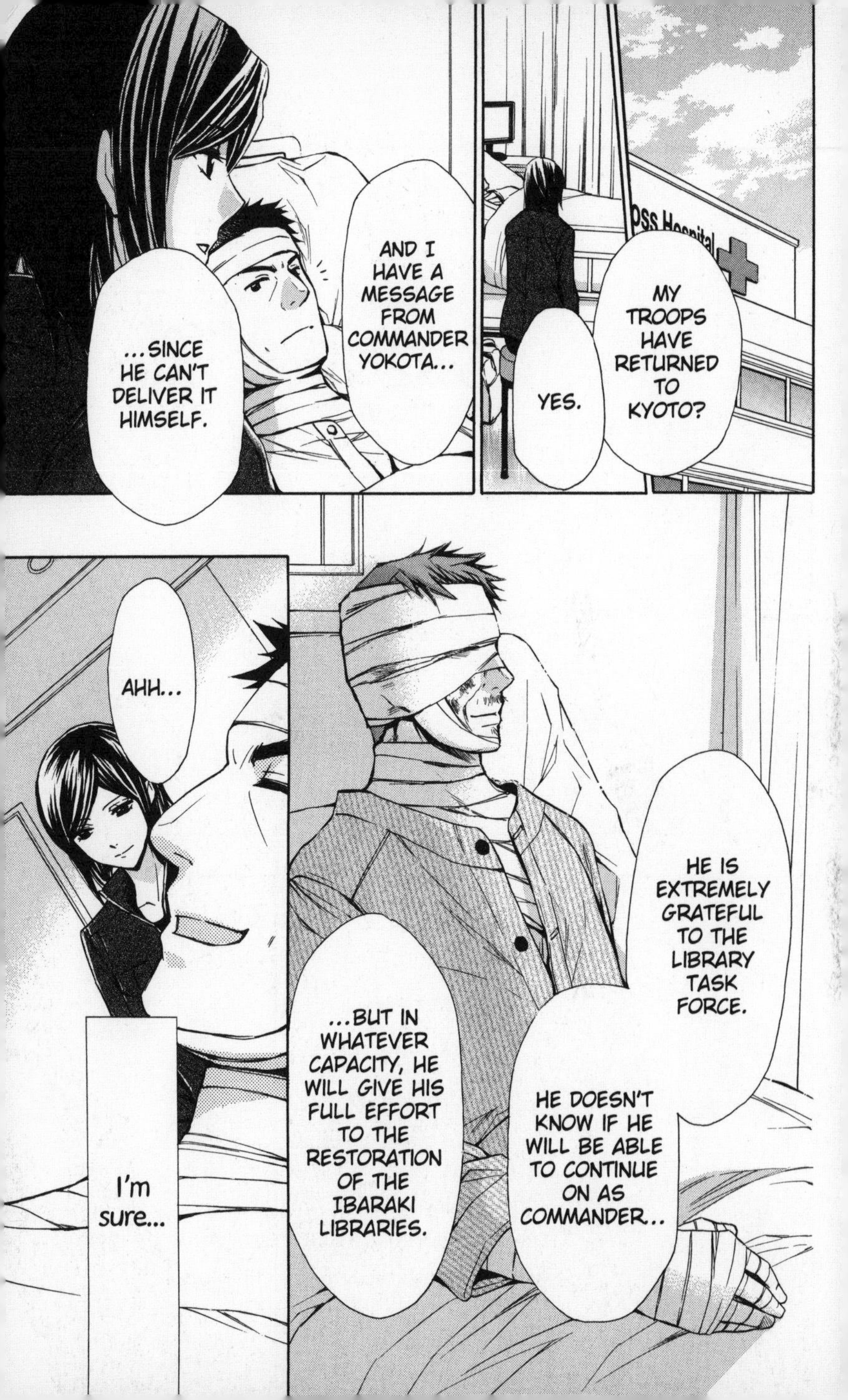
OSS Hospital
MY TROOPS HAVE RETURNED TO KYOTO?
YES.
AND I HAVE A MESSAGE FROM COMMANDER YOKOTA...
...SINCE HE CAN'T DELIVER IT HIMSELF.
HE IS EXTREMELY GRATEFUL TO THE LIBRARY TASK FORCE.
HE DOESN'T KNOW IF HE WILL BE ABLE TO CONTINUE ON AS COMMANDER...
...BUT IN WHATEVER CAPACITY, HE WILL GIVE HIS FULL EFFORT TO THE RESTORATION OF THE IBARAKI LIBRARIES.
AHH...
I'm sure...

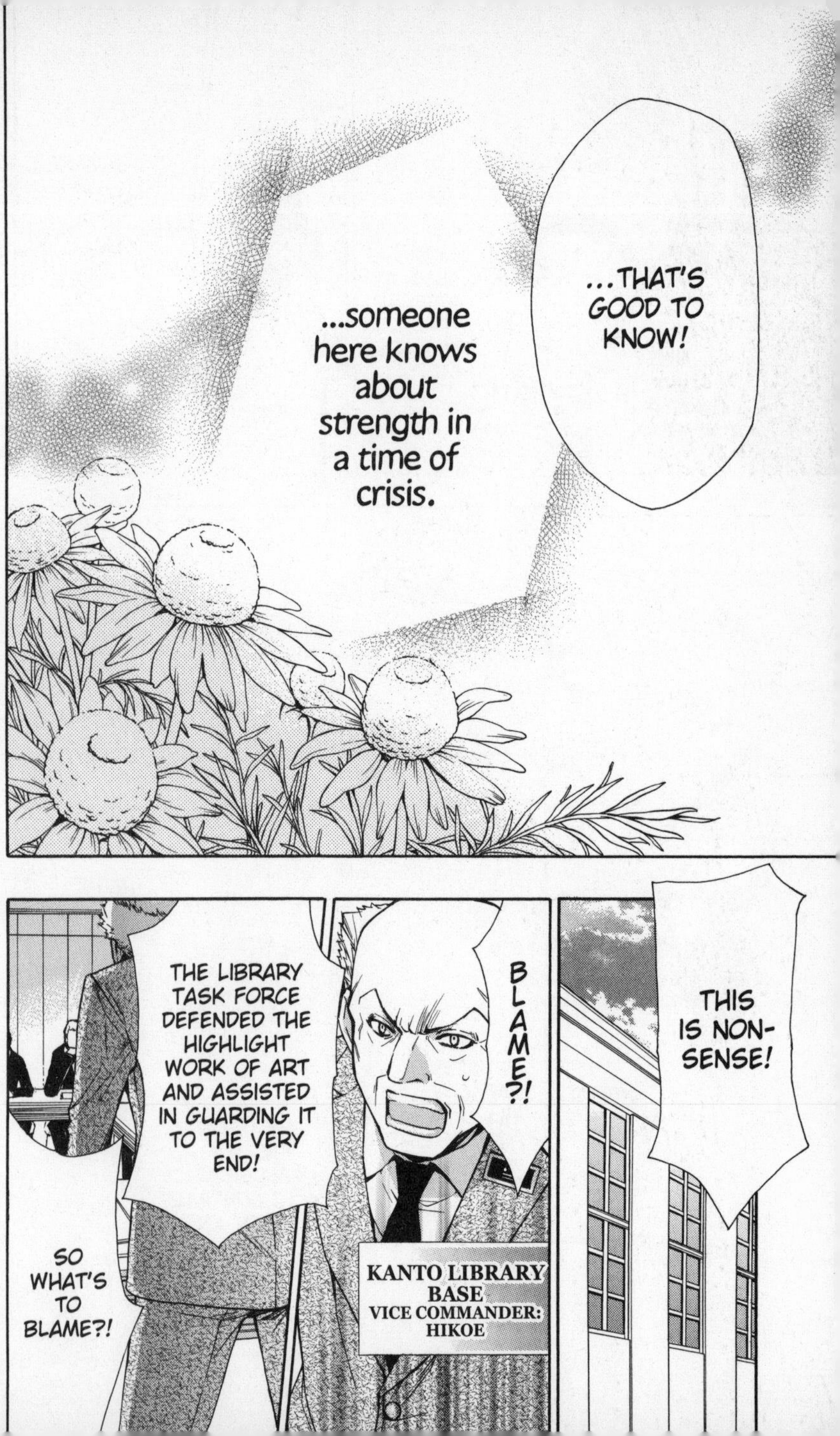

...THAT'S GOOD TO KNOW!
...someone here knows about strength in a time of crisis.
THIS IS NON-SENSE!
BLAME?!
THE LIBRARY TASK FORCE DEFENDED THE HIGHLIGHT WORK OF ART AND ASSISTED IN GUARDING IT TO THE VERY END!
KANTO LIBRARY BASE VICE COMMANDER: HIKOE
SO WHAT'S TO BLAME?!

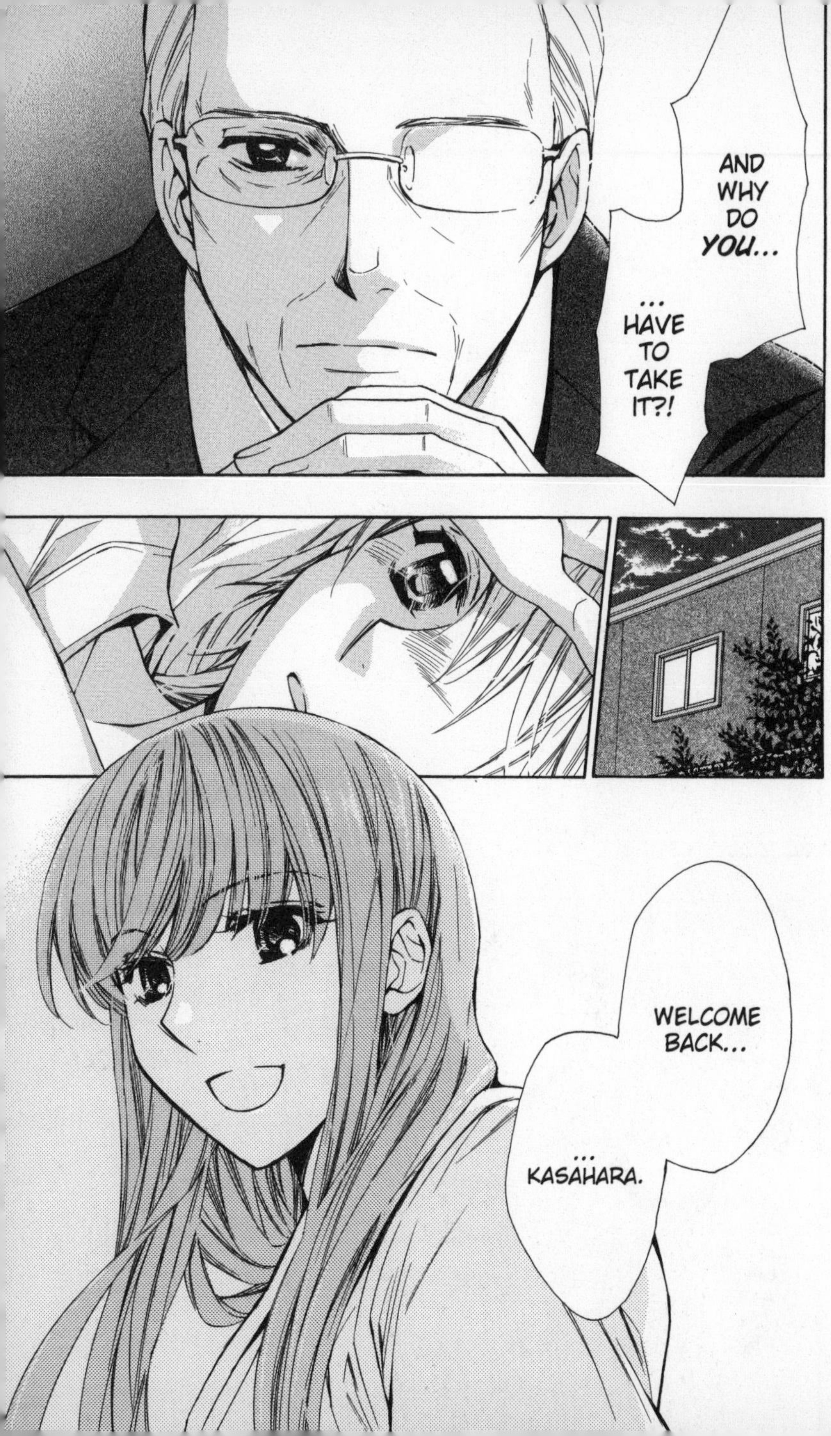
AND WHY DO *YOU*...
... HAVE TO TAKE IT?!
WELCOME BACK...
... KASAHARA.

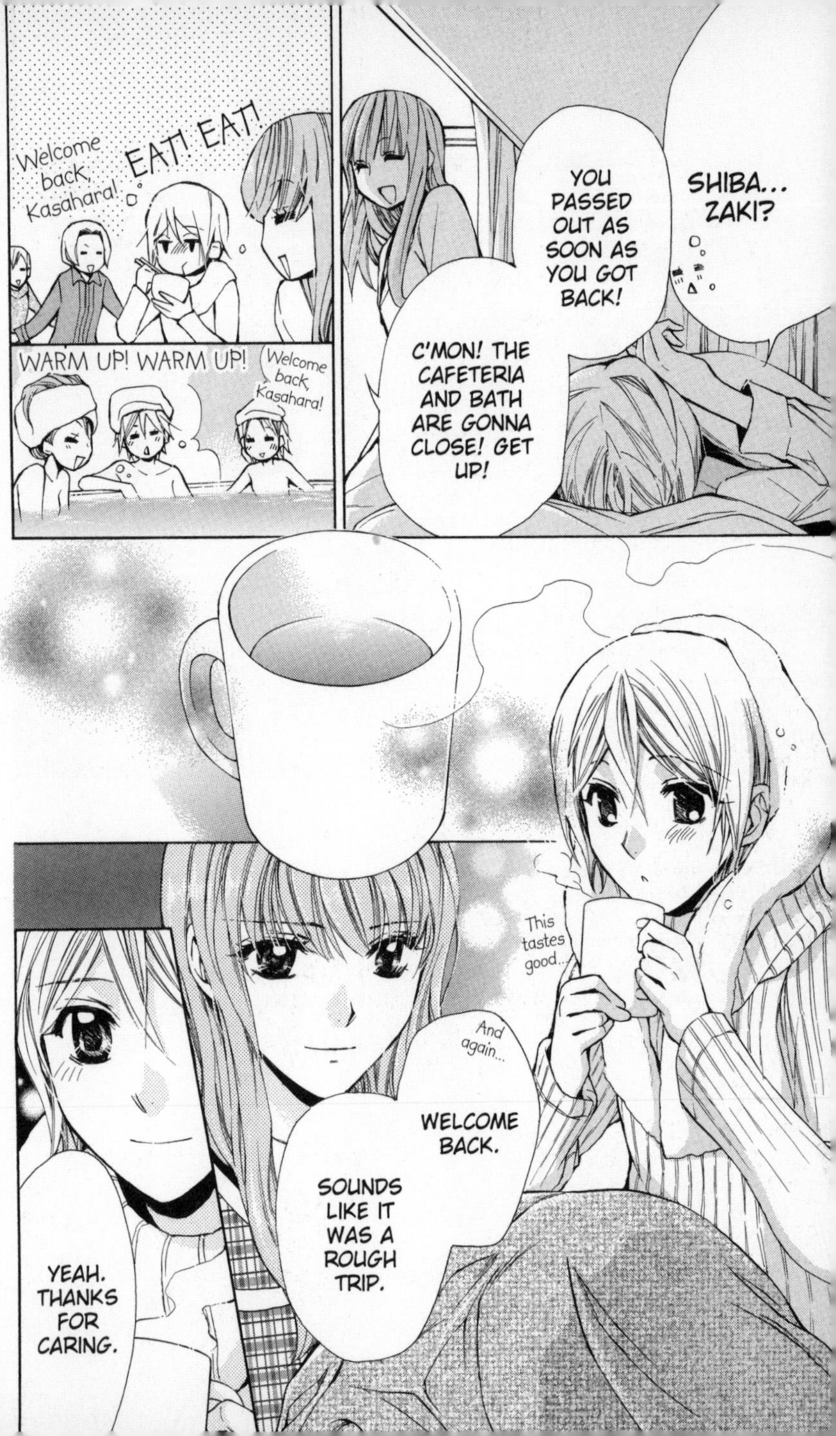
SHIBA... ZAKI?
YOU PASSED OUT AS SOON AS YOU GOT BACK!
C'MON! THE CAFETERIA AND BATH ARE GONNA CLOSE! GET UP!
EAT! EAT!
Welcome back, Kasahara!
Welcome back, Kasahara!
WARM UP! WARM UP!
This tastes good...
And again...
WELCOME BACK.
SOUNDS LIKE IT WAS A ROUGH TRIP.
YEAH. THANKS FOR CARING.

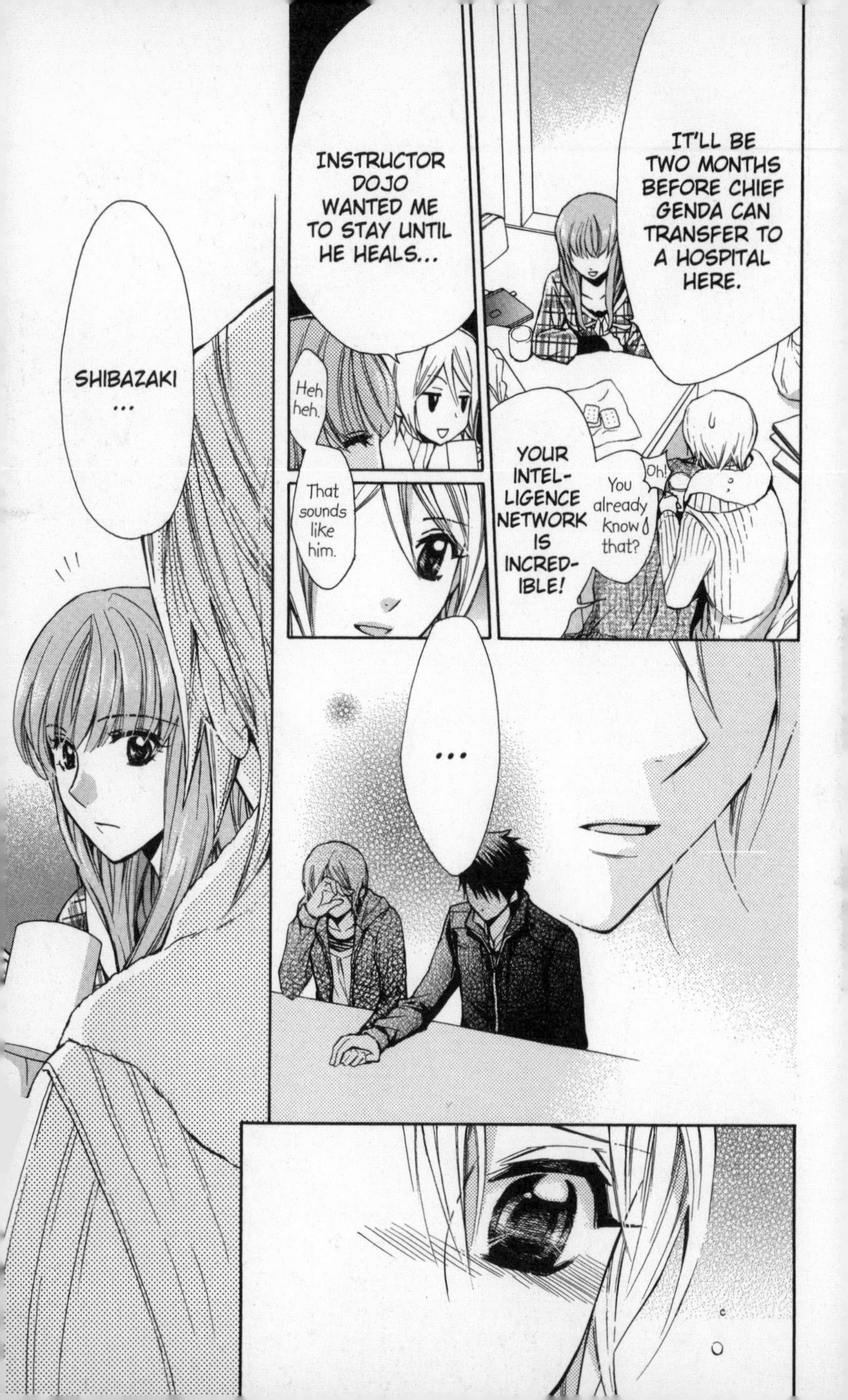
IT'LL BE TWO MONTHS BEFORE CHIEF GENDA CAN TRANSFER TO A HOSPITAL HERE.
Oh!
You already know that?
YOUR INTEL-LIGENCE NETWORK IS INCRED-IBLE!
INSTRUCTOR DOJO WANTED ME TO STAY UNTIL HE HEALS...
Heh heh.
That sounds like him.
...
SHIBAZAKI ...

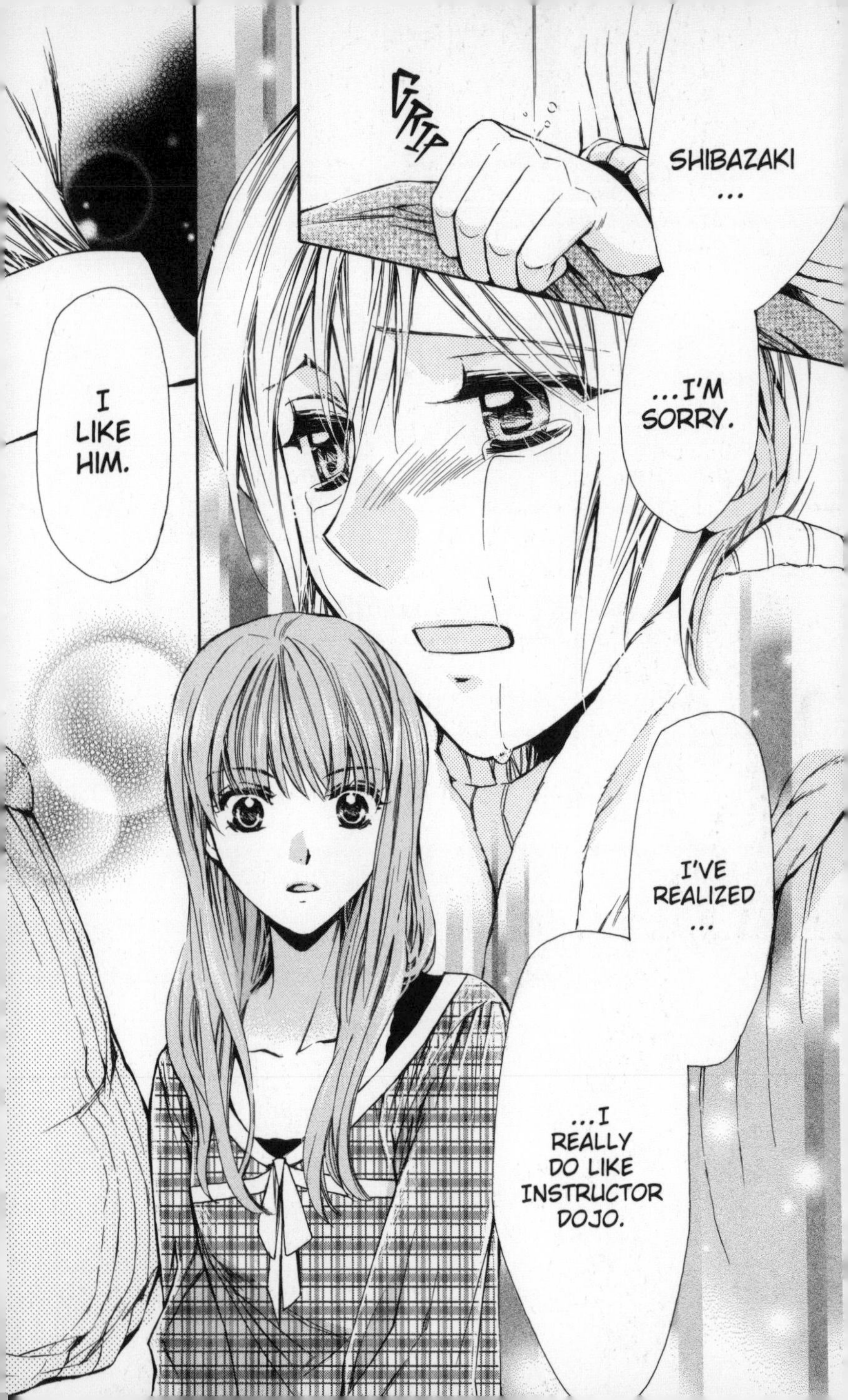
GRIP
SHIBAZAKI ...
...I'M SORRY.
I LIKE HIM.
I'VE REALIZED ...
...I REALLY DO LIKE INSTRUCTOR DOJO.

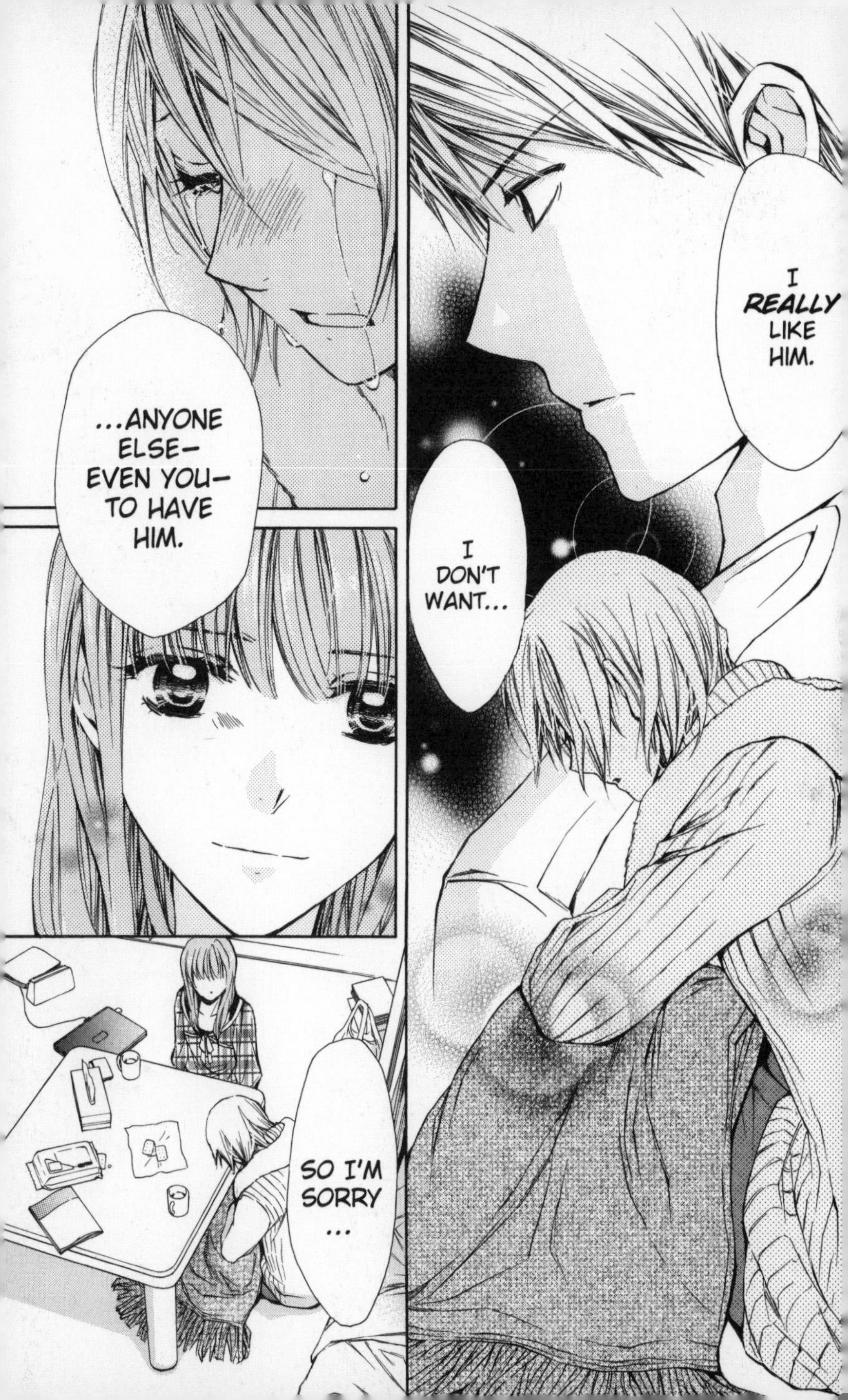
I *REALLY* LIKE HIM.
I DON'T WANT...
...ANYONE ELSE— EVEN YOU— TO HAVE HIM.
SO I'M SORRY ...

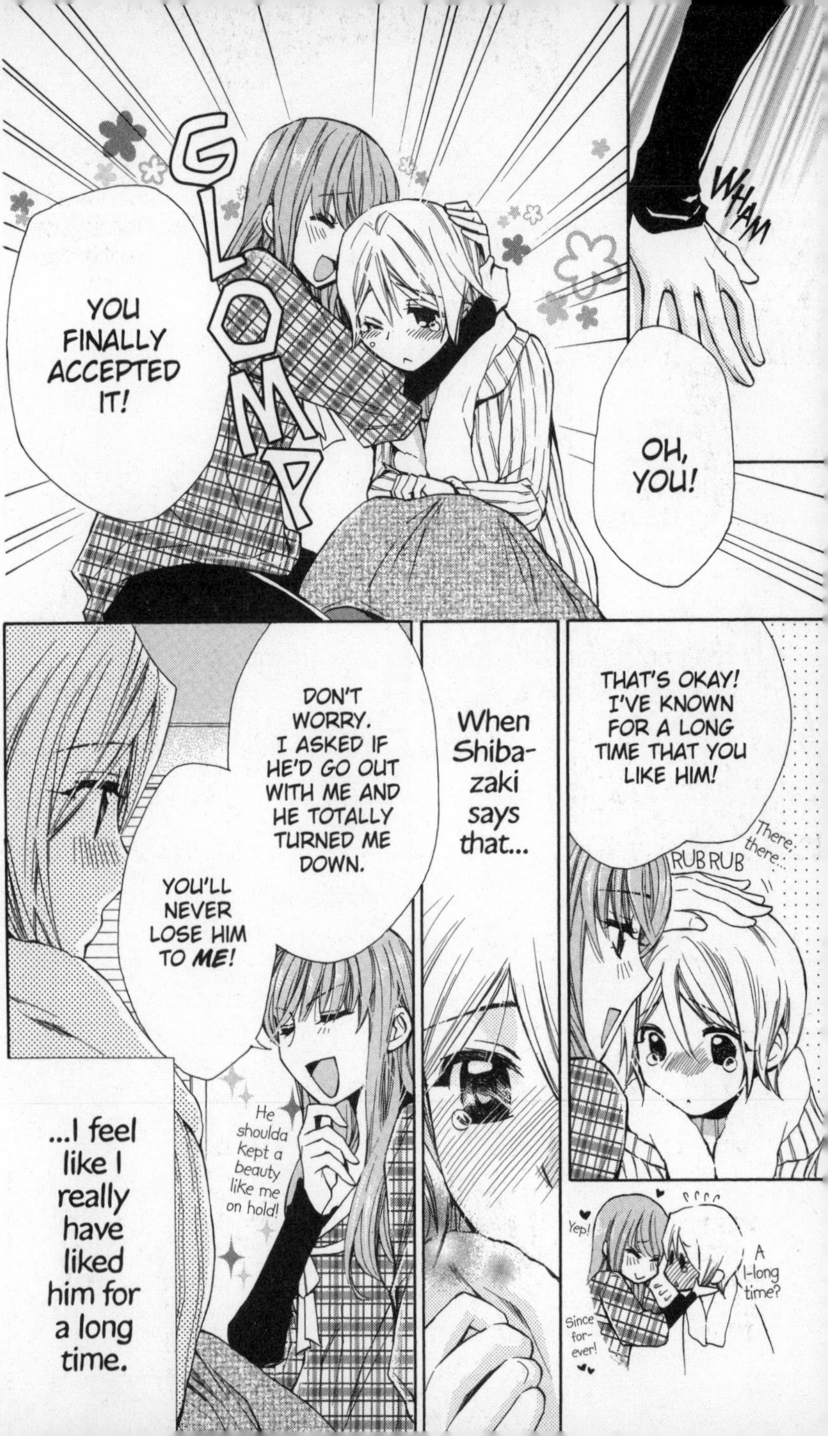
WHAM
OH, YOU!
GLOMP
YOU FINALLY ACCEPTED IT!
THAT'S OKAY! I'VE KNOWN FOR A LONG TIME THAT YOU LIKE HIM!
There, there...
RUB RUB
Yep!
A l-long time?
Since for-ever!
When Shiba-zaki says that...
DON'T WORRY. I ASKED IF HE'D GO OUT WITH ME AND HE TOTALLY TURNED ME DOWN.
YOU'LL NEVER LOSE HIM TO ME!
He shoulda kept a beauty like me on hold!
...I feel like I really have liked him for a long time.

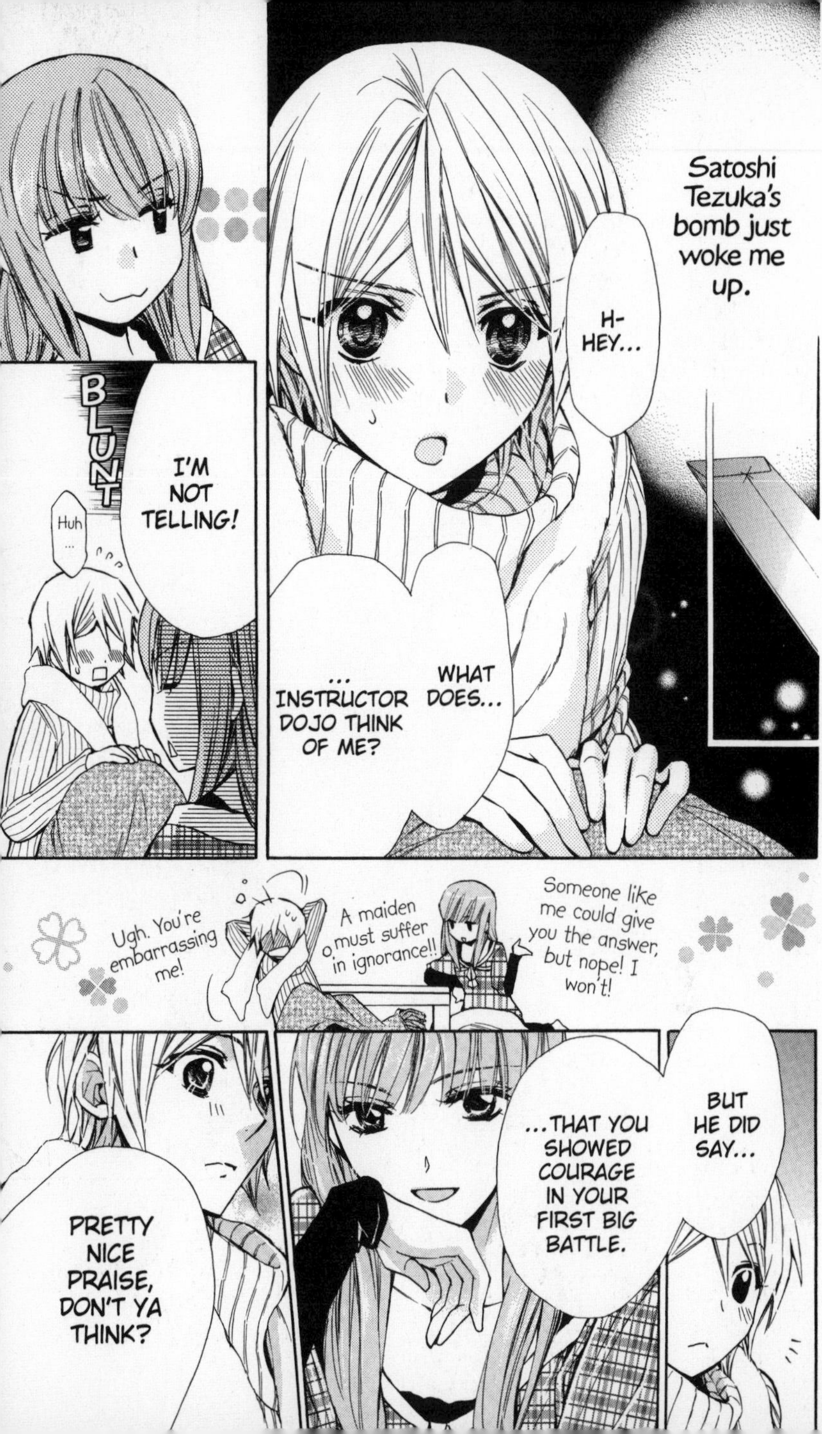
Satoshi Tezuka's bomb just woke me up.
H-HEY...
WHAT DOES...
...INSTRUCTOR DOJO THINK OF ME?
BLUNT
I'M NOT TELLING!
Huh...
Someone like me could give you the answer, but nope! I won't!
A maiden must suffer in ignorance!!
Ugh. You're embarrassing me!
BUT HE DID SAY...
...THAT YOU SHOWED COURAGE IN YOUR FIRST BIG BATTLE.
PRETTY NICE PRAISE, DON'T YA THINK?

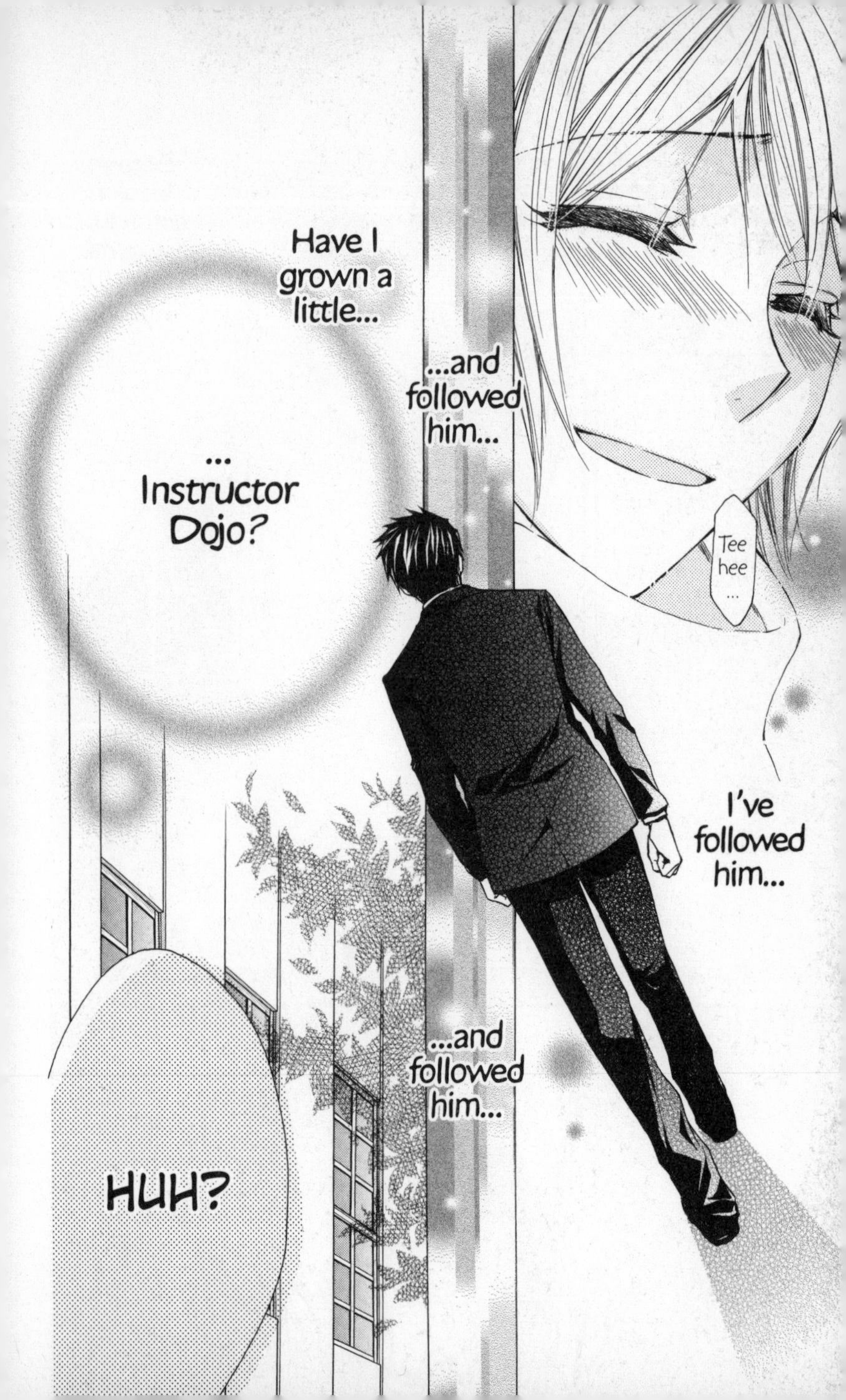
Tee hee ...
I've followed him...
...and followed him...
...and followed him...
Have I grown a little...
... Instructor Dojo?
HUH?

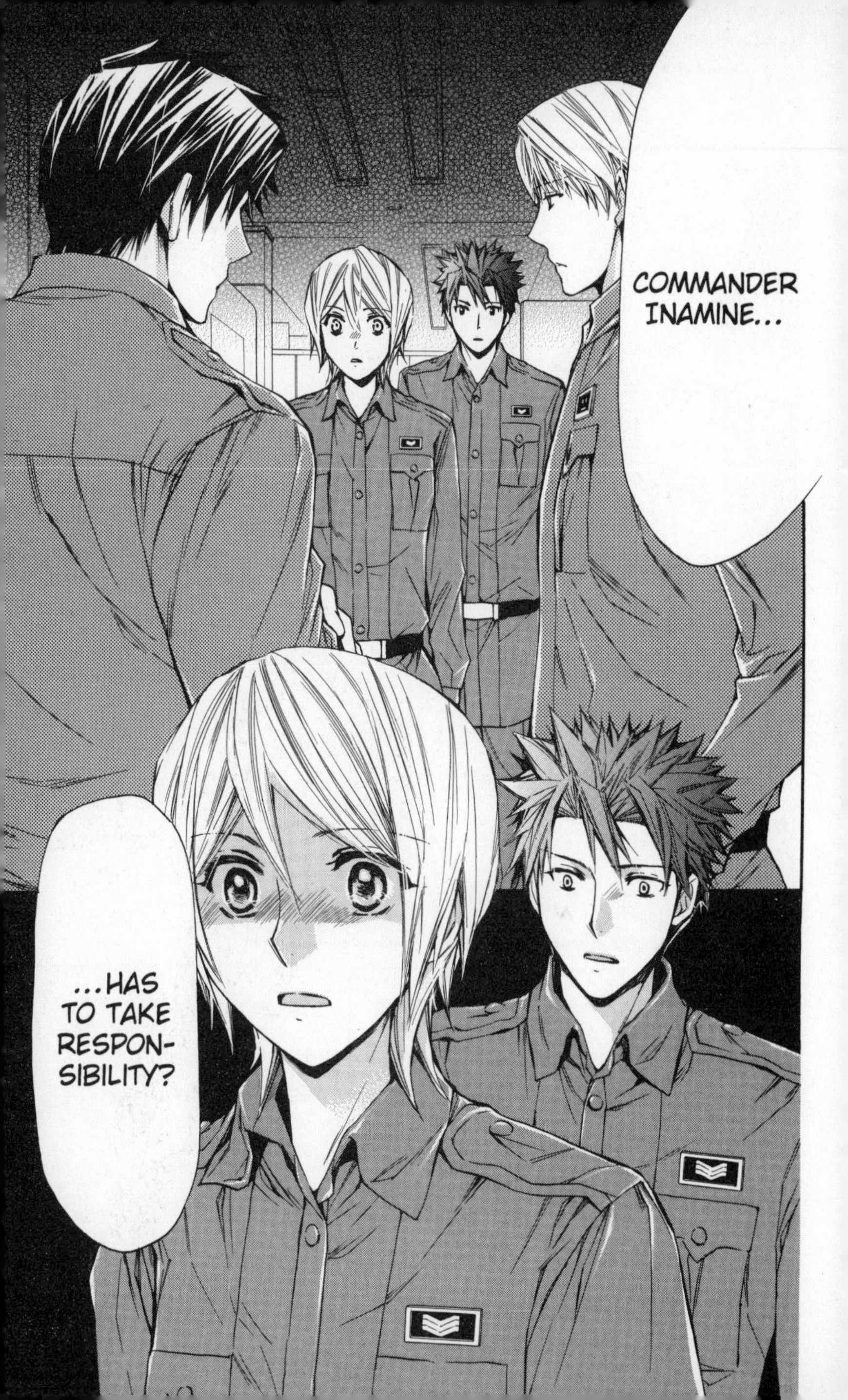
COMMANDER INAMINE...
...HAS TO TAKE RESPON-SIBILITY?

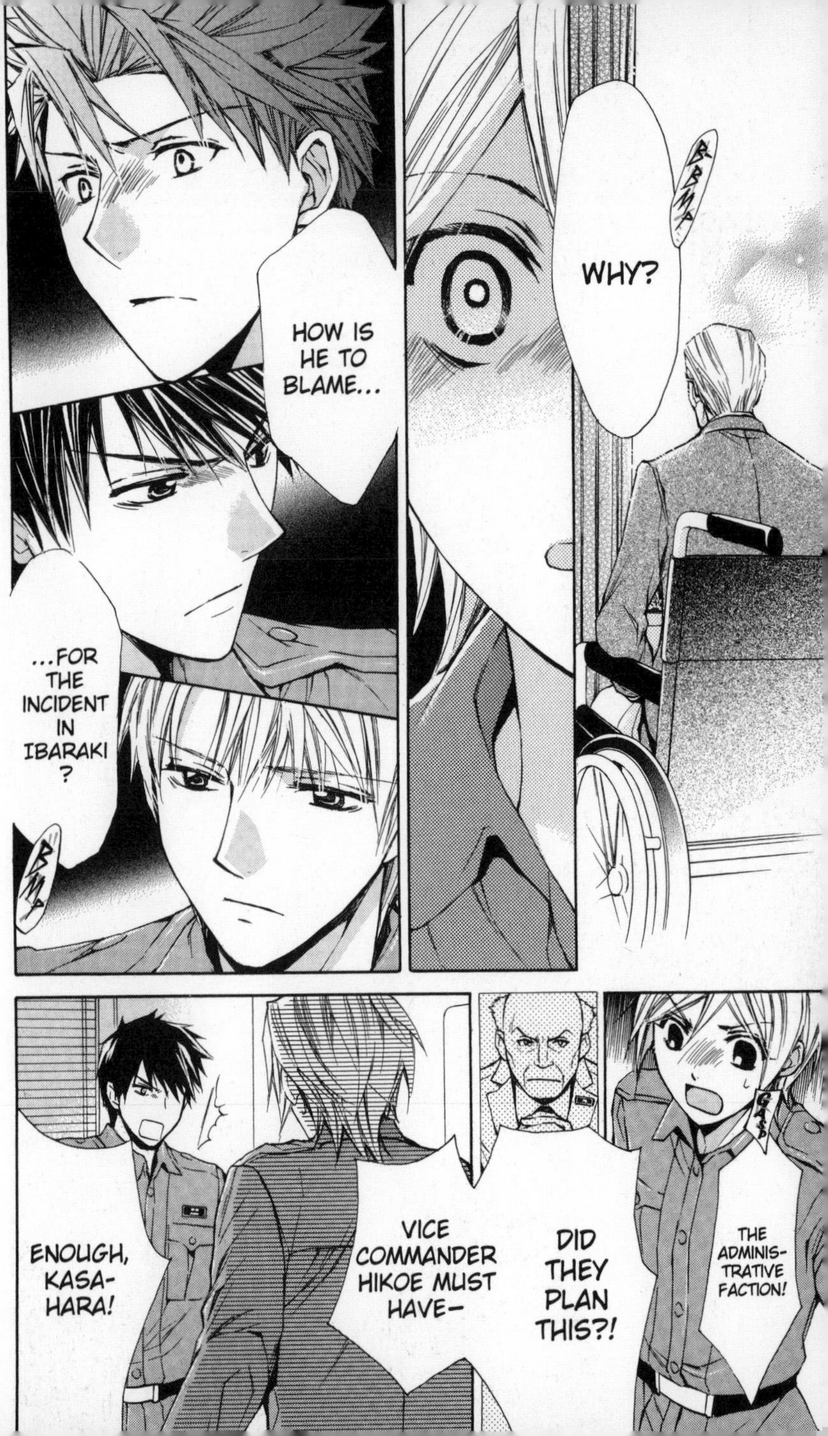
B-BMP...
WHY?
HOW IS HE TO BLAME...
...FOR THE INCIDENT IN IBARAKI?
BMP!
THE ADMINISTRATIVE FACTION!
GASP
DID THEY PLAN THIS?!
VICE COMMANDER HIKOE MUST HAVE–
ENOUGH, KASAHARA!

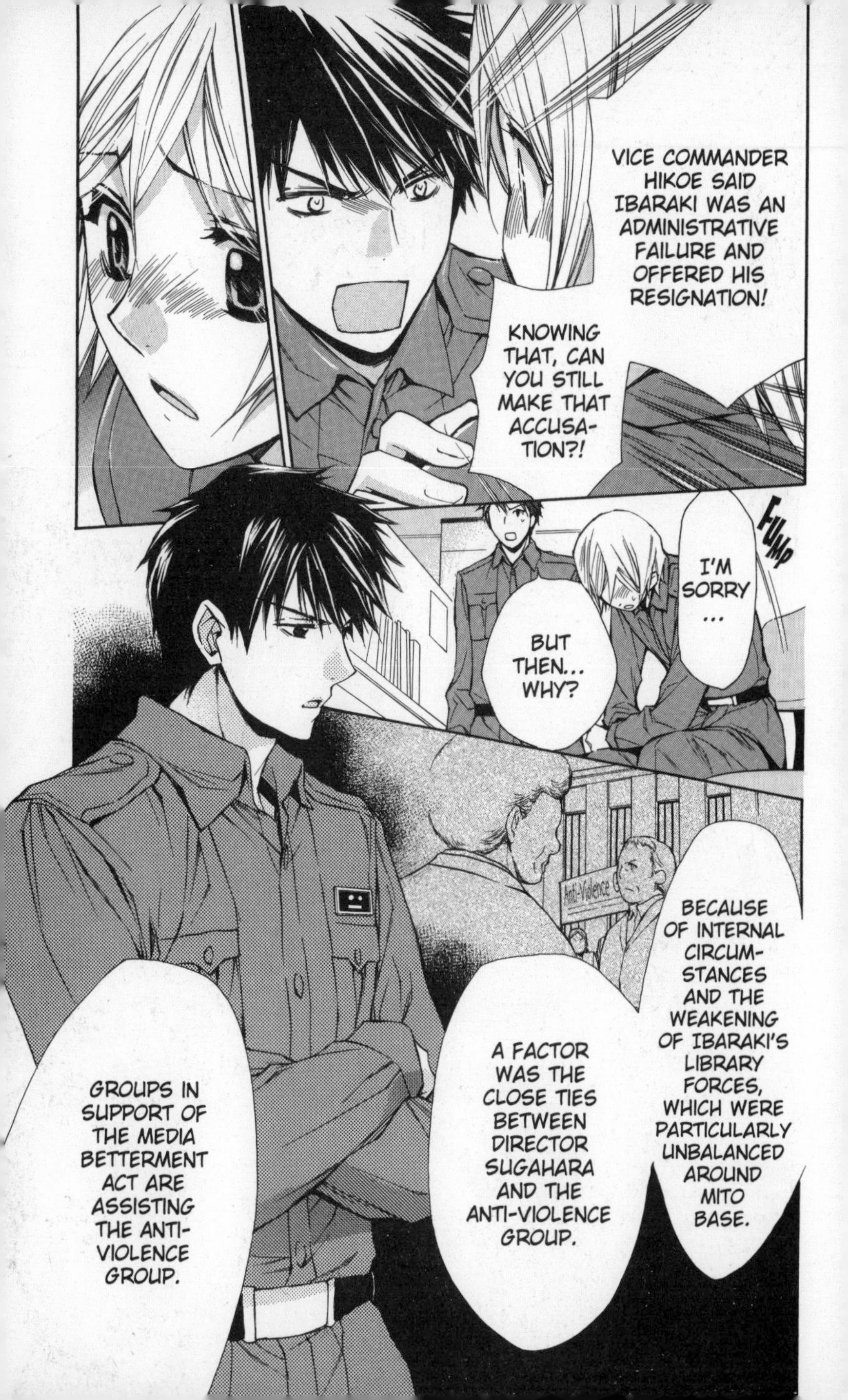
VICE COMMANDER HIKOE SAID IBARAKI WAS AN ADMINISTRATIVE FAILURE AND OFFERED HIS RESIGNATION!
KNOWING THAT, CAN YOU STILL MAKE THAT ACCUSA-TION?!
FUMP
I'M SORRY ...
BUT THEN... WHY?
Anti-Violence
BECAUSE OF INTERNAL CIRCUM-STANCES AND THE WEAKENING OF IBARAKI'S LIBRARY FORCES, WHICH WERE PARTICULARLY UNBALANCED AROUND MITO BASE.
A FACTOR WAS THE CLOSE TIES BETWEEN DIRECTOR SUGAHARA AND THE ANTI-VIOLENCE GROUP.
GROUPS IN SUPPORT OF THE MEDIA BETTERMENT ACT ARE ASSISTING THE ANTI-VIOLENCE GROUP.

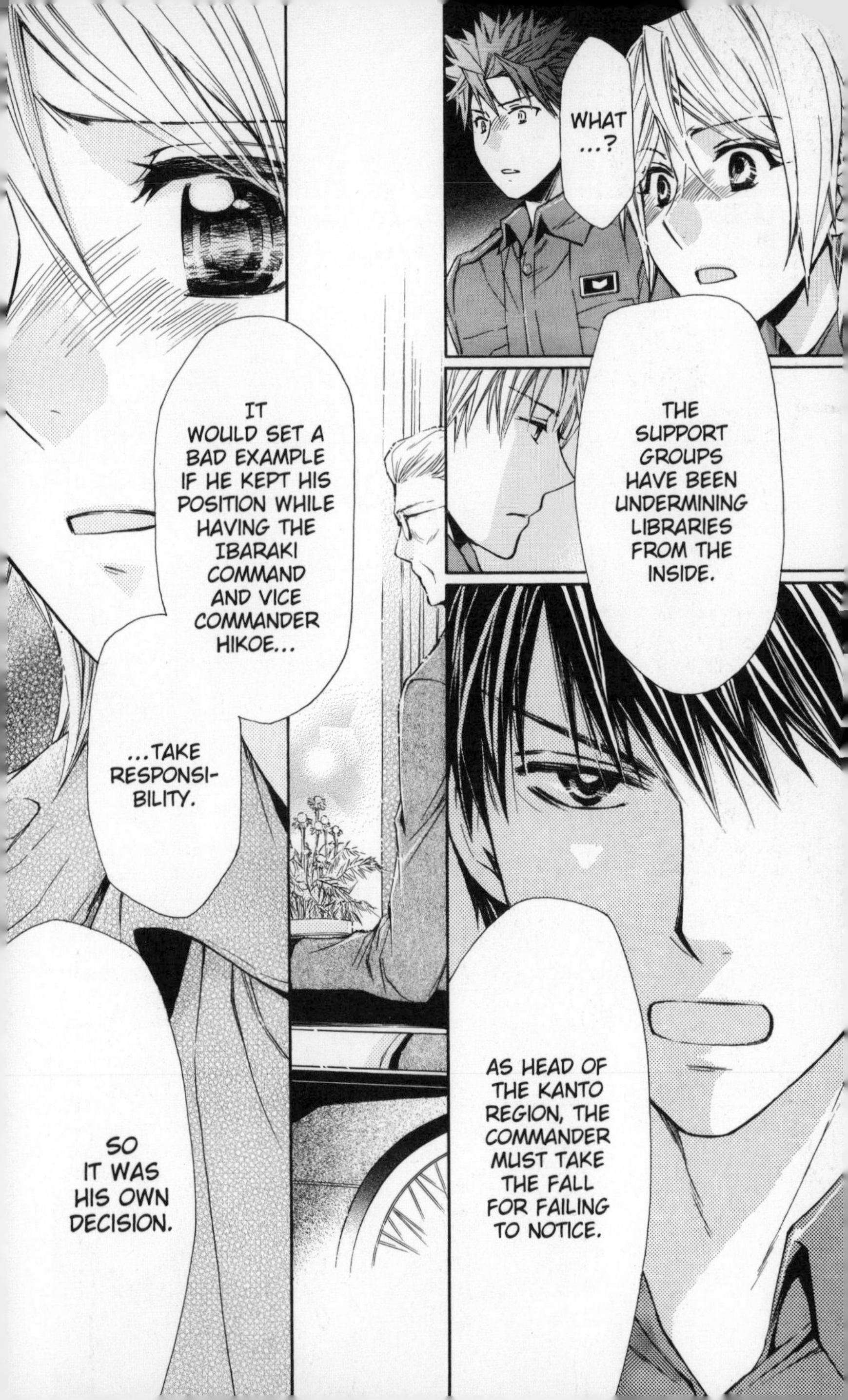
WHAT ...?
THE SUPPORT GROUPS HAVE BEEN UNDERMINING LIBRARIES FROM THE INSIDE.
AS HEAD OF THE KANTO REGION, THE COMMANDER MUST TAKE THE FALL FOR FAILING TO NOTICE.
IT WOULD SET A BAD EXAMPLE IF HE KEPT HIS POSITION WHILE HAVING THE IBARAKI COMMAND AND VICE COMMANDER HIKOE...
...TAKE RESPONSI-BILITY.
SO IT WAS HIS OWN DECISION.

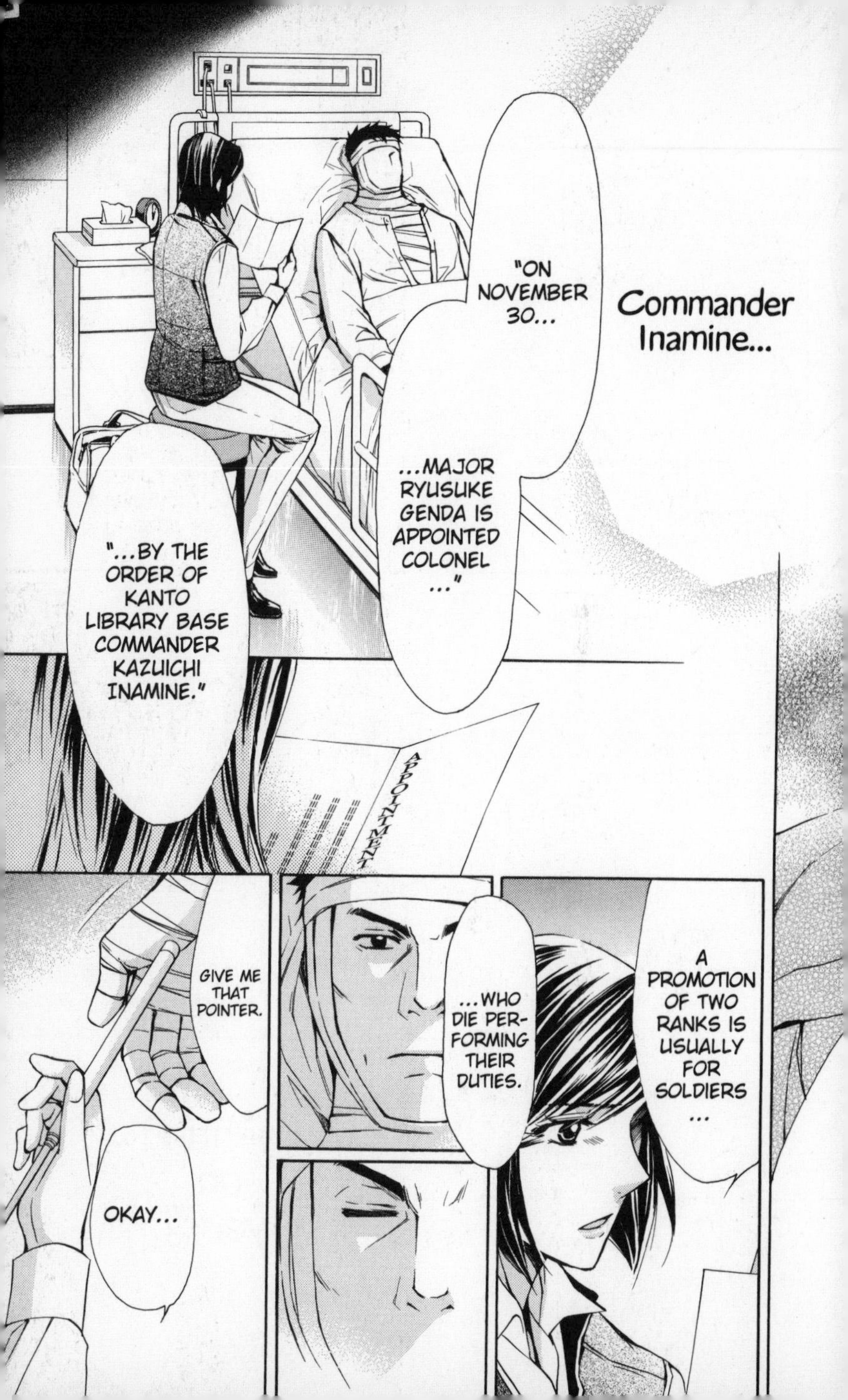
Commander Inamine...
"ON NOVEMBER 30...
...MAJOR RYUSUKE GENDA IS APPOINTED COLONEL..."
"...BY THE ORDER OF KANTO LIBRARY BASE COMMANDER KAZUICHI INAMINE."
APPOINTMENT
A PROMOTION OF TWO RANKS IS USUALLY FOR SOLDIERS...
...WHO DIE PERFORMING THEIR DUTIES.
GIVE ME THAT POINTER.
OKAY...

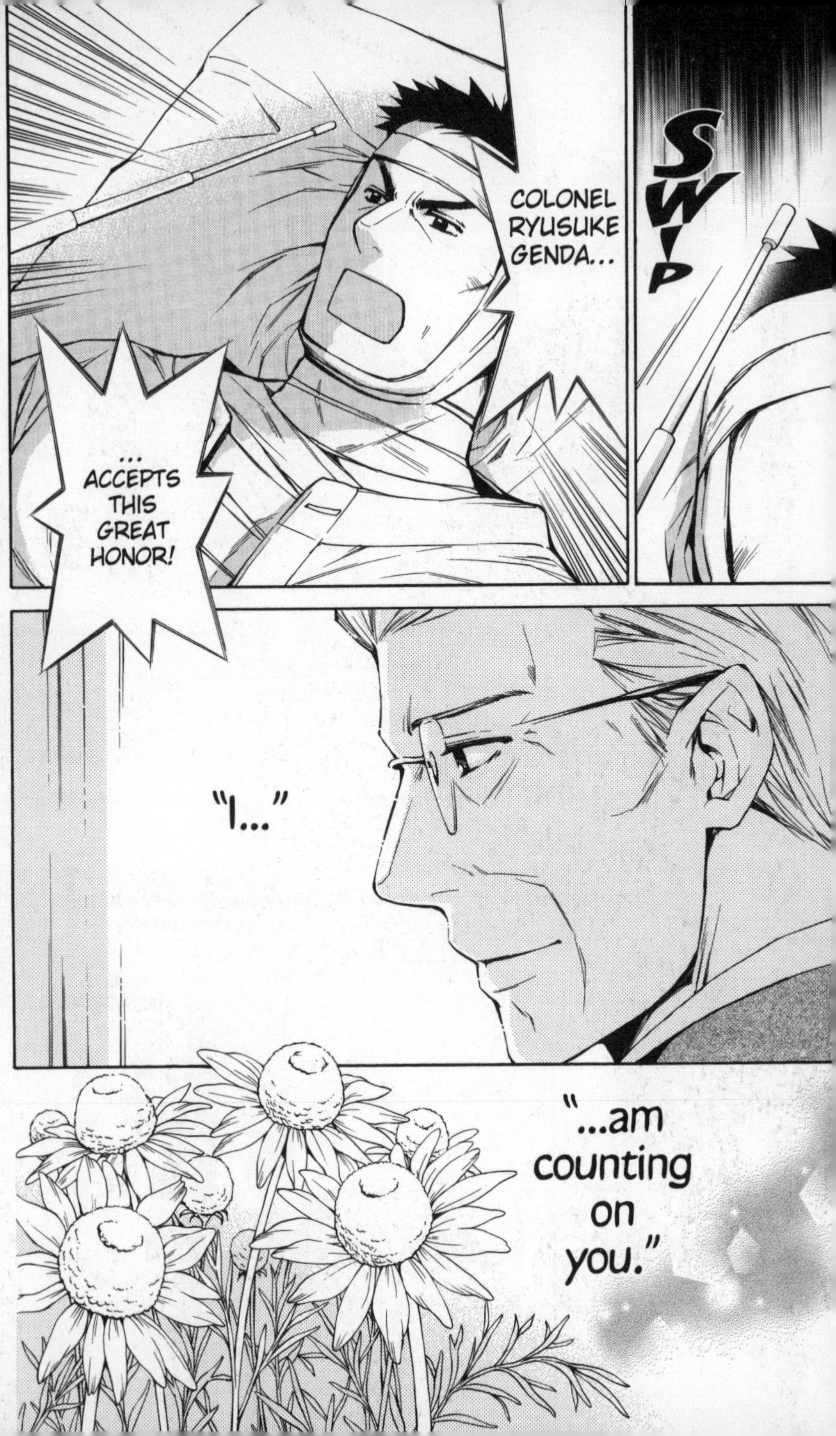
SWIP
COLONEL RYUSUKE GENDA...
...ACCEPTS THIS GREAT HONOR!
"I..."
"...am counting on you."

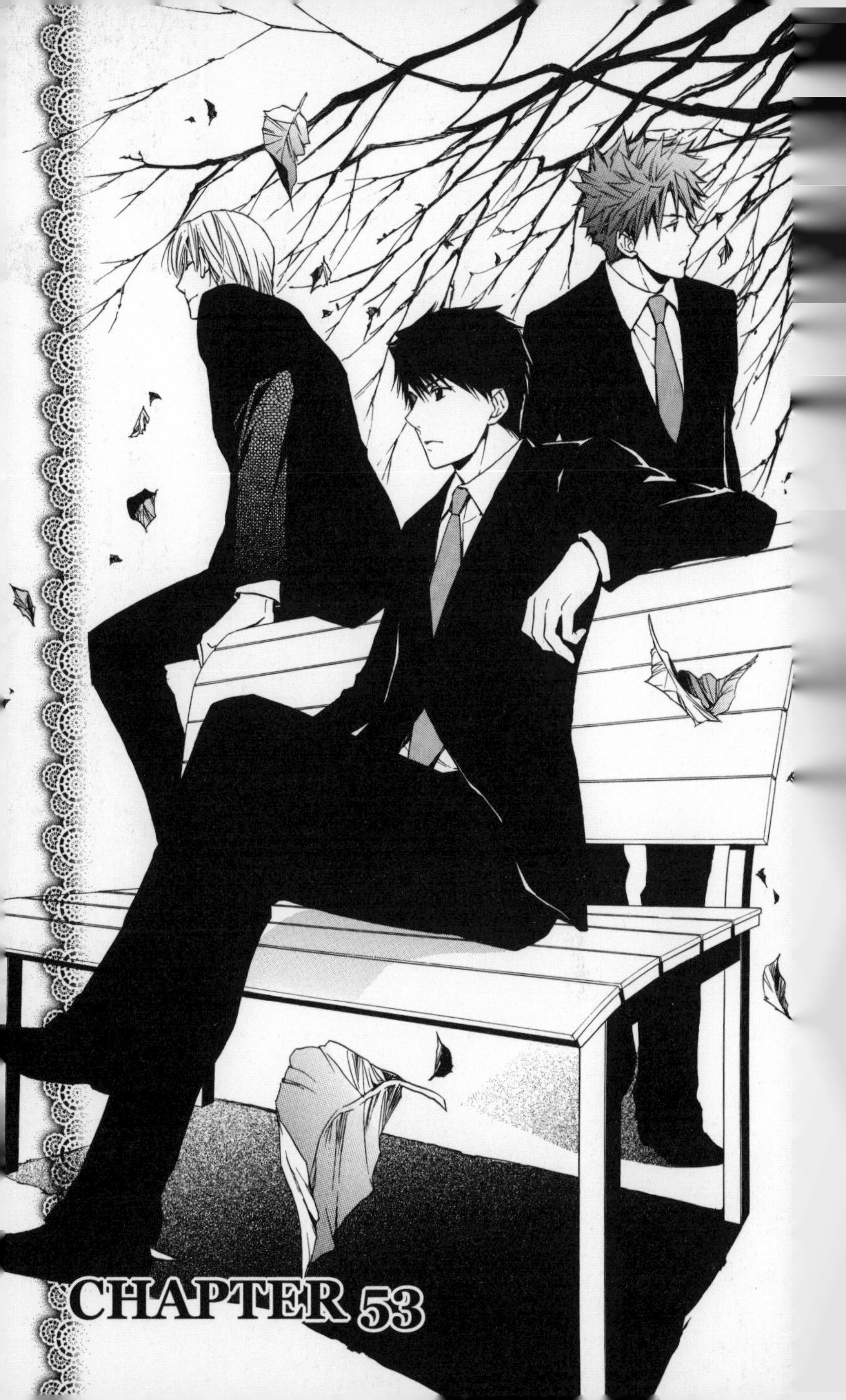
CHAPTER 53

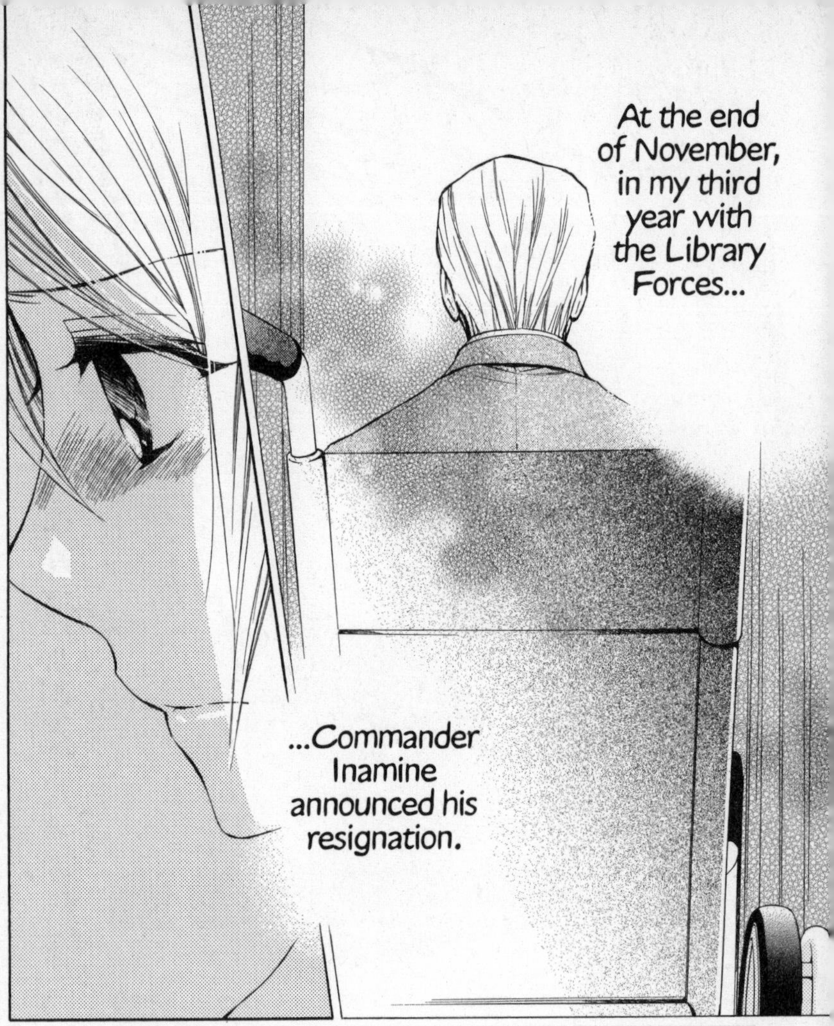
At the end of November, in my third year with the Library Forces...
...Commander Inamine announced his resignation.

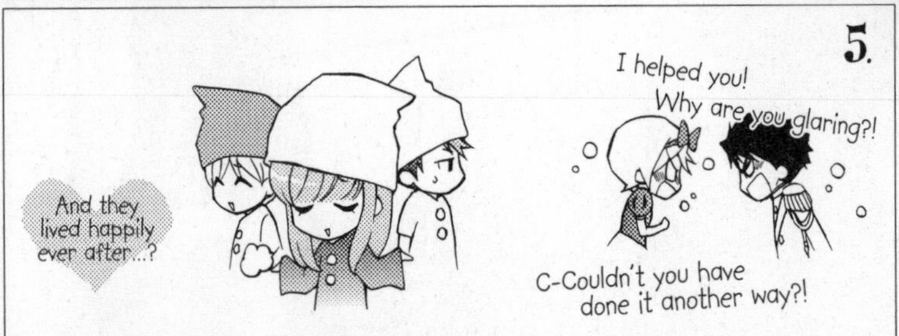
5.
I helped you! Why are you glaring?!
C-Couldn't you have done it another way?!
And they lived happily ever after...?

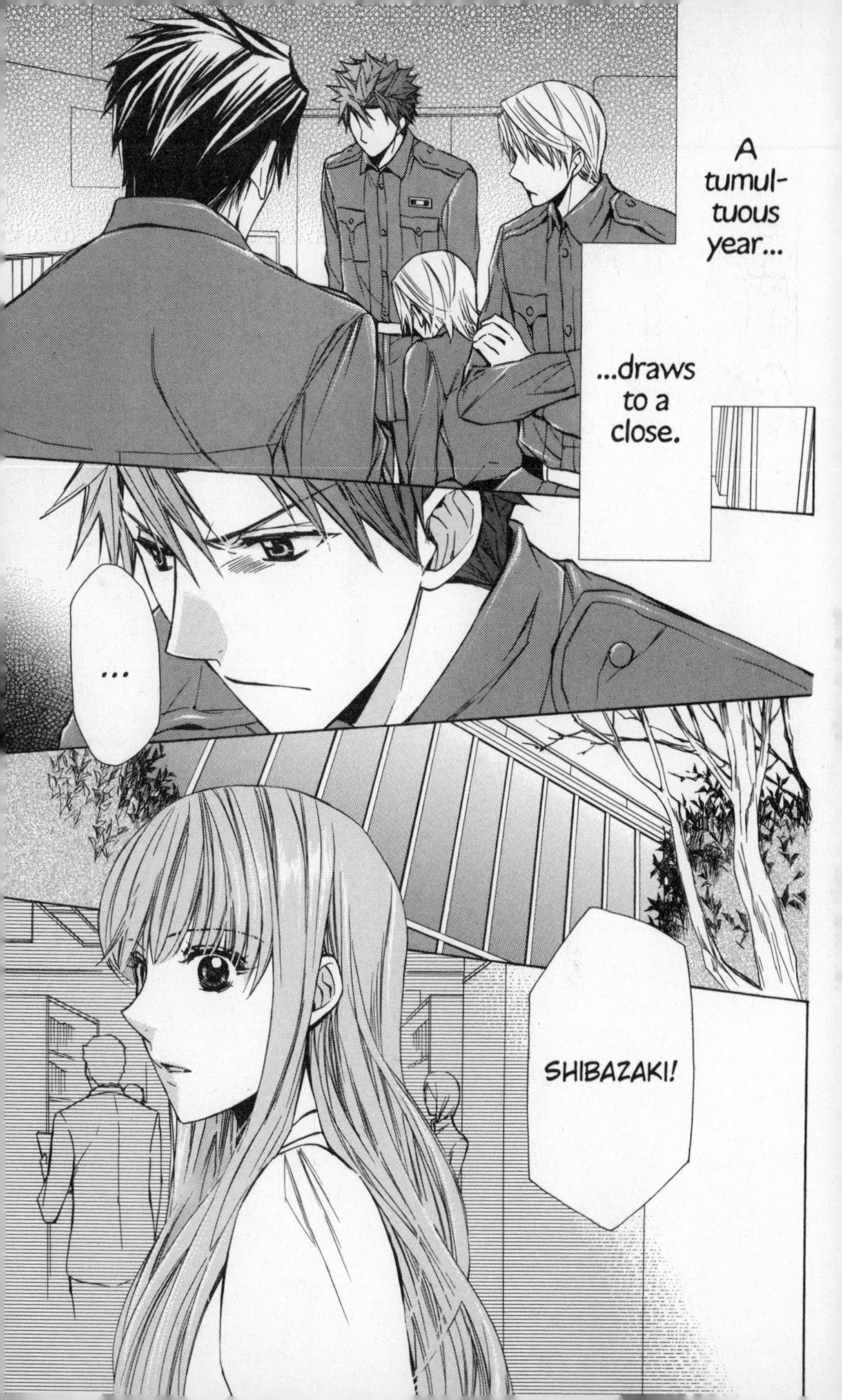
A tumul-tuous year...
...draws to a close.
...
SHIBAZAKI!

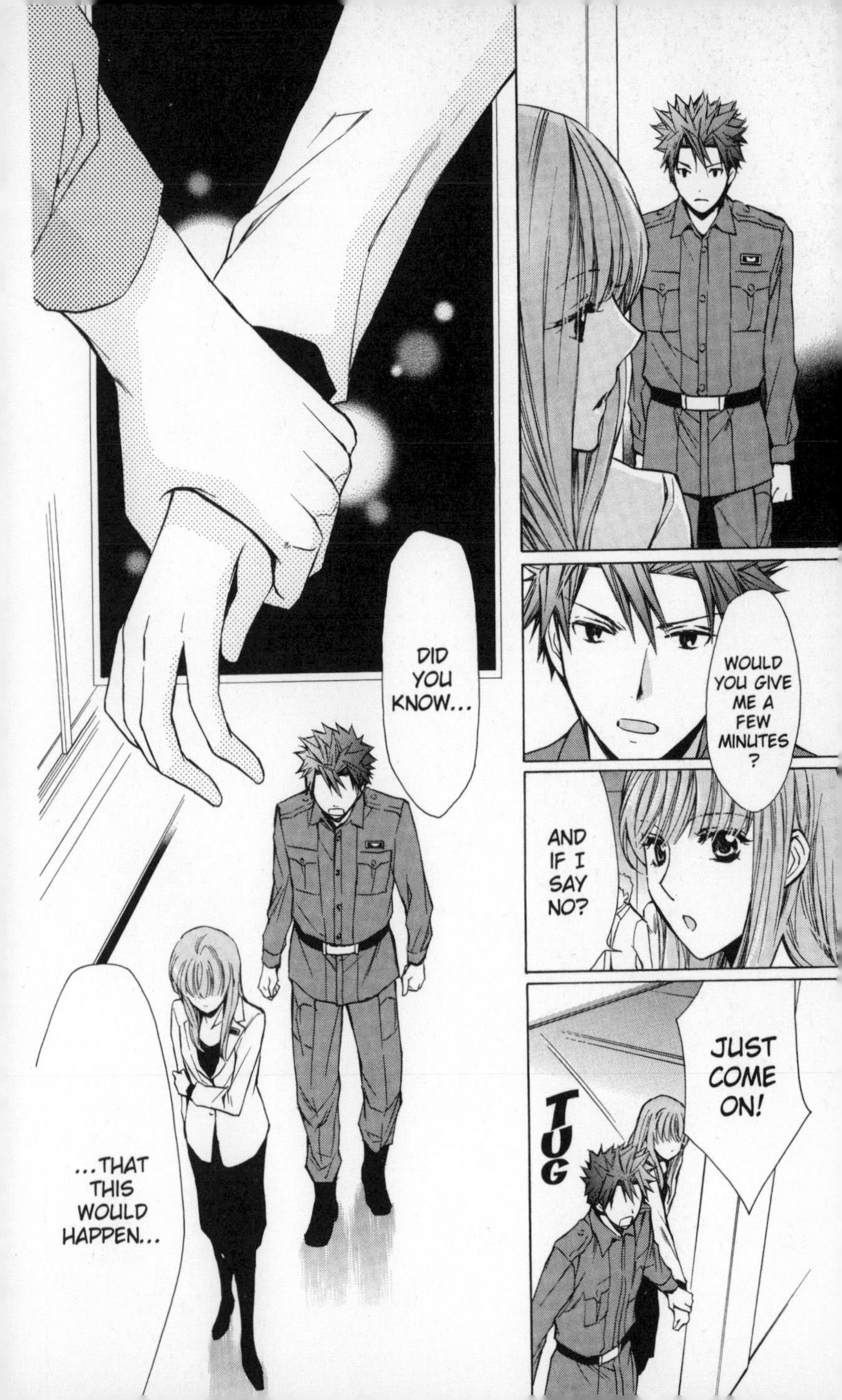
WOULD YOU GIVE ME A FEW MINUTES?
AND IF I SAY NO?
JUST COME ON!
TUG
DID YOU KNOW...
...THAT THIS WOULD HAPPEN...

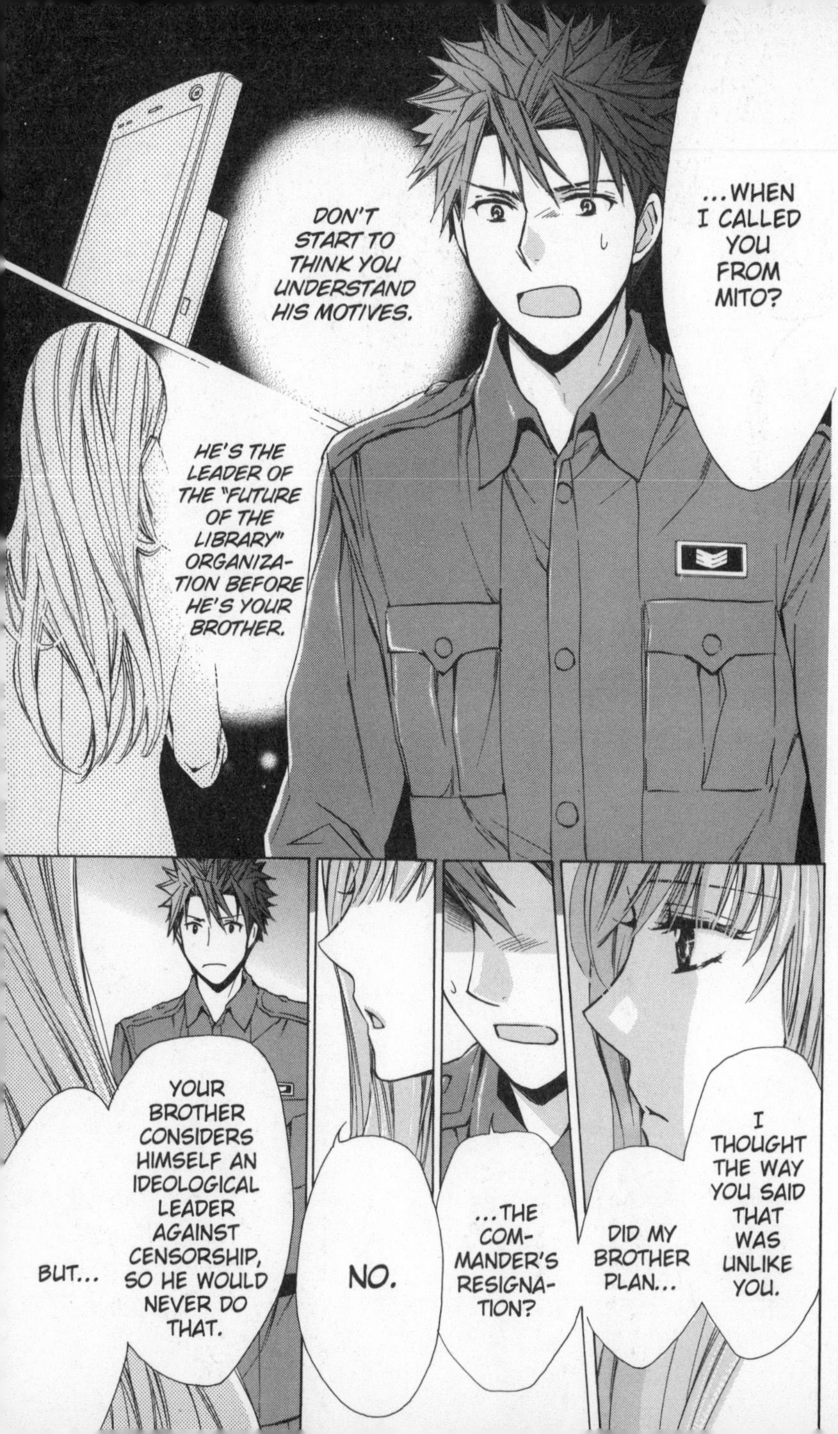
...WHEN I CALLED YOU FROM MITO?
DON'T START TO THINK YOU UNDERSTAND HIS MOTIVES.
HE'S THE LEADER OF THE "FUTURE OF THE LIBRARY" ORGANIZATION BEFORE HE'S YOUR BROTHER.
I THOUGHT THE WAY YOU SAID THAT WAS UNLIKE YOU.
DID MY BROTHER PLAN...
...THE COMMANDER'S RESIGNATION?
NO.
YOUR BROTHER CONSIDERS HIMSELF AN IDEOLOGICAL LEADER AGAINST CENSORSHIP, SO HE WOULD NEVER DO THAT.
BUT...

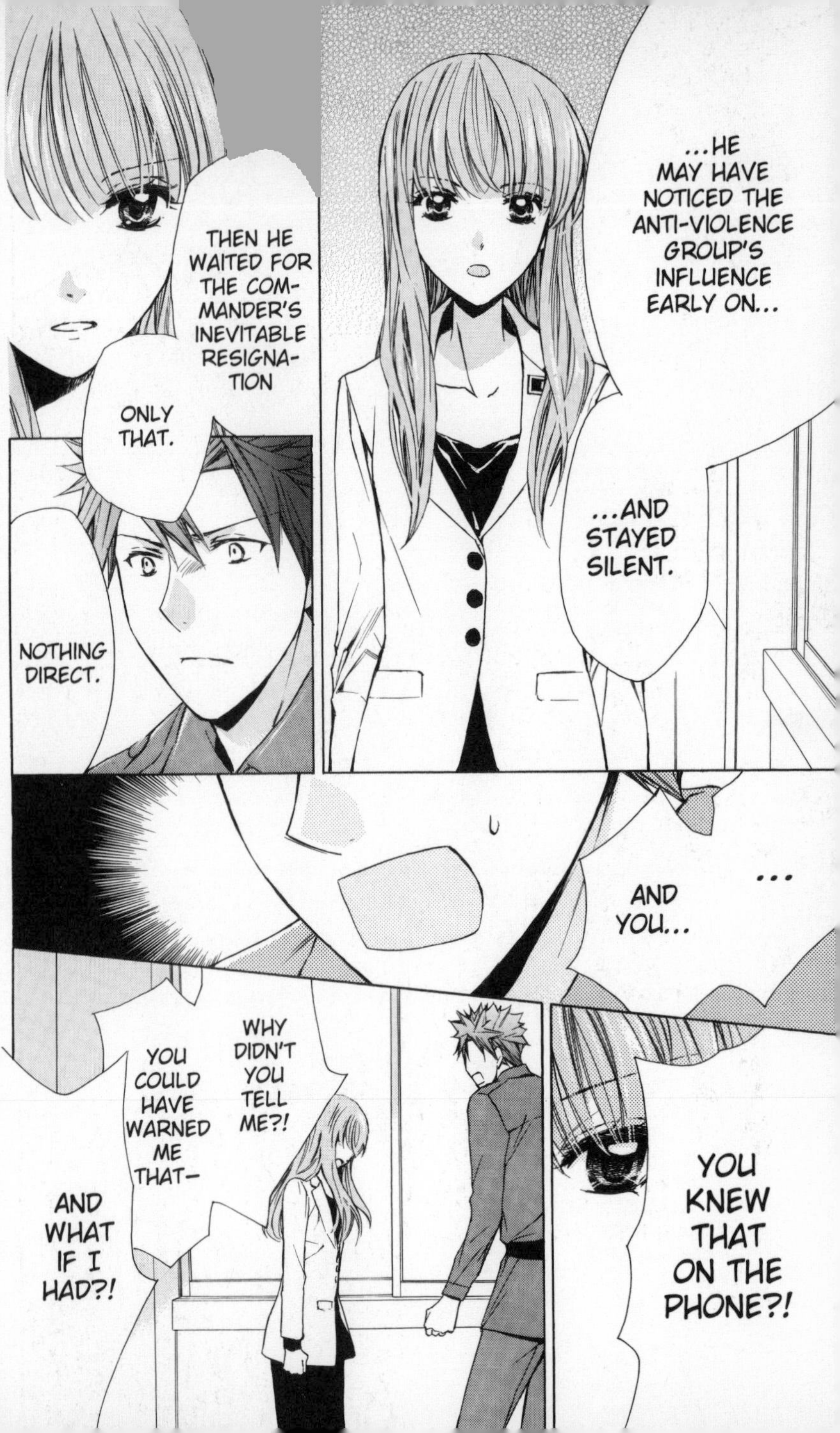
...HE MAY HAVE NOTICED THE ANTI-VIOLENCE GROUP'S INFLUENCE EARLY ON...
...AND STAYED SILENT.
THEN HE WAITED FOR THE COM-MANDER'S INEVITABLE RESIGNA-TION
ONLY THAT.
NOTHING DIRECT.
...
AND YOU...
YOU KNEW THAT ON THE PHONE?!
WHY DIDN'T YOU TELL ME?!
YOU COULD HAVE WARNED ME THAT—
AND WHAT IF I HAD?!

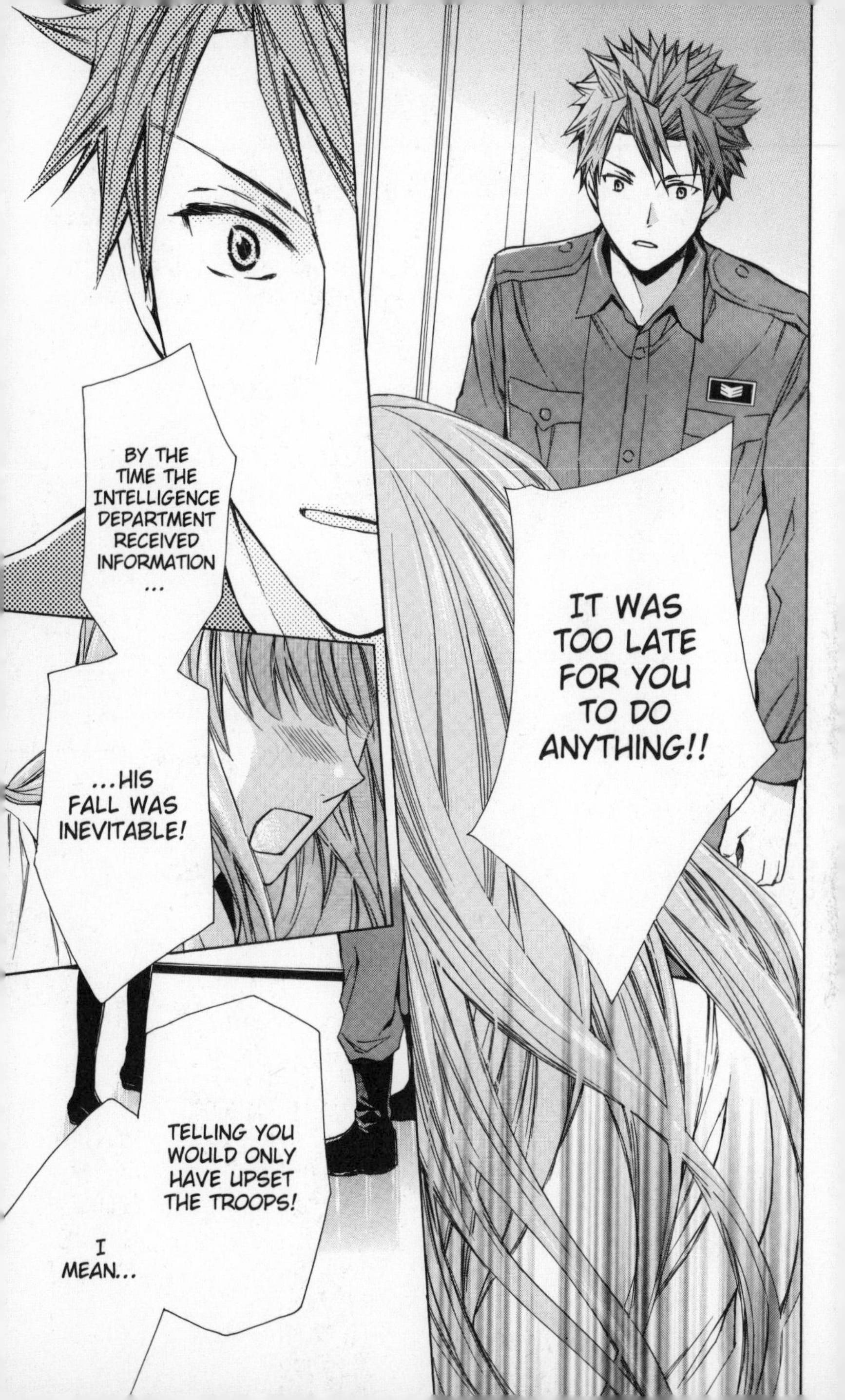
IT WAS TOO LATE FOR YOU TO DO ANYTHING!!
BY THE TIME THE INTELLIGENCE DEPARTMENT RECEIVED INFORMATION ...
...HIS FALL WAS INEVITABLE!
TELLING YOU WOULD ONLY HAVE UPSET THE TROOPS!
I MEAN...

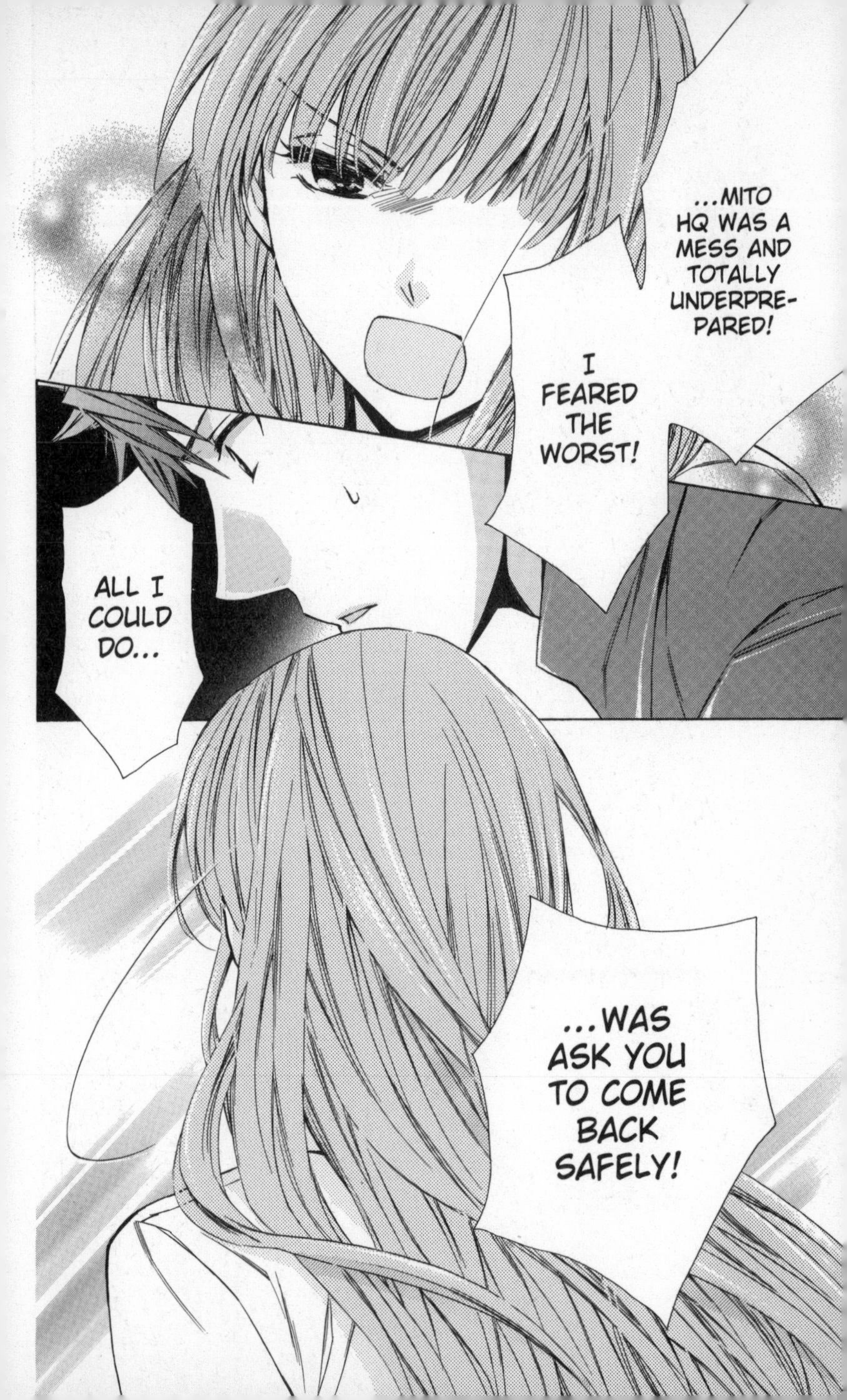
...MITO HQ WAS A MESS AND TOTALLY UNDERPRE-PARED!
I FEARED THE WORST!
ALL I COULD DO...
...WAS ASK YOU TO COME BACK SAFELY!

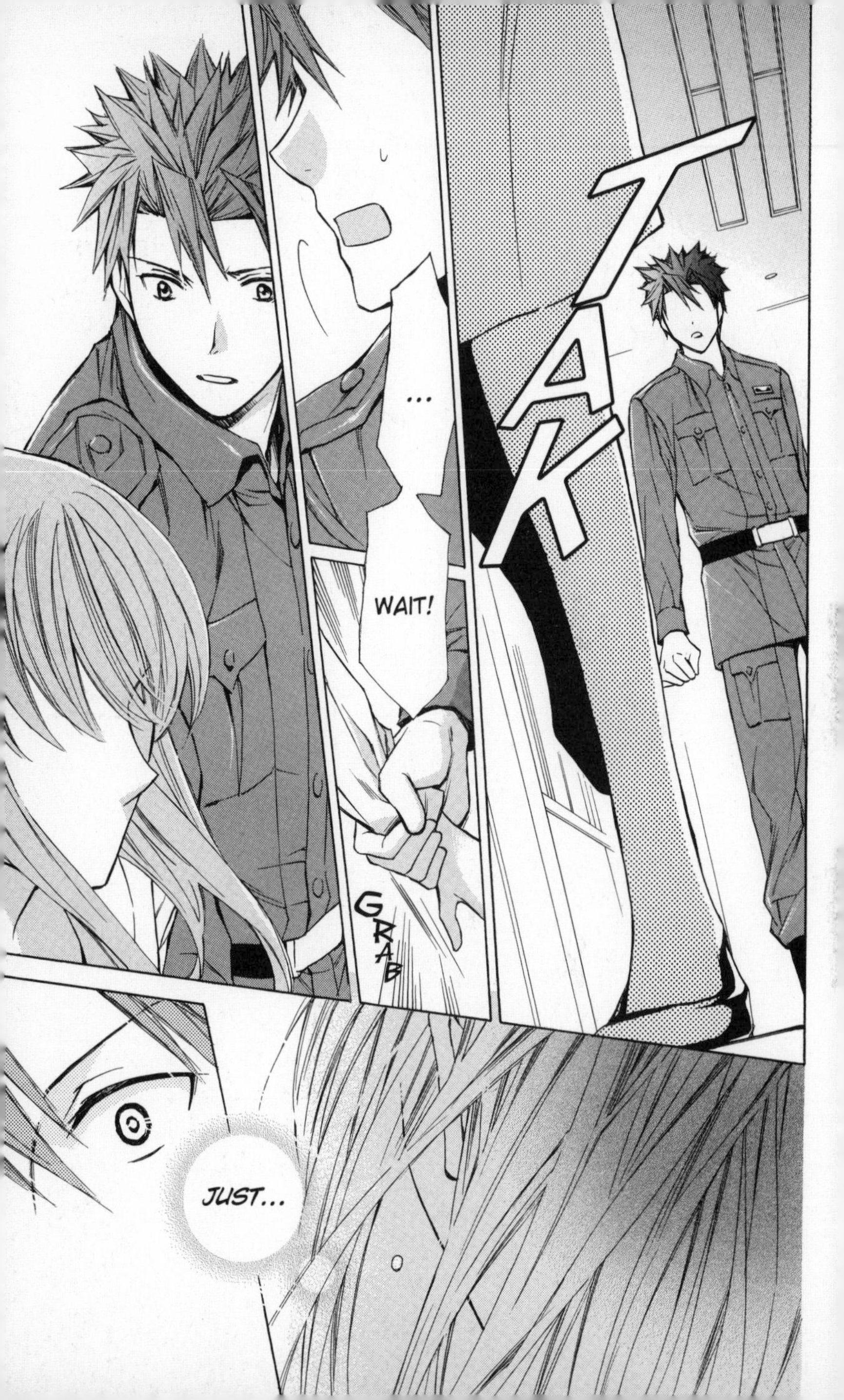
TAK
...
WAIT!
GRAB
JUST...

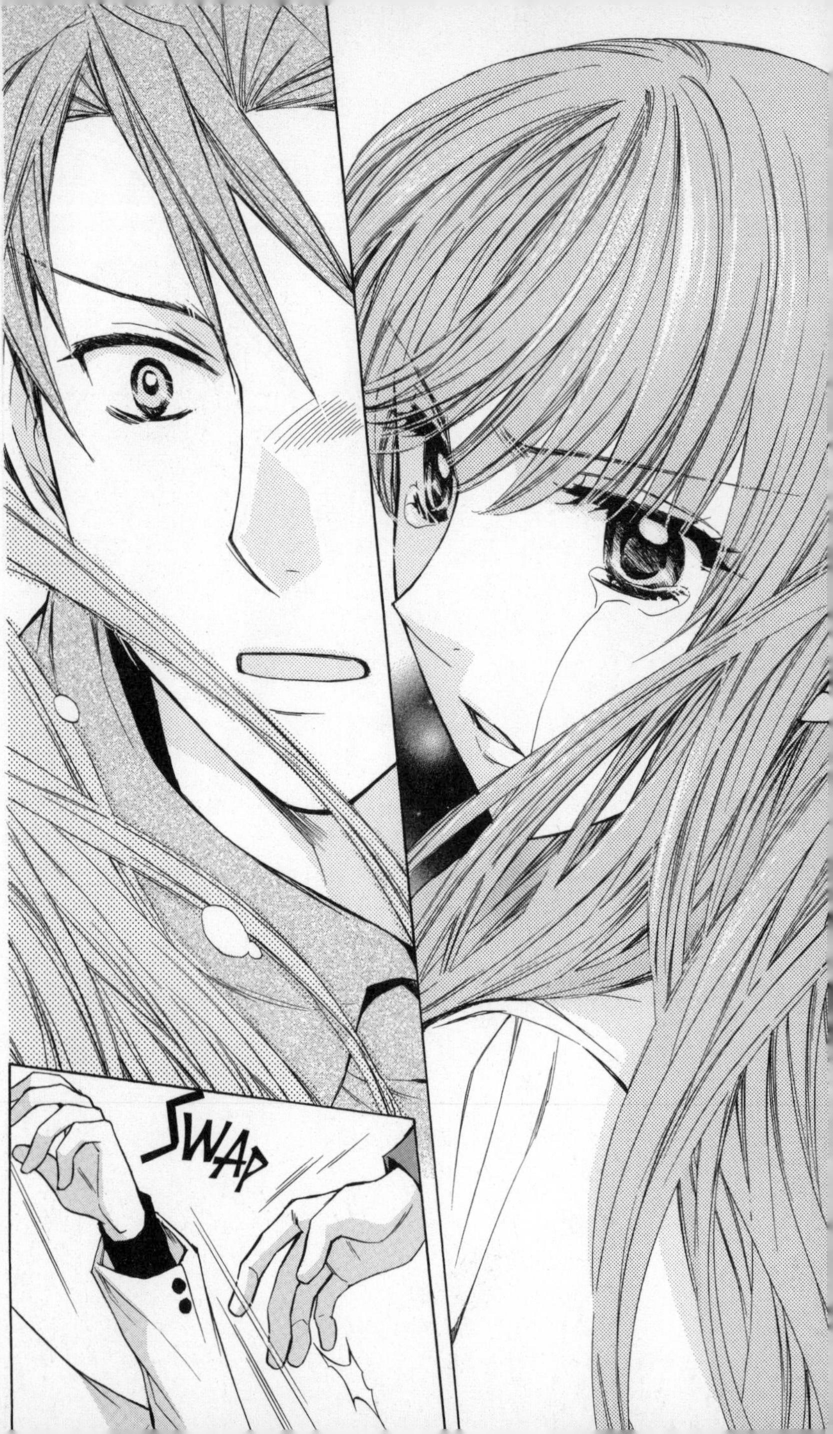
SWAP

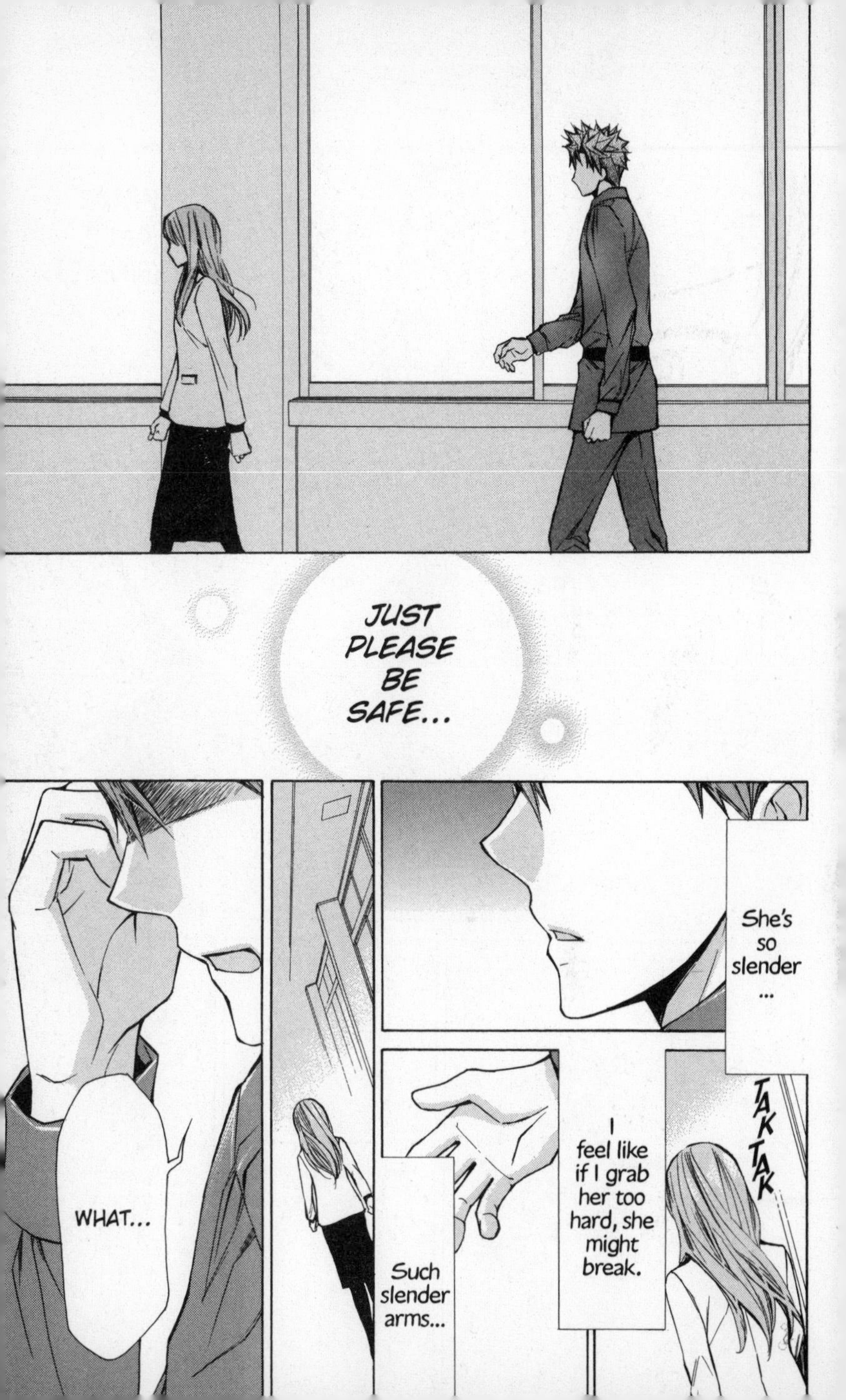
JUST PLEASE BE SAFE...
She's so slender ...
TAK TAK
I feel like if I grab her too hard, she might break.
Such slender arms...
WHAT...

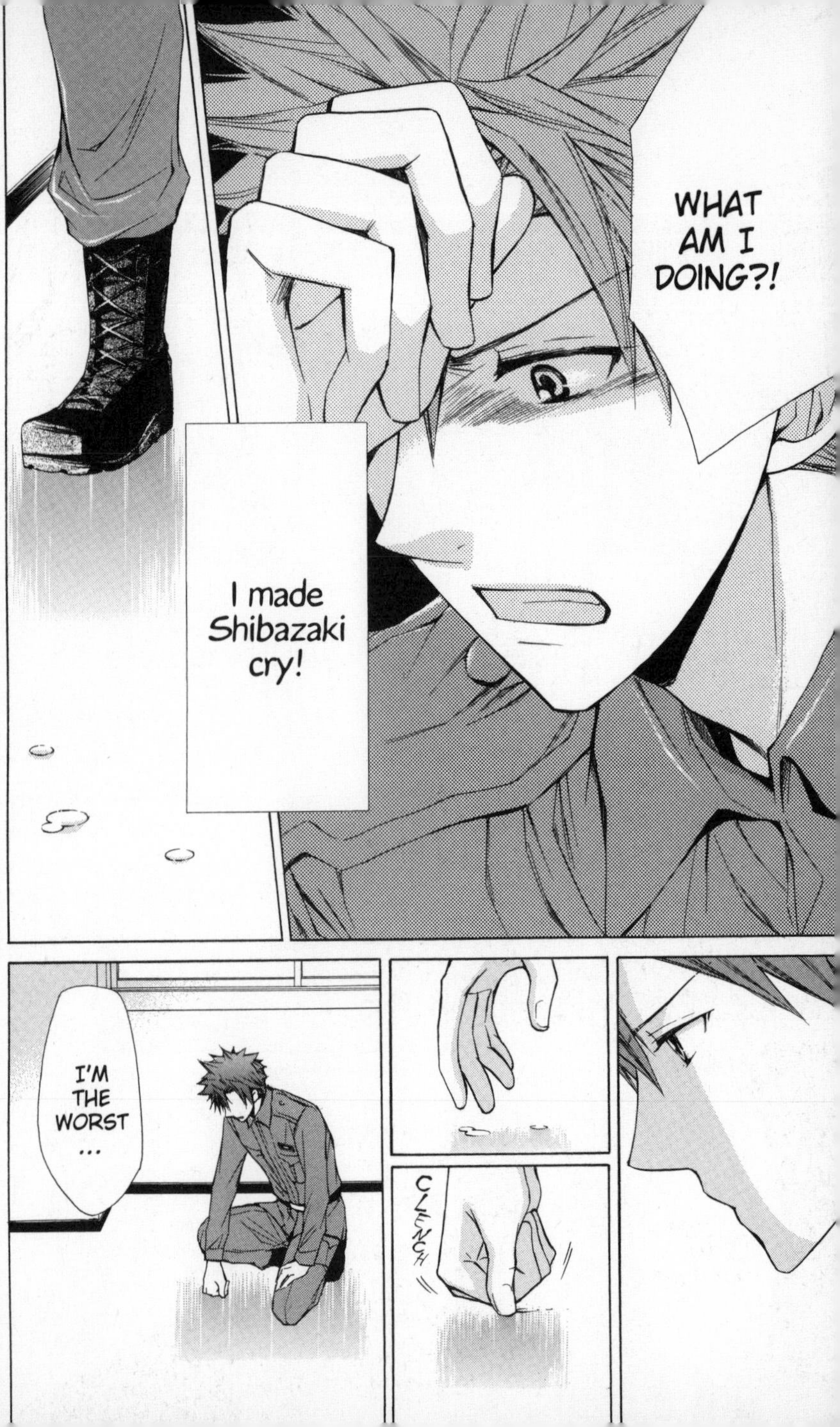
WHAT AM I DOING?!
I made Shibazaki cry!
CLENCH
I'M THE WORST ...

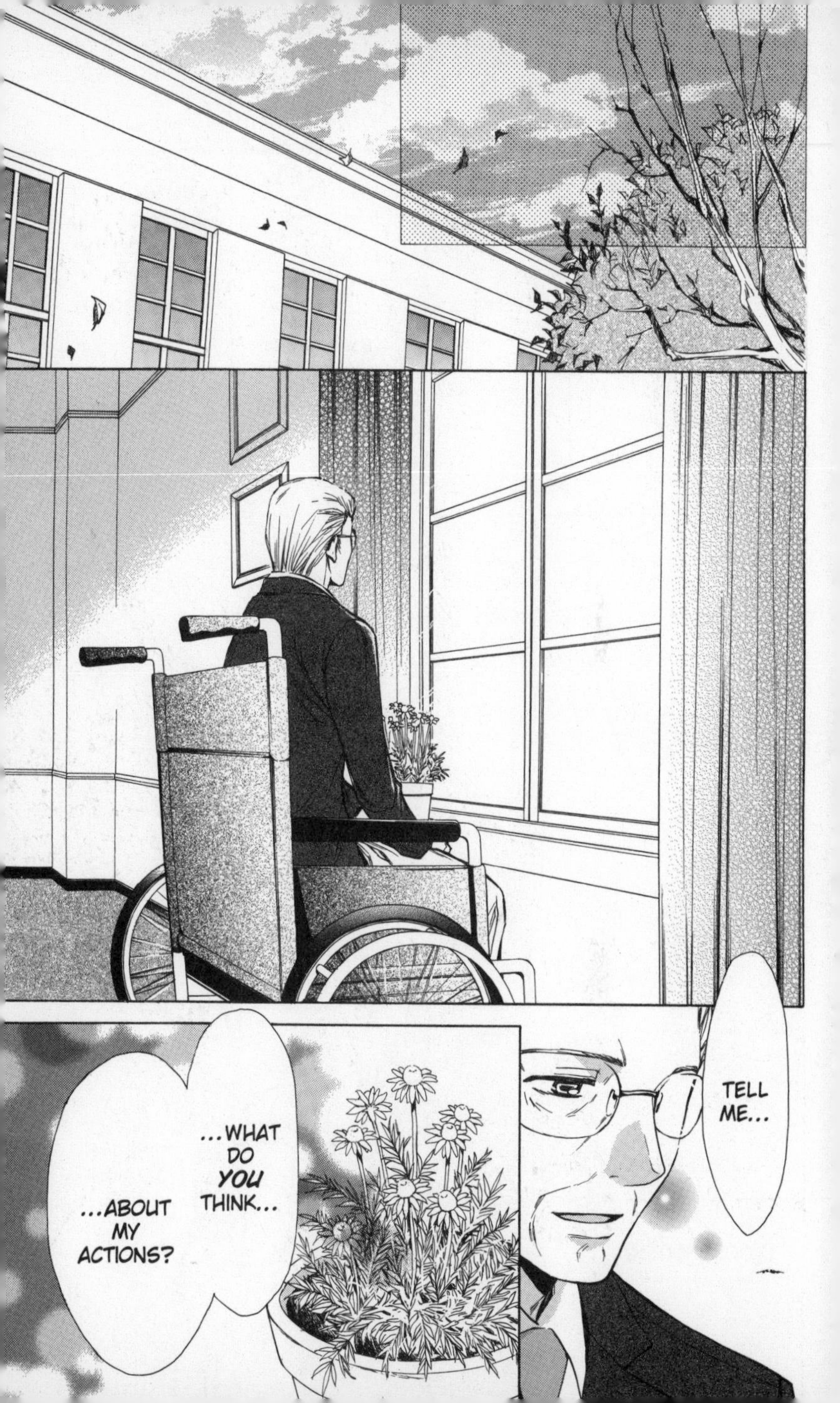
TELL ME...
...WHAT DO *YOU* THINK...
...ABOUT MY ACTIONS?

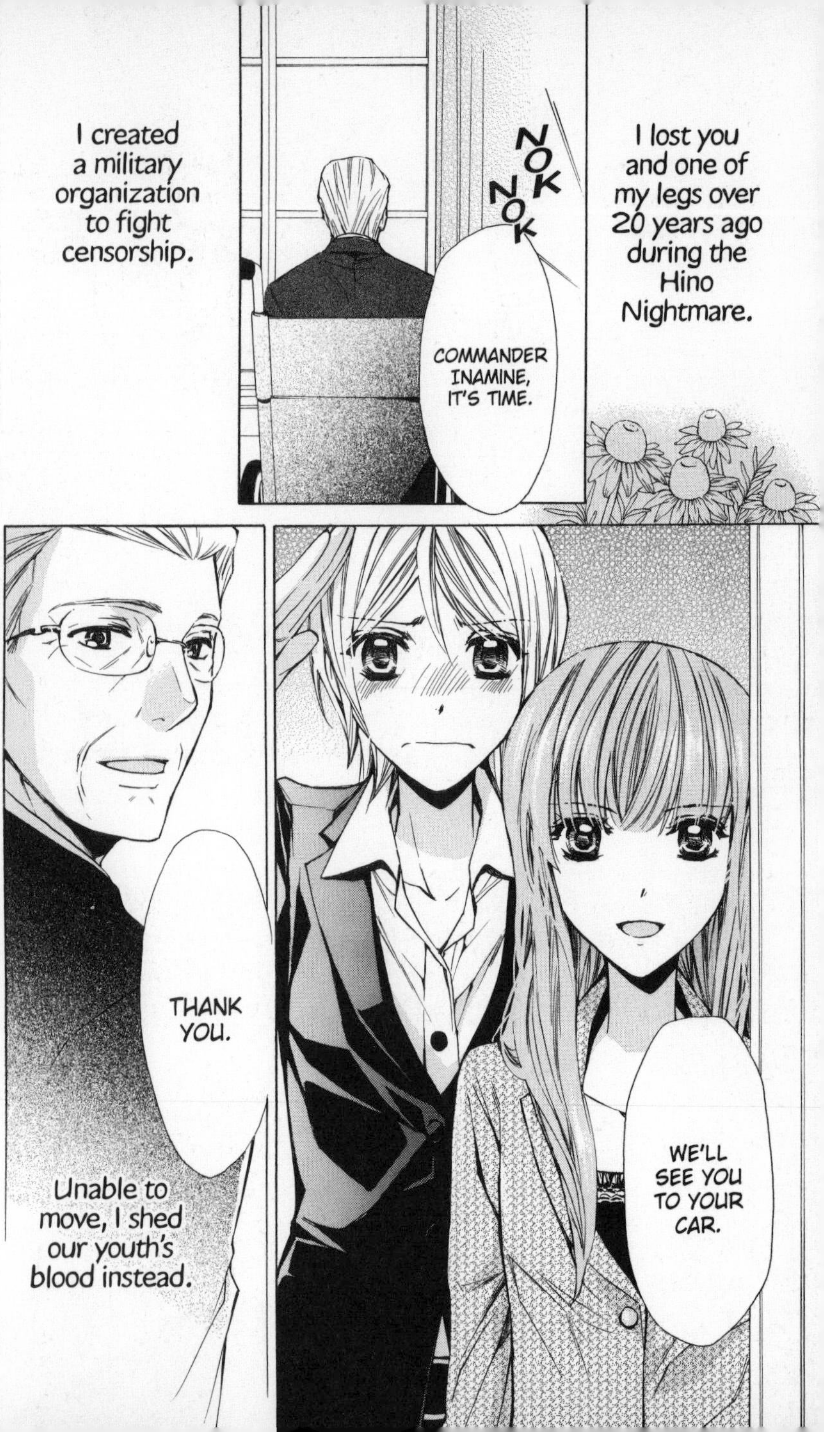
I lost you and one of my legs over 20 years ago during the Hino Nightmare.
NOK NOK
COMMANDER INAMINE, IT'S TIME.
I created a military organization to fight censorship.
WE'LL SEE YOU TO YOUR CAR.
THANK YOU.
Unable to move, I shed our youth's blood instead.

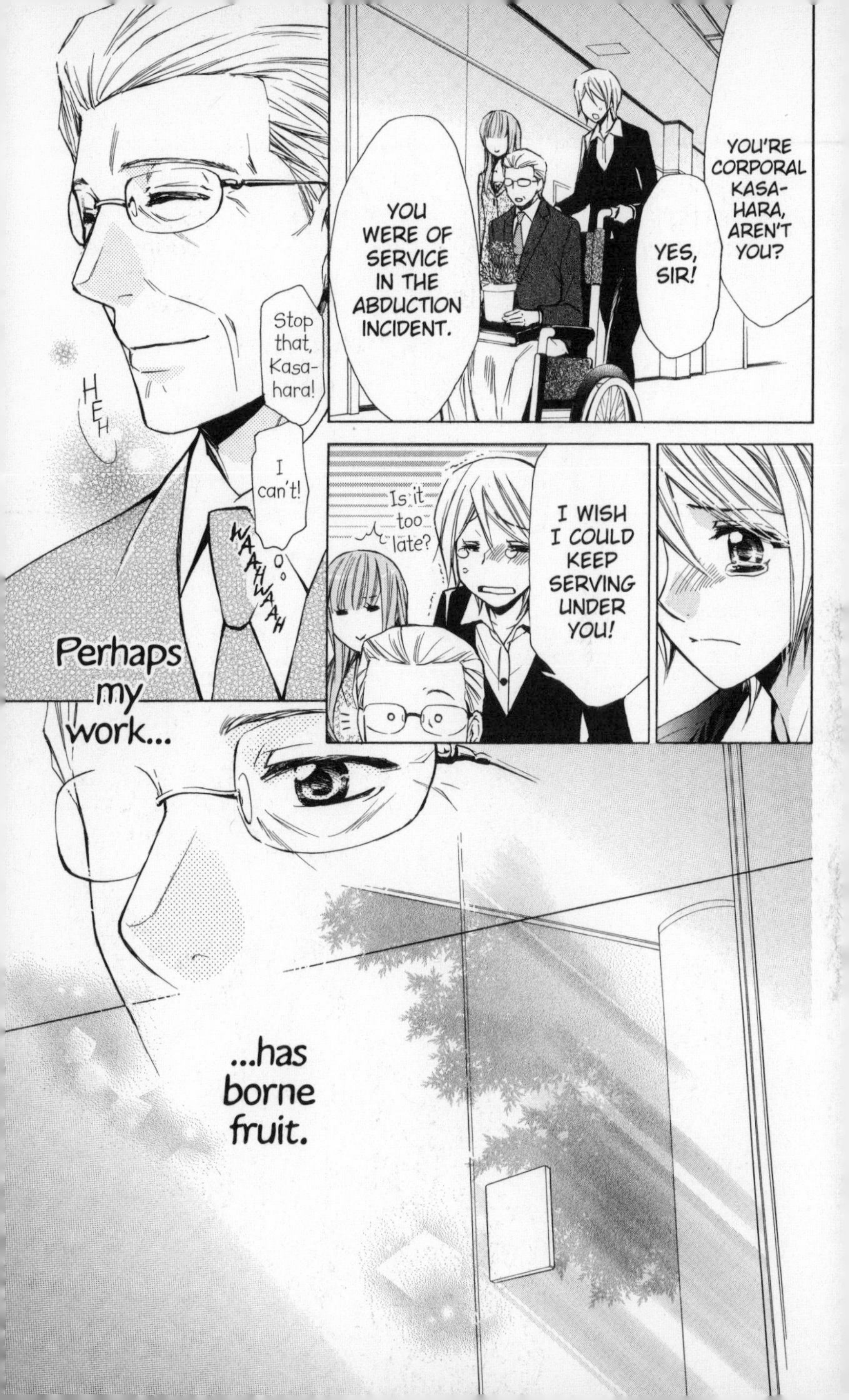
YOU'RE CORPORAL KASAHARA, AREN'T YOU?
YES, SIR!
YOU WERE OF SERVICE IN THE ABDUCTION INCIDENT.
I WISH I COULD KEEP SERVING UNDER YOU!
Is it too late?
Stop that, Kasahara!
I can't!
WAAHWAAH
HEH
Perhaps my work...
...has borne fruit.

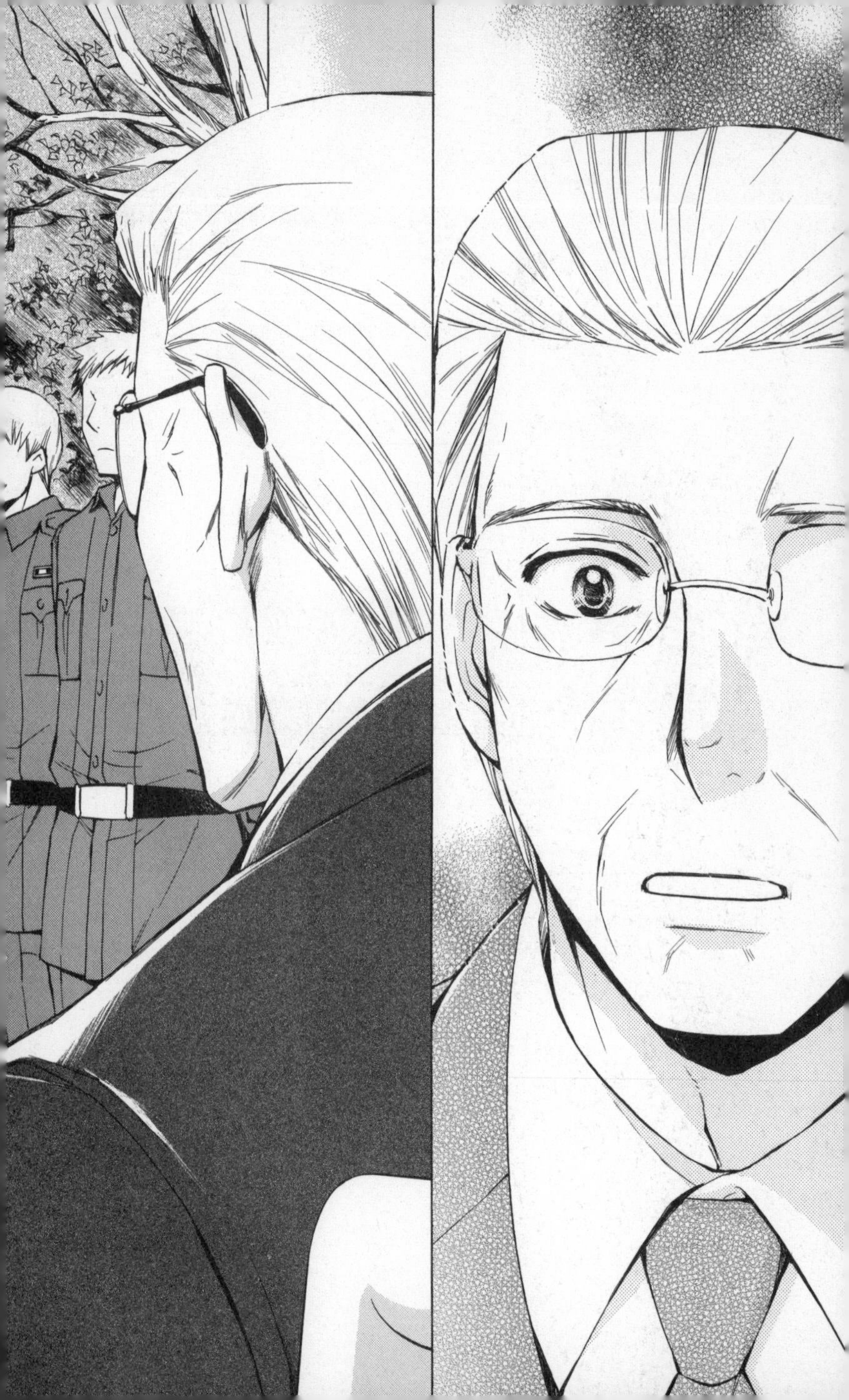

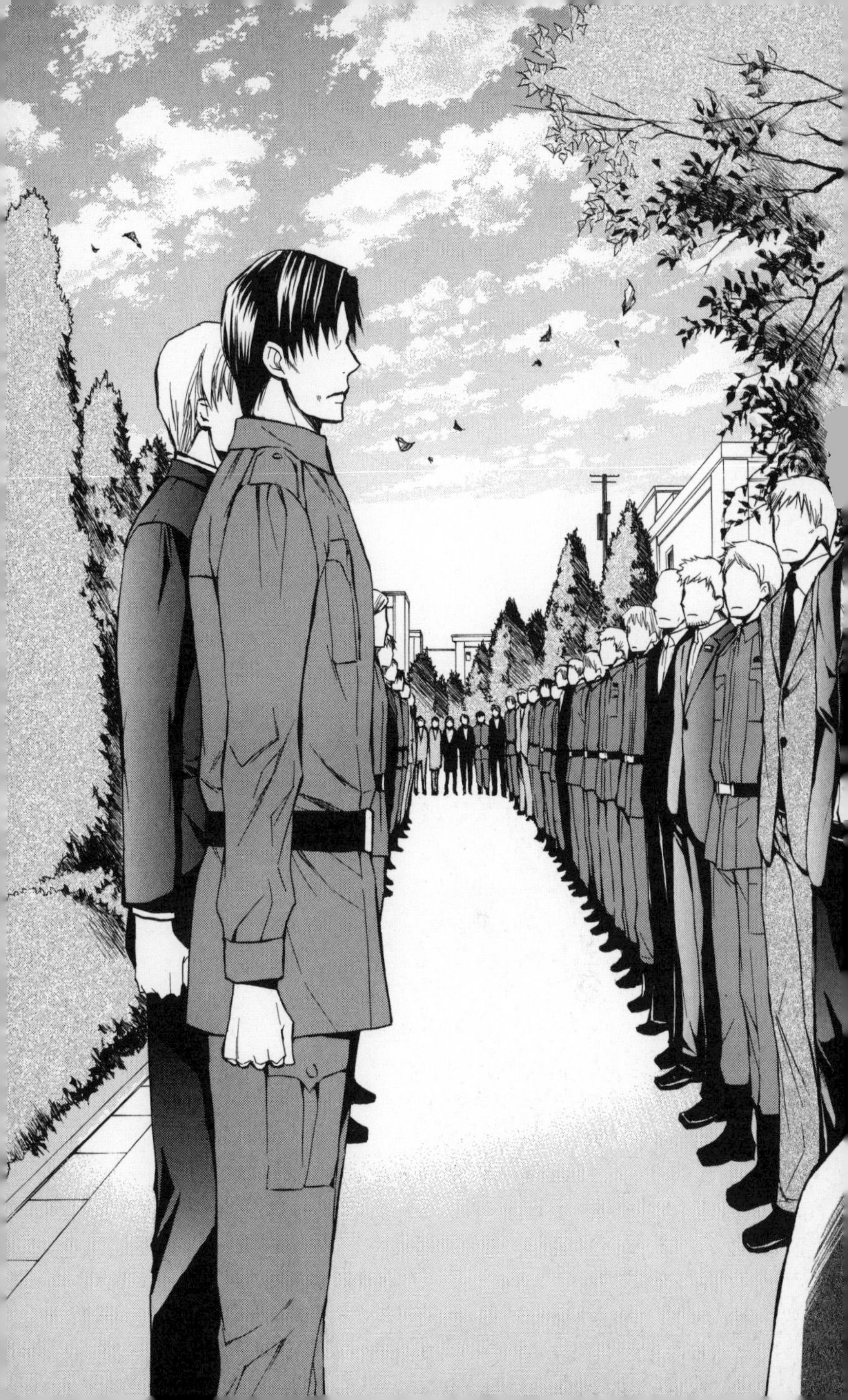

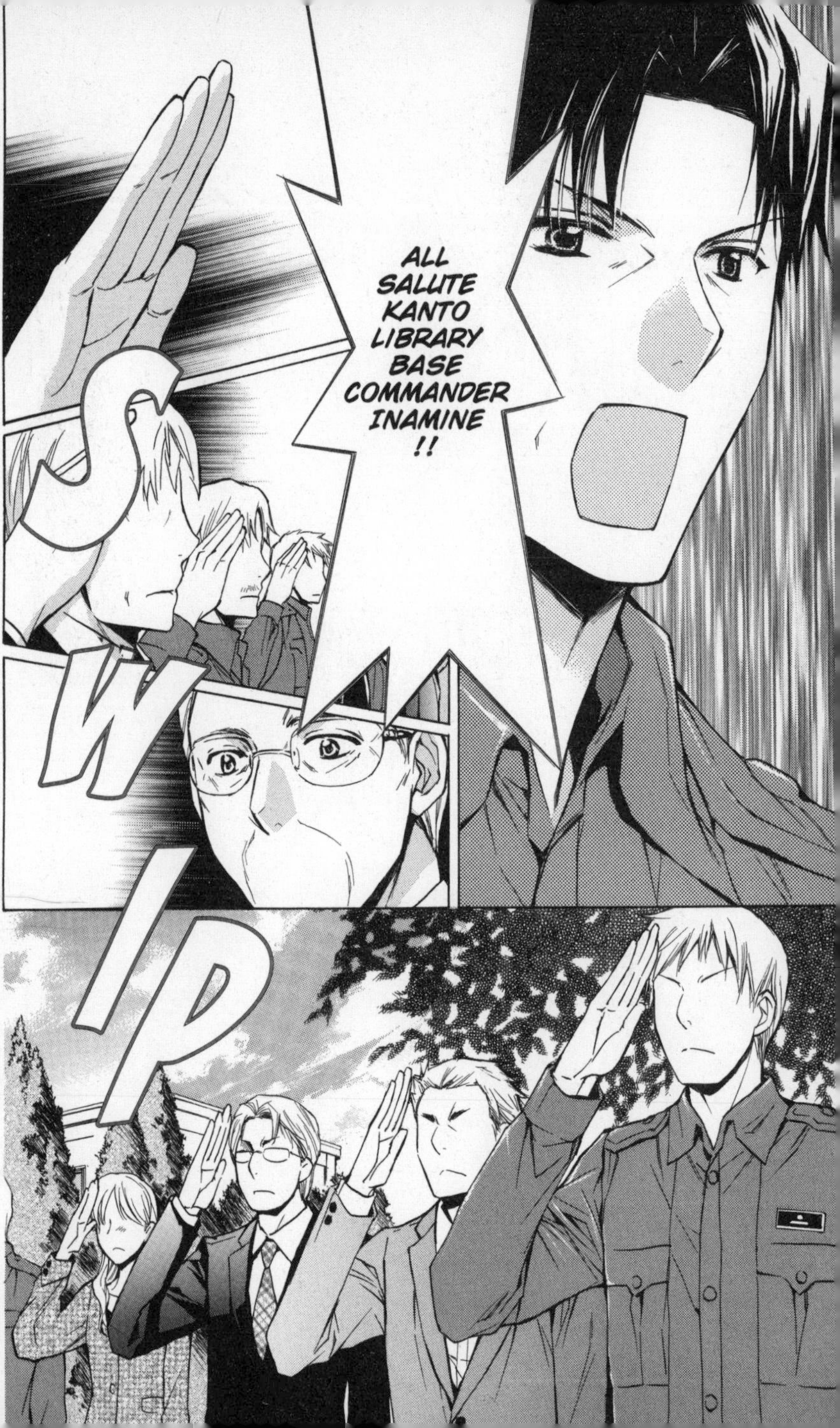
ALL SALUTE KANTO LIBRARY BASE COMMANDER INAMINE !!
SWIP

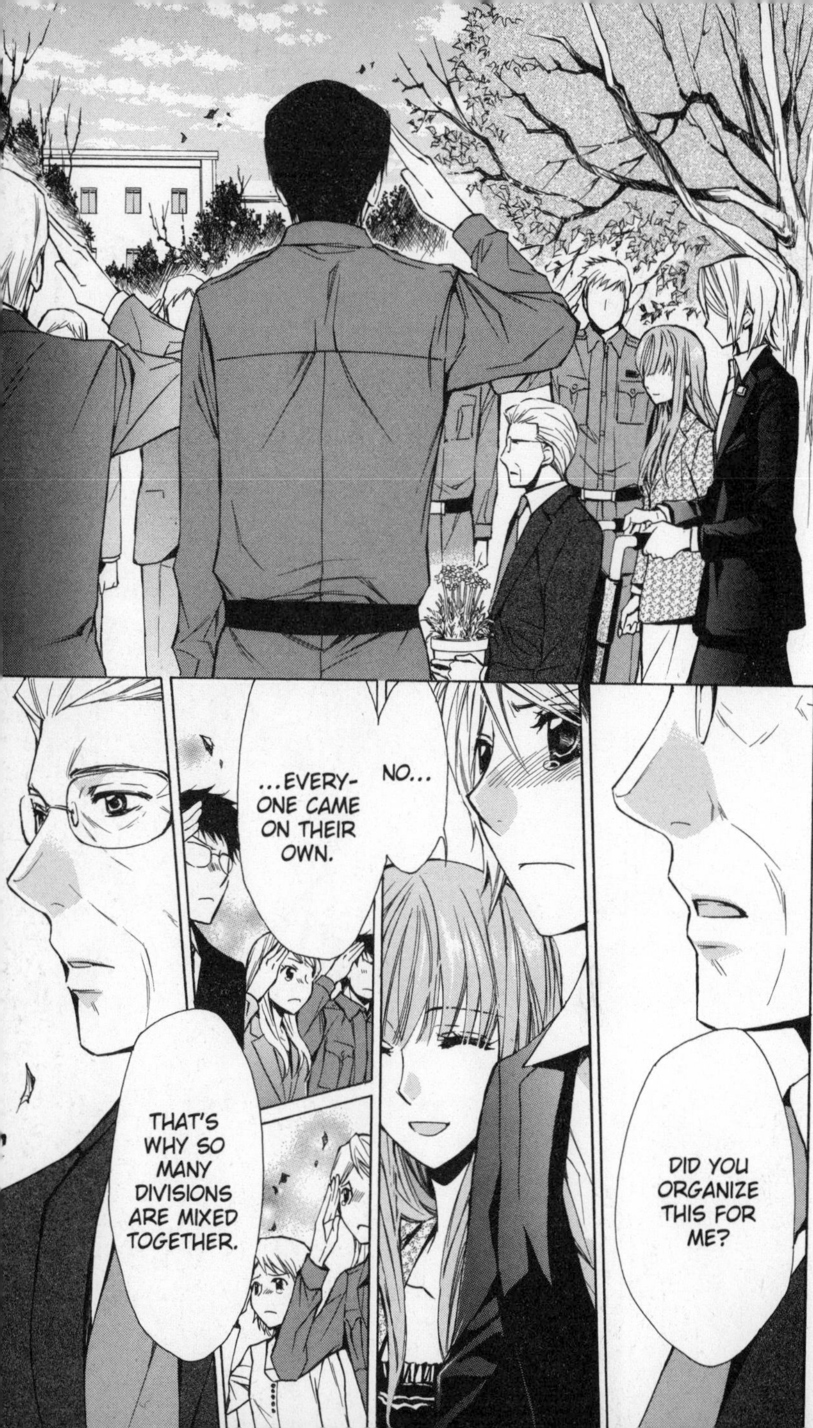
DID YOU ORGANIZE THIS FOR ME?
NO...
...EVERY-ONE CAME ON THEIR OWN.
THAT'S WHY SO MANY DIVISIONS ARE MIXED TOGETHER.

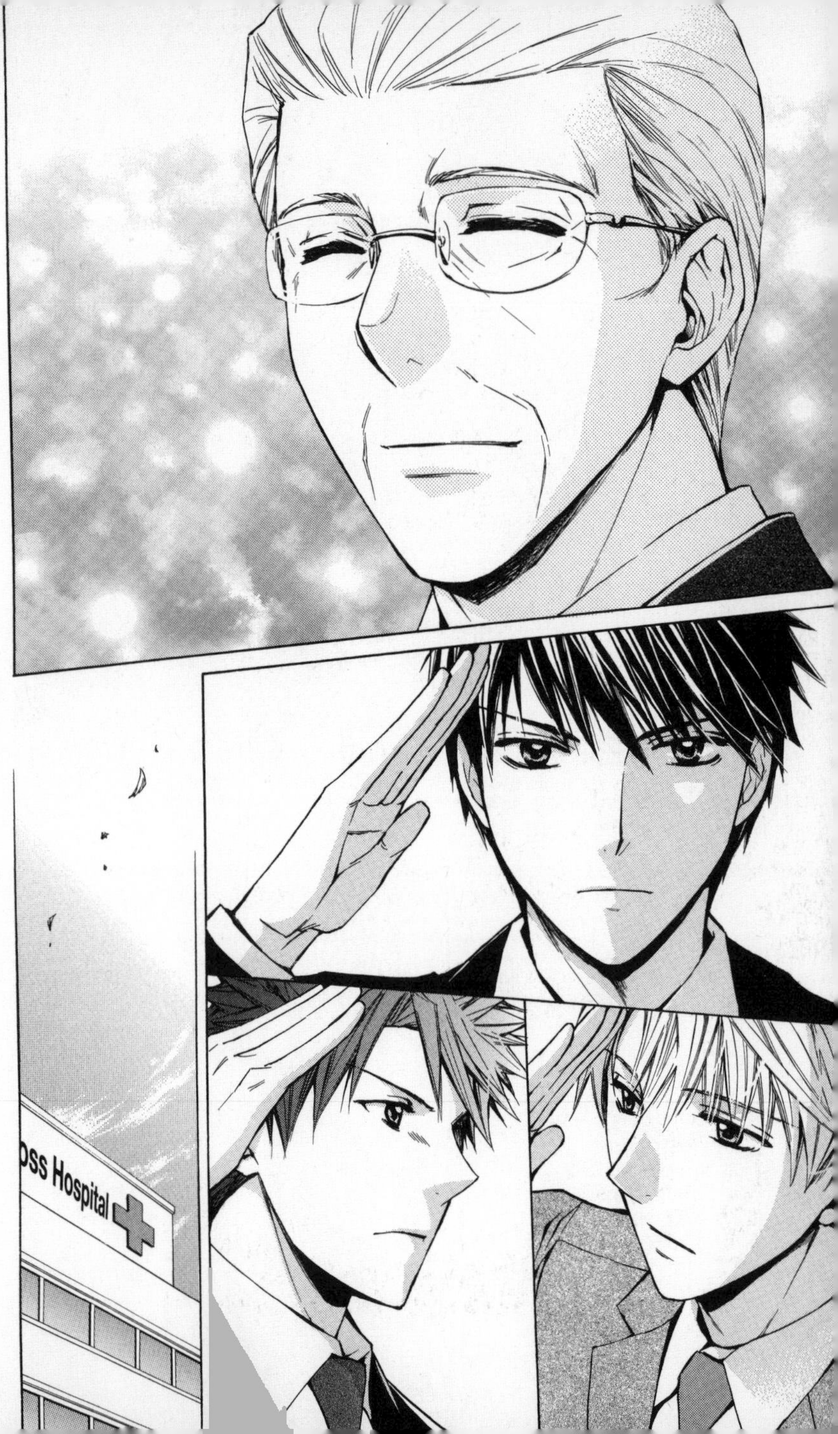
oss Hospital

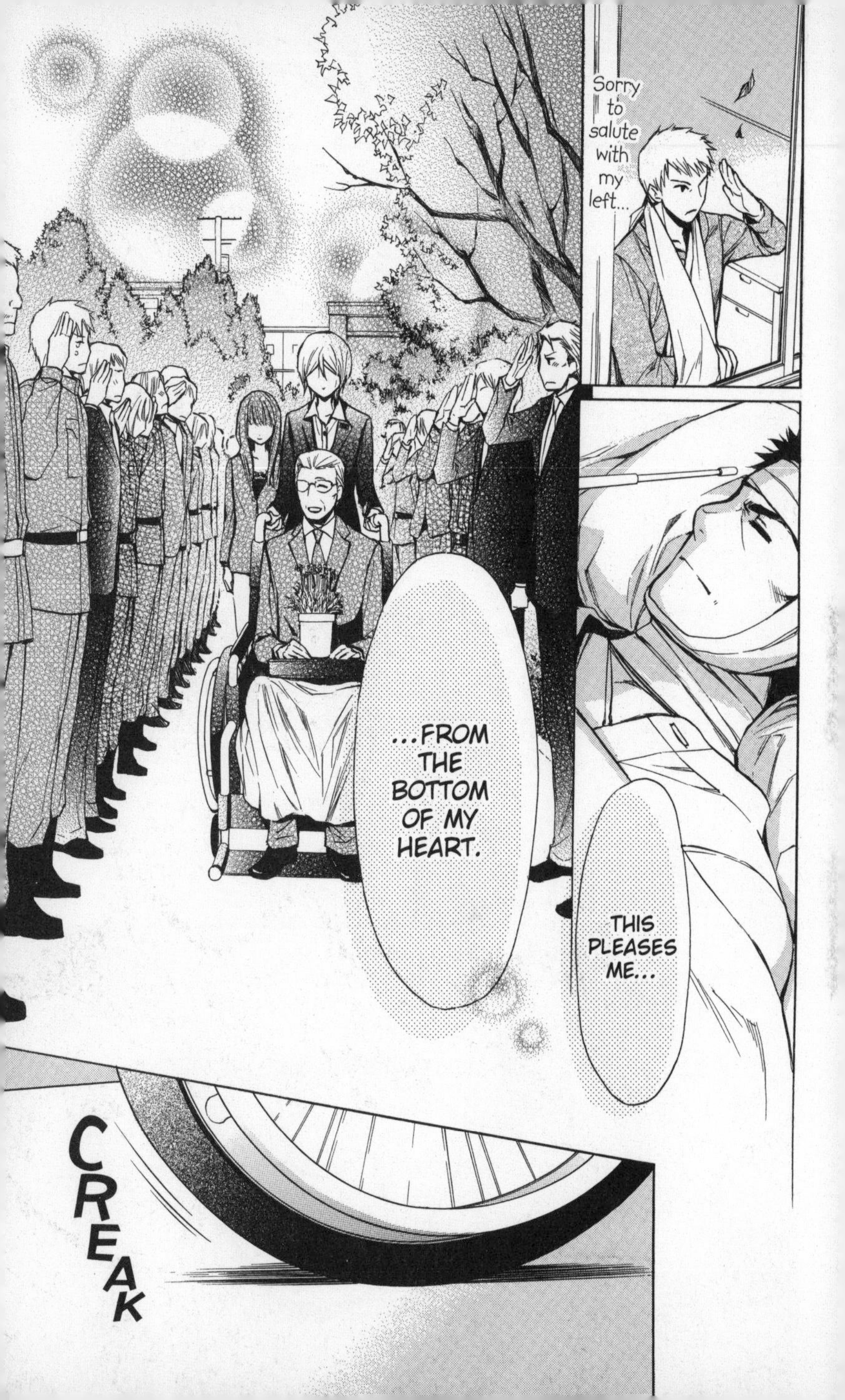
Sorry to salute with my left...
THIS PLEASES ME...
...FROM THE BOTTOM OF MY HEART.
CREAK

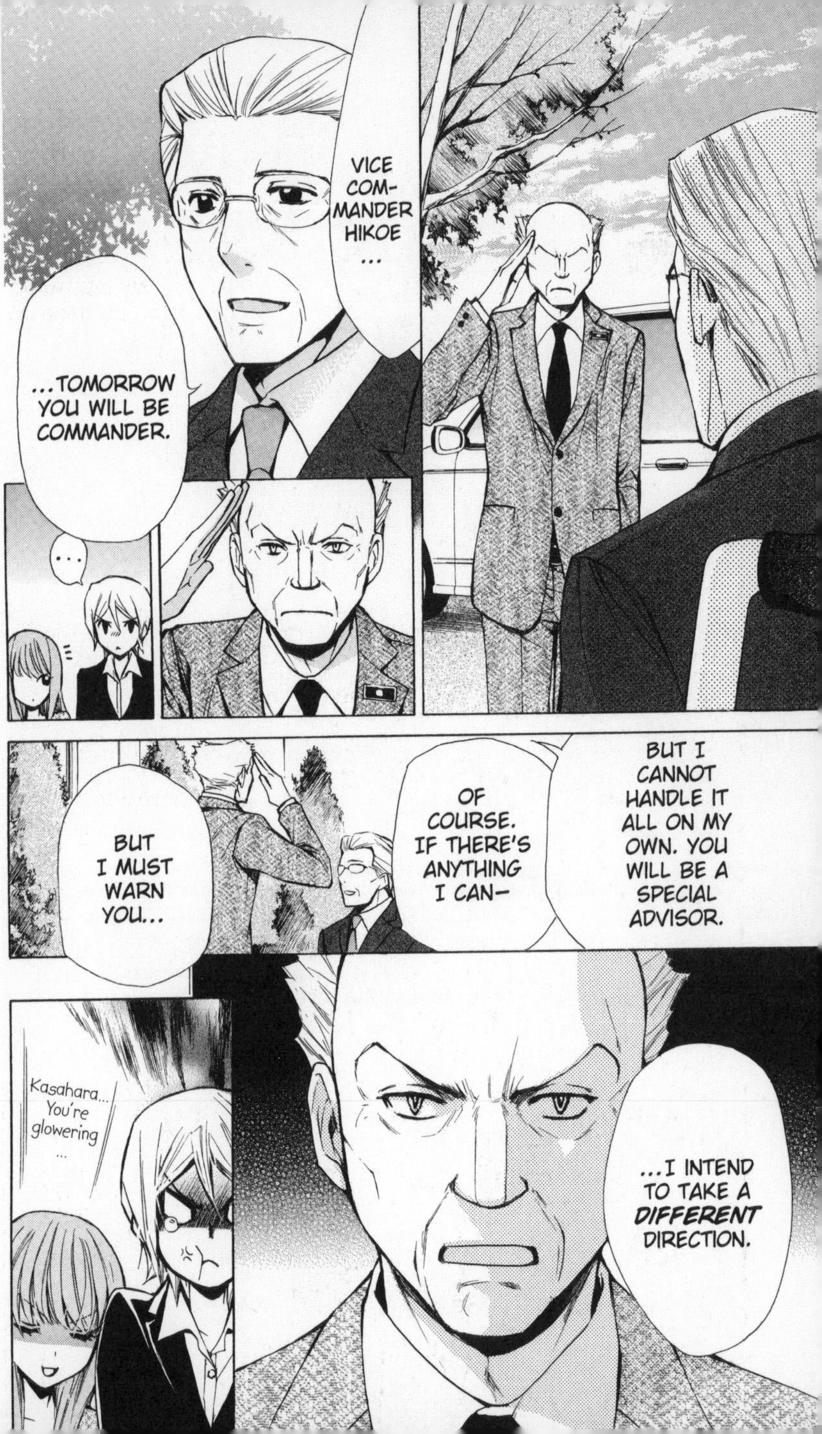
VICE COM-MANDER HIKOE ...
...TOMORROW YOU WILL BE COMMANDER.
...
BUT I CANNOT HANDLE IT ALL ON MY OWN. YOU WILL BE A SPECIAL ADVISOR.
OF COURSE. IF THERE'S ANYTHING I CAN-
BUT I MUST WARN YOU...
...I INTEND TO TAKE A *DIFFERENT* DIRECTION.
Kasahara... You're glowering ...

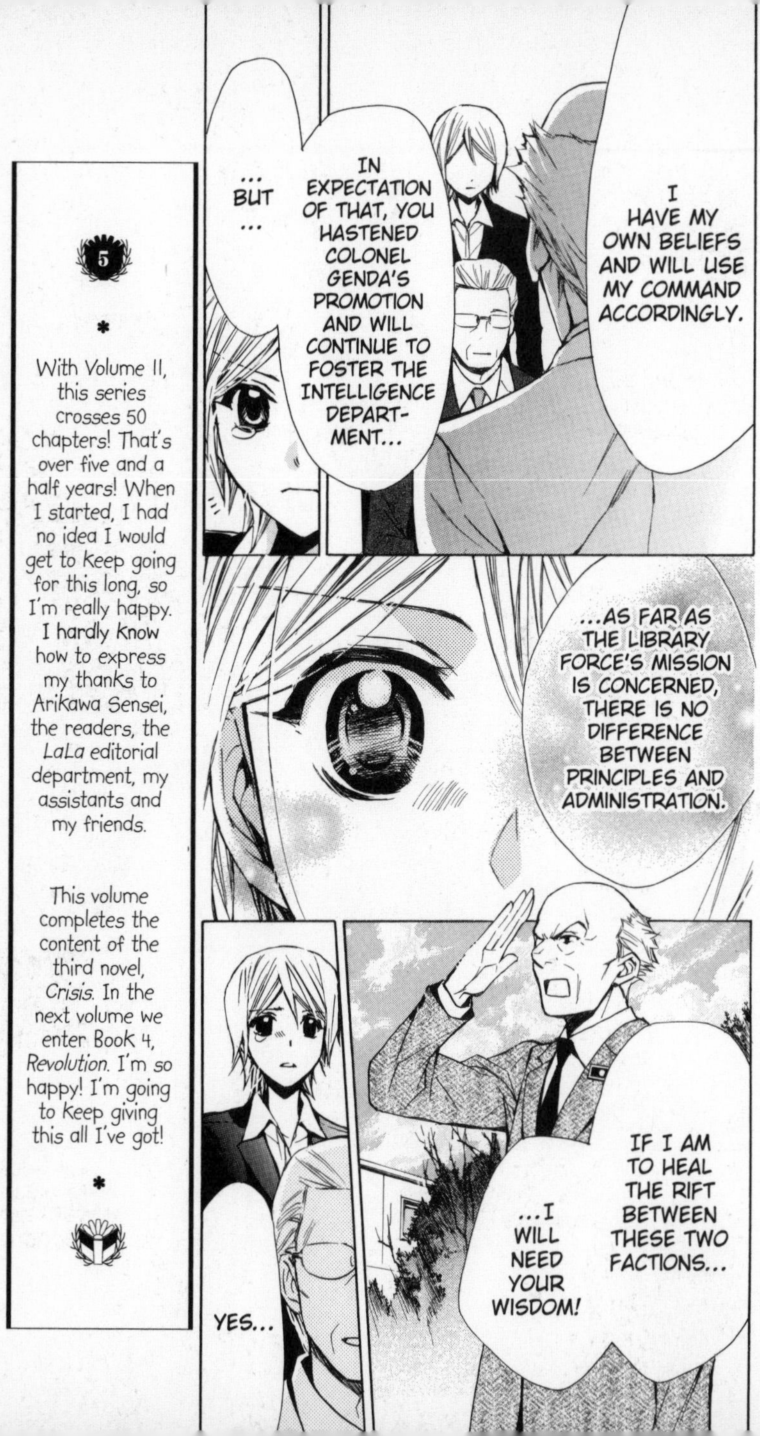
I HAVE MY OWN BELIEFS AND WILL USE MY COMMAND ACCORDINGLY.
IN EXPECTATION OF THAT, YOU HASTENED COLONEL GENDA'S PROMOTION AND WILL CONTINUE TO FOSTER THE INTELLIGENCE DEPART-MENT...
...BUT...
...AS FAR AS THE LIBRARY FORCE'S MISSION IS CONCERNED, THERE IS NO DIFFERENCE BETWEEN PRINCIPLES AND ADMINISTRATION.
IF I AM TO HEAL THE RIFT BETWEEN THESE TWO FACTIONS...
...I WILL NEED YOUR WISDOM!
YES...

5

*

With Volume 11, this series crosses 50 chapters! That's over five and a half years! When I started, I had no idea I would get to keep going for this long, so I'm really happy. I hardly know how to express my thanks to Arikawa Sensei, the readers, the *LaLa* editorial department, my assistants and my friends.

This volume completes the content of the third novel, *Crisis*. In the next volume we enter Book 4, *Revolution*. I'm so happy! I'm going to keep giving this all I've got!

*

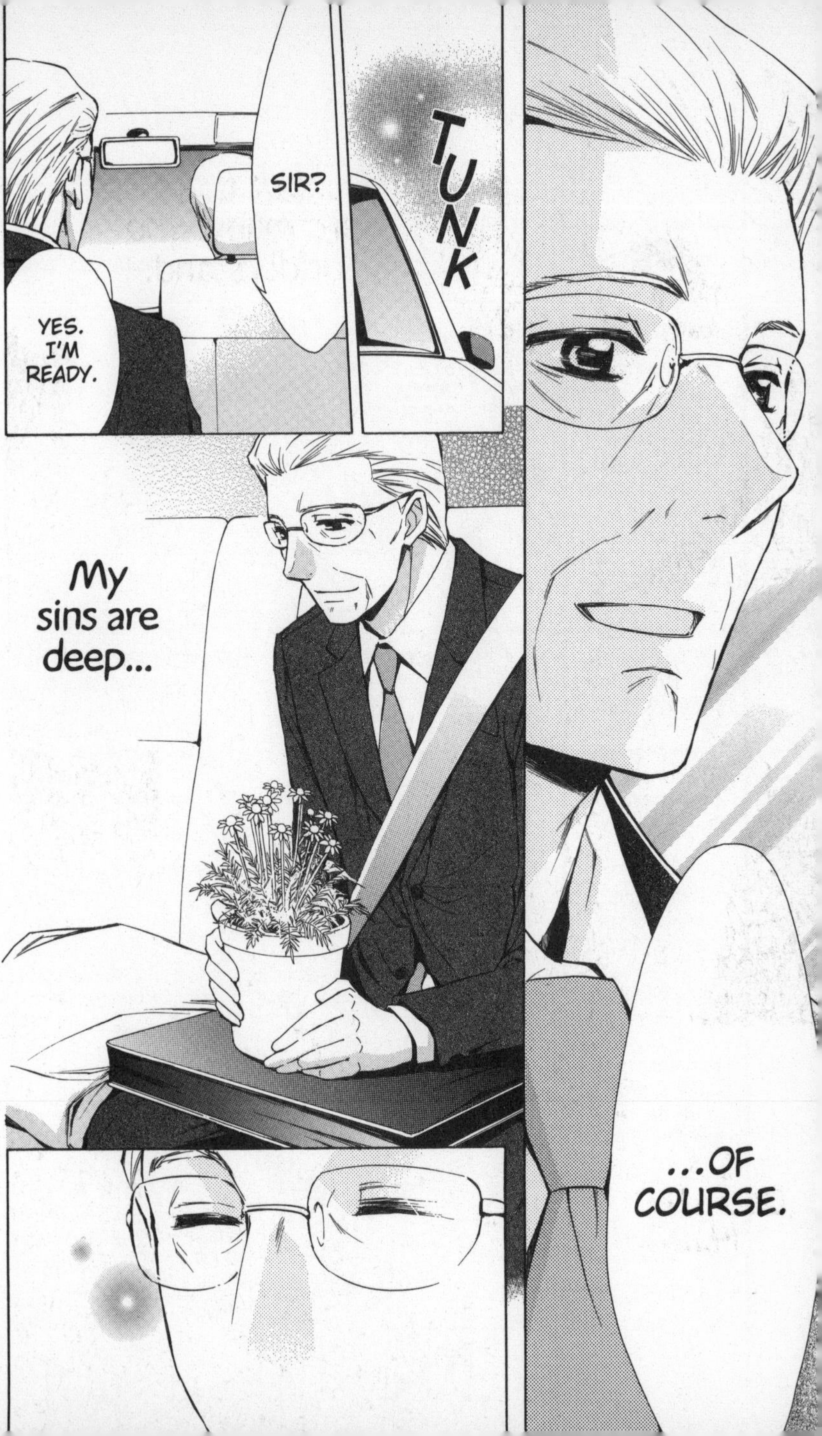
SIR?
TUNK
YES. I'M READY.
My sins are deep...
...OF COURSE.

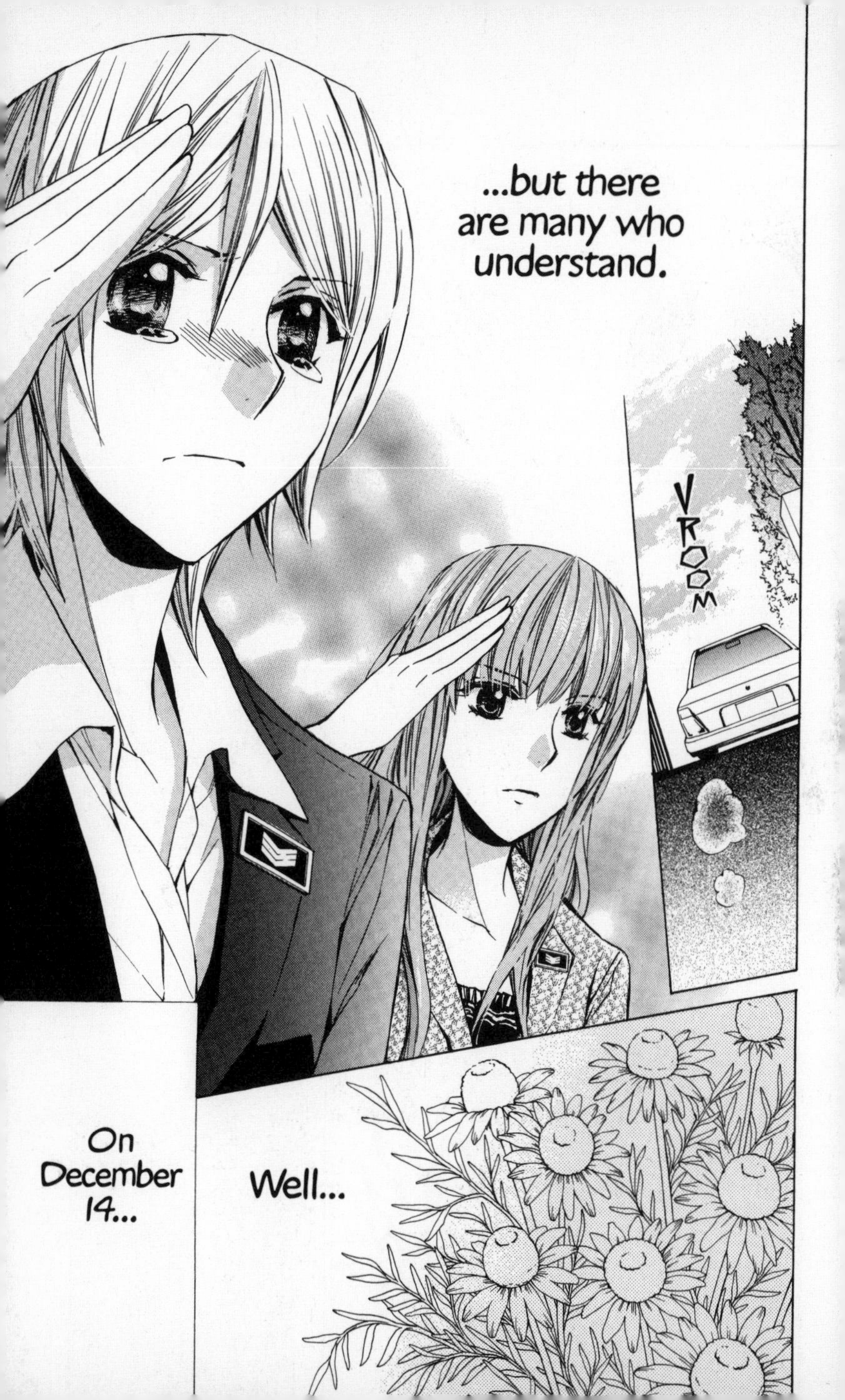
...but there are many who understand.
VROOM
Well...
On December 14...

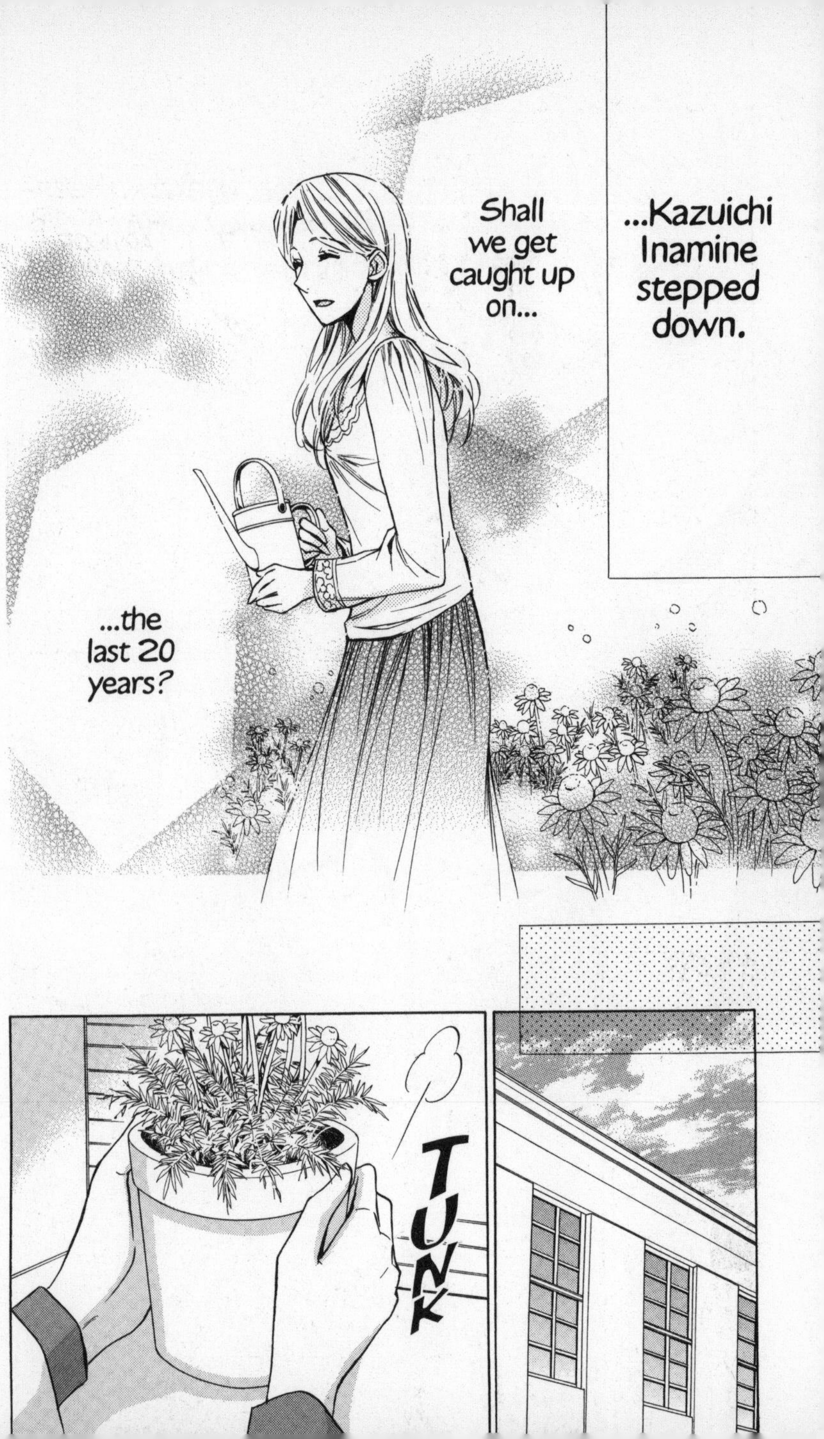
...Kazuichi Inamine stepped down.
Shall we get caught up on...
...the last 20 years?
TUNK

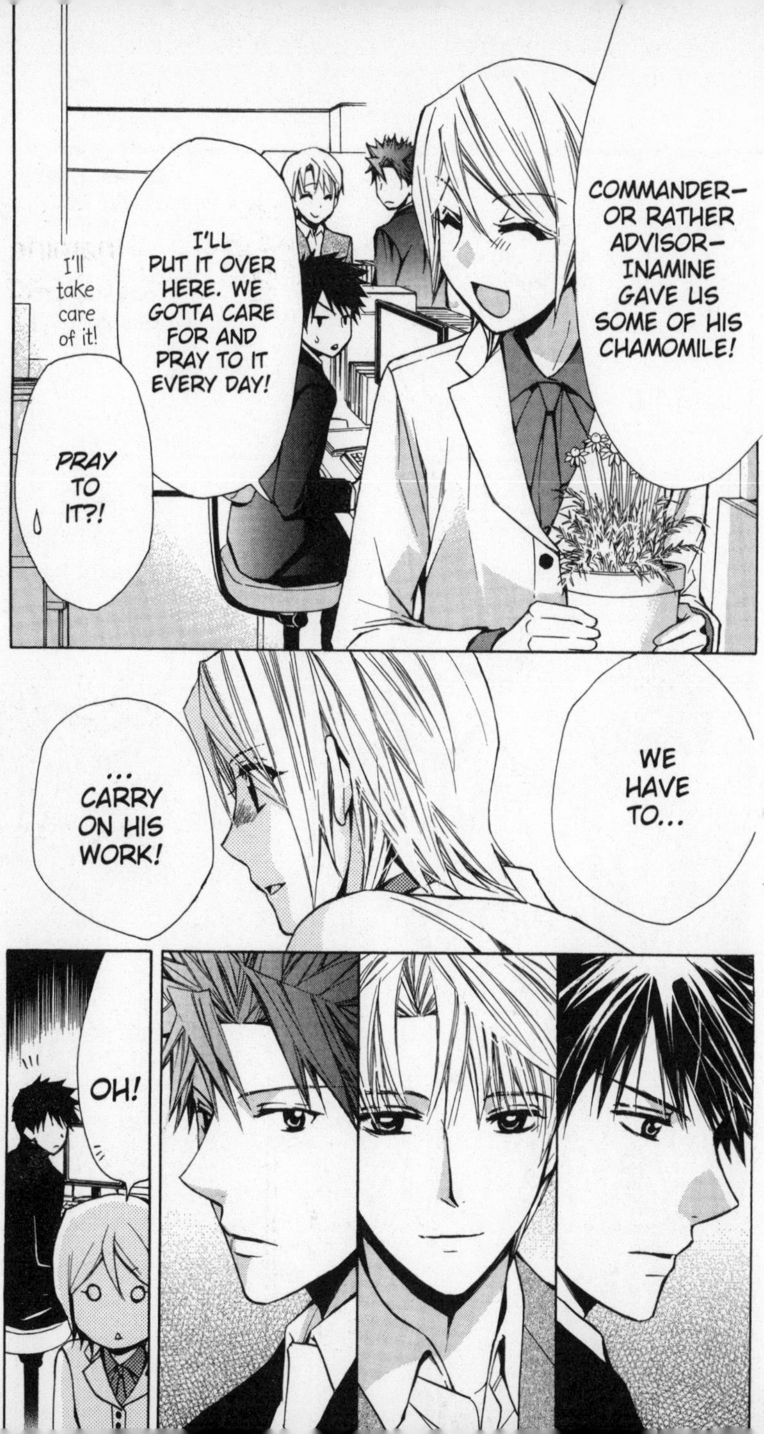
COMMANDER—OR RATHER ADVISOR—INAMINE GAVE US SOME OF HIS CHAMOMILE!
I'LL PUT IT OVER HERE. WE GOTTA CARE FOR AND PRAY TO IT EVERY DAY!
I'll take care of it!
PRAY TO IT?!
WE HAVE TO...
...CARRY ON HIS WORK!
OH!

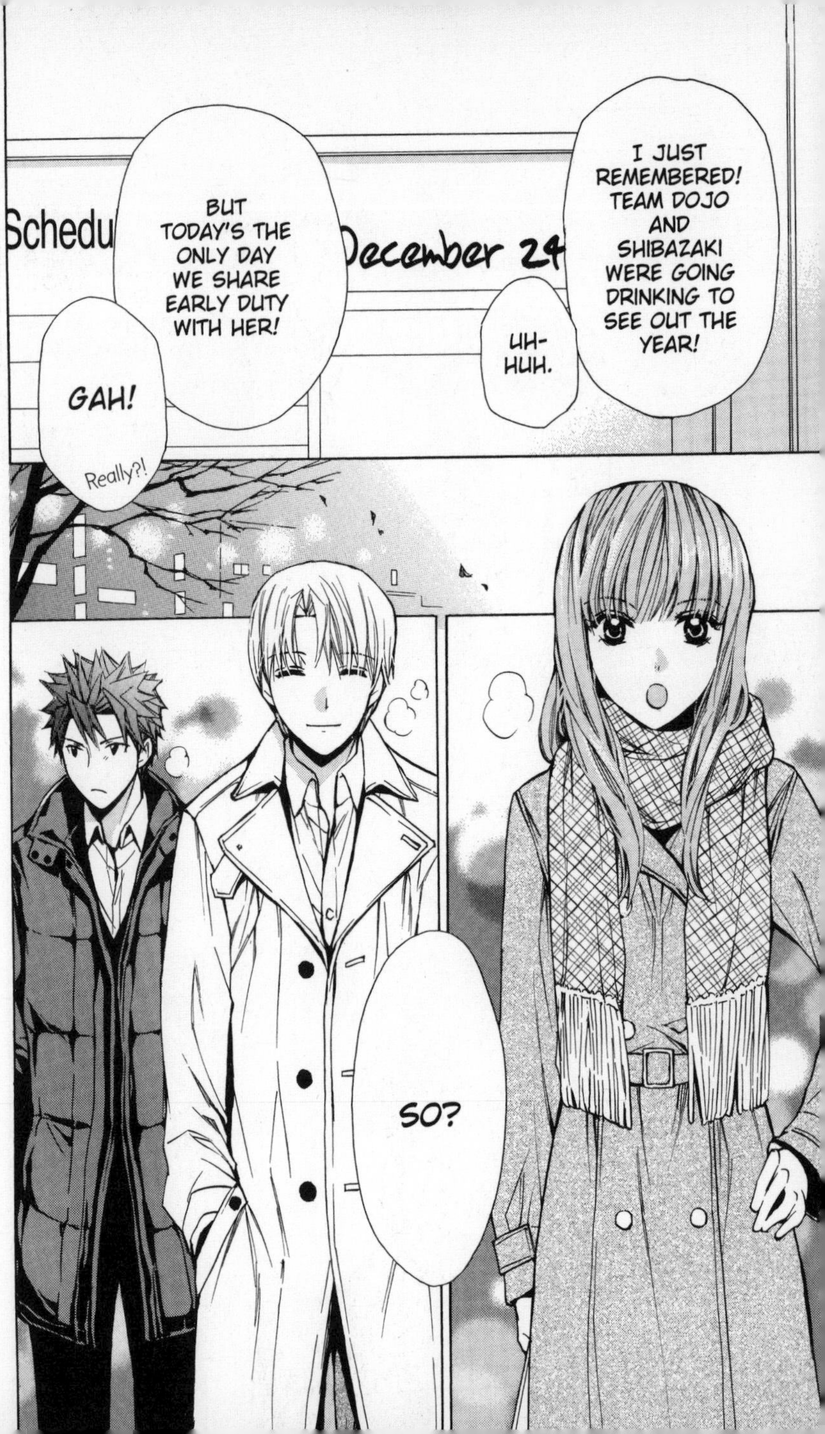
I JUST REMEMBERED! TEAM DOJO AND SHIBAZAKI WERE GOING DRINKING TO SEE OUT THE YEAR!
UH-HUH.
December 24
BUT TODAY'S THE ONLY DAY WE SHARE EARLY DUTY WITH HER!
Schedu
GAH!
Really?!
SO?

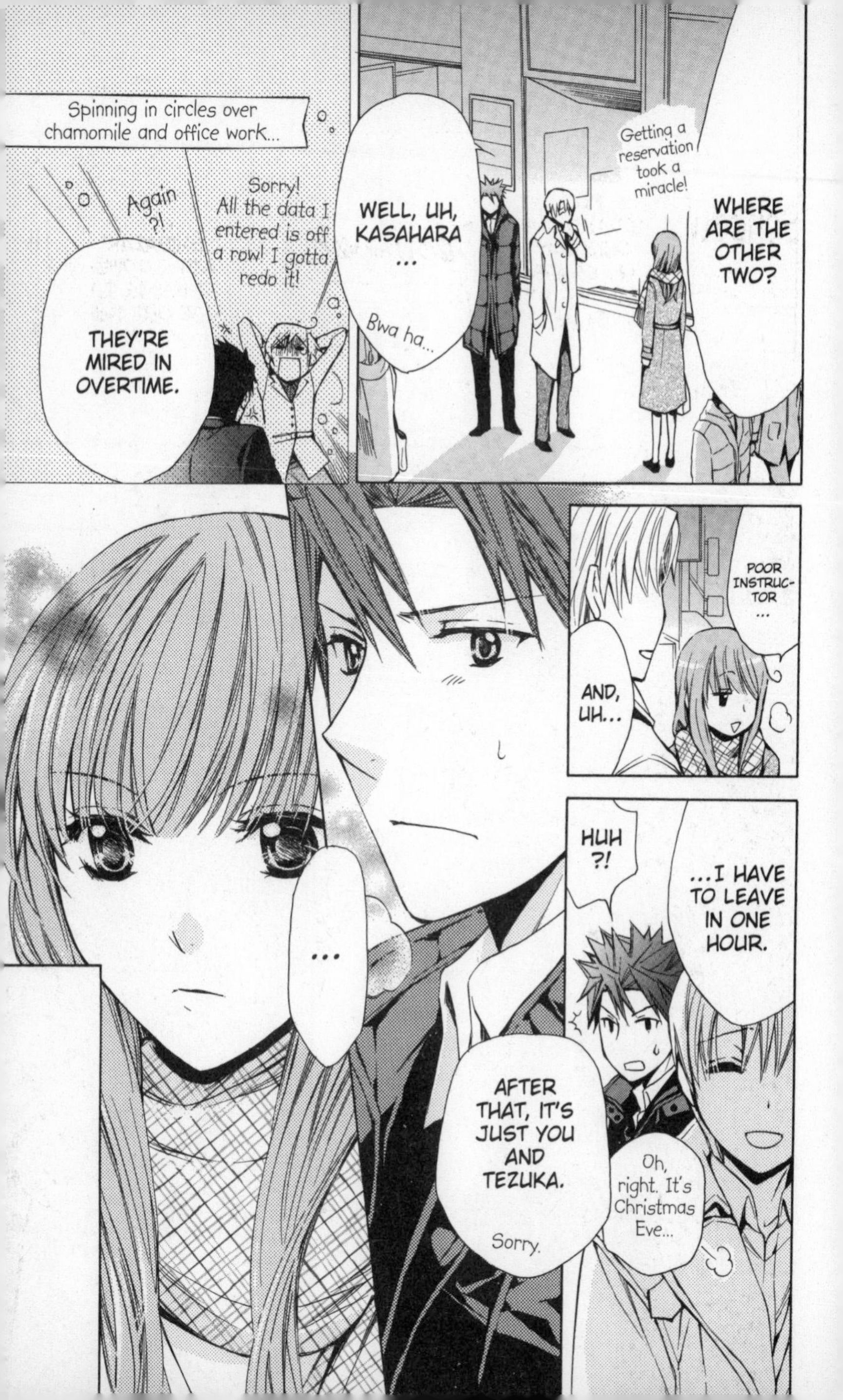

WHERE ARE THE OTHER TWO?
Getting a reservation took a miracle!
WELL, UH, KASAHARA ...
Bwa ha...
Spinning in circles over chamomile and office work...
Sorry! All the data I entered is off a row! I gotta redo it!
Again ?!
THEY'RE MIRED IN OVERTIME.
POOR INSTRUCTOR ...
AND, UH...
...I HAVE TO LEAVE IN ONE HOUR.
HUH ?!
Oh, right. It's Christmas Eve...
AFTER THAT, IT'S JUST YOU AND TEZUKA.
Sorry.
...

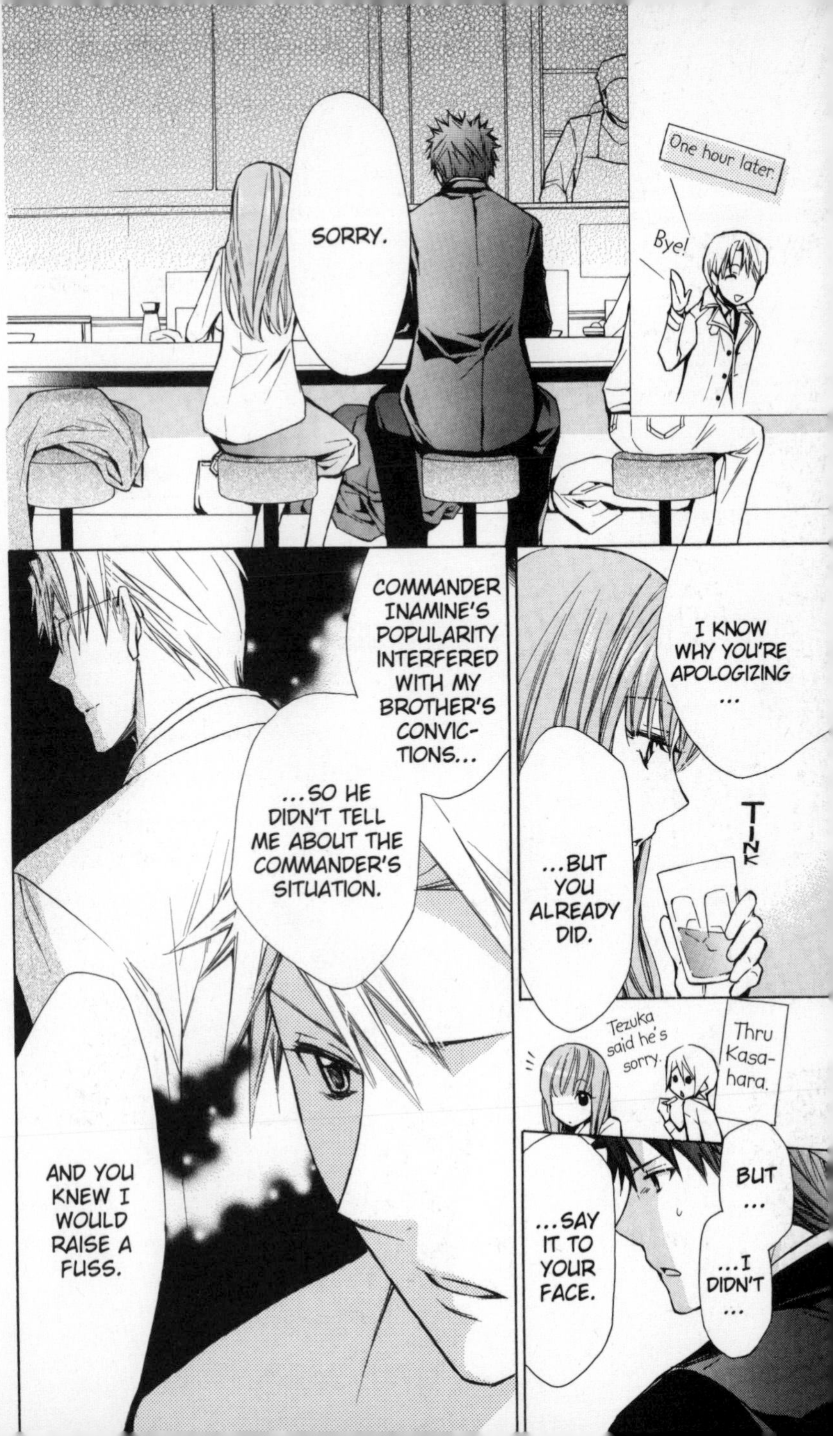
One hour later.
Bye!
SORRY.
I KNOW WHY YOU'RE APOLOGIZING ...
...BUT YOU ALREADY DID.
TINK
Thru Kasahara.
Tezuka said he's sorry.
BUT ...
...I DIDN'T ...
...SAY IT TO YOUR FACE.
COMMANDER INAMINE'S POPULARITY INTERFERED WITH MY BROTHER'S CONVICTIONS...
...SO HE DIDN'T TELL ME ABOUT THE COMMANDER'S SITUATION.
AND YOU KNEW I WOULD RAISE A FUSS.

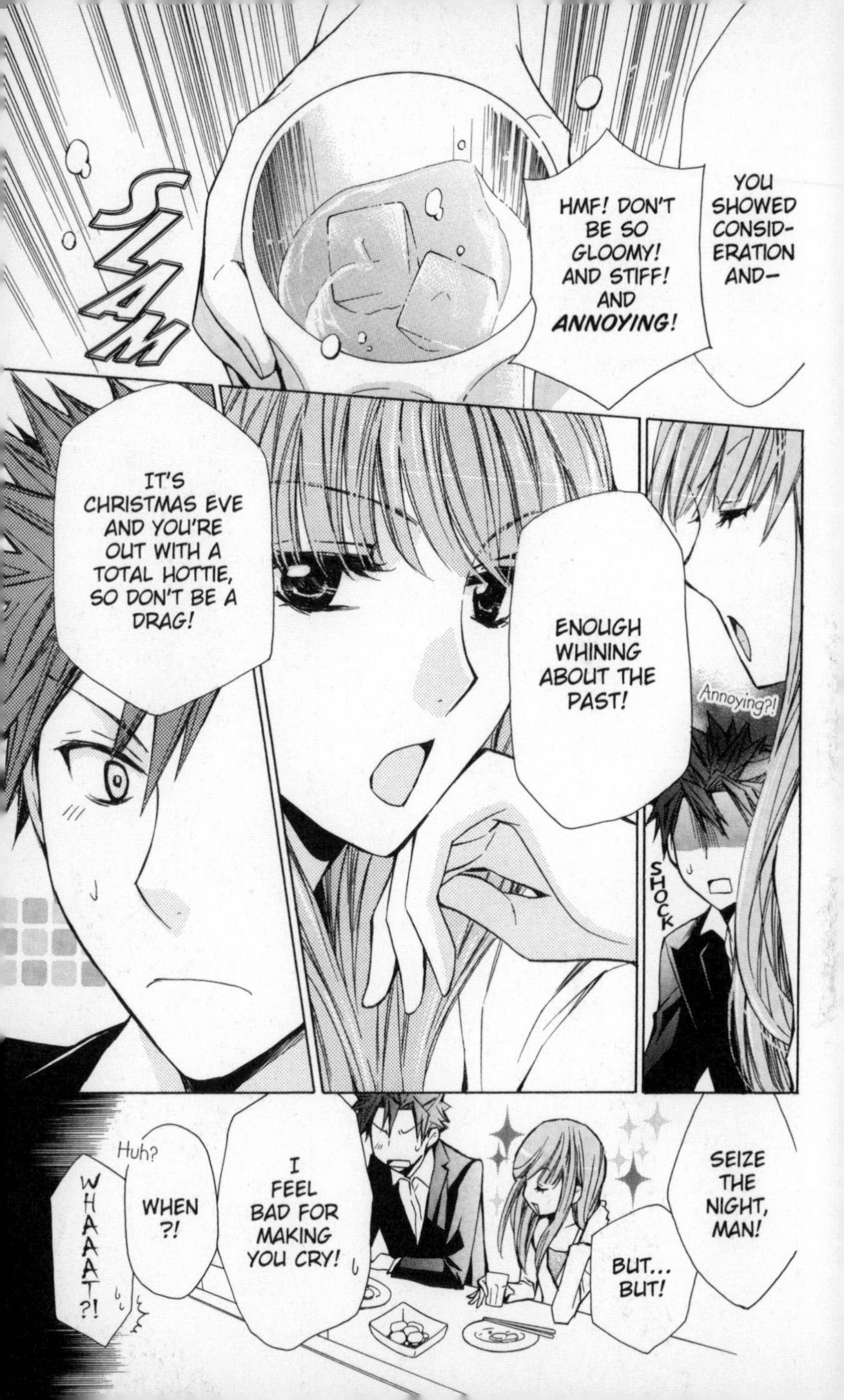
YOU SHOWED CONSID- ERATION AND—
HMF! DON'T BE SO GLOOMY! AND STIFF! AND ANNOYING!
SLAM
Annoying?!
SHOCK
ENOUGH WHINING ABOUT THE PAST!
IT'S CHRISTMAS EVE AND YOU'RE OUT WITH A TOTAL HOTTIE, SO DON'T BE A DRAG!
SEIZE THE NIGHT, MAN!
BUT... BUT!
I FEEL BAD FOR MAKING YOU CRY!
WHEN ?!
Huh?
WHAAAAT ?!

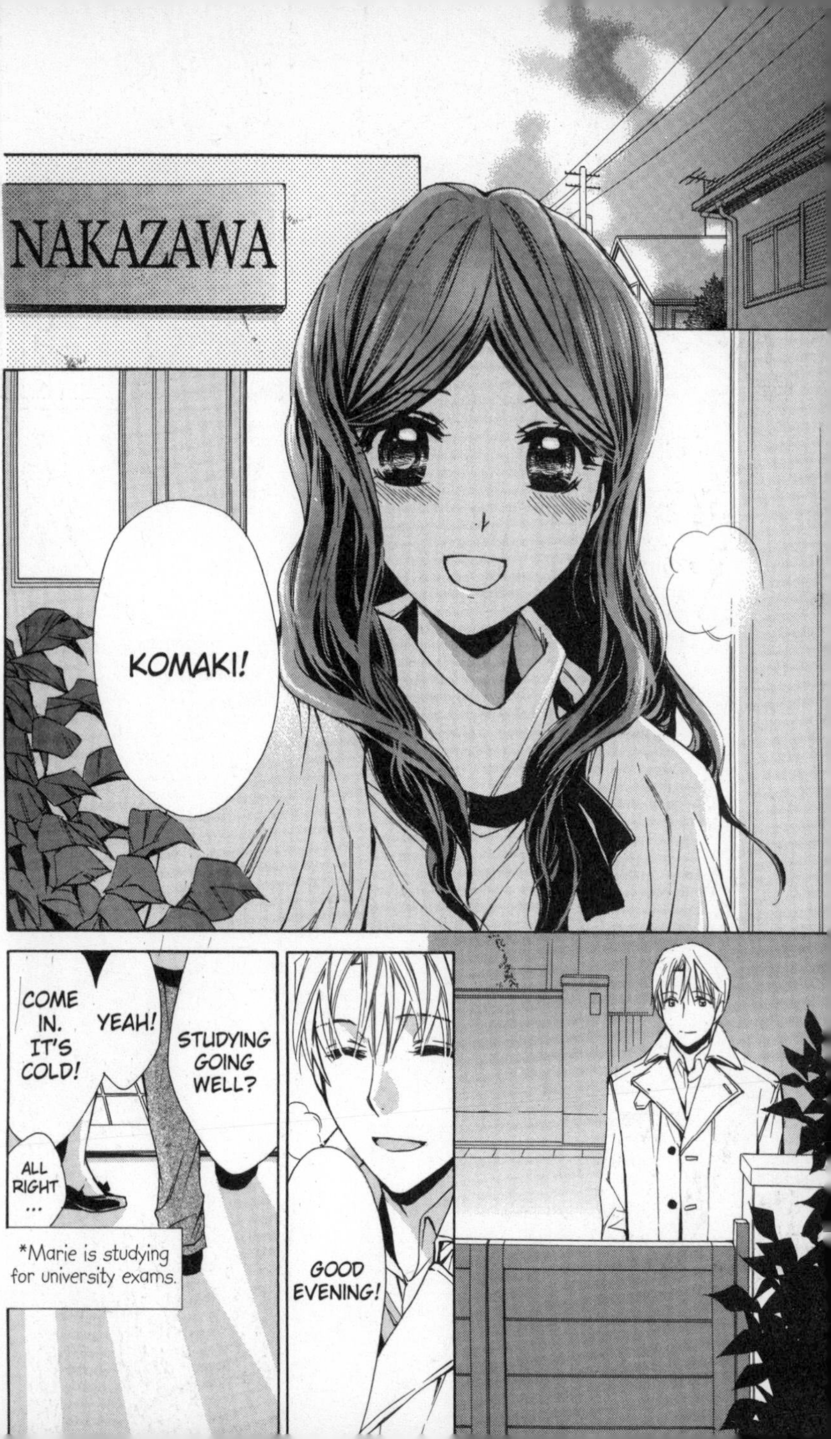
NAKAZAWA
KOMAKI!
GOOD EVENING!
STUDYING GOING WELL?
YEAH!
COME IN. IT'S COLD!
ALL RIGHT ...
*Marie is studying for university exams.

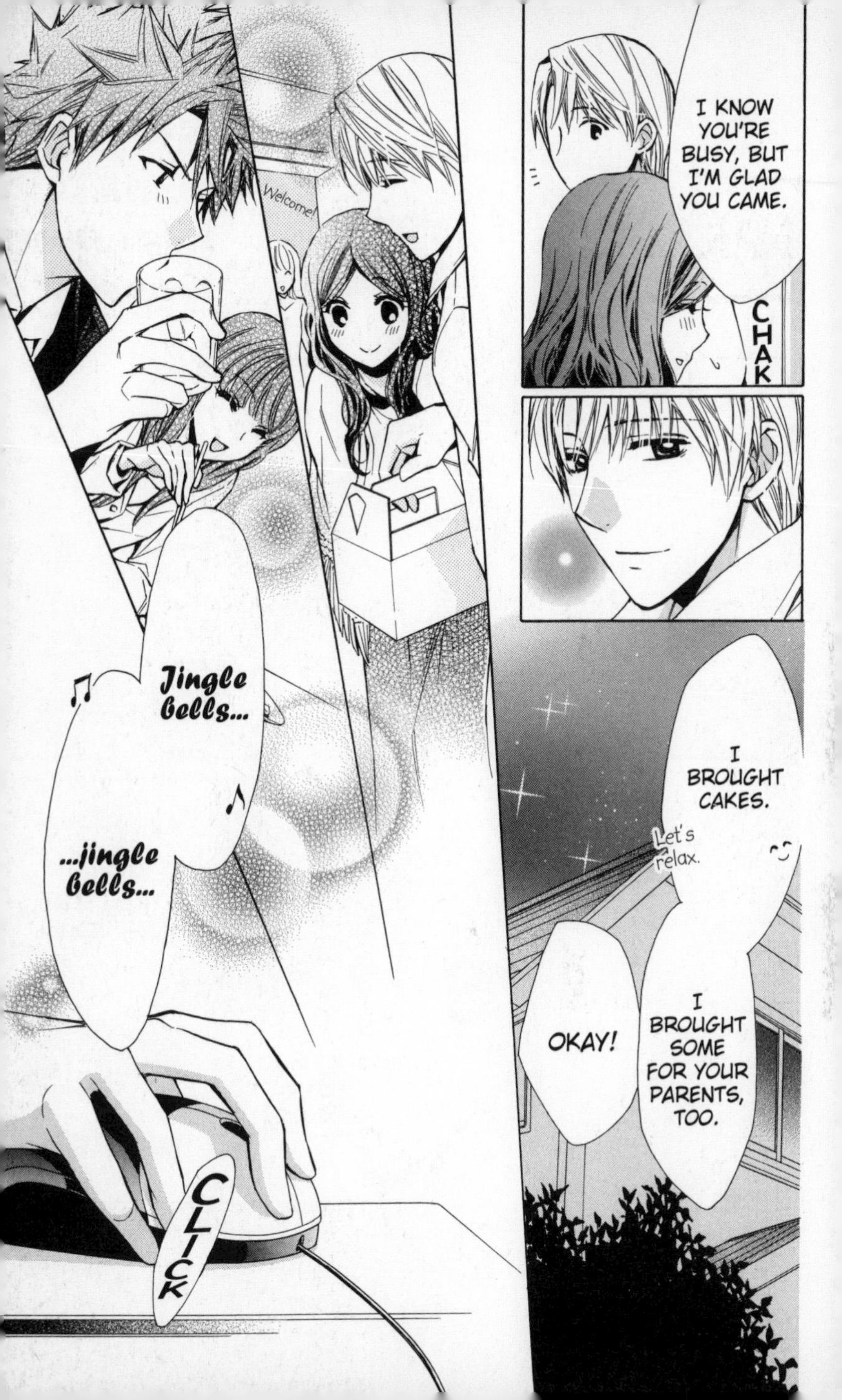
I KNOW YOU'RE BUSY, BUT I'M GLAD YOU CAME.
CHAK
I BROUGHT CAKES.
Let's relax.
I BROUGHT SOME FOR YOUR PARENTS, TOO.
OKAY!
Welcome!
Jingle bells...
...jingle bells...
CLICK

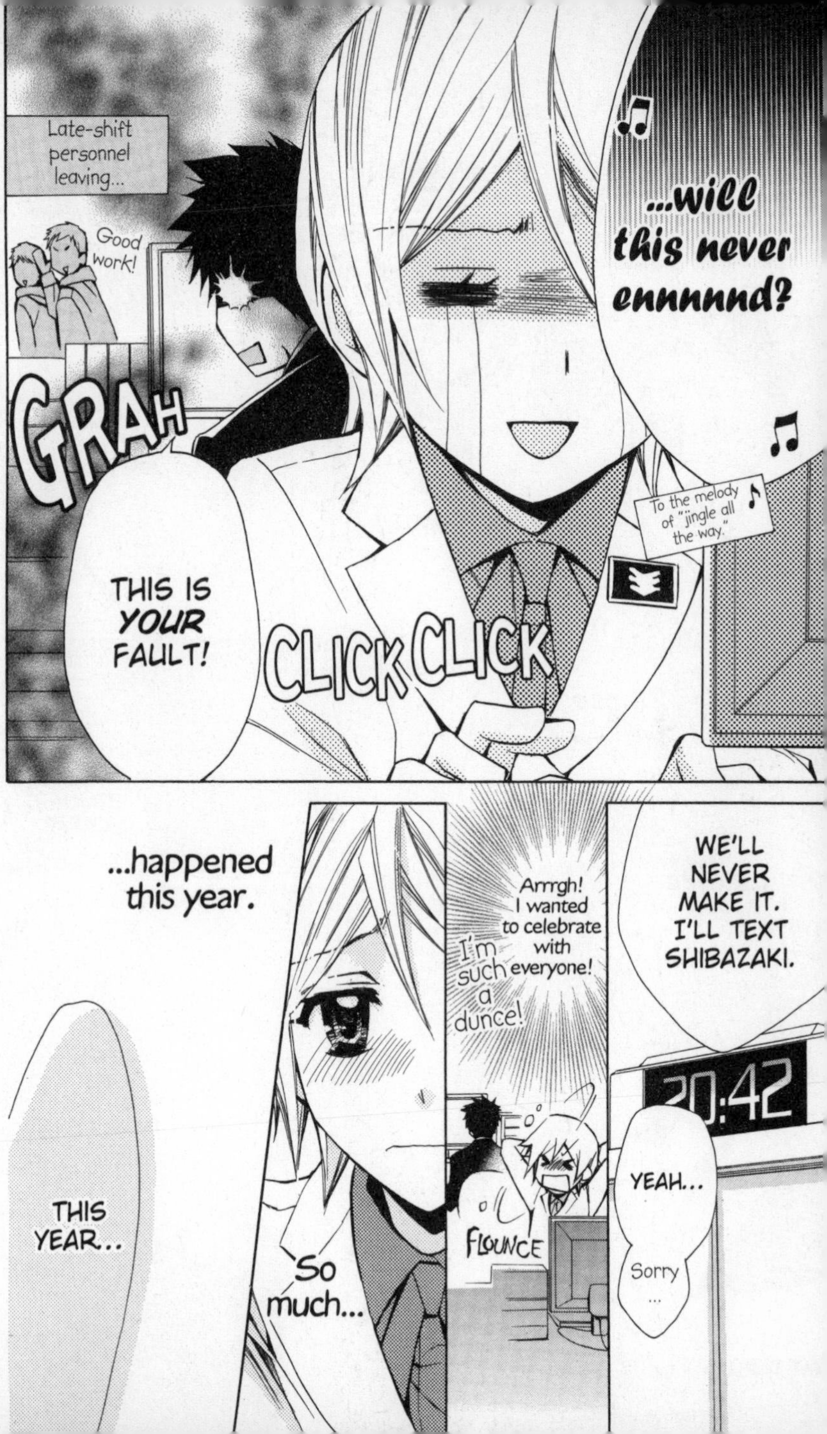
♫ ...will this never ennnnnd? ♫
To the melody of "jingle all the way." ♪
Late-shift personnel leaving...
Good work!
GRAH
CLICK CLICK
THIS IS *YOUR* FAULT!
WE'LL NEVER MAKE IT. I'LL TEXT SHIBAZAKI.
20:42
YEAH...
Sorry...
Arrrgh! I wanted to celebrate with everyone!
I'm such a dunce!
FLOUNCE
So much...
...happened this year.
THIS YEAR...

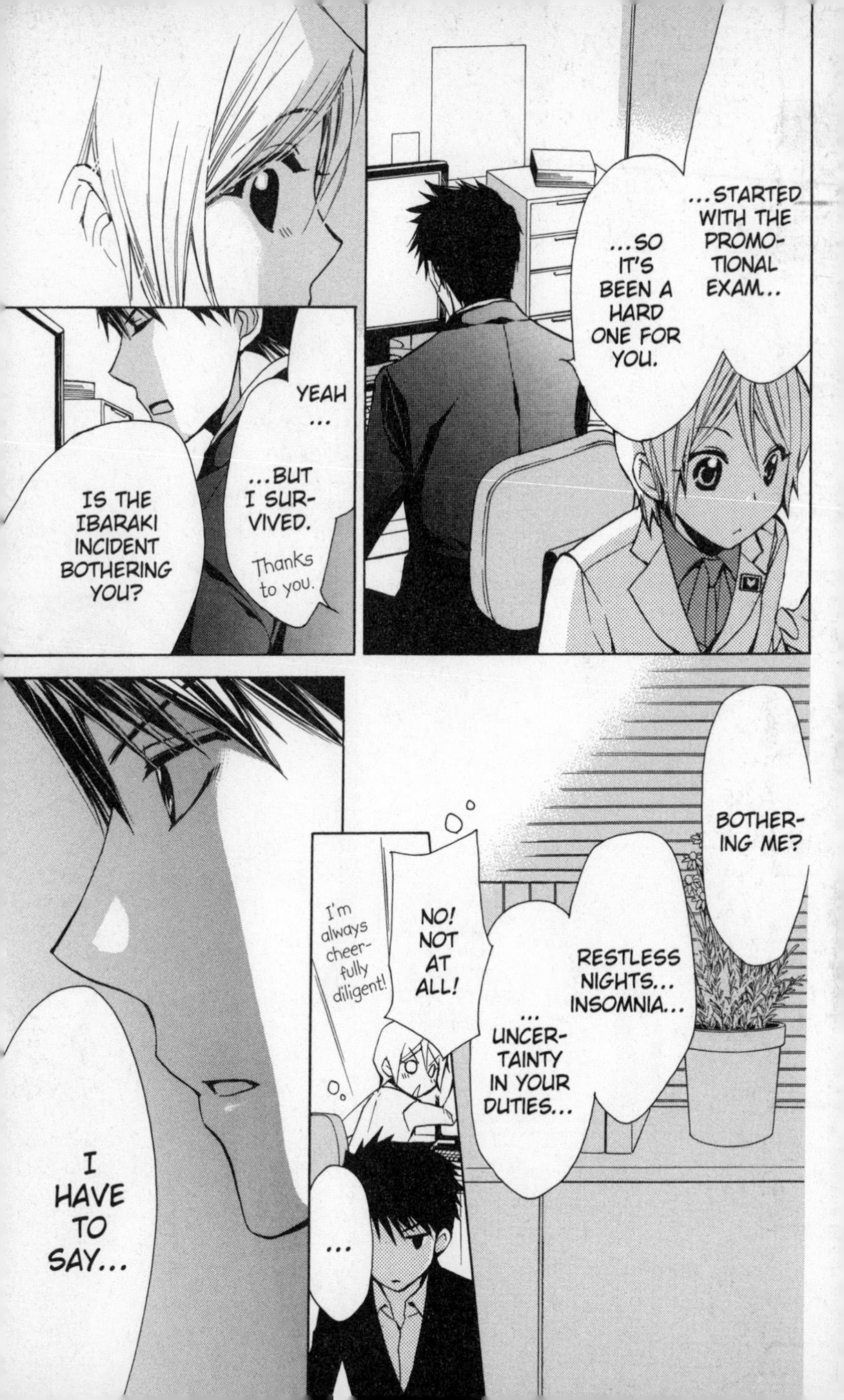
...STARTED WITH THE PROMOTIONAL EXAM...
...SO IT'S BEEN A HARD ONE FOR YOU.
YEAH ... ...BUT I SURVIVED.
Thanks to you.
IS THE IBARAKI INCIDENT BOTHERING YOU?
BOTHERING ME?
RESTLESS NIGHTS... INSOMNIA...
... UNCERTAINTY IN YOUR DUTIES...
NO! NOT AT ALL!
I'm always cheerfully diligent!
...
I HAVE TO SAY...

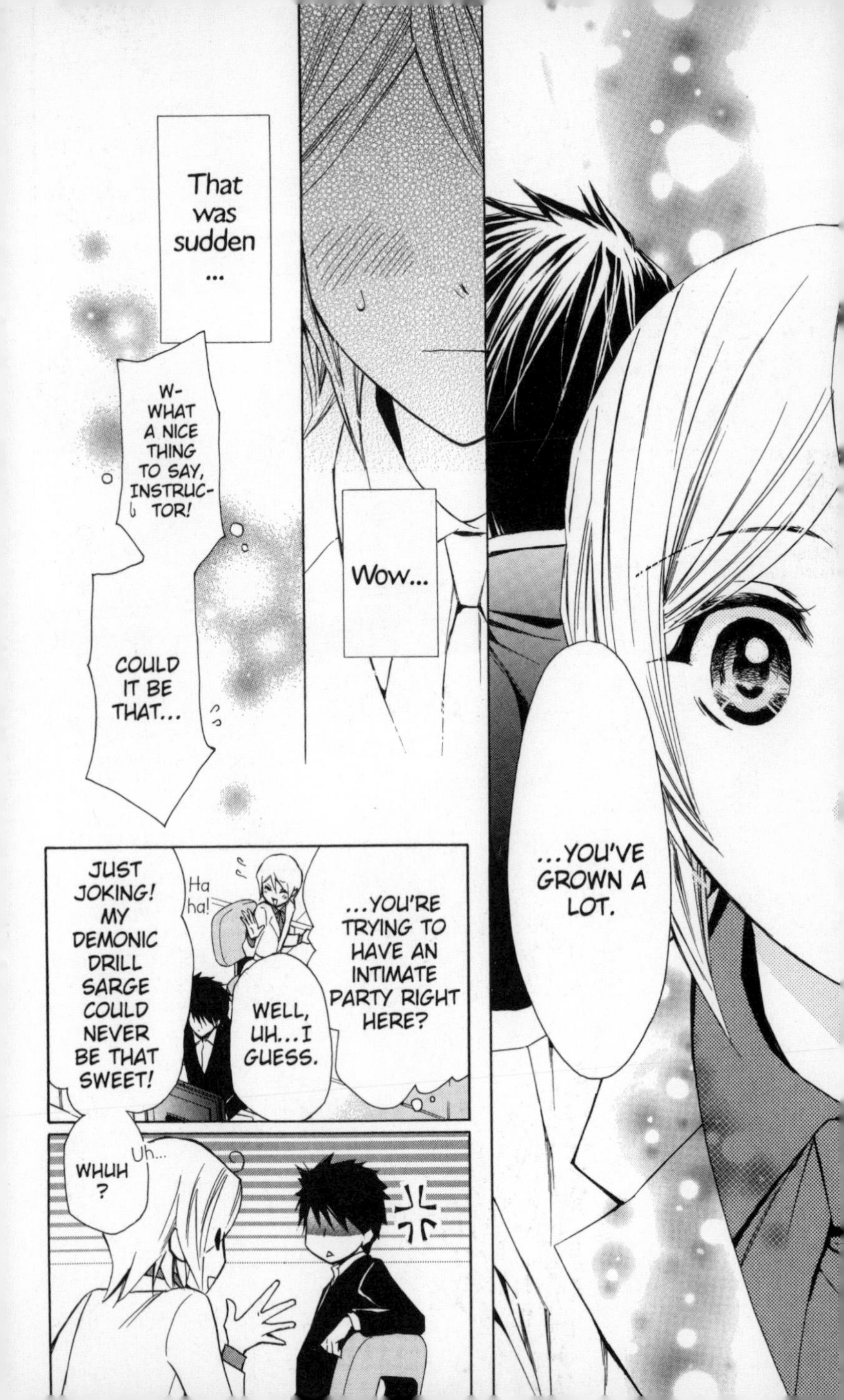
...YOU'VE GROWN A LOT.
Wow...
That was sudden...
W-WHAT A NICE THING TO SAY, INSTRUCTOR!
COULD IT BE THAT...
...YOU'RE TRYING TO HAVE AN INTIMATE PARTY RIGHT HERE?
WELL, UH...I GUESS.
Ha ha!
JUST JOKING! MY DEMONIC DRILL SARGE COULD NEVER BE THAT SWEET!
Uh...
WHUH?

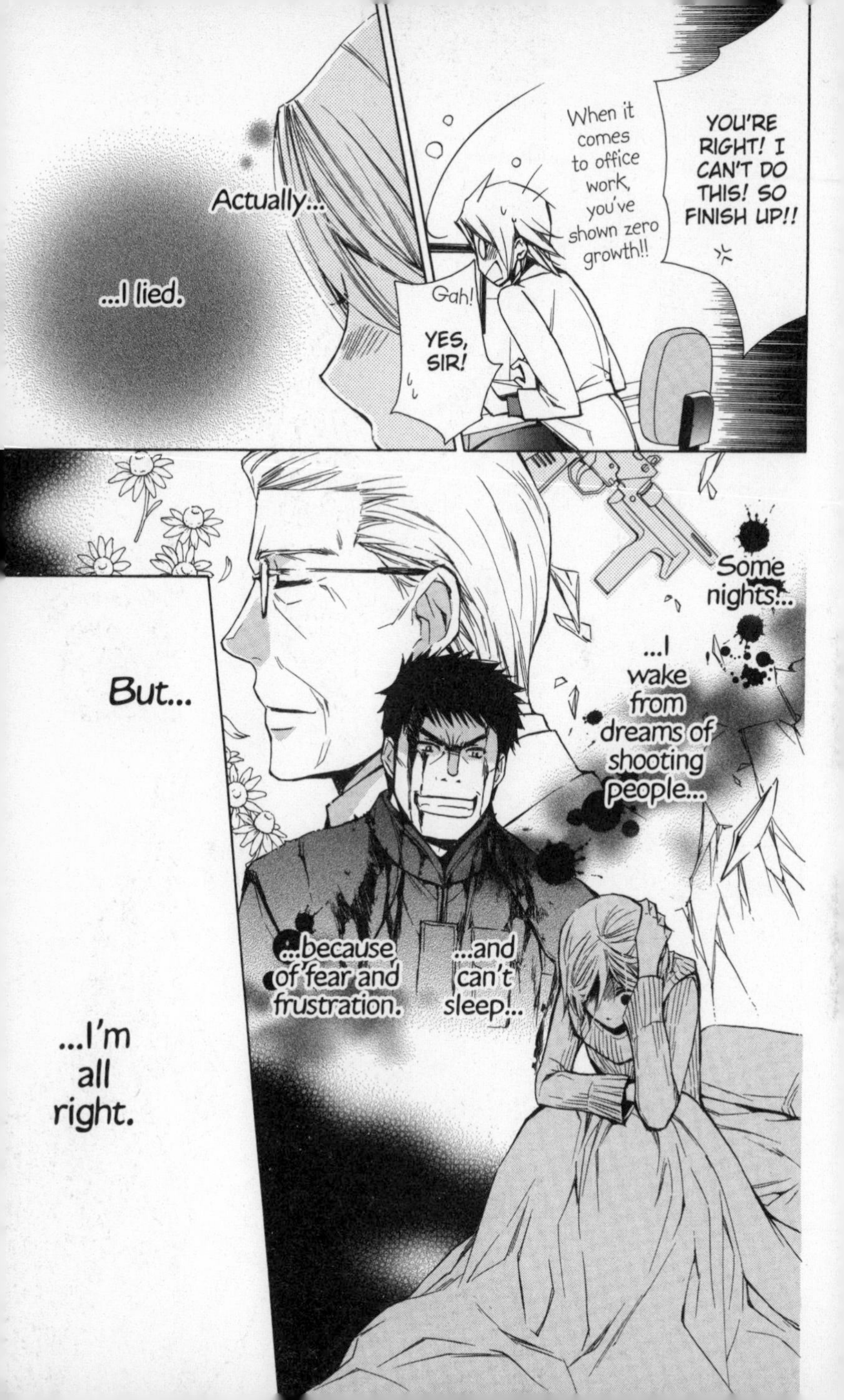
YOU'RE RIGHT! I CAN'T DO THIS! SO FINISH UP!!
When it comes to office work, you've shown zero growth!!
Gah!
YES, SIR!
Actually...
...I lied.
Some nights...
...I wake from dreams of shooting people...
...and can't sleep...
...because of fear and frustration.
But...
...I'm all right.

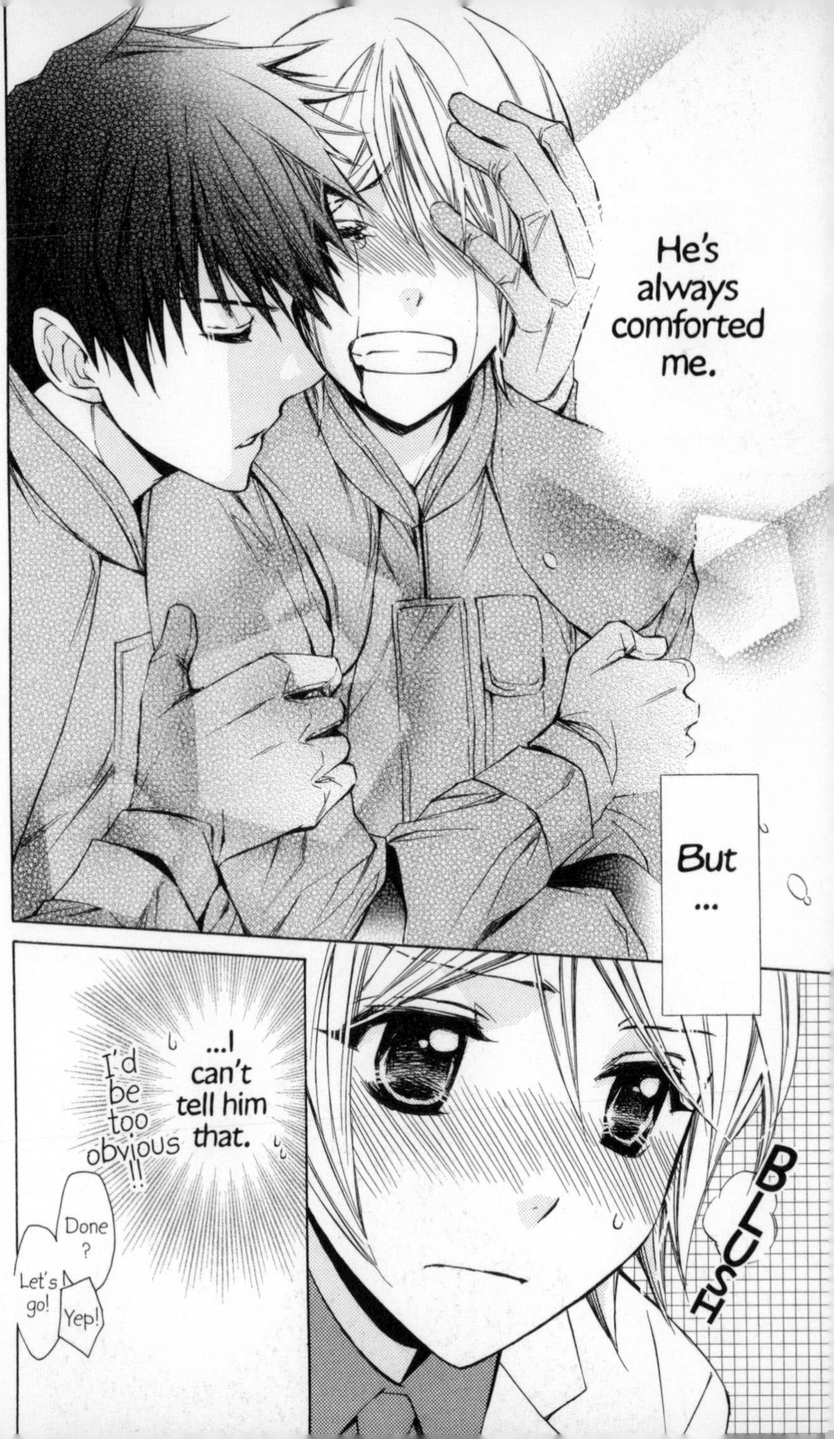
He's always comforted me.
But ...
...I can't tell him that.
I'd be too obvious!!
BLUSH
Done?
Yep!
Let's go!

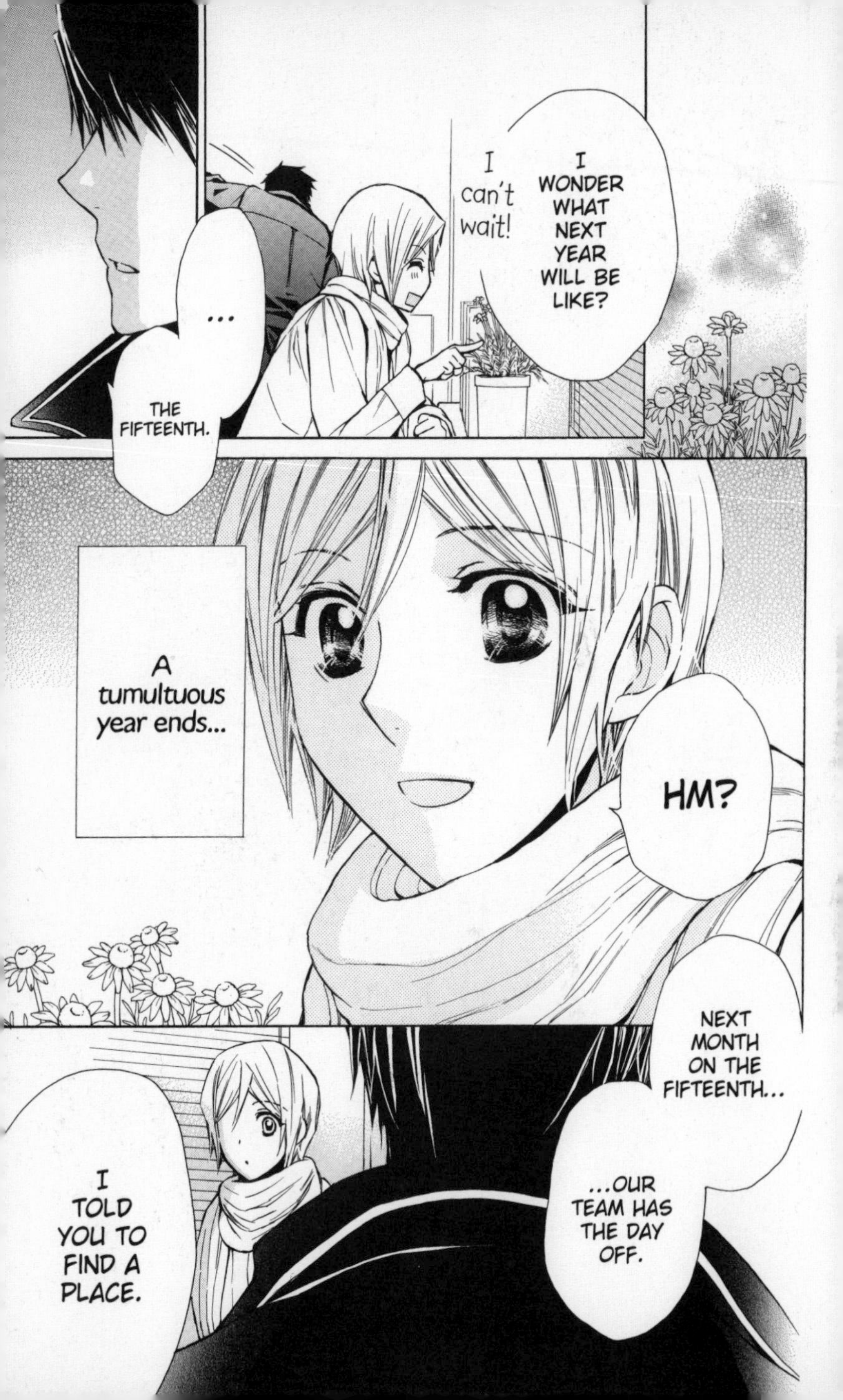
I WONDER WHAT NEXT YEAR WILL BE LIKE?
I can't wait!
...
THE FIFTEENTH.
HM?
A tumultuous year ends...
NEXT MONTH ON THE FIFTEENTH...
...OUR TEAM HAS THE DAY OFF.
I TOLD YOU TO FIND A PLACE.

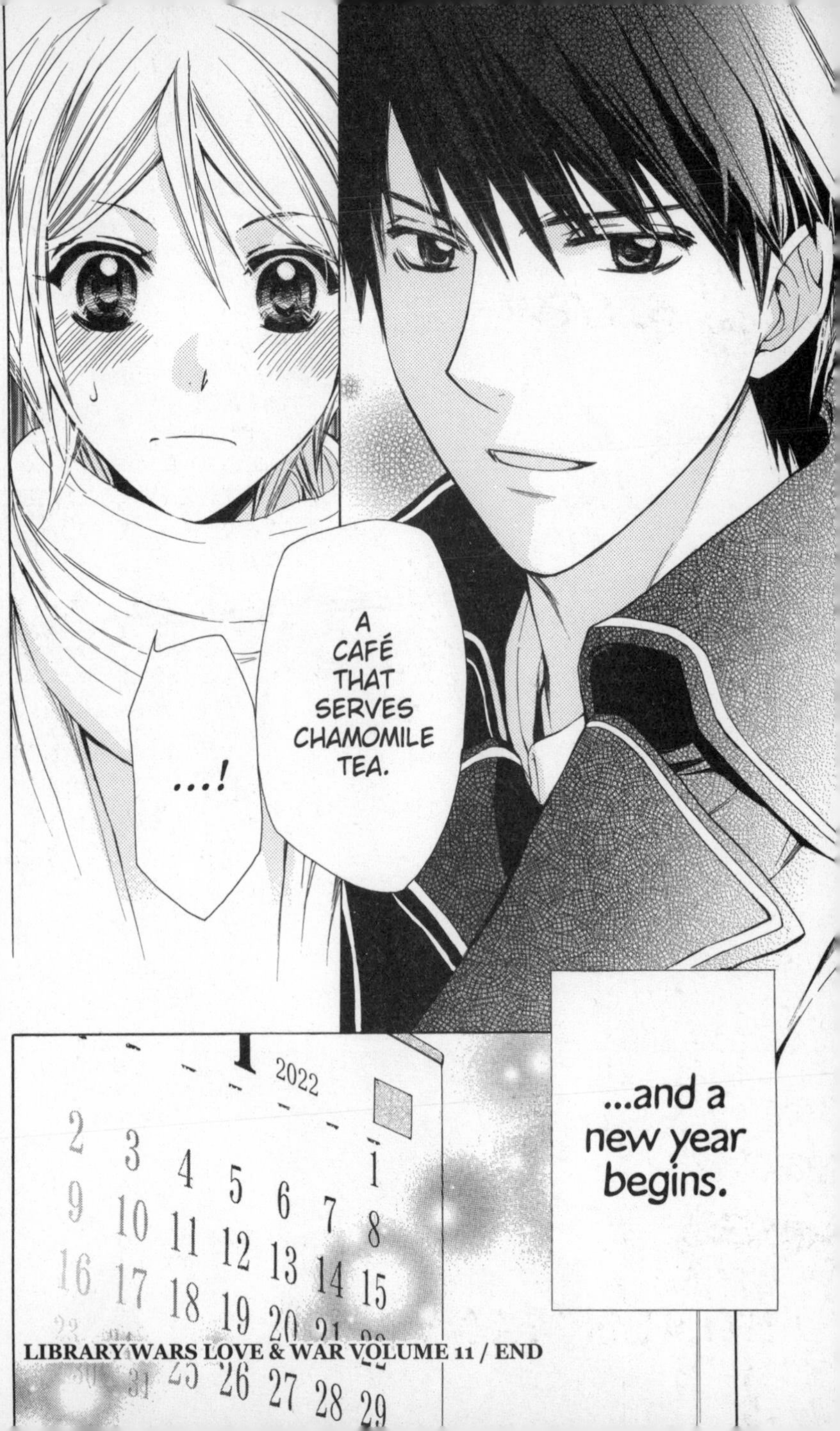
A CAFÉ THAT SERVES CHAMOMILE TEA.
...!
...and a new year begins.
LIBRARY WARS LOVE & WAR VOLUME 11 / END

BONUS MANGA

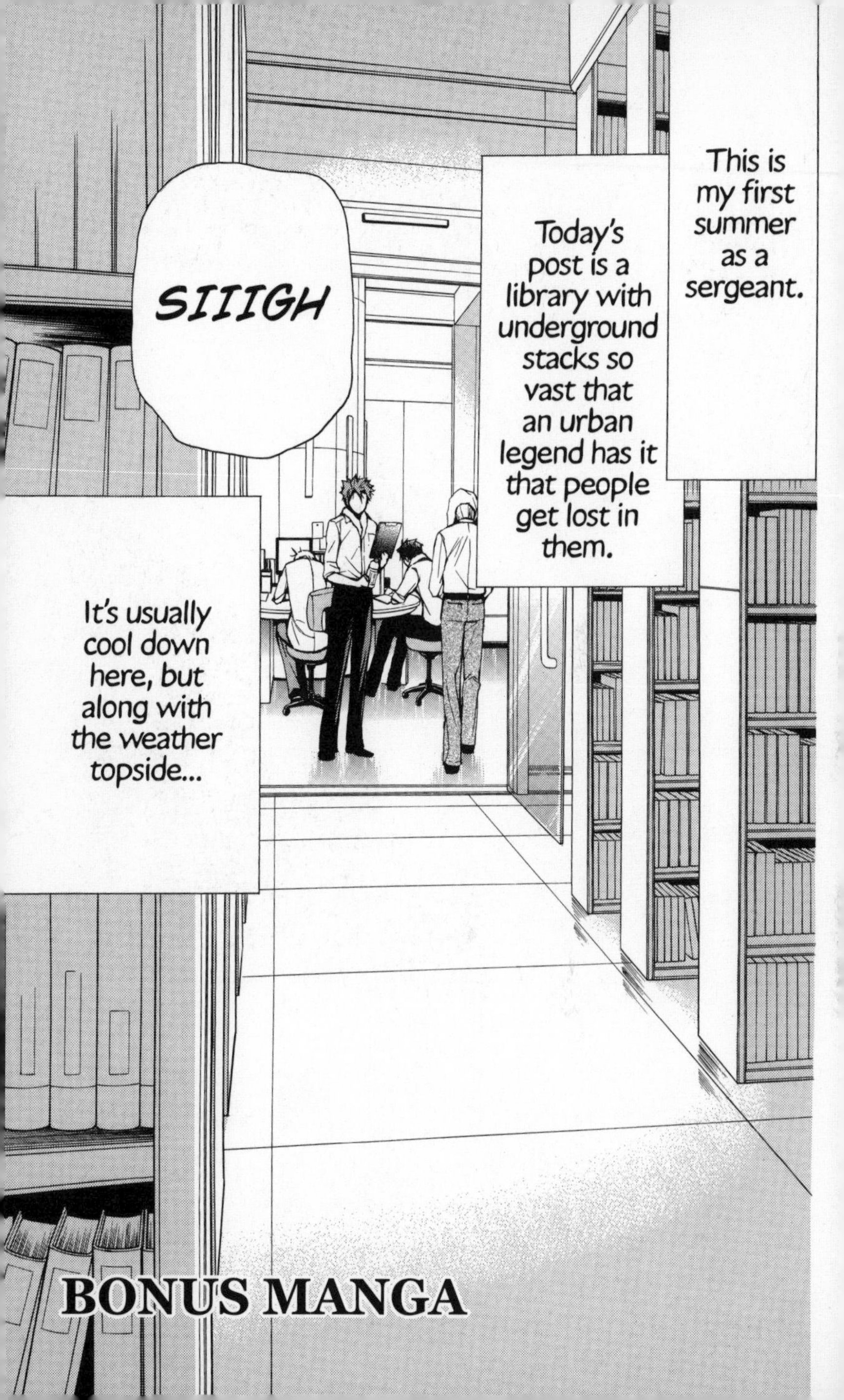
This is my first summer as a sergeant.
Today's post is a library with underground stacks so vast that an urban legend has it that people get lost in them.
SIIIGH
It's usually cool down here, but along with the weather topside...

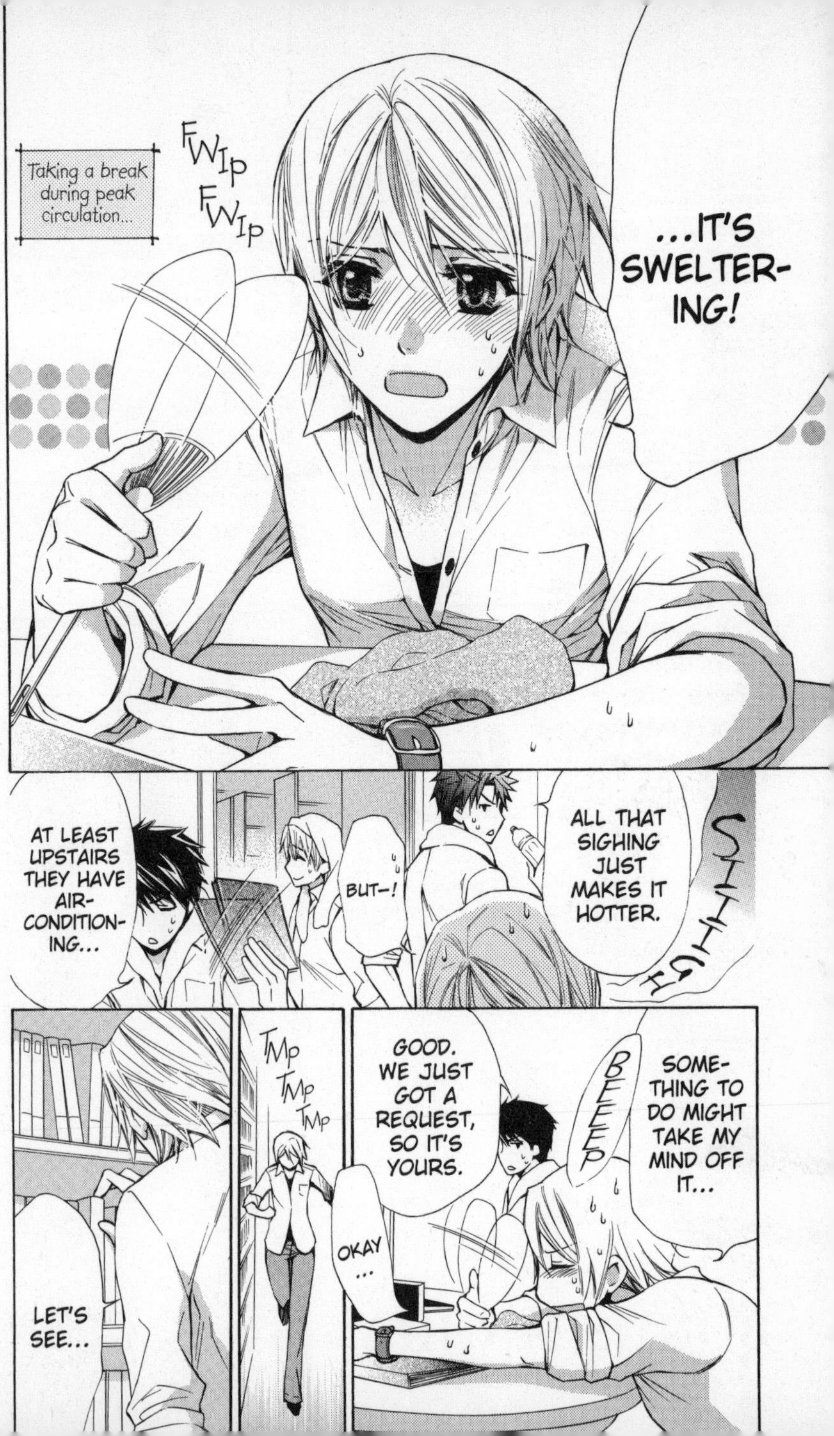

Taking a break during peak circulation...
FWIP FWIP
...IT'S SWELTER-ING!
SIIIGH
ALL THAT SIGHING JUST MAKES IT HOTTER.
BUT-!
AT LEAST UPSTAIRS THEY HAVE AIR-CONDITION-ING...
SOME-THING TO DO MIGHT TAKE MY MIND OFF IT...
BEEEP
GOOD. WE JUST GOT A REQUEST, SO IT'S YOURS.
OKAY ...
TMP TMP TMP
LET'S SEE...

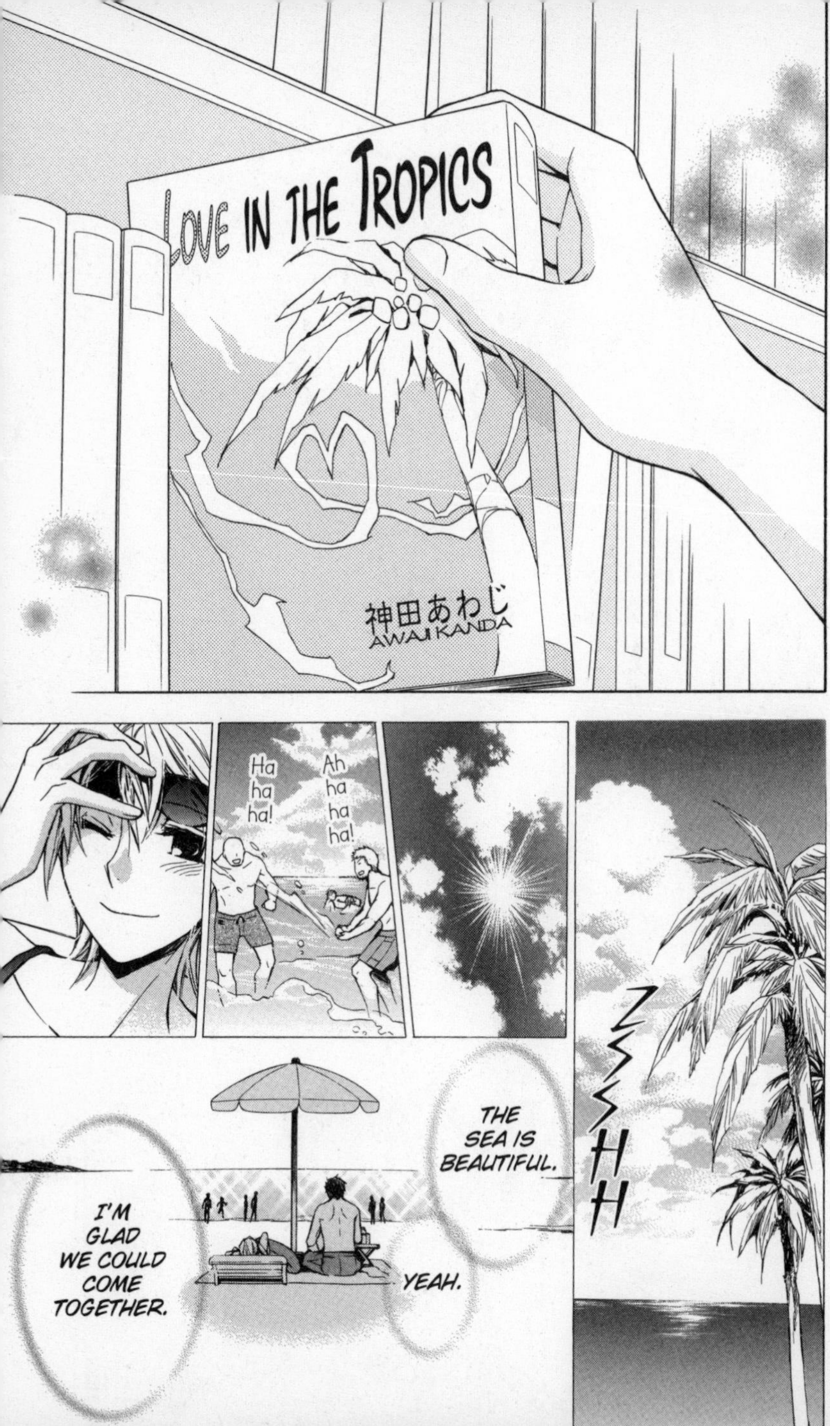

LOVE IN THE TROPICS
神田あわじ
AWAJI KANDA
ZSSHH
Ah ha ha ha!
Ha ha ha!
THE SEA IS BEAUTIFUL.
I'M GLAD WE COULD COME TOGETHER.
YEAH.

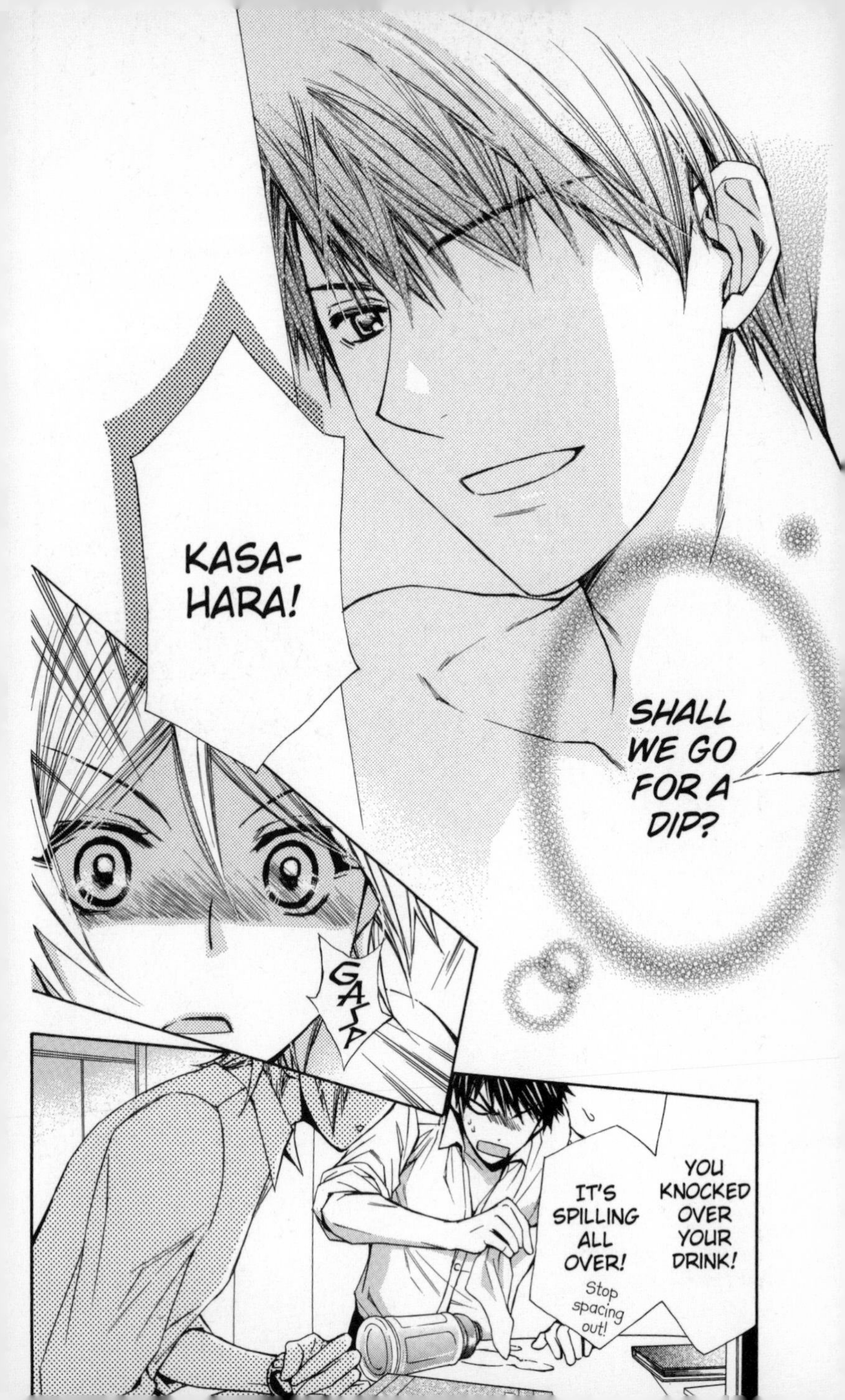
SHALL WE GO FOR A DIP?
KASA-HARA!
GASA
YOU KNOCKED OVER YOUR DRINK!
IT'S SPILLING ALL OVER!
Stop spacing out!

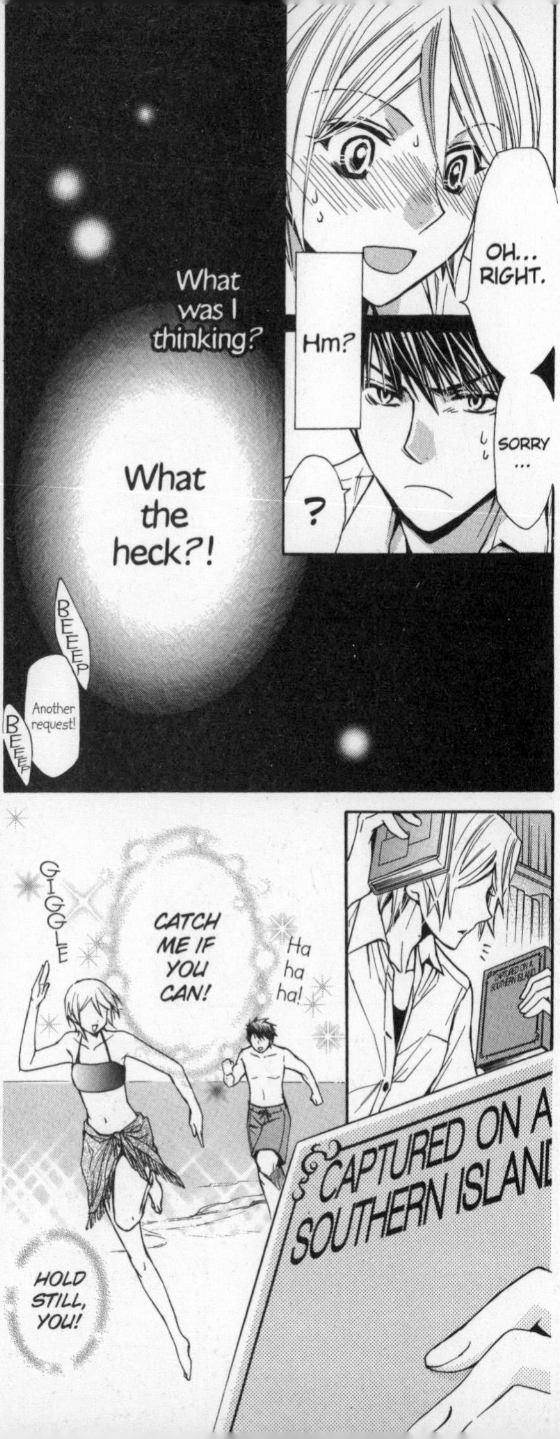
OH... RIGHT.
Hm?
SORRY...
?
What was I thinking?
What the heck?!
BEEEP
Another request!
BEEEP
CAPTURED ON A SOUTHERN ISLAND
CAPTURED ON A SOUTHERN ISLAND
GIGGLE
CATCH ME IF YOU CAN!
Ha ha ha!
HOLD STILL, YOU!

6

*

The last sidebar! Thanks for reading all this way. This time I was able to draw some of my favorite scenes from the novel. Yahoo!

I'm aware this manga has a lot of "What the heck?!" moments, but I hope you'll be kind enough to stick with me come what may. Bye!

Special thanks are at the back of the book.

Kiiro Yumi

*

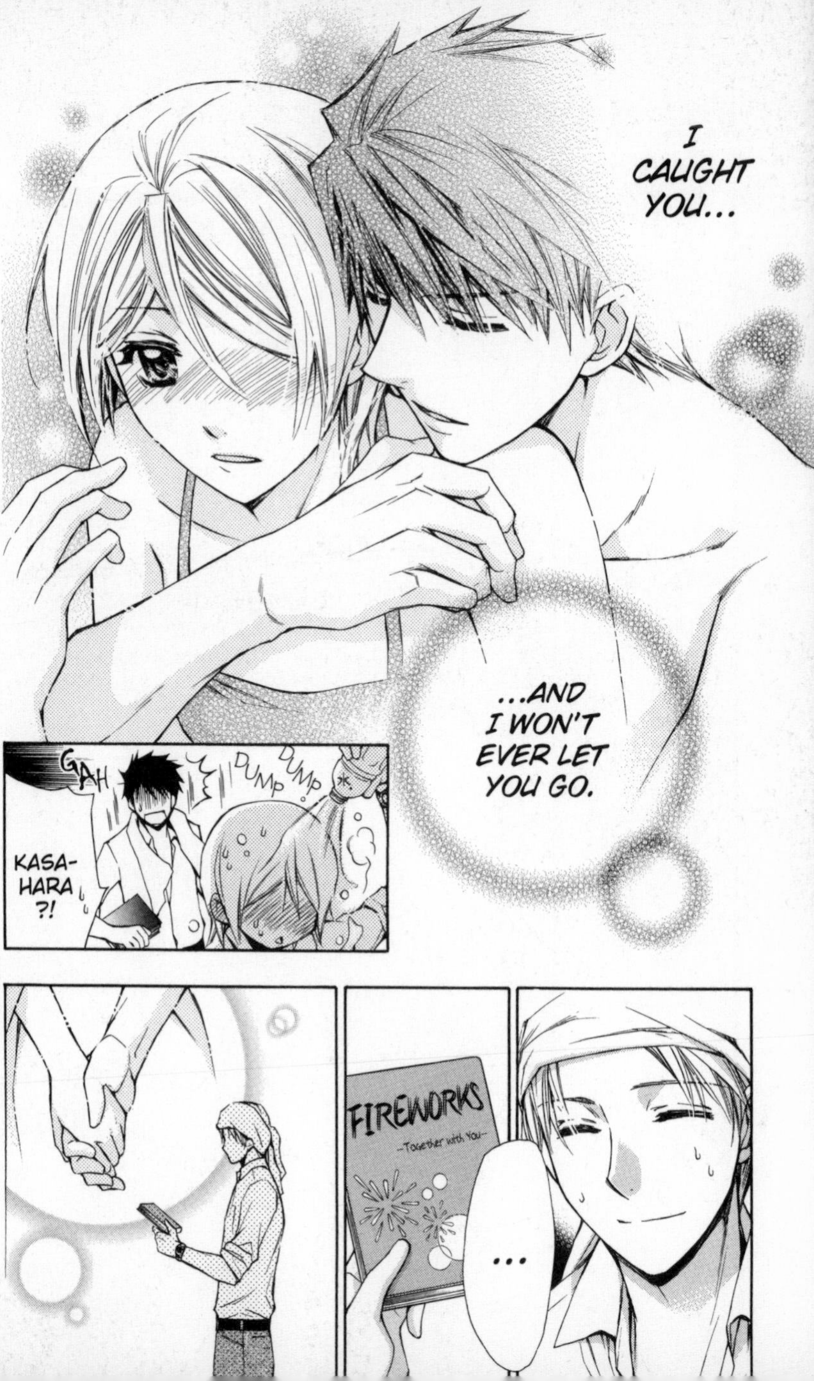
I CAUGHT YOU...
...AND I WON'T EVER LET YOU GO.
GAH
DUMP DUMP
KASA-HARA ?!
...
FIREWORKS
-Together with You-

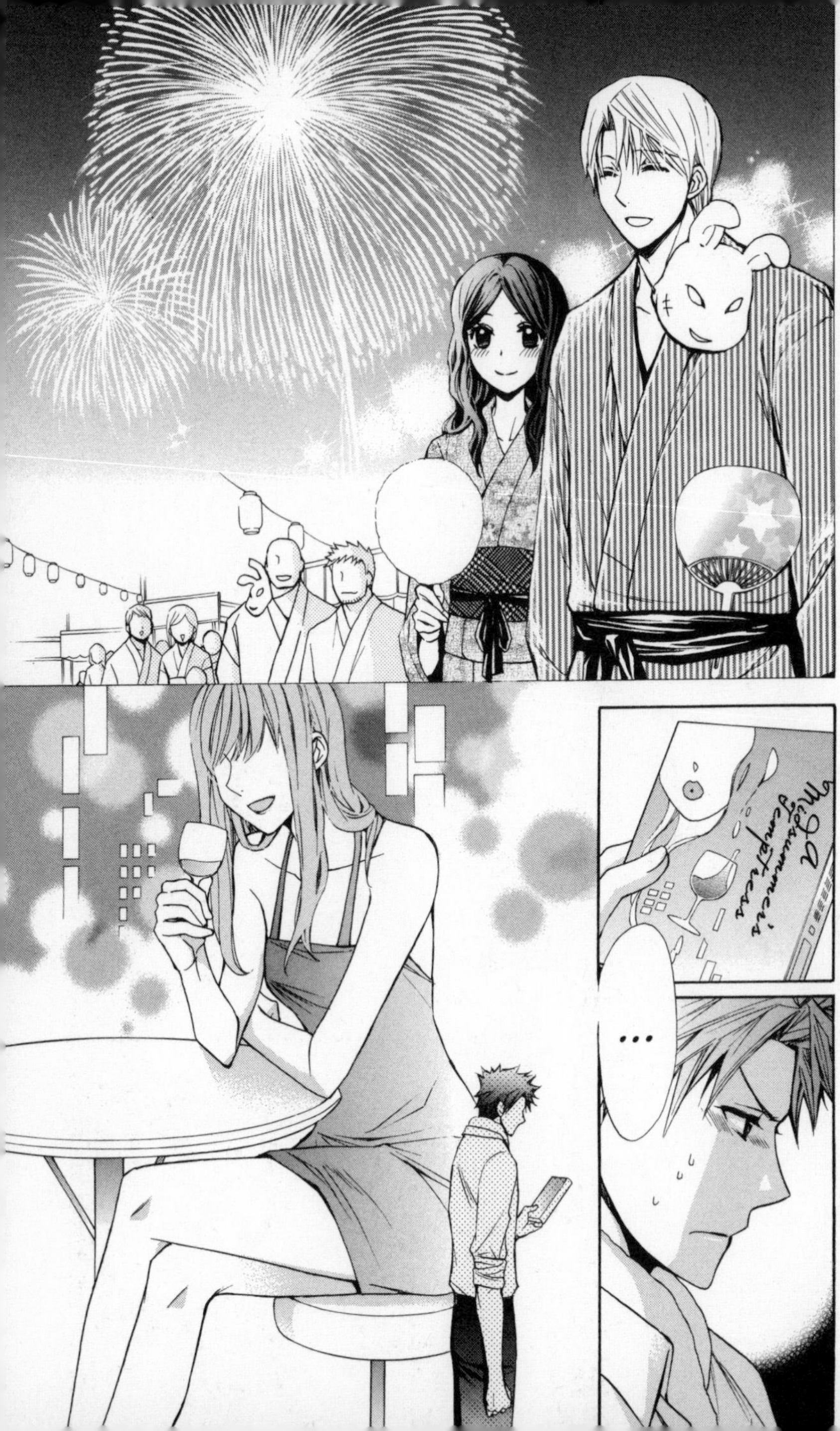
A Midsummer's Temptress
...

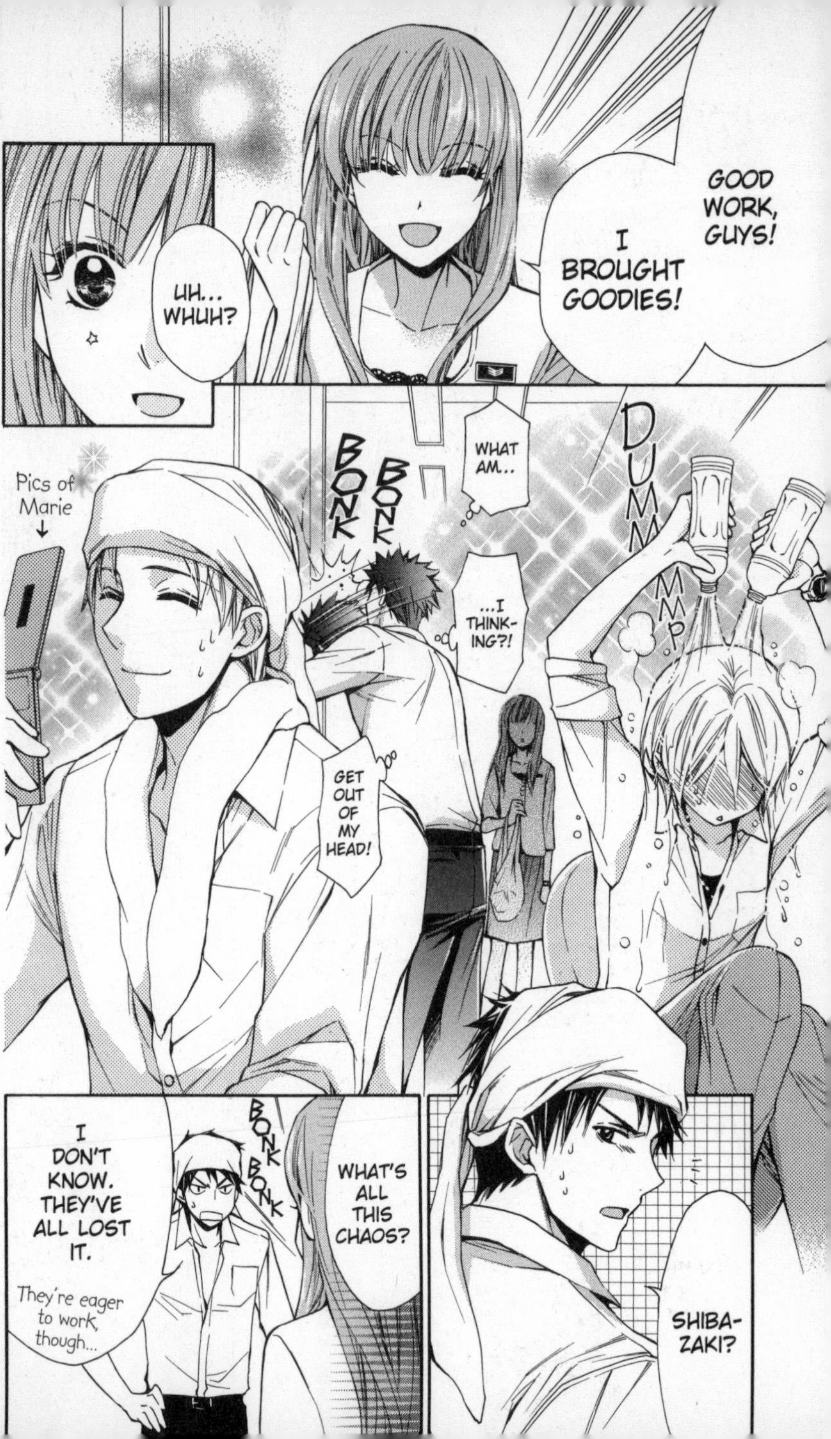
GOOD WORK, GUYS!
I BROUGHT GOODIES!
UH... WHUH?
DUMMMMP
WHAT AM...
...I THINKING?!
BONK BONK
GET OUT OF MY HEAD!
Pics of Marie ↓
SHIBA-ZAKI?
WHAT'S ALL THIS CHAOS?
BONK BONK
I DON'T KNOW. THEY'VE ALL LOST IT.
They're eager to work, though...

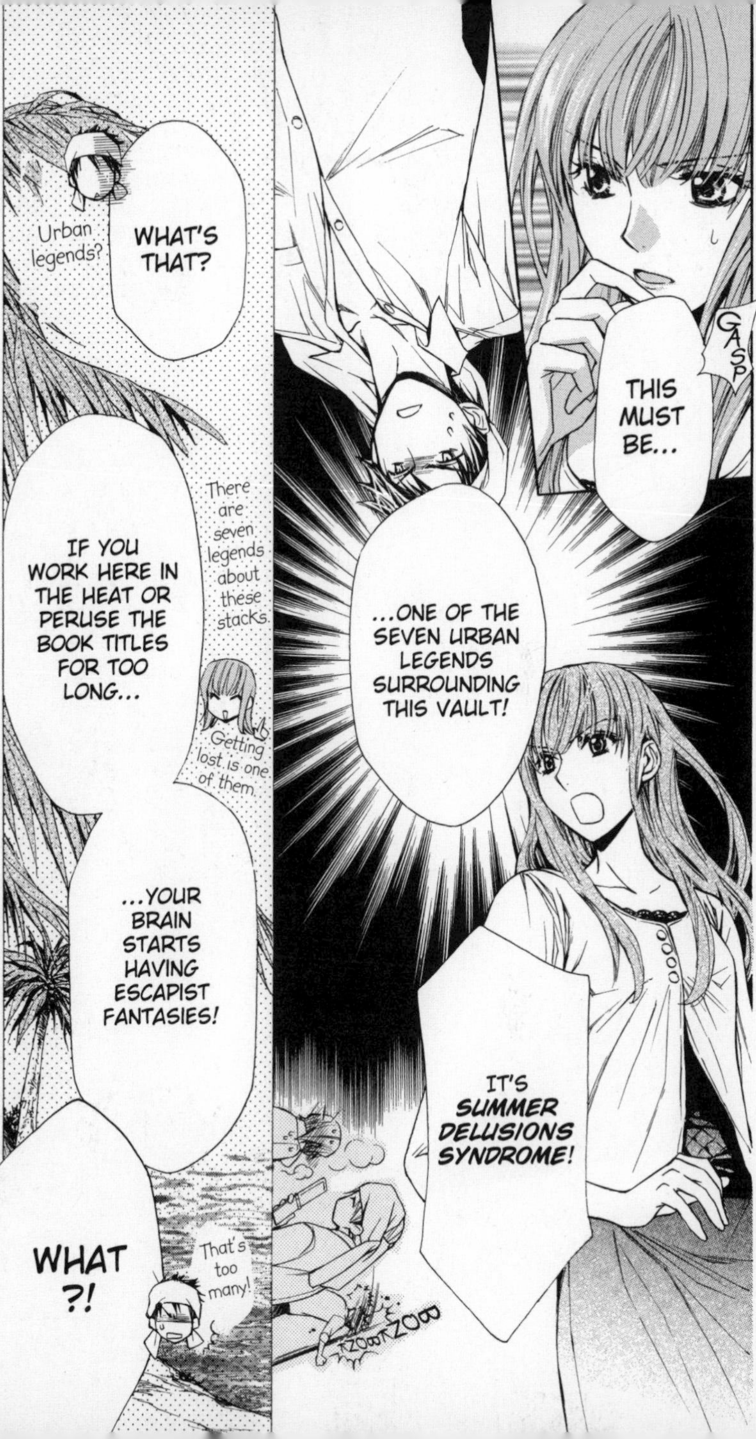
GASP
THIS MUST BE...
...ONE OF THE SEVEN URBAN LEGENDS SURROUNDING THIS VAULT!
IT'S SUMMER DELUSIONS SYNDROME!
Urban legends?
WHAT'S THAT?
There are seven legends about these stacks.
IF YOU WORK HERE IN THE HEAT OR PERUSE THE BOOK TITLES FOR TOO LONG...
Getting lost is one of them.
...YOUR BRAIN STARTS HAVING ESCAPIST FANTASIES!
WHAT ?!
That's too many!

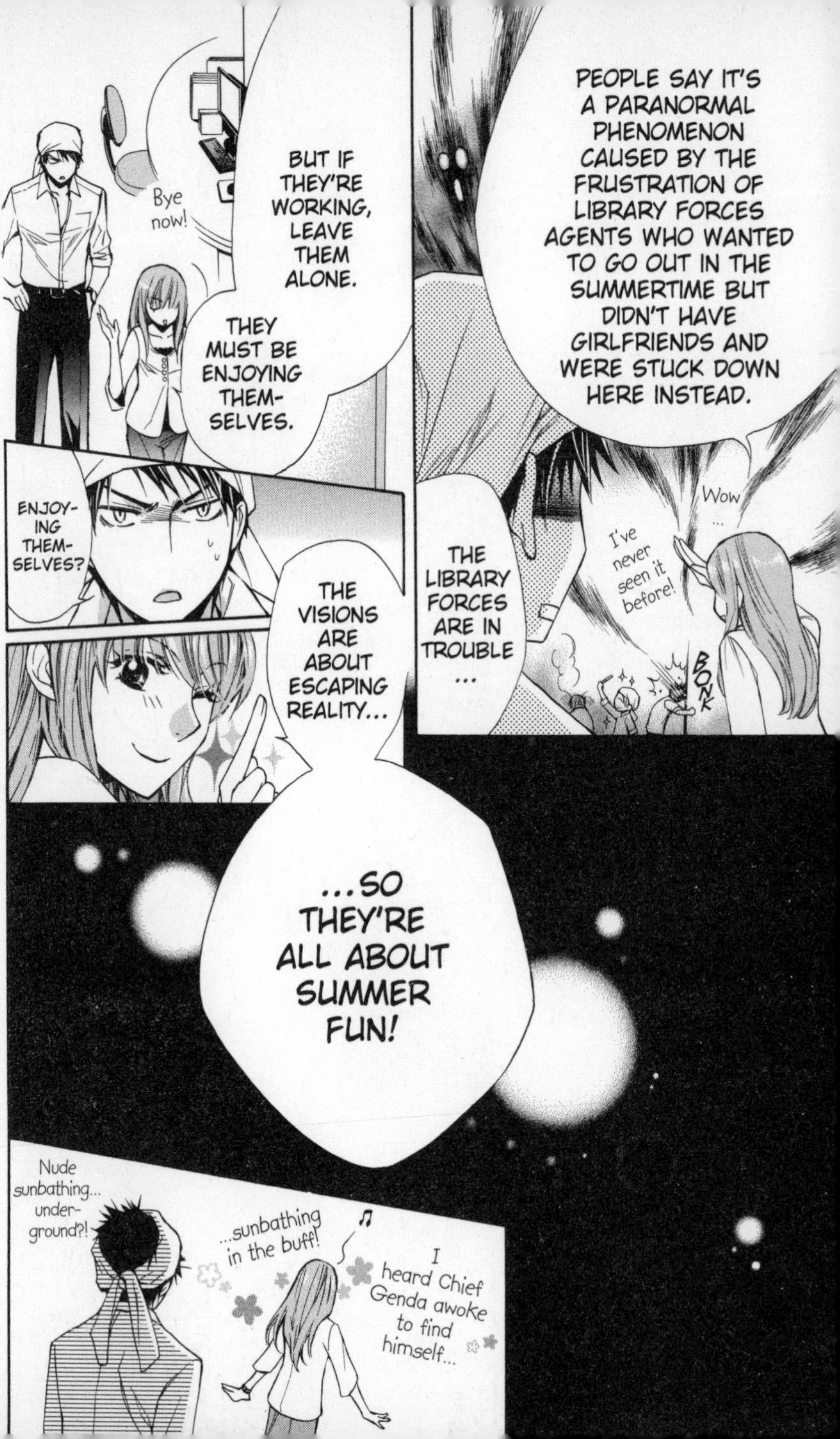
PEOPLE SAY IT'S A PARANORMAL PHENOMENON CAUSED BY THE FRUSTRATION OF LIBRARY FORCES AGENTS WHO WANTED TO GO OUT IN THE SUMMERTIME BUT DIDN'T HAVE GIRLFRIENDS AND WERE STUCK DOWN HERE INSTEAD.
Wow...
I've never seen it before!
BONK
THE LIBRARY FORCES ARE IN TROUBLE...
BUT IF THEY'RE WORKING, LEAVE THEM ALONE.
Bye now!
THEY MUST BE ENJOYING THEMSELVES.
ENJOYING THEMSELVES?
THE VISIONS ARE ABOUT ESCAPING REALITY...
...SO THEY'RE ALL ABOUT SUMMER FUN!
I heard Chief Genda awoke to find himself...
...sunbathing in the buff!
Nude sunbathing... underground?!

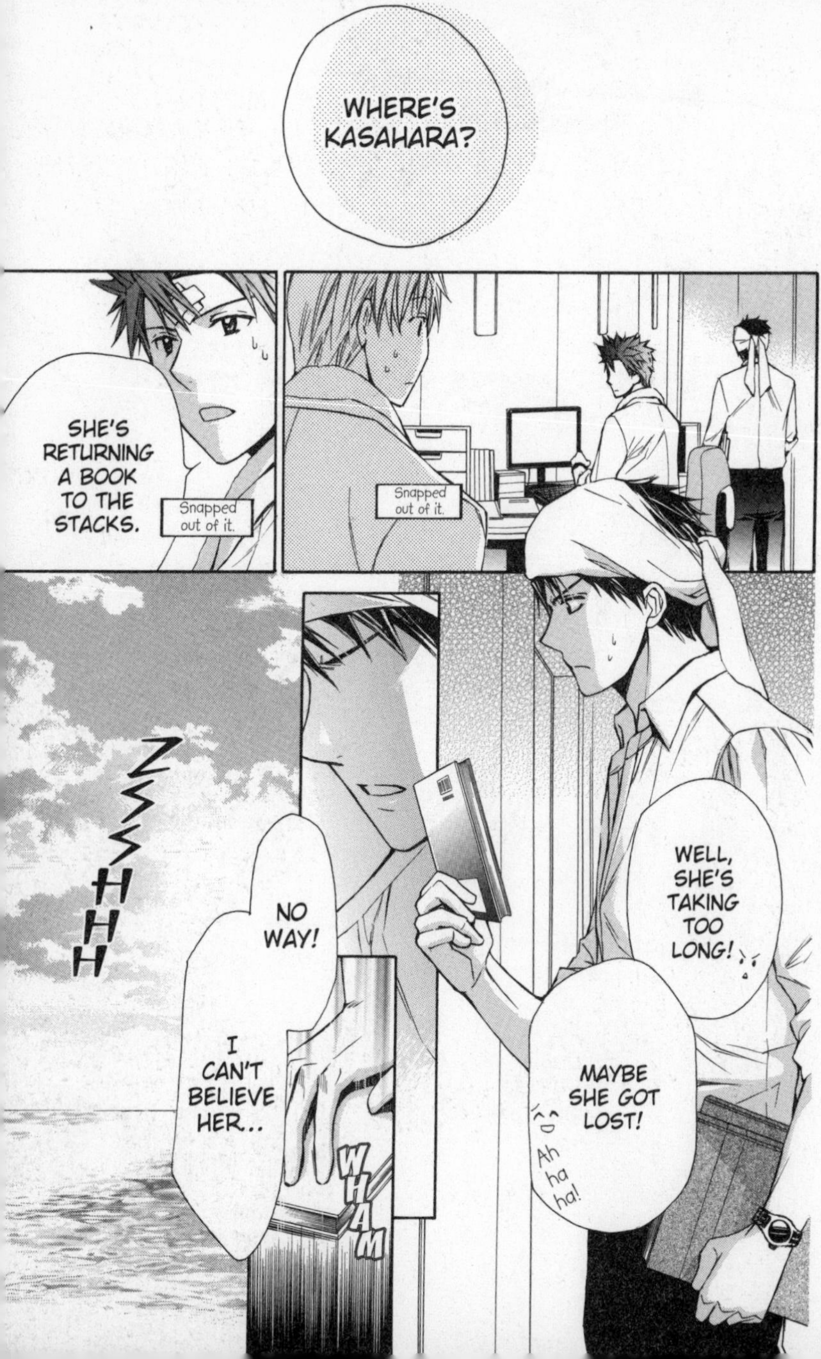
WHERE'S KASAHARA?
Snapped out of it.
SHE'S RETURNING A BOOK TO THE STACKS.
Snapped out of it.
WELL, SHE'S TAKING TOO LONG!
MAYBE SHE GOT LOST!
Ah ha ha!
NO WAY!
I CAN'T BELIEVE HER...
WHAM
ZSSHHH

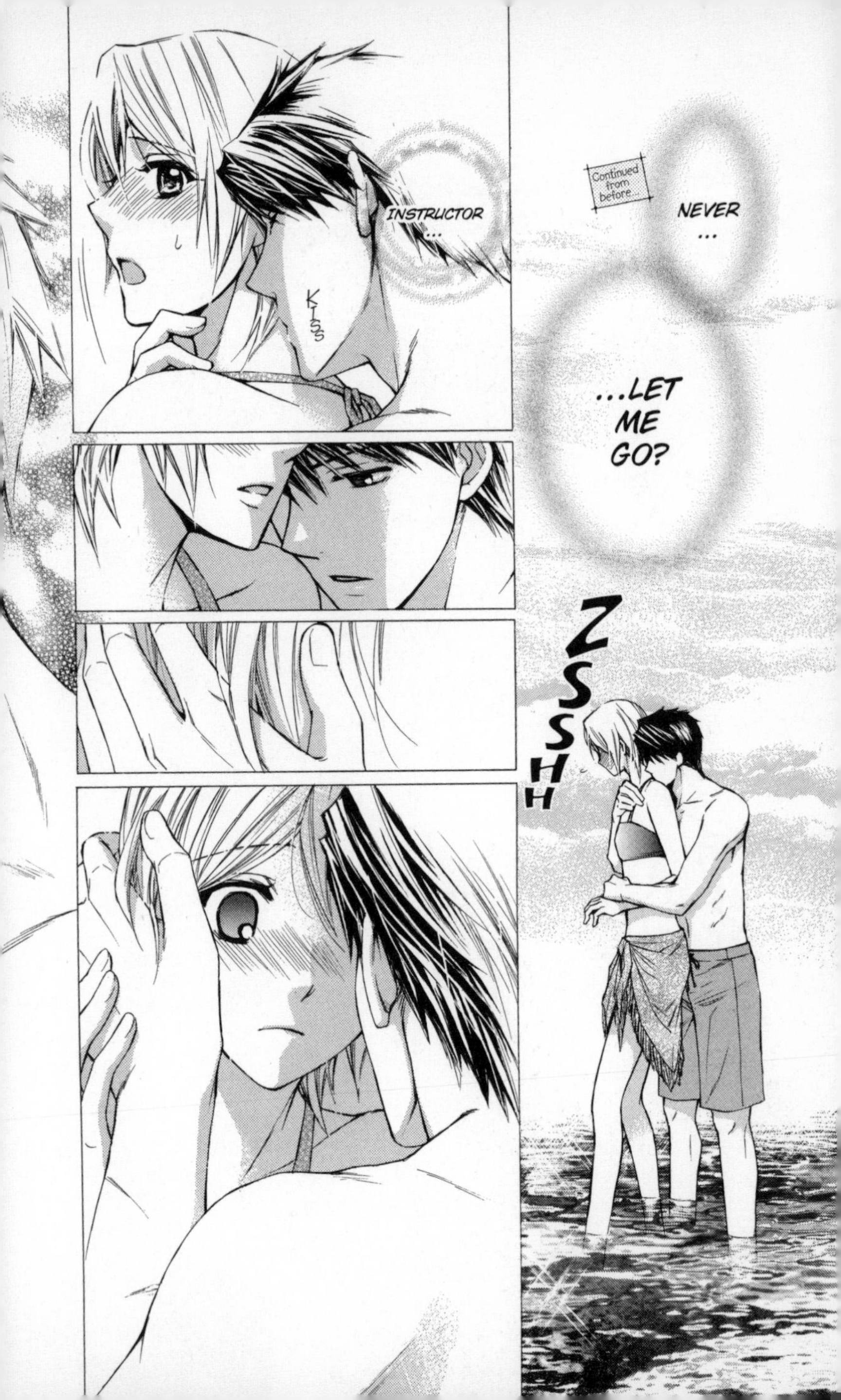
Continued from before...
NEVER ...
...LET ME GO?
ZSSHH
INSTRUCTOR ...
KISS

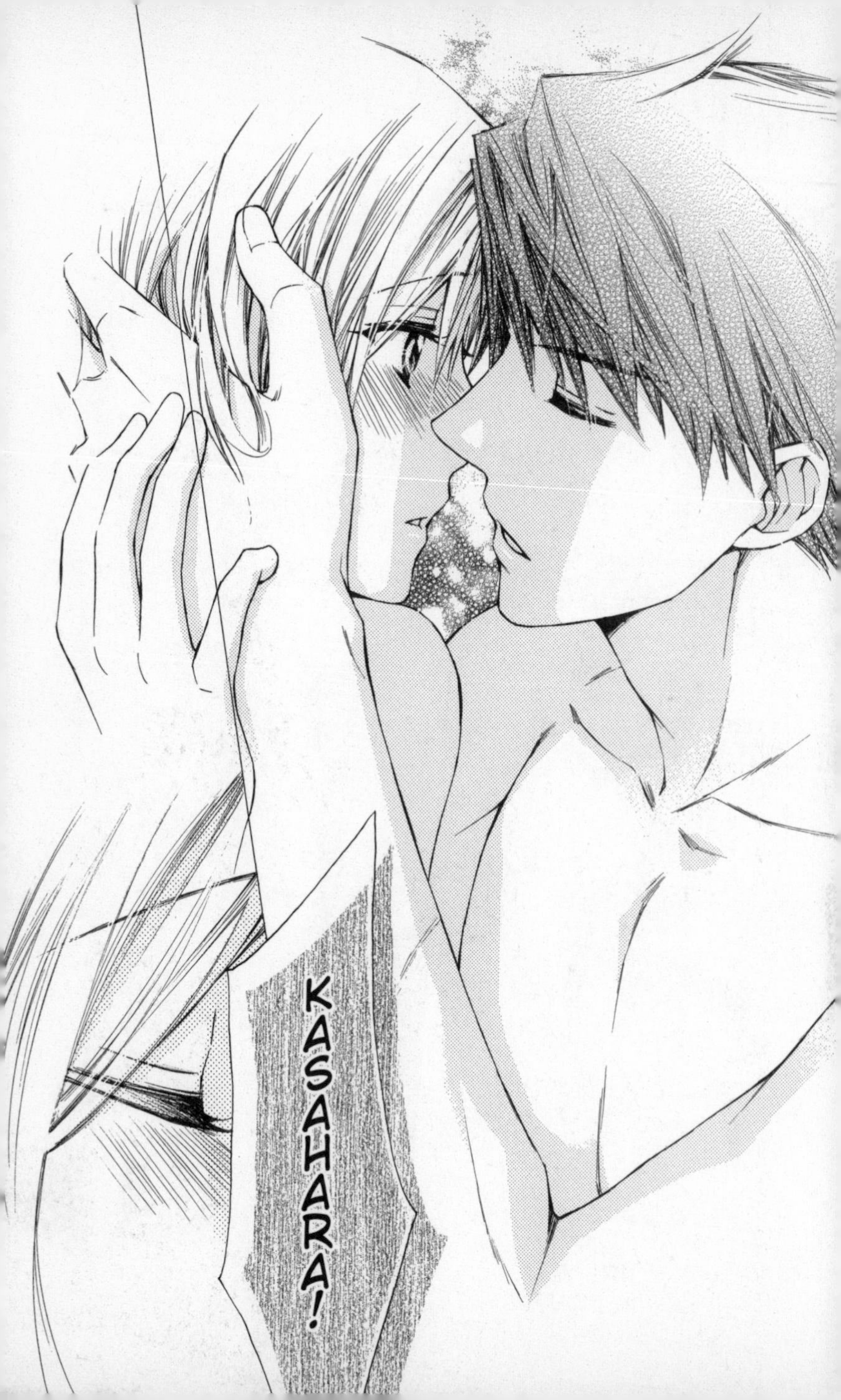
KASAHARA!

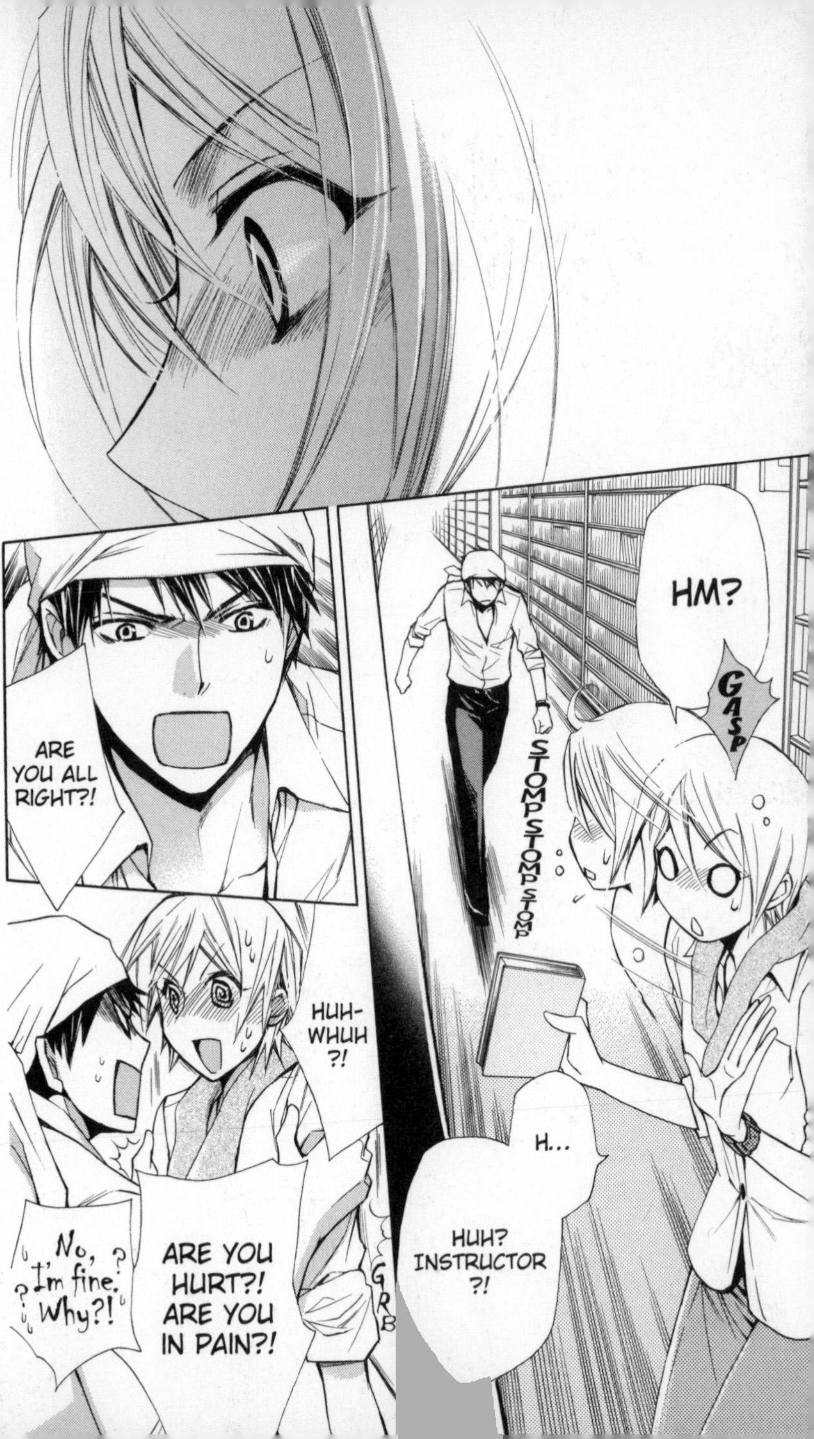
HM?
GASP
STOMPSTOMPSTOMP
H...
HUH? INSTRUCTOR?!
ARE YOU ALL RIGHT?!
HUH-WHUH?!
GRB
ARE YOU HURT?! ARE YOU IN PAIN?!
No, I'm fine. Why?!

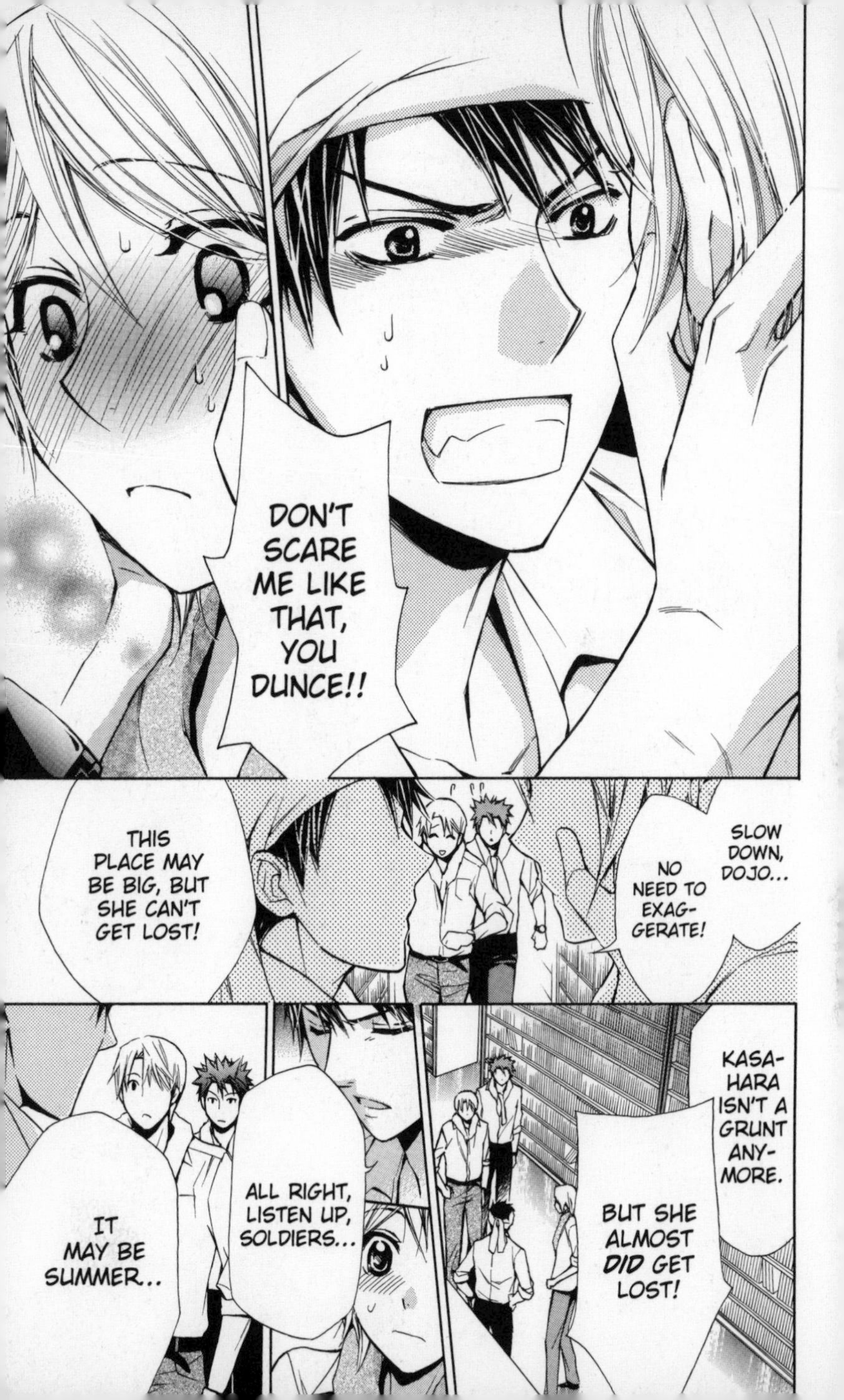
DON'T SCARE ME LIKE THAT, YOU DUNCE!!
SLOW DOWN, DOJO...
NO NEED TO EXAG-GERATE!
THIS PLACE MAY BE BIG, BUT SHE CAN'T GET LOST!
KASA-HARA ISN'T A GRUNT ANY-MORE.
BUT SHE ALMOST *DID* GET LOST!
ALL RIGHT, LISTEN UP, SOLDIERS...
IT MAY BE SUMMER..

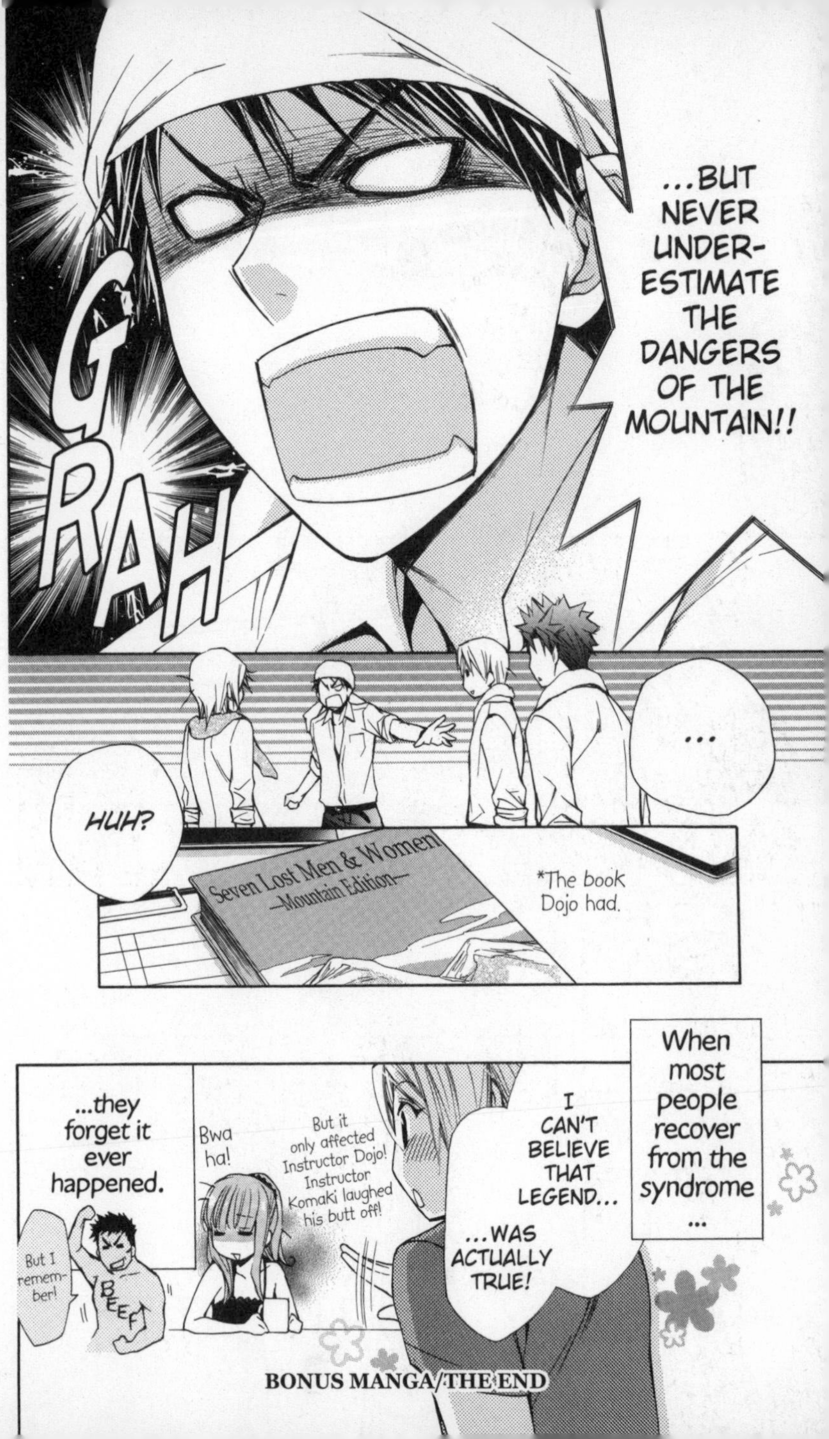
...BUT NEVER UNDER-ESTIMATE THE DANGERS OF THE MOUNTAIN!!
GRAH
...
HUH?
Seven Lost Men & Women —Mountain Edition—
*The book Dojo had.
When most people recover from the syndrome ...
I CAN'T BELIEVE THAT LEGEND...
...WAS ACTUALLY TRUE!
But it only affected Instructor Dojo! Instructor Komaki laughed his butt off!
Bwa ha!
...they forget it ever happened.
But I remember!
BEEF
BONUS MANGA/THE END

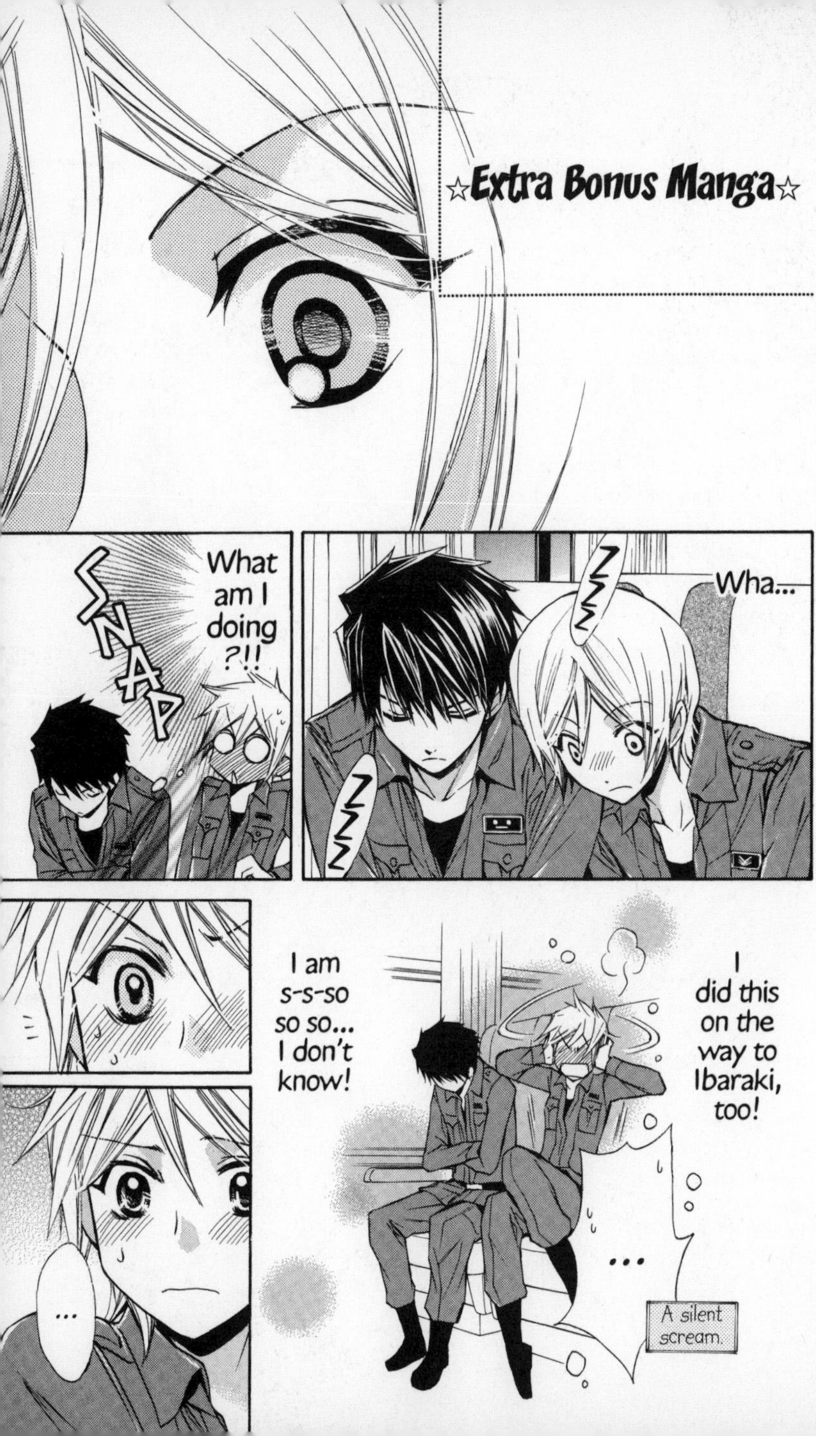
☆Extra Bonus Manga☆
Wha...
ZZZ
ZZZ
What am I doing?!!
SNAP
I did this on the way to Ibaraki, too!
I am s-s-so so so... I don't know!
...
A silent scream.
...

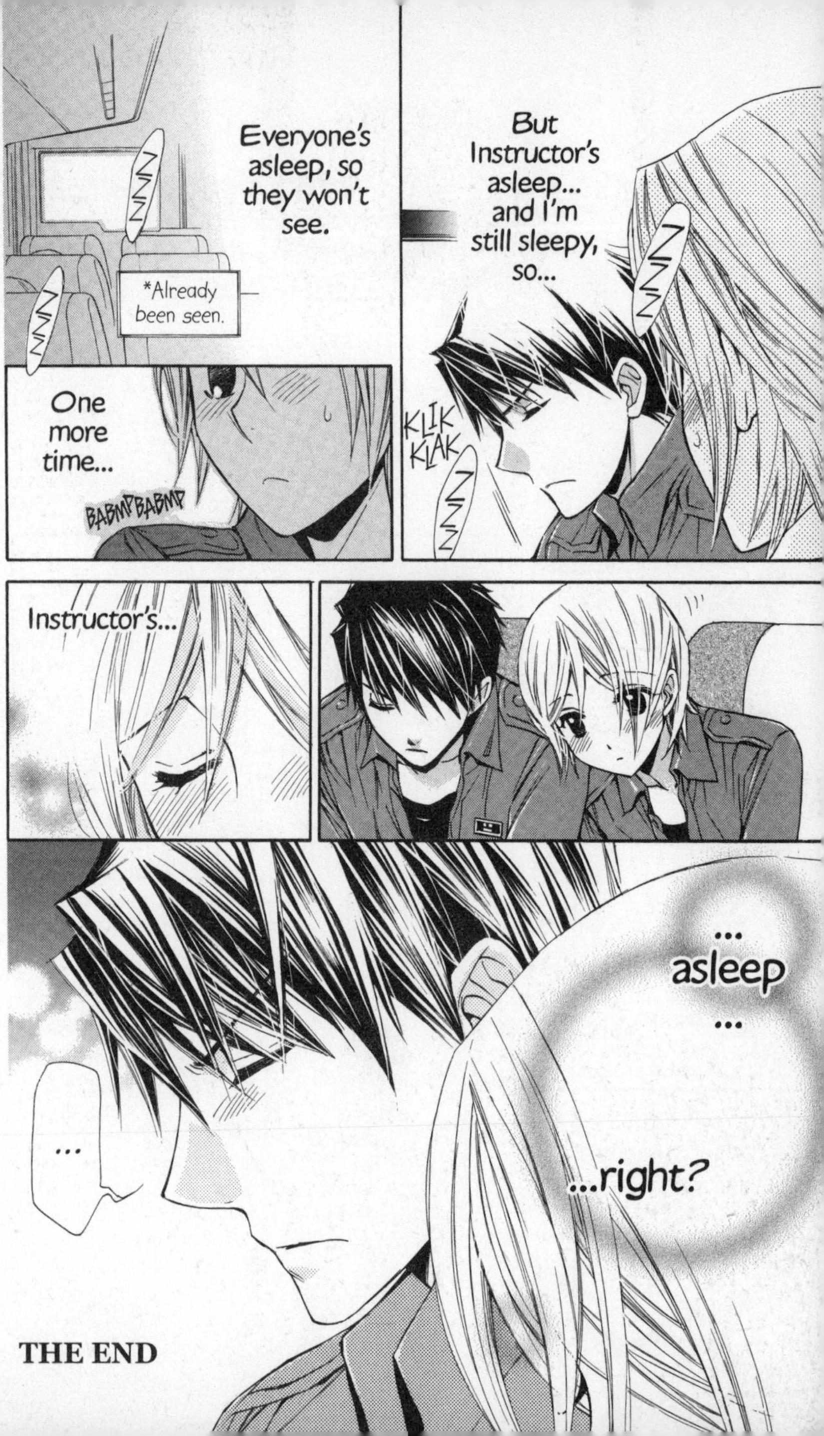
But Instructor's asleep... and I'm still sleepy, so...
ZZZ
KLIK KLAK
ZZZ
Everyone's asleep, so they won't see.
ZZZ
ZZZ
*Already been seen.
One more time...
BABMP BABMP
Instructor's...
... asleep ...
...right?
...
THE END

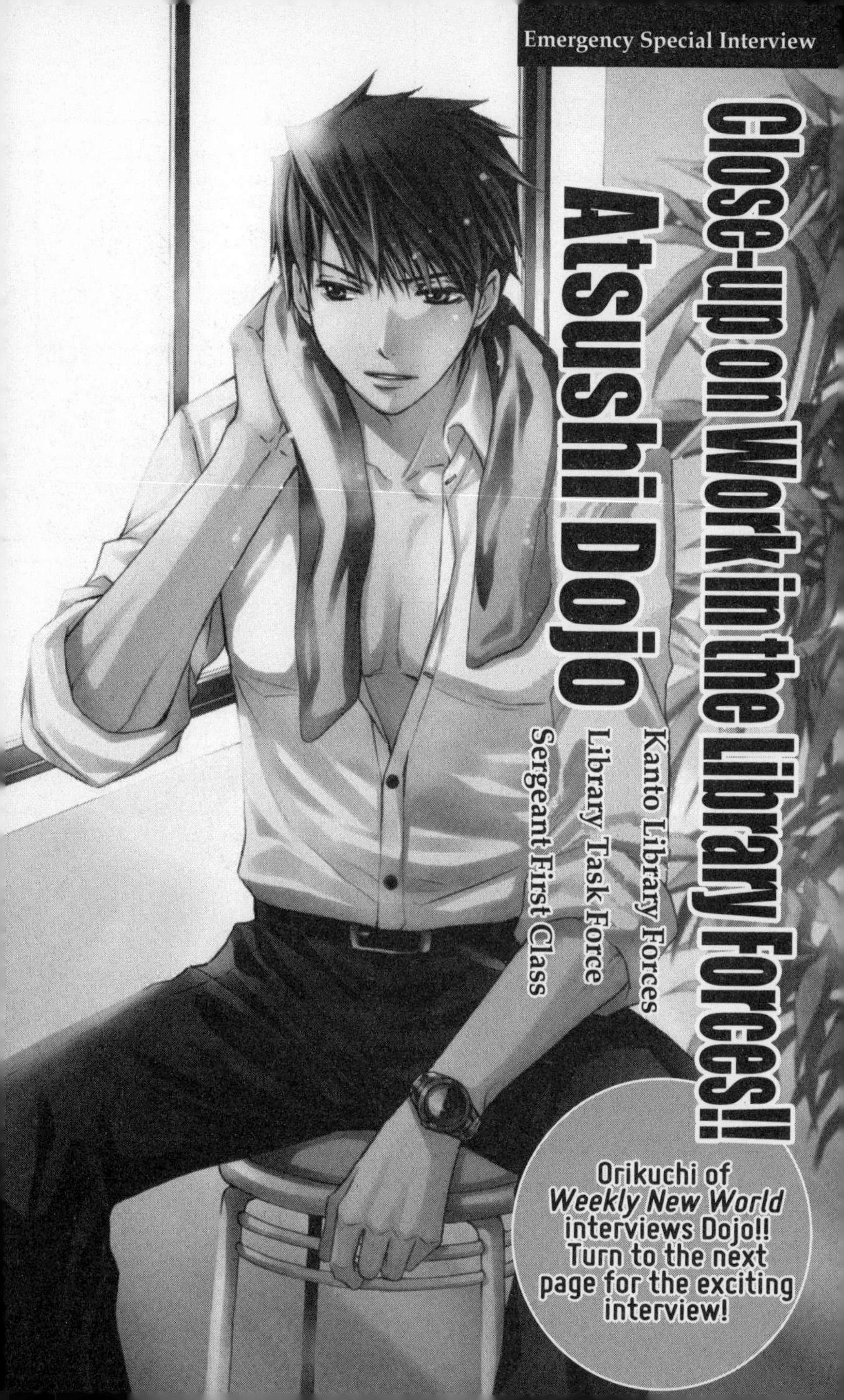
Emergency Special Interview
Close-up on Work in the Library Forces!!
Atsushi Dojo
Kanto Library Forces
Library Task Force
Sergeant First Class
Orikuchi of *Weekly New World* interviews Dojo!! Turn to the next page for the exciting interview!

IT'S BEEN 30 YEARS SINCE THE MEDIA BETTERMENT ACT
WAS ENACTED. THE MBA HAS BECOME A REGULAR PART OF
OUR LIVES, BUT THE CONTROVERSY CONTINUES. IN THIS
INTERVIEW WE FOCUS ON A LIBRARY FORCES AGENT WHO
FIGHTS AGAINST CENSORSHIP. WE'VE BEEN GRANTED ACCESS
TO AN AGENT ON THE FRONT LINES, SENT TO DEFEND
THE IBARAKI LIBRARY. WHAT'S IT LIKE IN THE CENTER
OF THE ACTION?

Maki Orikuchi: I'm Maki Orikuchi, head of the Editorial Department at *Weekly New World*. Thank you for granting this interview.

Atsushi Dojo, Sergeant FC: I'm Sergeant First Class Atsushi Dojo of the Kanto Library Force's Library Task Force. It's a pleasure.

Q1: What are the Library Forces?

Orikuchi: First, tell me about the Library Forces.

Dojo: As you know, in the final year of the Showa Period, the Media Betterment Act was enacted and enforced, which meant censorship of media deemed to be against public order and morality. This law, which infringes upon freedom of expression, initiated an era of book hunts. Only libraries could stand against the Media Betterment Committee, which uses military might to suppress free speech through means such as censorship, so the Library Forces are the libraries' own defense organization.

Q2: What is the Library Task Force?

Orikuchi: Tell me about the Library Task Force to which you belong.

Dojo: The Library Forces have a Defense Force, which primarily does the work of defending books. The members of the Library Task Force are chosen from this group.

Orikuchi: They are the select elite. Does that mean their job is more dangerous?

Dojo: Yes. Normally agents are assigned after accruing some experience.

Q3: About the new agents

Orikuchi: Nonetheless, your team has two members who joined immediately after completing basic training.

Dojo: Kasahara and Tezuka.

Orikuchi: Agent Hikaru Tezuka's grades were always at the top during training, weren't they?

LIBRARY WARS WORK INTERVIEW

Dojo: Yes. His inflexibility is a drawback, but he's quite skilled.

Q4: About female agents

Orikuchi: The other agent, Iku Kasahara, is the first ever female special defense agent.

Dojo: She possesses some remarkable physical abilities, but she's shallow, forgetful, childish...

Orikuchi: I suppose you find her need for attention to be endearing and can't take your eyes off her.

Dojo: I never said that. She was recently promoted to sergeant, so she's gradually becoming a reliable agent.

Orikuchi: It must hurt to see her gradually separating from you.

Dojo: I never said that!

Orikuchi: I hear she yearned to join the Library Forces because a "prince" protected a book for her when she was younger.

Dojo: ?!

Orikuchi: Isn't it true that you are that prince?

Dojo: ?!! (*WHAM*) How do you—

Orikuchi: And yet it appears that she is growing out of her prince...

Dojo: Hmph! She always does whatever she wants without any concern for me no matter how much I—

Orikuchi: No matter how much you what?

Dojo: What?!

Kasahara: Instructor Dojo! Are you doing an interview?

Dojo: Kasahara??! How long have you been there?!

Orikuchi: I understand your feelings, Sergeant Dojo. Thank you for your time.

Dojo: Hey! Ms. Orikuchi?! How much of that is going in your article?!

Kasahara: What was the interview about?

Dojo: Sh-Shut up! You nincompoop!!

New World will continue to follow the men and women who risk their lives to protect books.

Publisher: Sesousha

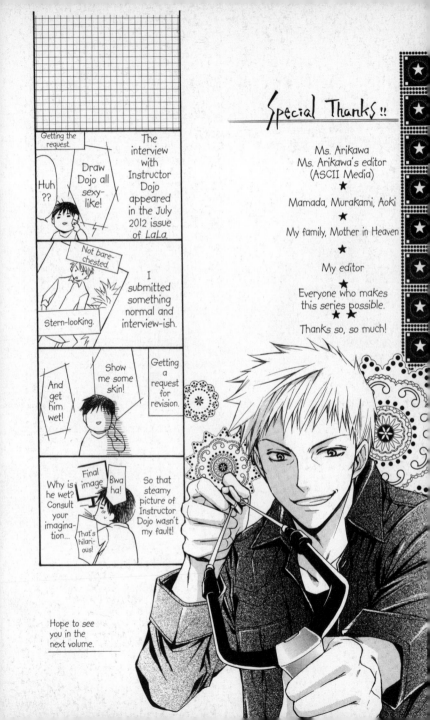

Special Thanks!!

Ms. Arikawa
Ms. Arikawa's editor
(ASCII Media)

★

Mamada, Murakami, Aoki

★

My family, Mother in Heaven

★

My editor

★

Everyone who makes
this series possible.

★★

Thanks so, so much!

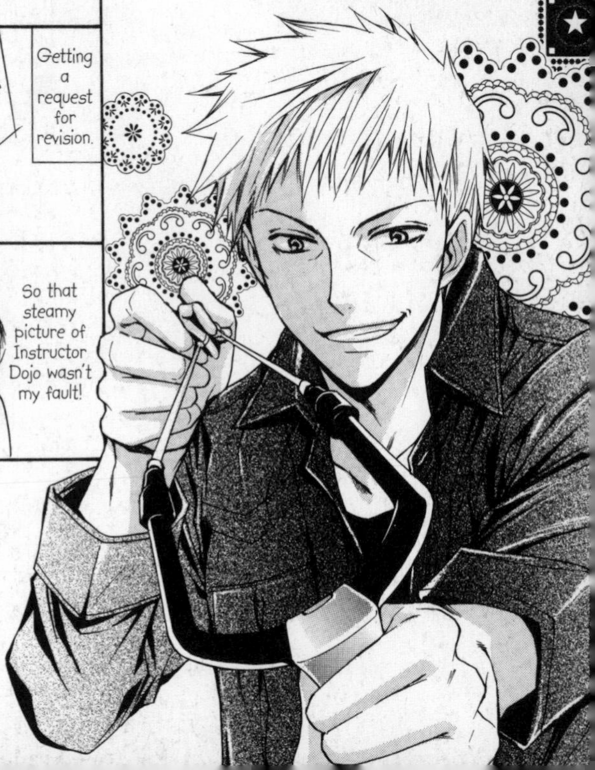

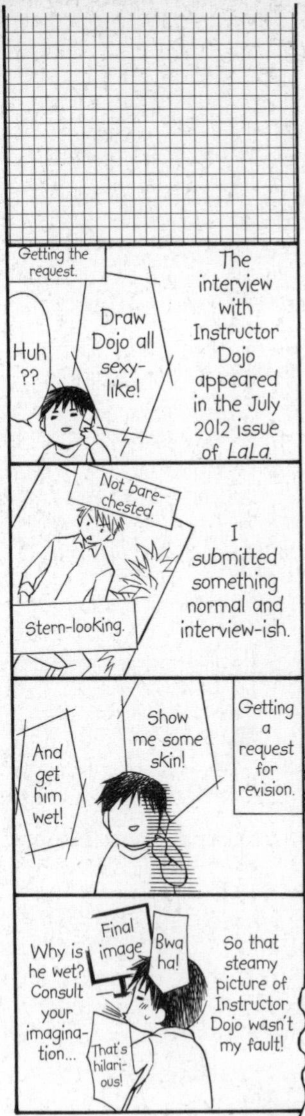
The interview with Instructor Dojo appeared in the July 2012 issue of LaLa.
Draw Dojo all sexy-like!
Getting the request.
Huh ??
I submitted something normal and interview-ish.
Not bare-chested.
Stern-looking.
Getting a request for revision.
Show me some skin!
And get him wet!
So that steamy picture of Instructor Dojo wasn't my fault!
Bwa ha!
Final image
That's hilari-ous!
Why is he wet? Consult your imagina-tion...

Hope to see
you in the
next volume.

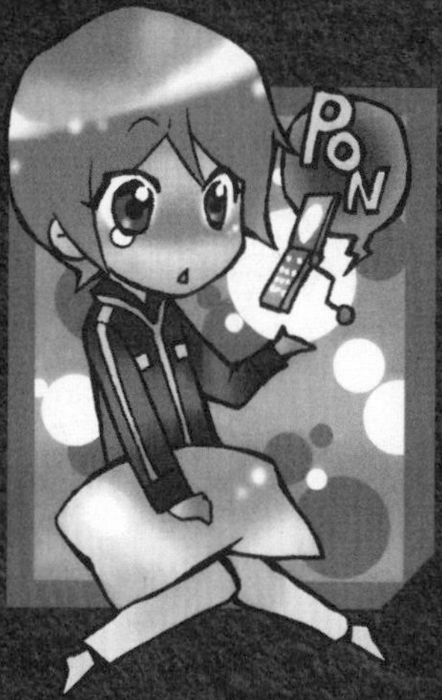
PON

Kiiro Yumi won the 42nd *LaLa* Manga Grand Prix Fresh Debut award for her manga *Billy Bocchan no Yuutsu* (Little Billy's Depression). Her latest series is *Toshokan Senso Love&War (Library Wars: Love & War)*, which runs in *LaLa* magazine in Japan and is published in English by VIZ Media.

Hiro Arikawa won the 10th Dengeki Novel Prize for her work *Shio no Machi: Wish on My Precious* in 2003 and debuted with the same novel in 2004. Of her many works, Arikawa is best known for the *Library Wars* series and her *Jieitai Sanbusaku* trilogy, which consists of *Sora no Naka* (In the Sky), *Umi no Soko* (The Bottom of the Sea) and *Shio no Machi* (City of Salt).

library wars

Volume 11
Shojo Beat Edition

Story & Art by **Kiiro Yumi**
Original Concept by **Hiro Arikawa**

ENGLISH TRANSLATION John Werry
LETTERING Annaliese Christman
DESIGN Amy Martin
EDITOR Megan Bates

Printed in Canada

Published by VIZ Media, LLC
P.O. Box 77010
San Francisco, CA 94107

10 9 8 7 6 5 4 3 2 1
First printing, April 2014

www.shojobeat.com   www.viz.com